# Contract Termination in International and Domestic Trade

This book highlights the right to terminate a contract, yielding invaluable insights to enable policymakers and legal practitioners to facilitate international trade.

In the modern landscape of globalised trade, the imperative of a harmonised legal framework of contract law capable of fostering stability and trust in cross-border trade has never been more pronounced. This is represented in the United Nations Convention on Contracts for the International Sale of Goods (CISG), providing rules that can be known, understood and abided by globally. This book focuses on the termination of contracts, one of the harshest remedies when a sale of goods contract is breached by the seller. Breaches by the seller dealt in this book are confined to breaches of contractual description, delivery time and quality of goods, which are the most common violations of sale of goods contracts. This book scrutinises the methods adopted for challenging or facilitating contractual termination by CISG as a transnational law, as well as the Sale of Goods Act 1979 (SGA) and Kuwaiti law (KLaw), both of which are national laws of non-contracting states of CISG. This study also draws attention to lacunae and practical issues, focusing on critical analyses of law and cases, and recognises the adopted themes underlying each law to find the degree of their legal clarity and the threshold upon which termination can be granted. This comprehensive analysis also provides inspiration for beneficial changes by weighing the pros and cons of each system.

The book will be of interest to practitioners, students, and scholars in the fields of contract law, trade law, commercial law and international law.

**Dr Bashayer Al-Mukhaizeem** holds a Ph.D. in law from the University of Sussex, complemented by a master's degree in private law from the University of Kuwait and additional master's degrees in international commercial law and information technology and intellectual property rights from the University of Sussex.

She served as a senior legal researcher at the Civil Service Commission of Kuwait. With experience as a teacher at Business Studies College and Kuwait International Law School, she is recognised for her expertise in private law, particularly in the domains of obligations, contract law, labour law, legal systems and evidence. She continues to contribute to her fields through research and practice.

# Contract Termination in International and Domestic Trade

## Buyers' Rights Under Contract Law

**Dr Bashayer Al-Mukhaizeem**

Routledge
Taylor & Francis Group
LONDON AND NEW YORK

First published 2025
by Routledge
4 Park Square, Milton Park, Abingdon, Oxon OX14 4RN

and by Routledge
605 Third Avenue, New York, NY 10158

*Routledge is an imprint of the Taylor & Francis Group, an informa business*



*British Library Cataloguing-in-Publication Data*
A catalogue record for this book is available from the British Library

ISBN: 978-1-032-71491-2 (hbk)
ISBN: 978-1-032-73825-3 (pbk)
ISBN: 978-1-003-46613-0 (ebk)

DOI: 10.4324/9781003466130

Typeset in Times New Roman
by Apex CoVantage, LLC

# Contents

# Acknowledgements

I express my greatest gratitude to God, who put in me the resilience, power, patience and determination to write this book.

I would like to express my love and gratitude to my parents, Muhammed Al-Mukhaizeem and Kadeja Al-Ibrahim, and my family for their endless support and their belief in me. I would also like to thank my dear grandmother, Latifa Al-Rushod, an inspirational woman, a beacon of self-reliance and wisdom.

I would like to express my sincere appreciation to Dr Sirko Harder for his insightful comments, helpful advice and invaluable support. I greatly appreciate the supportive role and assistance of Mr Paul Eden, including but not limited to providing me with books, either from the British Library or from his own collection. Dr Sirko Harder and Mr Paul Eden inspire me to help other people gain their goals.

# Abbreviations

- Al-Majalla of Islamic principles of obligations (Al-Majalla)
- Case Law of UNCITRAL Texts (CLOUT)
- Civil Code No. 67 of 1980 (KCIC)
- Commercial Code No. 68 of 1980 (KCOC)
- Directory of Open Access Journals (DOAJ)
- Explanatory Memorandum of Civil Code (EMKCIC)
- Gulf Cooperation Council (GCC)
- INCOTERMS Delivered Duty Paid Contract (DDP)
- Internationalisation of European Small and Medium-Sized Enterprises (SMEs)
- Kuwait Law Journal (KLJ)
- Principles of International Commercial Contracts 2016 (UPICC)
- The Sale of Goods Act 1979 (SGA)
- United Nations Commission on International Trade Law (UNCITRAL)
- United Nations Convention on Contracts for the International Sale of Goods (CISG)

# Table of Cases

## CISG Cases

- Acrylic blankets case (31/1/1997) 2U31/96 Appellate Court Koblenz <http://cisgw3.law.pace.edu/cases/970131g1.html>
- Agricultural machine case (12/12/1995) 2O246/95 (District Court Marburg) <http://cisgw3.law.pace.edu/cases/951212g1.html>
- Alpha Prime Development Corporation, Plaintiff v Holland Loader (6/7/2010) (District Court) <https://cisgw3.law.pace.edu/cases/100706u1.html>
- Aluminium hydroxide case (21/8/1997) (Appellate Court Oberlandesgericht) <http://cisgw3.law.pace.edu/cases/970821g1.html>
- ArensSondermaschinen GmbH v Smit Draad/DraadNijmegent B.V. (7/10/2008) 104.003.479 (Gerechtshof Appellate Court) <https://cisgw3.law.pace.edu/cases/081007n1.html>
- Audio CDs case (11/2/2003) HG.2001.11-HGK (Commercial Court St. Gallen) <http://cisgw3.law.pace.edu/cases/030211s1.html>
- Auto case (4/7/2007) 2 Ob 95/06v (Supreme Court) <https://cisgw3.law.pace.edu/cases/070704a3.html>
- Automobile case (11/1/2006) VIIIZR268/04 (Supreme Court) <http://cisgw3.law.pace.edu/cases/060111g1.html>
- Automobile case (2006) CISG/2006/03 (CIETAC arbitration proceeding) <http://cisgw3.law.pace.edu/cases/061200c1.html>
- Automobile case (27/4/1999) 9U146/98 (Appellate Court Naumburg) <https://cisgw3.law.pace.edu/cases/990427g1.html>
- Automobile case (31/3/2008) 6U220/07 (Appellate Court Stuttgart) <http://cisgw3.law.pace.edu/cases/080331g1.html>
- Beijing Light Automobile v Connell (5/6/1998) (Stockholm Chamber of Commerce Arbitration) <http://cisgw3.law.pace.edu/cases/980605s5.html>
- Bronneberg v Belvédère (20/2/1998) 16.442 (Supreme Court) <http://cisgw3.law.pace.edu/cases/980220n1.html>
- Brown & Root v Aerotech Herman Nelson (4/5/2004) MBCA 63 (Court of Appeal of Manitoba) <http://www.unilex.info/cisg/case/1009>
- BV BA G-2 v AS C.B. (25/4/2001) A/00/00665 (District Court Veurne) <https://cisgw3.law.pace.edu/cases/010425b1.html>

- Caito Roger v. Société française de factoring (13/9/1995) 93/4126 (Appellate Court Grenoble) <http://cisgw3.law.pace.edu/cases/950913f1.html>
- Canned food case (12/11/1997) S 97/324 (Turku Court of Appeal) <http://cisgw3.law.pace.edu/cases/971112f5.html>
- Canned oranges case (2006) CISG/2006/06 (CIETAC arbitration proceeding) <https://cisgw3.law.pace.edu/cases/060500c1.html>
- Carlos Manuel del Corazón de Jesús Bravo Barros, Sr v Salvador Martínez Gares (31/5/2007) 87484, Registro de Cámera No. 102.876/2002 (National Commercial Court of Appeals) <http://cisgw3.law.pace.edu/cases/070531a1.html>
- Case involving machine for repair of bricks (27/12/2007) (Appellate Court Navarra) <https://cisgw3.law.pace.edu/cases/071227s4.html>
- Catalogue case (21/9/1998) HG 960527/O (Commercial Court Zürich) <http://cisgw3.law.pace.edu/cases/980921s1.html>
- Caterpillar toys case (13/10/2005) 04/04128 (Appellate Court Versailles) <http://cisgw3.law.pace.edu/cases/051013f1.html>
- Chartbrook Ltd v Persimmon Homes Ltd [2009] 1 A.C. 1101, 1102 <https://cisgw3.law.pace.edu/cases/090701uk.html>
- Check valves case (21/12/2004) (Western Appellate Court) <http://cisgw3.law.pace.edu/cases/041221d1.html>
- Chemical compound case (1996) 8247 (ICC arbitration) <http://cisgw3.law.pace.edu/cases/968247i1.html>
- Chemical fertilizer case (1995) 8128 (Court of Arbitration of the International Chamber of Commerce) <http://cisgw3.law.pace.edu/cases/958128i1.html>
- Chicago Prime Packers v Northam Food Trading Co (2004) 01 C 4447 (Federal District Court) <http://cisgw3.law.pace.edu/cases/040521u1.html>
- Cisterns and accessories case (16/2/2009) (Tribunale di Forli District Court) <http://cisgw3.law.pace.edu/cases/090216i3.html>
- Clay case (26/9/2012) VIII ZR 100/11 (Supreme Court) <http://cisgw3.law.pace.edu/cases/120926g1.html>
- Cloth case (24/9/1998) 6O107/98 (District Court Regensburg) <http://cisgw3.law.pace.edu/cases/980924g1.html>
- Clothes case (18/4/1995) CISG/1995/06 (CIETAC arbitration proceeding) <https://cisgw3.law.pace.edu/cases/950418c1.html>
- Clothes case (21/12/1990) 4C549/90 (Lower Court Ludwigsburg) <https://cisgw3.law.pace.edu/cases/901221g1.html>
- Clothes case (3/6/2003) CISG/2003/01 (CIETAC arbitration proceeding) <http://cisgw3.law.pace.edu/cases/030603c1.html>
- CNC machine case (21/2/2005) C1 04 162 (Appellate Court Valais/Wallis) <http://cisgw3.law.pace.edu/cases/050221s1.html>
- Cobalt sulphate case (14/12/1994) 5 U 224/93 (Appellate Court Oberlandesgericht) <http://cisgw3.law.pace.edu/cases/941214g1.html>
- Cobalt sulphate case (3/4/1996) VIIIZR51/95 (Bundesgerichtshof Supreme Court) <https://cisgw3.law.pace.edu/cases/960403g1.html>
- Coke case (1994) 7565 (ICC arbitration) <http://cisgw3.law.pace.edu/cases/947565i1.html>

- Coke case (2/3/1994) 7 U 4419/93 (Appellate Court München) <http://cisgw3.law.pace.edu/cases/940302g1.html>
- Commercial vehicles case (10/3/2004) 7U147/03 (Appellate Court Celle) <http://cisgw3.law.pace.edu/cases/040310g1.html>
- Computer components case (1992) O 42/92 KfH I (District Court Heidelberg) <http://cisgw3.law.pace.edu/cases/920703g1.html>
- Condensate crude oil mix case (15/10/2002) 2319 (Netherlands Arbitration Institute) <https://cisgw3.law.pace.edu/cases/021015n1.html>
- CortemSpA v Controlmatic Pty Ltd (13/8/2010) VID 414 of 2008 (Federal Court of Australia) <http://cisgw3.law.pace.edu/cases/100813a2.html>
- Cotton bath towel case (26/10/1996) CISG/1996/49 (CIETAC arbitration proceeding) <http://cisgw3.law.pace.edu/cases/961026c1.html>
- Cotton gin motes case (2005) CISG/2005/01 (CIETAC arbitration proceeding) <http://cisgw3.law.pace.edu/cases/050407c1.html>
- Crudex Chemicals Oy v Landmark Chemicals S.A. (31/5/2004) S 01/269 (Hovioikeus/hovrätt Appellate Court Helsinki) <http://cisgw3.law.pace.edu/cases/040531f5.html>
- Deforche v Prins Gebroeders Bouwstoffenhandel (4/10/2004) 2003/AR/2763 (Appellate Court Ghent) <http://cisgw3.law.pace.edu/cases/041004b1.html>
- Delchi Carrier v Rotorex (6/12/1995) 185, 717, Dockets 95–7182, 95–7186 (Federal Appellate Court) <https://cisgw3.law.pace.edu/cases/951206u1.html>
- Delphic Wholesalers (Aust) Pty Ltd v Agrilex Co Ltd [2010] VSC 328 <http://cisgw3.law.pace.edu/cases/100806a2.html>
- Designer clothes case (14/10/2002) 16U77/01 (Appellate Court Köln) <http://cisgw3.law.pace.edu/cases/021014g1.html>
- Diversitel v Glacier (6/10/2003) 03-CV-23776 SR (Superior Court of Justice) <https://cisgw3.law.pace.edu/cases/031006c4.html>
- Dividing wall panels case (29/6/1999) 1Ob74/99k (Supreme Court Austria) <http://cisgw3.law.pace.edu/cases/990629a3.html>
- Doors case (13/1/1993) 1 U 69/92 (Appellate Court Saarbrücken) <http://cisgw3.law.pace.edu/cases/930113g1.html>
- Down jacket and winter coat case (22/3/1995) CISG/1995/05 (CIETAC arbitration proceeding) <http://cisgw3.law.pace.edu/cases/950322c1.html>
- Drukkerij Moderna v IVA Groep (28/6/2006) A.R. 06/1347 (Commercial Court Hasselt) <httcisgw3.law.pace.edu/cases/060628b1.html>
- Dust ventilator case (17/11/2006) 24U501/06 (Higher Regional Court of Munich) <http://cisgw3.law.pace.edu/cases/061117g1.html>
- Dust ventilator case (21/6/2006) 1 C 1025/05 (Lower Court Landsberg) <http://cisgw3.law.pace.edu/cases/060621g1.html>
- Dye for clothes case (20/6/1997) 755/95-C (Appellate Court Barcelona) <https://cisgw3.law.pace.edu/cases/970620s4.html>
- Electric heaters case (30/3/1999) CISG/1999/15 (CIETAC Arbitration) <https://cisgw3.law.pace.edu/cases/990330c3.html>
- Engines for hydraulic presses and welding machines case (23/6/1994) 31O231/94 (District Court Düsseldorf) <http://cisgw3.law.pace.edu/cases/940623g1.html>

- Eyroflam S.A. v P.C.C. Rotterdam B.V. (15/10/2008) 295401/HAZA07–2802 (Rechtbank District Court Rotterdam) <http://cisgw3.law.pace.edu/cases/081015n2.html>
- Fabrics case (10/2/1994) 6 U 119/93 (Appellate Court Düsseldorf) <http://cisgw3.law.pace.edu/cases/940210g2.html>
- Fabrics case (21/3/2003) (District Court Berlin) <http://cisgw3.law.pace.edu/cases/030321g1.html>
- Fallini Stefano v Foodik (19/12/1991) 900336 (District Court Roermond) <http://cisgw3.law.pace.edu/cases/911219n1.html>
- Fashion textiles case (24/4/1990) 5C73/89 (Lower Court Oldenburg) <http://cisgw3.law.pace.edu/cases/900424g1.html>
- FCF SA v Adriafil Commerciale Srl (15/9/2000) 4C105/2000 (Bundesgericht Supreme Court) <http://cisgw3.law.pace.edu/cases/000915s2.html>
- Flippe Christian v Douet Sport Collections (19/1/1998) 97 009265 (District Court Besançon) <http://cisgw3.law.pace.edu/cases/980119f1.html>
- Flowers case (3/6/1998) 1 U 703/97–143 (Appellate Court Saarbrücken) <http://cisgw3.law.pace.edu/cases/980603g1.html>
- Fluorite case (2006) (China CIETAC arbitration proceeding) <http://cisgw3.law.pace.edu/cases/060200c1.htm>
- Foliopack v Daniplast (24/11/1989) 77/89 (Preturacircondariale Court of First Instance) <http://cisgw3.law.pace.edu/cases/891124i3.html>
- Frozen chicken legs case (2/3/2000) 546/1999 (Appellate Court Granada) <http://cisgw3.law.pace.edu/cases/000302s4.html>
- Frozen fish case (27/2/2003) 2 Ob 48/02a (Supreme Court Austria) <http://cisgw3.law.pace.edu/cases/030227a3.html>
- Frozen pork case (2/3/2005) (Federal Supreme Court) VIII ZR 67/04 <http://cisgw3.law.pace.edu/cases/050302g1.html>
- Frozen pork liver case (25/1/2006) 7 Ob 302/05w (ObersterGerichtshof Supreme Court) <http://cisgw3.law.pace.edu/cases/060125a3.html]>
- Frozen vegetable case (29/11/2005) 5HKO10734/02 (District Court München) <http://cisgw3.law.pace.edu/cases/051129g1.html>
- Fryer Holdings Pty Ltd v Liaoning MEC Group Co Ltd [2012] NSWSC 18 <http://www.cisg-online.ch/content/api/cisg/urteile/2325.pdf>
- Furniture case (27/4/1992) 6252 (District Court Locarno Campagna) <http://cisgw3.law.pace.edu/cases/920427s1.html>
- Furniture case (6/4/2000) 12 HKO 4174/99 (District Court München) <https://cisgw3.law.pace.edu/cases/000406g1.html>
- Gantry v Research Consulting Marketing (19/9/1995) 1707/93 (District Court Nivelles) <http://cisgw3.law.pace.edu/cases/950919b1.html>
- Ginza v Vista Corporation (17/1/2003) WASC 11; CIV 1647 of 1998 (Supreme Court of Western Australia) <http://cisgw3.law.pace.edu/cases/030117a2.html>
- Globes case (27/2/2002) 5 HKO 3936/00 (Landgericht District Court) <http://cisgw3.law.pace.edu/cases/020227g1.html>
- GMS modules case (30/8/2007) A3/2006/79 (District Court Zug) <https://cisgw3.law.pace.edu/cases/070830s1.html>

- Granulated plastic case (25/6/1996) 7O147/94 (District Court Paderborn) <http://cisgw3.law.pace.edu/cases/960625g1.html>
- Hydraulic press case (20/1/1994) CISG/1994/02 (CIETAC arbitration proceeding) <http://cisgw3.law.pace.edu/cases/940120c1.html>
- Industrial equipment case (23/1/1997) 8611/HV/JK (ICC arbitration) <https://cisgw3.law.pace.edu/cases/978611i1.html>
- Industrial furnace case (26/7/2007) I.37/04 (Appellate Court Canton) <http://cisgw3.law.pace.edu/cases/070726s1.html>
- Inflatable triumphal arch case (5/11/2002) OR.2001.00029 (Commercial Court of the Canton of Aargau) <http://cisgw3.law.pace.edu/cases/021105s1.html>
- International Housewares v SEB (31/3/2003) (High Court, Auckland) <http://cisgw3.law.pace.edu/cases/030331n6.html>
- Iron molybdenum case (28/2/1997) 1U167/95 (Appellate Court Hamburg) <http://cisgw3.law.pace.edu/cases/970228g1.html>
- ISEA Industrie v Lu (13/12/1995) 95–018179 (Appellate Court Paris) <http://cisgw3.law.pace.edu/cases/951213f1.html>
- Italdecor v Yiu's Industries (20/3/1998) (Appellate Court Milan) <https://cisgw3.law.pace.edu/cases/980320i3.html>
- Key press case (18/11/1993) 6U228/92 (Appellate Court Düsseldorf) <http://cisgw3.law.pace.edu/cases/931118g1.html>
- Kunsthaus Mathias Lempertz v Wilhelmina van der Geld (9/2/1999) rolnr. 97/805 <http://www.unilex.info/cisg/case/452>
- La San Giuseppe v Forti Moulding (31/8/1999) 98-CV-142493CM (Ontario Superior Court of Justice) <http://cisgw3.law.pace.edu/cases/990831c4.html>
- Laminated glass case (19/12/2007) 9 Ob 75/07f (Supreme Court) <http://cisgw3.law.pace.edu/cases/071219a3.html>
- LDPE film case (2006) CISG/2006/18 (CIETAC arbitration proceeding) <https://cisgw3.law.pace.edu/cases/060500c2.html>
- Lumber case (28/5/2002) 4C.395/2001/rnd (Federal Supreme Court) <http://cisgw3.law.pace.edu/cases/020528s1.html>
- Machine case (10/3/2003) Proz Nr 433/02 (Cantonal Court Appenzell Auserrhoden) <https://cisgw3.law.pace.edu/cases/030310s1.html>
- Machine case (19/12/2002) 19U8/02 (Appellate Court Karlsruhe) <http://cisgw3.law.pace.edu/cases/021219g1.html>
- Machine for producing hygienic tissues case (3/11/1999) VIIIZR287/98 (Supreme Court) <http://cisgw3.law.pace.edu/cases/991103g1.html>
- Machinery case (30/7/2007) Chamber of National and International Arbitration Milan <http://cisgw3.law.pace.edu/cases/070730i3.html>
- Machines case (13/4/2000) 2 Ob 100/00w (Supreme Court Austria) <http://cisgw3.law.pace.edu/cases/000413a3.html>
- Machines case) 20/12/2006) 4C.314/2006 (Federal Supreme Court) <https://cisgw3.law.pace.edu/cases/061220s1.html>
- Machines, devices and replacement parts case (2002) 12/1997/322 (District Court Schaffhausen) <http://cisgw3.law.pace.edu/cases/020225s1.html>

- MacromexSrl v Globex International Inc (23/10/2007) 50181T 0036406 (American Arbitration Association) <https://cisgw3.law.pace.edu/cases/071023a5.html>
- Mansonville Plastics v Kurtz GmbH (21.8.2003) C993594 (British Columbia Supreme Court Canada) <http://www.unilex.info/cisg/case/1168>
- Marble slabs case (27/9/1991) 2U1899/89 Appellate Court Koblenz <http://cisgw3.law.pace.edu/cases/910927g1.html>
- Meat case (28/10/1998) 4C179/1998/odi (Bundesgerich Supreme Court) <http://cisgw3.law.pace.edu/cases/981028s1.html>
- Memory module case (12/11/2001) 13 U 102/01 (Appellate Court Hamm) <http://cisgw3.law.pace.edu/cases/011112g1.html>
- Metallic covers case (28/4/2004) 862/2003-B (Appellate Court Barcelona) <http://cisgw3.law.pace.edu/cases/040428s4.html>
- Miami Valley Paper v Lebbing Engineering & Consulting (26/3/2009) 1:05-CV-00702 (Federal District Court Ohio) <http://cisgw3.law.pace.edu/cases/090326u1.html>
- MiamiValleyPaper, LLC v LebbingEngineering&ConsultingGmbH (10/10/2006) 1:05-CV-00702 (Federal District Court Ohio) <http://cisgw3.law.pace.edu/cases/061010u1.html>
- Milling equipment case (2/2/2004) 7 U 4/03 (Appellate Court Zweibrücken) <http://cisgw3.law.pace.edu/cases/040202g1.html>
- Minibus case (29/7/2009) (District Court Arnhem) LJN BJ4645; 172927/HA ZA 08–1230 <https://cisgw3.law.pace.edu/cases/090729n1.html>
- Mitchell Aircraft Spares v European Aircraft Service (27/10/1998) 97 C 5668 (Federal District Court Illinois) <http://cisgw3.law.pace.edu/cases/981027u1.html>
- Mitias v Solidea Srl (11/12/2008) n.2280/2007 (Tribunale di Forli District Court) <http://cisgw3.law.pace.edu/cases/081211i3.html>
- Mobile car phones case (21/4/2004) 15U88/03 (Appellate Court Düsseldorf) <https://cisgw3.law.pace.edu/cases/040421g3.html>
- Mobile shear baler case (31/5/2010) T-10/09 (Foreign Trade Court) <https://cisgw3.law.pace.edu/cases/100531sb.html>
- Model locomotives case (27/1/2004) 11/1999/99 (District Court Schaffhausen) <http://cisgw3.law.pace.edu/cases/040127s1.html>
- New Zealand mussels case (8/3/1995) VIIIZR159/94 (Supreme Court) <http://cisgw3.law.pace.edu/cases/950308g3.html>
- Norfolk Southern Railway Company v Power Source Supply Inc. (25/7/2008) 07–140-JJf (Federal District Court) <https://cisgw3.law.pace.edu/cases/080725u1.html>
- NV Boco v S.r.l. LenziEgisto (8/11/2004) 2001/AR/1982 (Hof van Beroep Appellate Court Gent) <http://cisgw3.law.pace.edu/cases/041108b1.html>
- Old boxboard corrugated cartons case (8/3/1996) CISG/1996/12 (CIETAC arbitration proceeding) <http://cisgw3.law.pace.edu/cases/960308c1.html>
- Organic barley case (13/11/2002) 27 U 346/02 (Appellate Court München) <http://cisgw3.law.pace.edu/cases/021113g1.html>

- Oven case (27/4/2007) Canton Appellate Court Valais <https://cisgw3.law.pace.edu/cases/070427s1.html>
- Packaging machine case (8/11/2006) P-2004–152 (Civil Court Basil-Stadt) <https://cisgw3.law.pace.edu/cases/061108s1.html>
- Packaging machine case (26/9/2008) 16/2007/MEM/chi (Appellate Court Basel-Stadt Switzerland) <http://cisgw3.law.pace.edu/cases/080926s1.html>
- Packaging machine case (18/5/2009) 4A_68/2009 (Bundesgerichtshof Federal Supreme Court) <http://cisgw3.law.pace.edu/cases/090518s1.html>
- Palazzo Srl, Al v Bernardaud di Limoges SA (26/11/2002) 3095 (District Court Rimini) <http://cisgw3.law.pace.edu/cases/021126i3.html>
- Pallets case (11/12/2002) 1 C 419/01 (Lower Court Viechtach) <http://cisgw3.law.pace.edu/cases/020411g1.html>
- Paperboard containers case (12/1/2007) 19 U 11/07 (Appellate Court Köln) <http://cisgw3.law.pace.edu/cases/070112g1.html>
- Plants case (12/12/2006) 22 O 38/06 (District Court Coburg) <http://cisgw3.law.pace.edu/cases/061212g1.html>
- Plants case (23/10/2006) 2O51/02 (District Court Bamberg) <http://cisgw3.law.pace.edu/cases/061023g1.html>
- Plastic ketchup bottles case (15/9/2003) 3U19/03 (Appellate Court Rostock) <https://cisgw3.law.pace.edu/cases/030915g1.html>
- Pocket ash-trays case (10/10/2005) 4P.146/2005/biz (Supreme Court) <http://cisgw3.law.pace.edu/cases/051010s1.html>
- Poppy seed case (3/5/2007) 43Cg34/05f (Commercial Court Vienna) <http://cisgw3.law.pace.edu/cases/070503a3.html>
- Potato seedling case (19/12/2006) 05/03275 (Appellate Court Rouen) <http://cisgw3.law.pace.edu/cases/061219f1.html>
- Powdered milk case (9/1/2002) VIII ZR 304/00 (Supreme Court Germany) <http://cisgw3.law.pace.edu/cases/020109g1.html>
- Printed materials case (25/6/2007) HG050430/U/ei (Commercial Court Zürich) <http://cisgw3.law.pace.edu/cases/070625s1.html>
- Printed work case (29/5/2012) 88O57/11 District Court <https://cisgw3.law.pace.edu/cases/120529g1.html>
- Printing system and software case (4/12/1996) VIIIZR306/95 (Supreme Court) <http://cisgw3.law.pace.edu/cases/961204g1.html>
- Proof vest case (2009) 4505/2009 (Multi-Member Court of First Instance of Athens) <http://cisgw3.law.pace.edu/cases/094505gr.html>
- PVC and other synthetic materials case (21/10/1999) A3 1997 61 (District Court Zug Switzerland) <http://cisgw3.law.pace.edu/cases/991021s1.html>
- Racing carts case (25/3/2003) 3 O 196/01 (District Court Köln) <http://cisgw3.law.pace.edu/cases/030325g1.html>
- Rebar coil case (20/11/1997) CISG/1997/32 (CIETAC arbitration proceeding) <http://cisgw3.law.pace.edu/cases/971120c1.html>
- Recycling machine case (8/11/2005) 4Ob179/05k (Supreme Court) <http://cisgw3.law.pace.edu/cases/051108a3.html>

- Red pepper powder case (25/5/2012) 267/2012 (Appellate Court Murcia) <http://cisgw3.law.pace.edu/cases/120525s4.html>
- RJ & AM Smallmon v Transport Sales Limited and Grant Alan Miller (30/7/2010) CIV-2009–409–000363 (High Court of New Zealand) <http://cisgw3.law.pace.edu/cases/100730n6.html>
- RJ & AM Smallmon v Transport Sales Limited and Grant Alan Miller (22/7/2011) C A545/2010 [2011] NZ C A 340 (Court of Appeal of New Zealand) <http://cisgw3.law.pace.edu/cases/110722n6.html>
- Roland Schmidt GmbH v Textil-Werke Blumenegg AG (22/12/2000) 4C.296/2000/rnd (Federal Supreme Court Switzerland) <http://cisgw3.law.pace.edu/cases/001222s1.html>
- Rolled steel case (3/11/1997) 729/96-B (Appellate Court Barcelona) <https://cisgw3.law.pace.edu/cases/971103s4.html>
- Rynpoort Trading v MenebaMeel (23/4/2003) 99/474 (Appellate Court's-Gravenhage) <http://cisgw3.law.pace.edu/cases/030423n1.html>
- S.r.l. R.C. v BV BA R.T. (2001) 1997/AR/1554 (Appellate Court Antwerp) <http://cisgw3.law.pace.edu/cases/010627b1.html>
- Sacovini/M Marrazza v Les fils de Henri Ramel (23/1/1996) (Supreme Court) <http://cisgw3.law.pace.edu/cases/960123f1.html>
- Saltwater isolation tank case (26/4/1995) HG 920670 (Commercial Court Zürich) <http://cisgw3.law.pace.edu/cases/950426s1.html>
- Scaffold fittings case (1994) 7531(Court of Arbitration of the International Chamber of Commerce) <http://cisgw3.law.pace.edu/cases/947531i1.html>
- Schmitz-Werke GMBH Co v Rockland Industries Inc (21/06/2002) 1125 (US Court of Appeals) <http://cisgw3.law.pace.edu/cases/020621u1.html>
- Secondhand bulldozer case (28/10/1997) C1/97/167 (Appellate Court Valais) <http://cisgw3.law.pace.edu/cases/971028s1.html>
- SergueevHandelsagentur, Dr S v DAT-SCHAUB A/S (31/1/2002) H-0126–98 (Copenhagen Maritime Commercial Court) <http://cisgw3.law.pace.edu/cases/020131d1.html>
- Shanghai Anlili International Trading v J & P Golden Wings (25/12/2008) (Shanghai First Intermediate People's Court District Court) <http://cisgw3.law.pace.edu/cases/081225c1.html>
- Shoe case (6/7/2007) 4C4003/06 (Lower Court Freiburg) <http://cisgw3.law.pace.edu/cases/070706g1.html>
- Shoe leather case (11/5/2007) V CSK 456/06 (Supreme Court of Poland).
- Shoe soles case (29/7/1998) 3HKO43/98 (District Court Erfurt) <http://cisgw3.law.pace.edu/cases/980729g1.html>
- Shoes case (31/8/1989) 3KfHO97/89 (District Court Stuttgart) <http://cisgw3.law.pace.edu/cases/890831g1.html>
- Shoes case (1990) 41 O 198/89 (District Court Aachen) <http://cisgw3.law.pace.edu/cases/900403g1.html>
- Shoes case (3/4/1990) 41 O 198/89 (District Court Aachen) <http://cisgw3.law.pace.edu/cases/900403g1.html>

- Shoes case (17/9/1991) 5 U 164/90 (Appellate Court Frankfurt) <http://cisgw3.law.pace.edu/cases/910917g1.html>
- Shoes case (18/1/1994) 5U15/93 (Appellate Court Frankfurt) <https://cisgw3.law.pace.edu/cases/940118g1.html>
- Shoes case (14/6/1994) 3C75/94 (Lower Court Nordhorn) <https://cisgw3.law.pace.edu/cases/940614g1.html>
- Shoes case (15/9/1994) 52 S 247/94 (District Court Berlin) <http://cisgw3.law.pace.edu/cases/940915g1.html>
- Shoes case (24/4/1997) 6 U 87/96 (Düsseldorf Appellate Court) <http://cisgw3.law.pace.edu/cases/970424g1.html>
- Shoes case (21/11/2007) (Appellate Court Koblenz) <http://cisgw3.law.pace.edu/cases/071121g1.html>
- Skincare products case (30/7/1998) S 96/1215 (Helsinki Court of Appeal) <http://cisgw3.law.pace.edu/cases/980630f5.html>
- Souvenir coins case (2000) CISG/2000/17 (CIETAC arbitration proceeding) <http://cisgw3.law.pace.edu/cases/000000c1.html>
- Soy protein products case (22/8/2003) 33/2002/SAS/so (Canton Appellate Court Basel) <http://cisgw3.law.pace.edu/cases/030822s1.html>
- Spoldzielnia Pracy "A" in N v GmbH & Co KG in B (11/5/2007) V CSK 456/06 (Supreme Court of Poland) <http://cisgw3.law.pace.edu/cases/070511p1.html>
- Sport clothing case (5/4/1995) 54 O 644/94 (Landshut District Court) <https://cisgw3.law.pace.edu/cases/950405g1.html>
- Sports clothing case (29/6/1998) CI97–288 (Appellate Court Valais) <https://cisgw3.law.pace.edu/cases/980629s1.html>
- Srl RC v BV BA R.T (27/6/2001) 1997/AR/1554 (Appellate Court Antwerp) <http://cisgw3.law.pace.edu/cases/010627b1.html>
- Stainless steel plate case (23/1/2004) 17U110/02 (Appellate Court Düsseldorf) <http://cisgw3.law.pace.edu/cases/040123g1.html>
- Steel cylinders case (19/1/2000) CISG/2000/08 (CIETAC arbitration proceeding) <http://cisgw3.law.pace.edu/cases/000119c1.html>
- Steinbock-Bjonustan EHF v NV Duma (4/6/2004) AR21–36/2003 (District Court Kortrijk) <https://cisgw3.law.pace.edu/cases/040604b1.html>
- Stones case (21/11/2001) 419O48/01 (District Court Hamburg) <https://cisgw3.law.pace.edu/cases/011221g1.html>
- Technical equipment case (26/10/2004) 02/00109 (Appellate Court Poitiers) < http://cisgw3.law.pace.edu/cases/041026f1.html>
- Television sets case (28/5/2004) I-17 U 20/02 (Appellate Court Düsseldorf) <https://cisgw3.law.pace.edu/cases/040528g1.html>
- Textile manufacturing equipment case (18/7/2002) CISG/2002/20 (CIETAC arbitration proceeding) <https://cisgw3.law.pace.edu/cases/020718c1.html>
- Textile product machines case (2002) 10377/2002 (ICC Arbitration) <http://cisgw3.law.pace.edu/cases/020377i1.html>
- Thread case (21/4/2004) 15 U 222/02 (Appellate Court Düsseldorf) <http://cisgw3.law.pace.edu/cases/040421g2.html>

- Timber case (15/10/1998) 2Ob191/98x (Supreme Court) <http://cisgw3.law.pace.edu/cases/981015a3.html>
- Tinned cucumbers case (1993) 17U82/92 (Appellate Court Düsseldorf) <http://cisgw3.law.pace.edu/cases/930108g1.html>
- Trekking shoes case (27/8/1999) 1 Ob 223/99x (Supreme Court Austria) <http://cisgw3.law.pace.edu/cases/990827a3.html>
- Truffles case (24/1/1996) 13O142/95 (District Court Bochum) <http://cisgw3.law.pace.edu/cases/960124g1.html>
- Unavailable name (11/6/1997) 255/1994 (Arbitration proceeding) <http://cisgw3.law.pace.edu/cases/970611r1.html>
- Unavailable name (24/1/2000) (Arbitration proceeding Russia) 54/1999 <http://cisgw3.law.pace.edu/cases/000124r1.html>
- Unavailable name (6/6/2003) 97/2002 (Arbitration proceeding Russia) <http://cisgw3.law.pace.edu/cases/030606r1.html>
- Unavailable name (1/3/2006) 101/2005 (Tribunal of International Commercial Arbitration) <https://cisgw3.law.pace.edu/cases/060301r1.html>
- Unavailable name (3/4/2006) 105/2005 (Arbitration proceeding) <https://cisgw3.law.pace.edu/cases/060413r1.html>
- Used agricultural machine (14/4/1993) (Lower Court Cloppenburg) <http://cisgw3.law.pace.edu/cases/930414g1.html>
- Used automobiles case (17/1/2008) 81/2001 (Supreme Court Spain) <http://cisgw3.law.pace.edu/cases/080117s4.html>
- Used car case (21/5/1996) 22 U 4/96 (Appellate Court Köln Oberlandesgericht) <http://cisgw3.law.pace.edu/cases/960521g1.html>
- Used printing press case (24/5/1995) 20U76/94 (Appellate Court Celle) <http://cisgw3.law.pace.edu/cases/950524g1.html>
- Used shoes case (11/4/2005) (Landgericht District Court Frankfurt) <http://cisgw3.law.pace.edu/cases/050411g1.html>
- Valero Marketing & Supply Company v Greeni Trading Oy (19/7/2007) 06–3390/06–3525 (Federal Court of Appeals) <https://cisgw3.law.pace.edu/cases/070719u2.html>
- Valero Marketing v Greeni Oy (15/6/2005) CIV.01–5254 (DRD) (Federal District Court) <http://cisgw3.law.pace.edu/cases/050615u1.html>
- Valero Marketing v Greeni Oy (4/4/2006) Civ.01–5254 (Federal District Court) <https://cisgw3.law.pace.edu/cases/060404u1.html>
- Varnish and paint machine case (18/10/2005) 21/2005 (Arbitration proceeding Russia) <http://cisgw3.law.pace.edu/cases/051018r1.html>
- Vine wax case (24/3/1999) VIII ZR 121/98 (Supreme Court Germany) <http://cisgw3.law.pace.edu/cases/990324g1.html>
- Watermelon case (16/1/2009) 197586/KGZA08–659 (Rechtbank District Court Breda) <http://cisgw3.law.pace.edu/cases/090116n1.html>
- Weaving machines, tools and accessories case (5/9/1994) CIETAC Arbitration proceeding <http://cisgw3.law.pace.edu/cases/940905c2.html>
- Wine case (12/10/1995) 7 HO 78/95 (District Court Trier) <http://cisgw3.law.pace.edu/cases/951012g1.html>

- Wire and cable case (11/2/2004) 304/II/2003/wuda/scch (Appellate Court Bern) <http://cisgw3.law.pace.edu/cases/040211s1.html>

**English Cases**

- Alfred McAlpine Plc v BAI (Run-Off) Ltd [2000] 1 All ER (Comm) 545
- Alfred Toepfer v Continental Grain [1974] 1 Lloyd's Rep 11
- Alghussein Establishment v Eton College [1988] 1 WLR 587
- Ampurius Nu Homes Holdings Ltd v Telford Homes (Creekside) Ltd [2013] EWCA civ 577
- Andrews v Hopkinson [1957] 1 QB 229
- Andrews Bros v Singer [1934] 1 KB 17
- Antaios Compania Naviera SA v Salen Rederierna AB (The Antaios) [1985] AC 191(HL)
- Arcos Ltd v EA Ronaasen & Son [1933] AC 470
- Arden LJ in Valilas v Januzaj [2014] EWCA Civ 436
- Arnold v Britton [2015] UKSC 36
- Aron & Co Inc, J v Comptoir Wegimont SA[1921] 3 KB 435
- Aruna Mills Ltd v Dhanrajmal Gobindram [1968] 1 QB 655
- Ashington Piggeries Ltd v Christopher Hill Ltd [1972] AC 441
- Astea (UK) Ltd v Time Group Ltd [2003] EWHC 725 [144] (TCC)
- Aswan Engineering Establishment v Lupdine Ltd [1987] 1 WLR 1
- Attorney General of Belize v Belize Telecom Ltd [2009] UKPC 10
- Atwood v Emery 140 ER 45
- Bank Line Ltd v Arthur Capel & Co [1919] AC 435
- Bannerman v White 142 ER 685
- Beale v Taylor [1967] 1 WLR 1193, 1194
- Behn v Burness (1863) 122 ER 281
- Behzadi v Shaftesbury Hotels Ltd [1992] Ch 1
- Bentsen v Taylor Sons (No. 2) [1893] 2 QB 274, 281
- Berlian Laju Tanker TBK, PT v Nuse Shipping Ltd [2008] 1 CLC 967
- Bernstein v Pamson Motors (Golders Green) Ltd [1987] RTR 384
- Bettini v Gye (1876) 1 QBD 183
- Bisset v Wilkinson [1927] AC 177
- Bostock v Nicholson [1904] 1 KB 725
- Bowes v Shand (1877) 2 App Cas 455, 458
- Bradley & Sons, FC v Colonial Continental Trading [1964] 2 Lloyd's Rep 52
- Bramhill v Edwards [2004] EWCA Civ 403
- Bristol Tramways, & C, Carriage Company, Limited v Fiat Motors, Limited [1910] 2 KB 831
- British & Commonwealth Holdings Plc v Quadrex Holdings Inc [1995] CLC 1169
- Britvic Soft Drinks v Messer UK [2002] EWCA Civ 548
- Broadcrest CD Ltd v DOC Data (UK) Ltd [2000] 5 WLUK 124

- Fiat Auto Financial Services v Connelly [2007] SLT (Sh Ct) 111
- Fisher Reeves & Co Ltd v Armour & Co Ltd [1920] 3 KB 614
- Force India Formula One Team Ltd v Etihad Airways PJSC [2011] ETMR 10
- Freeman v Cooke (1848) 154 ER 652
- Geddling v Marsh [1920] 1 KB 668
- Gill & Duffus SA v Société pour l'Exportation des Sucres SA [1986] 1 Lloyd's Rep 322
- Gill & Duffus v Berger [1984] AC 382, 393
- Gillespie Bros & Co Ltd v Roy Bowles Transport Ltd [1973] QB 400
- Glass' Fruit Markets v Southwell (A) & Son (Fruit) [1969] 2 Lloyd's Rep 398
- Glynn v Margetson [1893] AC 351
- Godley v Perry [1960] 1 WLR 9
- Goldup v John Manson Ltd [1982] QB 161
- Grain Trade LLP (UK), RG v Feed Factors International [2011] EWHC 1889 (Comm)
- Green Ltd, RW v Cade Bros Farms [1978] 1 Lloyd's Rep 602
- Grenfell v E B Meyrowitz Ltd [1936] 2 All ER 1313
- Grimoldby v Wells (1874–75) LR 10 CP 391
- Guy-Pell v Foster [1930] 2 Ch 169
- Harbutt's Plasticine Ltd v Wayne Tank & Pump Co Ltd [1970] 1 QB 447
- Hare v Nicoll [1966] 2 QB 130
- Harling v Eddy [1951] 2 KB 739
- Harlingdon and Leinster Enterprises Ltd v Christopher Hull Fine Art Ltd [1991] 1 QB 564
- Harnor v Groves (1855) 139 ER 587
- Harrison, T&J v Knowles [1918] 1 KB 608
- Hartley v Hymans [1920] 3 KB 475
- Hazlewood Grocery Ltd v Lion Foods Ltd [2007] EWHC 1887.
- Heilbutt v Hickson (1871–72) LR 7 CP 438541
- Henry Kendall & Sons (a firm) v William Lillico & Sons Ltd and Others [1968] 2 All ER 444.
- Heyman v Darwins Ltd [1942] AC 356
- Hick v Raymond & Reid [1893] AC 22
- Honck v Muller (1881) 7 QBD 92
- Hong Kong Fir Shipping Co Ltd v Kawasaki Kisen Kaisha Ltd (The Hong Kong Fir) [1962] 2 QB 26
- Hopkins v Tanqueray (1854) 139 ER 369
- Hudson v Temple 54 ER 735
- Hydraulic Engineering Co Ltd v McHaffie Goslett & Co (1878) 4 QBD 670
- Investors Compensation Scheme Ltd v West Bromwich Building Society (No. 1) [1998] 1 WLR 896
- Jackson v Rotax Motor and Cycle Co [1910] 2 KB 937
- Jacobson van den Berg & Co (UK) v Biba [1977] 1 WLUK 254
- Jendwine v Slade (1797) 170 ER 459
- Jewson v Boyhan [2003] EWCA Civ 1030

- Phibro Energy AG v Nissho Iwai Corp (The Honam Jade) [1991] 1 Lloyd's Rep 38
- Phibro Energy Inc v Coastal (Bermuda) Ltd [1987] 4 WLUK 158
- Philip Head & Sons Ltd v Showfronts Ltd [1970] 1 Lloyd's Rep 140
- Pinnock Bros v Lewis & Peat Ltd [1923] 1 KB 690
- Porter v General Guarantee Corp [1982] RTR 384
- Postlethwaite v Freeland (1880) 5 App. Cas 599
- Poulton v Lattimore (1829) 109 ER 96
- Poussard v Speirs & Pond (1876) 1 QBD 410
- Power v Barham (1836) 111 ER 865
- Prenn v Simmonds [1971] 1 WLR 1381
- Proton Energy Group SA v Orlen Lietuva [2013] EWHC 2872 (Comm)
- Raineri v Miles [1981] AC 1050
- Rapalli v KL Take [1958] 2 Lloyd's Rep 469
- Reardon Smith Line Ltd v Hansen-Tangen (The Diana Prosperity) [1976] 1 WLR 989
- Reuter Hufeland v Sala (1879) 4 CPD 239
- Rice (t/a Garden Guardian) v Great Yarmouth BC [2000] 6 WLUK 829
- Robert A Munro & Co v Meyer [1930] 2 KB 312
- Rogers v Parish (Scarborough) Ltd [1987] QB 933
- Routledge v McKay v Nugent, Ashgrove, Mawson [1954] 1 WLR 615
- Rowland v Divall [1923] 2 KB 500
- Ruxley Electronics v Forsyth [1996] AC 344
- Saunt v Belcher and Gibbons [1920] All ER Rep 142
- Scandinavian Trading Co A/B v Zodiac Petroleum SA (The Al Hofuf) [1981] 1 Lloyd's Rep 81
- Schuler AG, L v Wickman Machine Tool Sales Ltd [1974] AC 235
- Shawton Engineering Ltd v DGP International Ltd (t/a Design Group Partnership) [2005] EWCA Civ 1359
- Shine v General Guarantee Corp [1988] 1 All ER 911
- Shore v Wilson 8 ER 450
- Skandia Property (UK) v Thames Water Utilities [1999] 7 WLUK 561
- Skanska Rasleigh Weatherfoil Ltd v Somerfield Stores Ltd [2006] EWCA Civ 1732
- Smith v Hughes (1870–71) LR 6 QB 597
- Soufflet Negoce SA v Bunge SA [2010] EWCA Civ 1102
- Stanton v Richardson (1873–74) LR 9 CP 390
- Steedman v Drinkle [1916] 1 AC 275
- Steels v Bleecker Bik [1956] 1 Lloyd's Rep 228
- Stickney v Keeble [1915] AC 386
- Stocznia Gdanska SA v Latvian Shipping Co (Repudiation) [2003] 1 CLC 282
- Suisse Atlantique Société d'Armement SA v NV Rotterdamsche Kolen Centrale [1967] 1 AC 361
- Sumner Permain v Webb [1922] 1 KB 55
- Susan Couch v The Attorney-General [2010] NZSC27.

- SW Tubes v Owen Stuart [2002] EWCA Civ 854
- Taylor v Caldwell [1989] SCCR 273
- Tele2 International Card Co SA v Post Office Ltd [2009] EWCA Civ 9
- Thain v Anniesland Trade Centre (1997) SLT (Sh Ct) 102
- Thames and Mersey Marine Insurance Co Ltd v Hamilton Fraser (1887) 12 App Cas 484
- The State Trading Corporation of India Limited v M. Golodetz Limited [1989] 7 WLUK 93
- Thomson v Weems (1884) 9 App Cas 671 (HL) 684
- Thornett & Fehr v Beers &Son [1919] 1 KB 486
- Thunderbird Industries LLC v Simoco Digital UK Ltd [2004] EWHC 209
- Toepfer v Warinco AG [1978] 2 Lloyd's Rep 569
- Torvald Klaveness A/S v Arni Maritime Corp (The Gregos) [1994] 1 W.L.R. 1465
- Tradax Export SA v European Grain & Shipping Ltd [1983] 2 Lloyd's Rep 100
- Tradax Internacional SA v Goldschmidt SA [1977] 2 Lloyd's Rep 604
- Travers (Joseph) v Longel (1948) 64 TLR 150
- Trollope & Colls Ltd v North West Metropolitan Regional Hospital Board [1973] 1 WLR 601
- Truk (UK) Ltd v Tokmakidis GmbH [2000] 2 All E.R. (Comm) 594
- Turnock v Fortune (1989) SLT (Sh Ct) 32
- Underwood Ltd v Burgh Castle Brick & Cement Syndicate [1922] 1 K.B. 343
- Union Eagle Ltd v Golden Achievement Ltd [1997] AC 514
- United Scientific Holdings Ltd v Burnley BC [1978] AC 904.
- Universal Cargo Carriers Corp v Citati (No. 2) [1958] 2 QB 254
- Vacwell Engineering v BDH Chemicals [1971] 1 QB 88
- Vallejo v Wheeler (1774) 98 ER 1012, 1017
- Van Wyk v Norden Laboratories 345 NW2d (Iowa 1984) 81–84
- Varley v Whipp [1900] 1 QB 513
- Vitol SA v Beta Renowable Group SA [2017] EWHC 1734
- Vitol SA v Norelf Ltd (The Santa Clara) [1996] AC 800
- Walker v Milner (1866) 176 ER 773
- Wallis Son & Wells v Pratt & Haynes [1911] AC 394
- Wärtsilä France SAS v Genergy plc [2003] EWHC 1966 (TCC)
- White Rosebay Shipping SA v Hong Kong Chain Glory Shipping Ltd [2013] 2 CLC 884
- Wilson v Rickett Cockerell [1954] 1 QB 598.
- Wimshurst v Deeley 135 ER 942
- Winnipeg Fish Co v Whitman Fish Co (1909) 41 SCR 453
- WJ Tatem Ltd v Gamboa [1939] 1 KB 132
- Wood v Capita Insurance Services Ltd [2017] UKSC 24
- Wormell v RHM Agricultural (East) Ltd[1987] 1 WLR 1091
- Wren v Holt [1903] 1 KB 610
- Yam Seng Pte Ltd v International Trade Corp Ltd [2013] EWHC 111.

### Australian Cases

- Savage, JJ v *Blakney (1970) 119 CLR 435*
- Grant v Australian Knitting Mills Ltd [1936] AC 85

### New Zealand Cases

- Easterbrook v Hopkins [1918] NZLR 428
- Susan Couch v The Attorney-General [2010] NZSC27
- Taylor v Combined Buyers Ltd [1924] GLR 51
- Turner v Anquetil [1953] NZLR 952

### Kuwaiti Cases

- Case 8/11/1970 Court of Cassation/Commercial 228/70
- Case 26/6/1990 Court of Cassation/Commercial 15/89
- Case 17/11/1991 Court of Cassation/Commercial 123/1990
- Case 30/12/1991 Court of Cassation/Commercial 214/90
- Case 29/3/1992 Court of Cassation/Commercial 233/90
- Case 17/4/1995 Appellate Court/Commercial-1 293/1995
- Case 17/4/1995 Appellate Court/Commercial-1 297/1995
- Case 22/5/1995 Appellate Court/Civil 2 17/95
- Case 9/10/1995 Appellate Court/Commercial 866/1995
- Case 7/11/1995 Court of Cassation/Commercial 4 400/1995
- Case 31/12/1995 Appellate Court/Civil 407/1995
- Case 29/1/1996 Appellate Court/Commercial-1 1302/95
- Case 6/2/1996 Appellate Court/Commercial 932/1995
- Case 13/2/1996 Appellate Court/Commercial 1429/95
- Case 25/3/1996 Appellate Court/Commercial 357/1995
- Case 31/3/1996 Court of Cassation/Commercial 3 439/95
- Case 15/4/1996 Appellate Court/Commercial-2 1346/1995
- Case 4/6/1996 Appellate Court/Commercial 933/1995
- Case 18/6/1996 Appellate Court/Commercial-4 1427/1995
- Case 15/10/1996 Appellate Court/Commercial-3 406/1996
- Case 11/11/1996 Appellate Court/Commercial 574/96
- Case 18/11/1996 Appellate Court/Commercial 1024/1995
- Case 27/11/1996 Appellate Court/Civil 439/1996
- Case 9/12/1996 Appellate Court/Commercial-4 1368/1995
- Case 4/1/1997 Appellate Court/Commercial-4 658/96
- Case 20/5/1998 Appellate Court/Commercial-5 793/98
- Case 30/9/1998 Appellate Court/Commercial-5 1416/1998
- Case 1/11/1998 Court of Cassation/Commercial 636/1997
- Case 17/2/1999 Appellate Court/Commercial 1453/1998
- Case 14/6/1999 Appellate Court/Commercial 1207/1998
- Case 11/10/1999 Appellate Court/Commercial 1988–2072/1998
- Case 19/6/2000 Court of Cassation/Civil 249/1999

- Case 27/12/2007 Court of Cassation/Commercial-1 417/2006
- Case 31/1/2008 Appellate Court/Commercial 2486–2529/2007
- Case 16/3/2008 Court of Cassation/Commercial 467, 476/2008
- Case 25/9/2008 Court of Cassation/Commercial 1314–1330/2005
- Case 30/12/2008 Court of Cassation/Commercial-3 92/2008
- Case 6/1/2009 Court of Cassation/Commercial 1 384/2006
- Case 8/1/2009 Appellate Court/Civil-4 1487–1491/2008
- Case 29/12/2009 Court of Cassation/Commercial 768,781/2007
- Case 27/4/2010 Court of Cassation/Commercial 865/2008
- Case 10/5/2010 Court of Cassation/Civil-2 98586
- Case 29/6/2010 Court of Cassation/Commercial 3 656/2007
- Case 2/11/2010 Court of Cassation/Commercial 1175/2008
- Case 3/10/2011 Court of Cassation/Civil 783/2010
- Case 20/12/2011 Court of Cassation/Commercial 2009/1498
- Case 7/2/2012 Court of Cassation/Commercial 188, 225, 237/2010
- Case 14/2/2012 Court of Cassation/Commercial 499/2011
- Case 5/3/2012 Court of Cassation/Civil 435/2010
- Case 16/4/2012 Court of Cassation/Civil 165/2011
- Case 17/4/2012 Court of Cassation/Commercial-1 1720/2010

**Kuwaiti Cases in Ministry of Justice: The Legal Principles Decided by the Court of Cassation During Forty Years, in Civil Provisions, Volume 11 (2016)**

- Case 23/4/1989 Court of Cassation/Commercial 333/88
- Case 13/11/1989 Court of Cassation 116/89
- Case 20/11/1989 Court of Cassation/Commercial 180/98
- Case 18/12/1989 Court of Cassation/Commercial 170–172/89
- Case 10/5/1993 Court of Cassation/Commercial 194/92
- Case 14/6/1993 Court of Cassation/Commercial 212/92
- Case 28/6/1993 Court of Cassation/Commercial 222–232/93
- Case 7/2/1995 Court of Cassation/Commercial 193/94, 5–6
- Case 28/4/1997 Court of Cassation/Commercial 298/96
- Case 6/3/2003 Court of Cassation/Commercial 549/2003
- Case 25/5/2005 Court of Cassation/Commercial 857/2003
- Case 15/10/2006 Court of Cassation/Commercial 876/2005
- Case 20/3/2007 Court of Cassation/commercial 291/2003
- Case 16/12/2007 Court of Cassation/Commercial 1062/2006
- Case 27/4/2010 Court of Cassation/Commercial 865, 872/2008
- Case 29/6/2010 Court of Cassation/Commercial 656/2007

**Kuwaiti Cases in Ministry of Justice, The Legal Principles Decided by the Court of Cassation During Forty Years, in Commercial Provisions, Volume 9 (2016)**

- Case 14/12/1983 Court of Cassation/Commercial 70/83
- Case 6/11/1985 Court of Cassation/Commercial 18/85

- Case 12/1/1987 Court of Cassation/Civil 18/86
- Case 1/6/1987 Court of Cassation/Civil 11/87
- Case 5/6/1988 Court of Cassation/Commercial 55/88
- Case 25/6/1990 Court of Cassation/Commercial 62/90
- Case 18/1/1993 Court of Cassation 94/92
- Case 21/2/1993 Court of Cassation/Commercial 147/92
- Case 6/11/1998 Court of Cassation/Commercial 85
- Case 27/11/2000 Court of Cassation/Commercial 145/99

# Legislations

**Transnational Law**

- United Nations Convention on Contracts for the International Sale of Goods (CISG)
- Vienna Convention on the Law of Treaties 1969

**Soft Law**

- INCOTERMS 2000
- UNIDROIT Principles of International Commercial Contracts 2016 (UPICC)

**Legislations in England**

- The Sale of Goods Act 1979 01/02/1991c 54 (SGA)

**Legislations in Kuwait**

- Al-Majalla of Islamic Principles of Obligations 1876 (Al-Majalla)
- Civil and Commercial Procedure Law (Part 2) No. 17 1960
- Civil Code No. 67 of 1980 (KCIC)
- Commercial Code No. 68 of 1980 (KCOC)
- Explanatory Memorandum of Civil Code 1980 (EMKCIC)
- Law on Evidence of Civil and Commercial Provisions No. 39 1980

**Other Laws**

- French Civil Code 2016
- German Civil Code 2002
- Iraqi Civil Code 1951
- Lebanese Law (The Code of Obligations and Contracts of 1932)
- Moroccan Obligations Law 2016

# 1 Introduction

## 1.1 Theoretical and Brief Historical Background

### *1.1.1 International Sale of Goods and CISG*

Each country has limited natural resources, making the notion of self-sufficiency fictitious,[1] and this has contributed to a dramatic increase in the exchange of goods worldwide.[2] International sales account for two-thirds of world trade, and 40% of world trade occurs between intercontinental corporations.[3] International sales have led some companies to be economically greater than a number of countries. Mitsubishi, for instance, is the 22nd largest economy in the world, larger than the economies of Denmark, Saudi Arabia, Malaysia, Chile, Turkey and Thailand.[4] International trade aids nations attaining economic prosperity,[5] exploiting productive ability,[6] fostering the alleviation of poverty[7] and contributing to cultural understanding.[8] In 2019, the world's reciprocal merchandise reached $37.7 trillion.[9]

The final report by the European Commission, 'Internationalisation of European Small and Medium-Sized Enterprises' (SMEs), reveals some of the barriers preventing the globalisation of SMEs: namely, laws and regulations in foreign countries and a lack of accessible legal information, affecting the potential of these

1 Frederick Ploeg, 'Natural Resources: Curse or Blessing?' (2011) 49(2) JEL 366, 399.
2 Joseph Stiglitz, *Globalization and Its Discontents* (Penguin Books 2002) 9.
3 Michael Woodin; Caroline Lucas, *Green Alternatives to Globalisation* (Pluto Press 2004) 18.
4 ibid.
5 Stiglitz (n 2) 4; Peter Bossche; Werner Zdouc, *The Law and Policy of the World Trade Organization* (4th edn, CUP 2017) 6.
6 ibid Bossche; Zdouc 20.
7 Stiglitz (n 2) 5.
8 Bossche; Zdouc (n 5) 16, 17, 21. See also Chibli Mallat, 'Commercial Law in the Middle East: Between Classical Transactions and Modern Business' (2000) 48(1) AmJCompL 81, 92.
9 Department of Economic and Social Affairs Statistics Division, *International Trade Statistics Yearbook Volume I* (UN 2020) 2 <https://comtrade.un.org/pb/downloads/2019/VolI2019.pdf>.

DOI: 10.4324/9781003466130-1

businesses to expand abroad.[10] This has stimulated the process of harmonising laws, which is likely to promote international commerce, permitting merchants to carry out business in multiple jurisdictions under one set of internationally recognised terms.[11] This could be easily applied, regardless of the merchants' conflicting beliefs, cultures and/or legal systems.[12] In 1980, the United Nations Commission on International Trade Law (UNCITRAL) promulgated the United Nations Convention on Contracts for the International Sale of Goods (CISG),[13] which contains a set of substantive rules governing the formation of and obligations under international contracts for the sale of goods. CISG has become one of the most widely implemented treaties in the field of commercial law. By November 2023, 97 states had adopted CISG,[14] including 9 of the 10 biggest national global traders.[15] With high levels of global acceptance, the Convention is becoming increasingly applicable.[16]

### *1.1.2 Sale of Goods and the UK (A Common Law Country)*

The UK is still reticent to join CISG, even though it had an effective role in drafting the Convention[17] and despite its high level of engagement in international sales. In September 2020, the total goods exported from the UK amounted to £25.9 billion, and imports were equivalent to £50 billion.[18] The following tables demonstrate the top ten countries exported to and the top ten goods exported from the UK in September 2020:

10 European Commission, *Internationalisation of European SMEs* (Entrepreneurship 2010) 60, 61.

11 Paul Berman, 'From International Law to Law and Globalization' (2005) 43 ColumJTransnatlL 485, 490; Jan Dalhuisen, *Dalhuisen on Transnational Comparative, Commercial, Financial and Trade Law Volume 3: Financial Products, Financial Services and Financial Regulation* (5th edn, Hart Publishing 2013) 627–629.

12 Silvia Nikolova, 'UK's Ratification of the CISG - An Old Debate or a New Hope for the Economy of the UK on Its Way out of the Recession: The Potential Impact of the CISG on the UK's SME'(2012) Pace Int Law Rev Online Companion 69, 76.

13 United Nations Commission on International Trade Law <http://www.uncitral.org/uncitral/en/uncitral_texts/sale_goods/1980CISG.html> accessed 21/3/2021.

14 Institute of International Commercial Law, 'CISG: Table of Contracting States' <https://iicl.law.pace.edu/cisg/page/cisg-table-contracting-states> accessed 18/11/2023.

15 Ingeborg Schwenzer, *Commentary on the UN Convention on the International Sale of Goods (CISG)* (4th edn, OUP 2016) 29 [4].

16 ibid.

17 Bruno Zeller, 'The Development of Uniform Laws – A Historical Perspective' (2002) 14(1) Pace Int Law Rev 163, 168, 169.

18 National Statistics, UK Overseas Trade in Goods Statistics: September 2020 <https://www.gov.uk/government/statistics/uk-overseas-trade-in-goods-statistics-september-2020> accessed 21/3/2021.

*Table 1.1* British Exportation of Goods – Top Ten Countries, September 2020[19]

| *September 2020* | |
|---|---|
| *Partner Country* | *Total (£ Millions)* |
| USA | 3,271 |
| Germany | 2,564 |
| Republic of Ireland | 1,907 |
| France | 1,745 |
| Netherlands | 1,494 |
| China | 1,249 |
| Belgium | 959 |
| Norway | 845 |
| Italy | 818 |
| Spain | 734 |
| Others | 10,279 |
| **Total EU** | 12,571 |
| **Total Non-EU** | 13,296 |
| **Total Exports** | **25,866** |

*Table 1.2* British Exportation – Top Ten Commodities, September 2020[20]

| *September 2020* | |
|---|---|
| *Commodity Description* | *Total (£ Millions)* |
| Mechanical appliances | 3,822 |
| Motor vehicles | 2,844 |
| Precious metals | 1,946 |
| Electronic equipment | 1,720 |
| Pharmaceutical products | 1,437 |
| Mineral fuels | 1,274 |
| Measuring devices and gauges | 1,178 |
| Aircraft | 923 |
| Plastics and plastic products | 726 |
| Other products | 704 |
| Others | 9,292 |
| **Total Exports** | **25,866** |

The following tables demonstrate the top ten countries imported from and the top ten goods imported into the UK in September 2020:

19 HM Revenue and Customs, UK Overseas Trade in Goods Statistics: September 2020 <https://assets.publishing.service.gov.uk/government/uploads/system/uploads/attachment_data/file/934482/OTS_Release_092020.pdf> 4.

20 ibid 7.

*Table 1.3* British Importation of Goods – Top Ten Countries, September 2020[21]

| *September 2020* | |
|---|---|
| *Partner Country* | *Total (£ Millions)* |
| China | 5,881 |
| Germany | 5,754 |
| USA | 3,875 |
| Russia | 3,079 |
| Netherlands | 2,969 |
| Hong Kong | 2,874 |
| Switzerland | 2,871 |
| Belgium | 2,231 |
| France | 2,191 |
| Italy | 1,574 |
| Others | 16,667 |
| **Total EU** | **21,492** |
| **Total Non-EU** | **28,476** |
| **Total Imports** | **49,967** |

*Table 1.4* British Exportation – Top Ten Commodities, September 2020[22]

| *September 2020* | |
|---|---|
| *Commodity Description* | *Total (£ Millions)* |
| Precious metals | 12,021 |
| Motor vehicles | 4,676 |
| Mechanical appliances | 4,530 |
| Electronic equipment | 3,902 |
| Mineral fuels | 2,142 |
| Pharmaceutical products | 1,624 |
| Plastics and plastic products | 1,476 |
| Measuring devices and gauges | 1,379 |
| Clothes, not knitted | 1,176 |
| Knitwear | 971 |
| Others | 16,071 |
| **Total Imports** | **49,967** |

The Sale of Goods Act 1979 01/02/1991C 54 (SGA) is a UK law, regarded as one of the major single enactments created for national commerce, which historically has earned a remarkable reputation for resolving international mercantile disputes.[23] SGA

21 ibid 11.

22 ibid 14.

23 Anna Rogowska, 'Some Considerations on the Desirability of Accession to the CISG by the UK' (2013) 5(2) EJCCL 31, 40.

came into force on 1 January1980,[24] incorporating the previous provisions of Sale of Goods Act 1893 and amendments. SGA applies in England, Wales and Northern Ireland, but there are substantial differences in its application in Scotland.[25]

In previous eras, limited types of goods were sold, and the buyer had the ability to examine the goods before purchase,[26] recognise defects and negotiate prices.[27] Therefore, the *caveat emptor* principle prevailed, placing the responsibility on the buyer to take precautions before purchasing goods, especially as the seller may have had no obligations so long as the exchange was not fraudulent.[28] Nevertheless, due to the industrial revolution, the sheer variety and quantity of goods produced and the desire of sellers to maintain a good reputation saw attitudes in court change accordingly.[29] The implied terms in SGA shifted the *caveat emptor* principle to the *caveat venditor* principle,[30] which imposes the responsibility on the seller.

### *1.1.3 Sale of Goods and Kuwait (A Civil Law Country)*

The international sale of goods has historically been regarded as crucial in Kuwait. During the 18th and 19th centuries, when large Kuwaiti vessels were engaged in trade with India, Kuwait depended on the transit of goods between Baghdad, Aleppo and Bahrain.[31] The pearl industry also dominated when merchants and captains dealt with international pearl markets.[32] Furthermore, the English East India Company increased the distribution of English goods to the East and West and bought Eastern goods for resale to Europe through Kuwait.[33] Nowadays, despite the fact that the Kuwaiti government, agents and traders are regularly parties to international sale of goods contracts, Kuwait is still a non-contracting state of CISG. The total value of goods exported from Kuwait in 2018 was $71.9 billion, and imports were $35.9 billion.[34] Table 1.5 details Kuwait's most imported and exported commodities, as well as statistics regarding its major trading partners by country in September 2020, according to the Central Statistical Bureau:

24 SGA s. 64(2).

25 Michael Blair, *Sale of Goods Act 1979* (Butterworths 1980) 1.

26 Marco Pistis, 'From *Caveat Emptor* to *Caveat Venditor*: A Brief History of English Sale of Goods Law' [2006] Mondaq Business Briefing 1, 2.

27 ibid 1.

28 Andrew Burrows, *Principles of English Commercial Law* (OUP 2015) 70; Michael Bridge, *The Sale of Goods* (4th edn, OUP 2019) [7.03]; Michael Bridge, *Benjamin's Sale of Goods* (11th edn, Sweet & Maxwell 2021) [11–024].

29 Pistis (n 26) 2.

30 *Beale v Taylor* [1967] 1 WLR 1193, 1196; Michael Furmston, *Law of Contract* (17th edn, OUP 2017) 187; Christian Twigg-Flesner; Rick Canavan, *Atiyah and Adams' Sale of Goods* (14th edn, Pearson 2021) 113.

31 Ismael Jacqueline, *Kuwait: Social Change in Historical Perspective* (Syracuse UP 1982) 30, 31; Ahmad Abu-Hakima, *The Modern History of Kuwait (1750–1965)* (Luzac & Company Limited 1983) 93.

32 ibid Jacqueline 33; Zahra Freez, *Kuwait Was My Home* (That Al-Salasel 1997) 156.

33 Abu-Hakima (n 31) 98.

34 Department of Economic and Social Affairs Statistics Division (n 9) 200.

*Table 1.5* Commodities Imported and Exported by Kuwait and the Top Countries Acting as Partners in International Sale of Goods Contracts With Kuwait in September 2020[35]

| *Foreign Trade by BEC Rev 4* | | |
|---|---|---|
| *Value in 1000 KD* | *2020 ربمتبس*<br>*September 2020* | |
| | القيمة<br>*Value* | الحصة (%)<br>*Share (%)* |
| **Exports** | | |
| **Total** | **1,084,663** | **100** |
| Food and beverages | 10,542 | 1.0 |
| Industrial supplies not specified elsewhere | 87,626 | 8.1 |
| Fuels and lubricants | 925,364 | 85.3 |
| Capital goods (except transport equipment) and parts and accessories thereof | 19,631 | 1.8 |
| Transport equipment and parts and accessories thereof | 32,337 | 3.0 |
| Consumer goods not specified elsewhere | 7,416 | 0.7 |
| Goods not specified elsewhere | 1,747 | 0.2 |
| **Imports** | | |
| **Total** | **702,807** | **100** |
| Food and beverages | 135,442 | 19.3 |
| Industrial supplies not specified elsewhere | 169,462 | 24.1 |
| Fuels and lubricants | 3,742 | 0.5 |
| Capital goods (except transport equipment) and parts and accessories thereof | 144,361 | 20.5 |
| Transport equipment and parts and accessories thereof | 72,554 | 10.3 |
| Consumer goods not specified elsewhere | 175,463 | 25.0 |
| Goods not specified elsewhere | 1,783 | 0.3 |

*(Continued)*

35 Central Statistical Bureau of Kuwait <https://www.csb.gov.kw/Pages/Statistics_en?ID=38&ParentCatID=4> accessed 12/2/2021.

*Table 1.5* (Continued)

*Imports by Major Partner Countries*

| *Value in 1000 KD* | | سبتمبر 2020<br>*September 2020* | |
|---|---|---|---|
| *Rank/Country* | القيمة<br>*Value* | الحصة (%)<br>*Share (%)* | التغيير %<br>*Change (%)* |
| **Total** | **702,807** | **100.0** | |
| 1 People's Republic of China | 108,954 | 15.5 | −23.4 |
| 2 United Arab Emirates | 73,326 | 10.4 | 19.6 |
| 3 United States of America | 61,651 | 8.8 | −21.9 |
| 4 Saudi Arabia | 41,639 | 5.9 | −12.3 |
| 5 India | 37,862 | 5.4 | −16.8 |
| 6 Germany | 30,871 | 4.4 | −41.6 |
| 7 Italy | 30,149 | 4.3 | −16.3 |
| 8 Japan | 25,648 | 3.6 | −37.4 |
| 9 Turkey | 22,587 | 3.2 | 38.0 |
| 10 France | 19,598 | 2.8 | −40.0 |
| 11 Switzerland | 18,632 | 2.7 | 45.0 |
| 12 Vietnam | 13,963 | 2.0 | 22.4 |
| 13 Bahrain | 13,574 | 1.9 | 39.6 |
| 14 United Kingdom | 13,396 | 1.9 | −37.3 |
| 15 Thailand | 10,117 | 1.4 | −28.9 |
| 16 Netherlands | 9,178 | 1.3 | 11.8 |
| 17 Brazil | 8,715 | 1.2 | 3.8 |
| 18 Sultanate of Oman | 8,542 | 1.2 | 87.4 |
| 19 South Korea | 8,047 | 1.1 | −50.3 |
| 20 Spain | 7,922 | 1.1 | −11.4 |
| Others | 138,436 | 19.7 | −15.1 |

*Non-Oil Exports by Major Partner Countries*

| *Value in 1000 KD* | سبتمبر 2020<br>*September 2020* | | |
|---|---|---|---|
| *Rank/Country* | القيمة<br>*Value* | الحصة (%)<br>*Share (%)* | التغيير %<br>*Change (%)* |
| **Total** | **1,084,663** | **100.0** | |
| 1 United Arab Emirates | 27,612 | 2.5 | 47.2 |
| 2 People's Republic of China | 22,058 | 2.0 | −20.8 |
| 3 Iraq | 18,805 | 1.7 | −53.4 |
| 4 Saudi Arabia | 18,588 | 1.7 | 8.1 |
| 5 India | 17,985 | 1.7 | −12.3 |
| 6 Sultanate of Oman | 12,332 | 1.1 | 88.9 |

*(Continued)*

*Table 1.5* (Continued)

| *Non-Oil Exports by Major Partner Countries* | | | |
|---|---|---|---|
| *Value in 1000 KD* | *2020 سبتمبر*<br>*September 2020* | | |
| *Rank/Country* | *القيمة*<br>*Value* | *الحصة (%)*<br>*Share (%)* | *التغيير %*<br>*Change (%)* |
| 7 Qatar | 7,006 | 0.6 | −14.3 |
| 8 Philippines | 5,482 | 0.5 | 2137.6 |
| 9 Pakistan | 3,825 | 0.4 | −48.9 |
| 10 Jordan | 3,594 | 0.3 | 30.5 |
| 11 Thailand | 1,836 | 0.2 | 396.2 |
| 12 Bahrain | 1,760 | 0.2 | 1.0 |
| 13 Portugal | 1,593 | 0.1 | −36.7 |
| 14 Egypt | 1,484 | 0.1 | 77.1 |
| 15 Turkey | 1,409 | 0.1 | 121.2 |
| 16 Vietnam | 1,365 | 0.1 | −18.6 |
| 17 Netherlands | 1,253 | 0.1 | 284.4 |
| 18 United States of America | 1,178 | 0.1 | 62.7 |
| Others | 935,498 | 86.2 | −33.9 |

In 1876, the Al-Majalla of Islamic Principles of Obligations (Al-Majalla) was established pursuant to the Hanafi School by the Ottoman Empire. It subsequently became the civil law in all Arab countries under Ottoman control and the operative law in Kuwait.[36] In 1961, Kuwait was indirectly influenced by the Code of Napoleon (French Code of 1804)[37] through Egypt, which adopted this law in 1883 and revised it in 1948 in accordance with Islamic principles and decisions of the Egyptian court.[38] In 1977, the Council of Ministries in Kuwait ordered the drafting of new legislation addressing the un-codified issues and revising the existent laws in light of the Constitution, Islamic law and Kuwaiti traditions.[39] In 1980, the new Civil Code No. 67 of 1980 (KCIC), its Explanatory Memorandum (EMKCIC) and Commercial Code No. 68 of 1980[40] (KCOC) were formally enacted.[41]

36 Mahendra Kumar, 'The Political and Legal Status of Kuwait' (1962) 11(1) ICLQ 108, 116; Nicholas Kourides, 'The Influence of Islamic Law on Contemporary Middle Eastern Legal Systems: The Formation and Binding Force of Contracts' (1970) 9(2) ColumJTransnatlL 384, 385; W Ballantyne, *Commercial Law in the Arab Middle East: The Gulf States* (Springer 1986) 50.

37 Jacqueline McCormack, 'Commercial Contracts in Muslim Countries of the Middle East: A Comparison with the United States' (2009) 37(1) IJLI 1, 7.

38 ibid 13; Husny Al-Masry, *Commercial Law of Kuwait* (Dar AlKotob) 43.

39 Isa Huneidi, 'Twenty-Five Years of Civil Law System in Kuwait' (1986) 1(2) Arab Law Q 216, 217.

40 Abdulrasool Abdulreda, *Hidden Defects* (Dar AlKotob 1998) 49; Abdulla Al-Hayan, *Explanation of Commercial Law* (Kuwait University 2015) 13.

41 Huneidi (n 39) 217; Ballantyne (n 36) 50.

### *1.1.4 Impact of Termination on Sale of Goods Contracts*

Contract law ensures 'contractual discipline' by delivering on promises, and this aids resource production and distribution worldwide while increasing social and economic welfare.[42] When a party does not adhere to the contractual obligations or legal requirements, the innocent party may find terminating the contract by disbandment of the contractual bond and returning the parties to the pre-conclusion of the contract[43] a suitable remedy in order to be released from a contract with an unreliable party. However, terminating a contract for the benefit of the innocent buyer due to *any* breach committed by the breaching seller,[44] even if such failure is insignificant to the contract's aims or is realistically minor to the aggrieved buyer, could be problematic. It would discard a series of laborious and time-consuming stages, such as negotiation, offer, acceptance and execution of the contract, and could create an obstacle to the flow of goods, both domestically and between nations.[45] As stated in the UNIDROIT Principles of International Commercial Contracts 2016 (UPICC),[46] '[T]ermination will often cause serious detriment to the non-performing party, whose expenses in preparing and tendering performance may not be recovered.'[47] Termination of a contract is costly, requiring re-shipment of the goods,[48] even those that are flawless,[49] and accruing associated expenses for transportation, storage, insurance and the administrative and health procedures necessary for the handling of the goods. The exposure of the goods to damage in transit, the refund (with interest)[50] and fluctuations of exchange rates add further pressure.[51] More problematically, an aggrieved party may view any breach as a pretext for terminating the contract, wishing to be released from the obligations imposed upon them[52] or to find another, more beneficial transaction. Consequently,

42 J Harker, 'The Nature and Scope of Rescission as a Remedy for Breach of Contract in American and South African Law' [1980] AJ 61–63.

43 Case 20/5/1998 Appellate Court/Commercial 793/98, 3; Andrew Burrows, *A Casebook on Contract* (7th edn, Hart 2020) 354.

44 Harker (n 42) 79.

45 Sonja Kruisinga, 'Incorporation of Standard Terms under the CISG and Electronic Communication,' in Ingeborg Schwenzer; Lisa Spagnolo, *Towards Uniformity: The 2nd Annual Maa Schlechtriem CISG Conference* (2nd edn, Eleven International Publishing 2010) 75.

46 UNIDROIT is an international organisation founded in 1926 with the aim of unifying private law. Giuditta Cordero-Moss, *International Commercial Contracts* (CUP 2014) 34.

47 UPICC 254.

48 Eduardo Grebler, 'Fundamental Breach of Contract under the CISG: A Controversial Rule' (2007) 101 ASIL 407, 409, 410.

49 Abdulreda (n 40) 396.

50 Egyptian Supreme Court (12/11/1974) 568 Y 39 Q S 25 P 1266 reproduced in Ahmed Ateya, *Nullity and Termination of Sale Contract* (Dar AlFeker 2012)266 ; Anwer Talaba, *Contractual Termination* (The Modern University Office 2004) 127, 128.

51 Muhsen Shafiq, *The UN Convention on the International Sale of Goods* (Dar Alnahda 1988) 33, 34.

52 Bader Al-Yaqob, *Principles of Obligation in Kuwaiti Civil Law* (Kuwait University 2012) 310, 311.

a certain degree of seriousness is crucial for termination,[53] and, if the breach is insignificant, resorting to other, less harsh remedies, such as payment of damages or a price reduction, would be more appropriate.[54]

## 1.2 The Scope of the Book

The field of this book is private law and its substantive and procedural rules with regard to the contractual relationship between buyer and seller. It tackles the differences between transnational law (CISG), which aims to harmonise commercial law, and two non-contracting states from different legal systems (England and Kuwait) in addressing the termination of sale of goods contracts. Where it is relevant, UPICC, which is a non-binding supplementary tool to other international instruments[55] in particular CISG,[56] will be mentioned. At the heart of the study is the right of the buyer who does not breach the contract to terminate the contract as a result of the seller's breach, particularly when the goods have been delayed in delivery, do not comply with contractual description or are of inferior quality. These issues are dealt with throughout the book, assuming the absence of the parties' implicit or explicit agreement to regulate the disputed matter contrary to law and assuming that the seller's breach is not due to force majeure. It is not the purpose of this study to analyse the meaning of 'internationality' in CISG or to scrutinise any other parties' rights, such as claims of damages.

CISG is chosen as a core for this book because it is 'a milestone in the movement to codify the private international law of the sale of goods and has achieved strong worldwide approval.'[57] A stable increase of approximately 5% in the use of transnational commercial law, particularly CISG, was recorded annually between 2004 and 2008.[58] Interestingly, global exchanges rose almost proportionately during that period.[59] SGA and KLaw have been selected because they are non-signatory to CISG. Parties all over the world have adopted SGA as their governing law and deem London to be their judicial forum, even when none of the parties are English.[60] KLaw has not pursued the legal development of either French or Egyptian

53 Harker (n 42) 79.

54 Lisa Spagnolo, *CISG Exclusion and Legal Efficiency* (KLI 2014) 52; Schwenzer, *Commentary on CISG* (n 15) 421 [9].

55 It is mentioned in the preamble that it can 'be used to interpret or supplement international uniform law instruments.' <http://www.unidroit.org/english/principles/contracts/principles2010/blackletter2010-english.pdf> accessed 10/12/2014.

56 Michael Bonell, *An International Restatement of Contract Law: The UNIDROIT Principles of International Commercial Contracts* (3rd edn, Transnational Publishers 2005) 305.

57 Andrew Babiak, 'Defining "Fundamental Breach" under the United Nations Convention on Contracts for the International Sale of Goods' (1992) 6(1) TempleIntlCompLJ 113.

58 Ingeborg Schwenzer; C Kee, Global Sales Law: Theory and Practice, in Schwenzer; Spagnolo, *Towards Uniformity* (n 45) 157.

59 ibid.

60 Angelo Forte, 'The United Nations Convention on Contracts for the International Sale of Goods: Reason and Unreason in the United Kingdom' (1997) 26(3) UBLR 51, 58; Ricardo Borges, 'The

jurisdictions as Egypt codified a new commercial law reflecting the influence of CISG in 1999,[61] and the French Civil Code was recently amended to follow UPICC,[62] which is compatible with CISG's general aims and purpose.

This book presumes a valid contract has been concluded, which produced its legal effects in the creation of obligations for both parties,[63] and excludes 'rescission,' which is associated with defective consent, such as mistake, fraud or duress.[64] A 'contract' can be defined as a mandatory bond between parties, which is effective once an offer is linked with acceptance,[65] to establish business dealings by fulfilling legal obligations.[66] This study supposes that the contract is concluded between traders in the course of business. Many examples presented here, though, can be relevant to consumer sales under SGA and KLaw. 'Sale' is defined as the transfer of ownership of property in return for the payment of money[67] while 'goods' encompasses all tangible movables,[68] excluding the sale of stocks, shares, money,[69] ships, aircrafts[70] and electricity,[71] as they are outside CISG's sphere.

There is little controversy associated with any term used in this study except for 'termination.' In CISG, the term 'avoidance' is used, although some cases use the

---

United Kingdom and the UN Convention on Contracts for the International Sale of Goods (CISG): To Ratify or not to Ratify?' (2008) 14(4) JIML 331, 335; Rogowska, 'Some Considerations on the Desirability of Accession to the CISG (n 23) 34.

61 McCormack (n 36) 13.

62 Mohamed Mattar, 'Integrating the Unidroit Principles of International Commercial Contracts as a Source of Contract Law in Arab Civil Codes' (2017) 22(1) UniflRev 168.

63 Al-Yaqob (n 52) 311.

64 Richard Stone; James Devenney, *Text, Cases and Materials on Contract Law* (4th edn, Routledge 2017) 644; Elizabeth Macdonald; Ruth Atkins, *Koffman and Macdonald's Law of Contract* (9th edn, OUP 2018) 447; Joseph Chitty, *Chitty on Contracts Volume 1 General Principles* (33rd edn, Sweet & Maxwell 2019) [24–049]. See also Edwin Peel, *Treitel: The Law of Contract* (15th edn, Sweet & Maxwell 2020) 955–956 [18–001].

65 KCIC Art. 31.

66 Farisa Tasneem, 'Electronic Contracts and Cloud Computing' (2014) 9(2) JICLT 105, 106.

67 KCIC Art. 454; *PVC and other synthetic materials* (21/10/1999) A3 1997 61 (District Court Zug Switzerland) <;http://cisgw3.law.pace.edu/cases/991021s1.html>; *Al Palazzo Srl v Bernardaud di Limoges SA* (26/11/2002) 3095 (District Court Rimini) <;http://cisgw3.law.pace.edu/cases/021126i3.html>; Peter Schlechtriem, 'Requirements of Application and Sphere of Applicability of the CISG' (2005) 36 Vic Univ Wellington Law Rev 781, 787; Larry DiMatteo; Lucien Dhooge; Stephanie Greene; Virginia Maurer; Marisa Pagnattaro, *International Sales Law: A Critical Analysis of CISG Jurisprudence* (CUP 2005) 103; Davies Martin; David Snyder, *International Transactions in Goods* (OUP 2014) 54; Stefan Kröll; Loukas Mistelis; Pilar Viscasillas, *UN Convention on Contracts for the International Sale of Goods (CISG)* (2nd edn, Hart 2018) 28 [25]; Ralph Folsom; Michael Alstine; Michael Ramsey, *International Business Transactions* (11th edn, West Academic Publishing 2020) 61.

68 ibid Martin; Snyder 48. See also Michael Bridge, *The International Sale of Goods* (4th edn, OUP 2017) 571 [10.8].

69 CISG Art. 2(d).

70 CISG Art. 2(e).

71 CISG Art. 2(f).

word 'termination,'[72] whereas in SGA, there is variation in terms used to express the case of ending the contract, such as 'repudiation,' 'bringing the contract to an end,'[73] 'discharging the contract,'[74] 'withdrawal,' 'rejection,'[75] 'avoidance,'[76] 'cancellation'[77] and 'termination.'[78] 'Termination' is used here as a neutral phrase, concerning all legal systems. In relation to KLaw, all translations from Arabic to English were conducted by the author.

## 1.3 The Purpose of the Book

'The growing significance of [CISG] before national courts requires consideration of the converse trend':[79] namely, scrutinising domestic laws that address the same issues as CISG. As Clausson asserted, '[I]t is advisable to study the interpretation of similar provisions in national legal systems.'[80] Therefore, transnational law cannot be isolated from national legal regimes; there must be a relation between them in order to identify whether there is consistency or each law renders different rulings.

Establishing what grounds and justifications can lead to the acute remedy of terminating a contract under the aforementioned laws is crucial. The reader will identify whether these laws support the upholding of contracts, reduce the possibility of contracts being terminated and confine termination to grave breaches or grant hypersensitive aggrieved buyers the liberty to end contractual relationships and to find substitute transactions for any breach by a seller, no matter how slight.

For the sake of this book, there are two important terms the reader should consider – 'certainty' and 'flexibility' – which have been used when undertaking the comparative analysis sections and assessing the law theoretically and practically. These terms are defined as follows: 'Certainty' is a useful element for all branches of law but is of greater importance in the domain of contract law. 'Certainty'

72 *Shanghai Anlili International Trading v J & P Golden Wings* (25/12/2008) (Shanghai First Intermediate People's Court District Court) <http://cisgw3.law.pace.edu/cases/081225c1.html>.

73 For example, *ERG Raffinerie Mediterranee SpA v Chevron Usa Inc* [2007] 1 CLC 807, 808.

74 Michael Bridge, 'Discharge for Breach of the Contract of Sale of Goods' (1983) 28(4) McGillLJ 867; Furmston (n 30) 208.

75 *Kwei Tek Chao v British Traders and Shippers Ld* [1954] 3 WLR 496.

76 *Parkin v Thorold* (1852) 51 ER 698, 699.

77 *Raffinerie* (n 73) 808. See also Mindy Chen-Wishart, *Contract Law* (6th edn, OUP 2019) 469 [12.2].

78 *Maredelanto Compania Naviera SA v Bergbau-Handel GmbH* [1971]1 QB 164; *Cie Commerciale Sucres et Denrees v C Czarnikow Ltd* [1990] 1 WLR 1337, 1338; *BNP Paribas v Wockhardt EU Operations (Swiss) AG* [2009] EWHC 3116 (Comm) [40]; Neil Andrews, *Contractual Duties: Performance, Breach, Termination and Remedies* (Sweet & Maxwell 2011) 249; Bridge, *The Sale of Goods* (n 28) [10.01].

79 Anthea Roberts, 'Comparative International Law: The Role of National Courts in Creating and Enforcing International Law' (2011) 60(1) ICLQ 57, 58.

80 Olof Clausson, 'Avoidance in Nonpayment Situations and Fundamental Breach Under the 1980 U.N. Convention on Contracts for the International Sale of Goods' (1984) 6(1) NYLSchJIntl&CompL 93, 97.

of both the legal rule and the consequences of breaching it could reduce cases of breached contract law because the breaching party understands the outcome of their actions.[81] Additionally, both parties know beforehand where they stand if a seller breaches the contract. 'Certainty' also lessens the recourse to litigation as the rule is clear and would not need judicial interpretation. On the other hand, a drawback of 'certainty' is that it requires strict rules, and this strictness prevents the possibility of their being shaped according to the great variety of situations and scenarios encountered in contract law. This facilitates the termination of contracts by innocent parties, not because of the breaches themselves but because of the parties' disadvantageous positions. Thus, 'flexible rules,' shaped according to the circumstances of the case in question,[82] could attain fairer results as every contract has its own unique qualities. 'Flexibility' prevents the harsh application of one rule and its associated results to *all* contracts, regardless of their particularities. Striking a balance between 'certainty' and 'flexibility' and finding out which rules need which of these approaches are key in contract law.

## 1.4 Contributions of the Book

This book makes vital contributions to the study of law:

### *1.4.1 Judicial Importance in Applying CISG in Non-Contracting States*

It is important to look at CISG through the lens of non-signatory states, especially as there is the possibility, according to Article 7(2) CISG, of applying their domestic laws by virtue of the private international law's rules to fill a gap in CISG. There is another possibility of national courts of non-contracting states (e.g, English and Kuwaiti courts) being competent to look at the issue at hand and apply CISG when the parties have chosen it as their applicable law by virtue of the party autonomy principle. Therefore, with the differences between the laws highlighted, judges are able to work alongside CISG's philosophy without being affected by their national laws, achieving the objective of homogenisation. This, accordingly, would avoid the 'search for the most favourable forum,'[83] as well as the scenario of *Schmitz-Werke v Rockland*,[84] in which the court resorted to homeward trends to interpret an issue not settled under CISG's terms, citing merely domestic cases, and turned a blind eye to court and arbitral decisions and literature on CISG.

81 Lon Fuller, *The Morality of Law* (YUP 1969) 63.

82 Babiak (n 57) 123, 124.

83 Teija Poikela, 'Conformity of Goods in the 1980 United Nations Convention of Contracts for the International Sale of Goods' (2003) 1 Nord J Commer Law 1, 67.

84 *Schmitz-Werke GMBH Co v Rockland Industries Inc* (21/06/2002) 1125 (Court of Appeals) <http://cisgw3.law.pace.edu/cases/020621u1.html>.

### *1.4.2 Judicial Importance of Interpreting Domestic Laws*

Legal literature can assist with the comprehension of law to assess the appropriateness of rules and decisions, their coherence and their level of transparency and reasoning.[85] This research contributes significantly to the better understanding of one 'jurisdiction by analysing how other jurisdictions handle the same issue.'[86] This interdisciplinary association between international and national law can affect decision-makers,[87] providing judges with fit and proper answers to formulate their legal opinions. Therefore, judges can be well informed and better problem solvers in a way that fills the lacuna in law by borrowing an international standard and following 'the accepted practices of international transactions [and incorporating] trade usages into its framework.'[88]

### *1.4.3 Legislative Importance*

This study could enhance the willingness of the governing institutions of non-contracting states to take action in solving legal problems by adopting CISG for international commerce and possibly even domestic contracts. Although some commentators believe that ratifying CISG would have a negative impact[89] on SGA's prestigious legal position in the international commercial arena,[90] especially as CISG is a result of 'multi-cultural compromises,' and this might weaken its merit, coherence and consistency more than SGA,[91] others think that not adopting CISG in the UK may adversely impact London as a judicial prosecution and arbitration forum.[92] The adoption of CISG by Kuwait may help those looking to suggest legal amendments as a step towards KLaw reform, as CISG could be resorted to as a model law.[93] This is not for the purpose of achieving harmonisation but for the belief that the solutions adopted in the Convention would be very practical for the nation's commercial field, even for contracts within the boundaries of a

85 Stephen Smith, *Contract Theory* (OUP 2004) 36; Forte (n 60) 52.

86 Indiana University, 'Legal Dissertation: Research and Writing Guide' <https://law.indiana.libguides.com/dissertationguide> accessed 22/3/2021.

87 Michael Byers, 'The Law and Politics of the Pinochet Case' (2003) 10(2) DukeJComp&IntlL 415, 416; Angelo Chianale, 'The CISG as a Model Law: A Comparative Law Approach'(2016) 1(2016) Sing J Legal Stud 29, 33.

88 Poikela (n 83) 65.

89 Sally Moss, 'Why the United Kingdom has Not Ratified the CISG' (2005) (1–2) JL & Com 483, 485.

90 Charles Percy, *Hearing Before the Committee on Foreign Relations United States Senate Ninety-eighth Congress* (2nd edn, United States Senate 1984) 44 [8]; Borges (n 60) 335; Rogowska, 'Some Considerations on the Desirability of Accession to the CISG' (n 23) 34.

91 J Hobhouse, 'International Conventions and Commercial Law: The Pursuit of Uniformity' (1990) 106 LQR 530, 533.

92 Moss (n 89) 485.

93 Louis Duca, 'Developing Global Transnational Harmonization Procedures for the Twenty-First Century: The Accelerating Pace of Common and Civil Law Convergence'(2007) 42(3) TexIntlLJ 625, 631.

country. Kuwait is the founder of the Gulf Cooperation Council (GCC),[94] and its ratification of CISG would have an impact on other GCC countries regionally,[95] urging them to participate in the international trading process.

### *1.4.4 Contractual Importance*

Identifying the ambiguities and differences of the concerned systems, reviewing their advantages and disadvantages and proposing an assessment of existing laws provides a stronger awareness of the obstacles that may be encountered by merchants. They allow the contractual parties, legal advisors and practitioners to recognise the best law for the contract concerned by outlining effective tools for dealing with international or even domestic sales of goods contracts.This will also help practitioners of international commerce who are from England or Kuwait, have their domicile there, or are dealing with parties from these countries in formulating their contracts.

### *1.4.5 Desired Benefits for Law Students/Professionals*

'Many fields of law, such as contract law, are not susceptible to any approach other than that of the black-letter tradition,'[96] which is regarded as a 'framework of interpretation,'[97] crystallises into 'a critical conceptual analysis of all relevant legislation and case law to reveal a statement of the law relevant to the matter under investigation.'[98] This critical approach, which possesses a combination of law in books and law in courts,[99] reaffirms the underlying belief, recognises harmonious relationships and identifies what law ought to be.[100] This also assists the reader/professional in identifying the legal gaps and rationales of the law, not only to evaluate its strengths and weaknesses[101] but also to offer the best solutions.[102] Furthermore, this advanced scrutiny has a role in assisting the reader/professional in evaluating the judicial process.[103]

94 Kuwait News Agency (KUNA), Kuwaiti Efforts in Establishing the Cooperation Council for the Arab States of the Gulf (24/5/2002) <https://www.kuna.net.kw/ArticleDetails.aspx?id=1256299&language=ar>.

95 No GCC member states except Bahrain are parties to CISG.

96 Michael Salter; Julie Mason, *Writing Law Dissertations* (Pearson 2007) 111.

97 ibid 46.

98 Terry Hutchinson, 'Vale Bunny Watson: Law Librarians, Law Libraries, and Legal Research in the Post-Internet Era' (2014) 106 (4) AALL 579, 584.

99 Csaba Varga, 'Law and Its Doctrinal Study: On Legal Dogmatics' (2008) 49(3) Hung J Leg Stud 253, 254.

100 Salter; Mason (n 96) 46.

101 John Honnold, 'The Uniform Law for the International Sale of Goods: The Hague Convention of 1964' (1965) 30(2) Law&ContempProbs 326, 349; Dawn Watkins; Mandy Burton, *Research Methods in Law* (2nd edn, Routledge 2018) 146.

102 Indiana University (n 86).

103 Watkins; Burton (n 101) 108.

Despite the importance of *doctrinalism*,[104] 'comparing domestic law with the way the same area has been regulated in one or more countries has become almost compulsory in doctrinal legal research'[105] because it 'allows us to perceive [the concerned] problems (largely) independently from the doctrinal framework of each of the compared legal systems.'[106] Comparative legal studies contribute to legal interdependence[107] by reaching an appropriate balance between conflicting interests[108] in the concerned systems, especially as a law cannot be assessed in isolation. This mechanism, which combats attitudes of provincialism and parochialism, plays a positive role in the understanding and application of any law[109] and promotes intelligibility[110] in terms of consistency or conflict with other laws for the sake of

104 'Doctrinalism has been accused of being rigid, dogmatic, formalistic, and close-minded.' Douglas Vick, 'Interdisciplinarity and the Discipline of Law' (2004) 31(2) CanJL&Society 163, 181. However, there are many benefits in pursuing this method in comparative studies: a. 'Contrary to a social science approach, the black-letter methodology . . . rigorously exclude[s] supposedly 'external' factors' (Salter; Mason [n 96] 45). It focuses on textual sources and cases, which allows critical analysis to reach a coherent system of rules, and deploys 'a distinctly *deductive* form of legal reasoning from legal principles' (ibid). This uncovers plenty of underpinning, unwritten notions that appear to have either contrasting meanings or at least different doctrines. This approach also defines the 'relationship between individual cases and . . . legal rules (and vice-versa)' (ibid 51) and discovers 'whether individual cases feed off, build on, confirm, extend, erode, displace or overturn other cases' (William Twining, *Blackstone's Tower: The English Law School* [Sweet & Maxwell 1994]) 104; b. This 'rules-centred approach' allows the application of 'theories of interpretation and hermeneutics' beyond literalism, offering an 'authoritative exposition' and highlighting judicial elucidation, concerns, underlying principles, and '[l]ogical implications from the basic axioms of contract law' (Salter; Mason [n 96] 45, 50). As Smith asserts: An interpretive theory is a theory that helps us to better understand the law by illuminating the significance of, and connections between, its different parts. . . . Interpretive theories are assessed according to: (1) how well they fit the rules and decisions that make up contract law, (2) how coherent they are, and (3) how well they explain the way that legal actors themselves explain what they are doing. The third criterion can be subdivided into two parts: (1) how well does the theory explain law's claims to authority (the claim that law is a legitimate or morally justified authority), and (2) how well does the theory explain law's claim to transparency (the claim that legal reasoning is meaningful)? (Smith, *Contract Theory* [n 85] 36.) c. Practical and doctrinal illumination of legal systems can be reached by comparability, which is the heart of legal contribution, illustrating the wider picture, and makes the issue at hand clearer by providing a profound perspective on the techniques employed in different laws. Werro (n 109) 1230, 1226; Watkins; Burton (n 101) 108.Comparison in the field of contract law is considered an effective 'laboratory' in which to promote a better perception of irreconcilable differences and peculiarities of each legal system, to achieve improvement to the status quo and to attain ideal legal frameworks in the future. Örücü; Nelken (n 107) 264; Watkins; Burton (n 101) 119–121, 134, 135. This benefits practitioners by answering the question of how they can tackle analogous contention in different techniques. Salter; Mason (n 96) 182, 183.

105 Mark Hoecke, 'Methodology of Comparative Legal Research' (2015) 12 Law and Method 1.

106 ibid 9.

107 Esin Örücü; David Nelken, *Comparative Law: A Handbook* (Hart 2007) 3.

108 Salter; Mason (n 96) 183.

109 Franz Werro, 'Notes on the Purpose and Aims of Comparative Law' (2001) 75 TulLRev 1225, 1233.

110 Watkins; Burton (n 101) 108.

legal changes.[111] This comparability assists in finding a way to balance what is ideal with what is practical by identifying how the laws function and how effective they are.[112]

Because *doctrinalism* 'focuses on cases, rules and principles'[113] and because '[t]here is no statutory authority for many of the fundamental rules of private law . . . they must in some sense have been devised by the courts themselves.'[114] Therefore, case law carries a significant weight in this book.[115] The precedents set by CISG are likely to have a degree of persuasive power and will provide guidance to assist the adjudicator in comprehending the Convention's terms, although they are non-binding.[116] In the UK, SGA's provisions override common law rules[117] based on precedents and judicial cases, but common law rules can be resorted to for interpretations and explanations of vague provisos, for filling SGA's gaps[118] or for establishing disciplines.[119] This English philosophy reflects the:

> ingrained belief in gradualism, and indeed in pragmatism . . . to sheer away from wide generalisations, from abstract principles, and even from ideals enshrined in principles. [Through this approach] a gradual, step-by-step development [can be noticed].[120]

According to the legal hierarchy, to answer legal questions in relation to commercial contracts under Kuwaiti law (KLaw), KCOC will be applied, and if no legal text regulates the issue at hand, KCIC is the complementary reference.[121] For cases in which issues are not regulated even in KCIC, judges should rule according to Islamic principles, which are compatible with reality and the interests of the country.[122] Thus, the statutes are the primary and, in many cases, the only source

111 Rob Gestel; Hans-W Micklitz; Edward Rubin, *Rethinking Legal Scholarship: A Transatlantic Dialogue* (CUP 2017) 210.
112 Edward Eberle, 'The Methodology of Comparative Law' (2011) 16(1) RWULawReview 51, 61, 63, 66.
113 Salter; Mason (n 96) 48.
114 John Cartwright, *Contract Law: An Introduction to English Law for the Civil Lawyer* (3rd edn, Hart 2016) 34, 35.
115 CISG cases are mainly from <http://www.cisg.law.pace.edu/>, English cases are mainly from <https://uk.westlaw.com/> and Kuwaiti cases are from <ccda.kuniv.edu.ku>.
116 Sandra Saiegh, 'Avoidance under the CISG and Its Challenges Under International Organizations Commercial Transactions' (2005) 25(1–2) JL & Com 443, 462.
117 Cartwright (n 114) 17.
118 ibid 19, 20.
119 Lord Goff of Chieveley, 'The Role of the Judge in England' (1994) 58(3) RabelsZ 443, 447.
120 ibid 446.
121 KCOC Art. 96; Ballantyne (n 36) 107; Al-Masry, *Commercial Law of Kuwait* (n 38) 65.
122 KCIC Art. 1(2).

of law.[123] Precedents, pre-judicial rulings and the principles of legal studies are utilised as the sources of reference or guidance.[124]

Notably, some English and Kuwaiti cases not related to sale of goods contracts have been used in this study either for the use of a common rule or as viable sources from which to deduce general principles. These could be applied in the sphere of sale of goods contracts by analogy. S.62(2) SGA encourages resorting to common law rules where there are no contradictions with SGA.[125] As Roskill LJ stated in *Cehave*,

> In principle it is not easy to see why the law relating to contracts for the sale of goods should be different from the law relating to the performance of other contractual obligations. . . . Sale of goods law is but one branch of the general law of contract.[126]

Additionally, some useful cases relating to the 1893 Act are used for interpreting the current version of SGA.[127]

## 1.5 The Structure of the Book

The gap in the literature that focuses on contractual termination as a mechanism at the hand of the buyer comparing KLaw, CISG and SGA may result in misapprehension, misapplication and inadequate reflection of transnational law. Consequently, this book provides testimonials reflecting the realistic practice and success of addressing a significant aspect of contract life in a transnational instrument, as well as in national laws. This book focuses on thematic aims – namely, the degree of dependency on the termination and the degree of clarity of its rules, which affect the predictability of judicial outcomes on either terminating the contract or refusing it under the three legal systems. As Hoecke states, 'there is no agreement on the kind of [comparative legal methodology] to be followed.'[128] Thus, the method chosen for this study differs from the stereotypical reasoning. In each chapter, there is a comparative analysis section in which all laws are applied to either actual cases from one of the regimes or hypothetical scenarios. This is not only to identify the similarities and differences of the legal systems but also to find the answers to the questions regarding the thematic aims mentioned earlier.

The reader should be aware that some subheadings may be repeated in more than one chapter, but the content varies according to the type of the breach. Chapter 2

123 Cartwright (n 114) 16.

124 Al-Masry, *Commercial Law of Kuwait* (n 38) 60.

125 Tony Weir, 'The Buyer's Right to Reject Defective Goods' (1976) 35(1) CLJ 33, 38.

126 *Cehave NV v Bremer Handels GmbH (The Hansa Nord)* [1976] QB 44, 71.

127 Poikela (n 83) footnote 182; John Adams; Hector MacQueen, *Atiyah's Sale of Goods* (12th edn, Longman 2010) 159; Bridge, *The Sale of Goods* (n 28) [7.35]; Twigg-Flesner; Canavan (n 30) 3. See Bridge, *Benjamin's* (n 28) [11–039].

128 Hoecke (n 105) 1.

discusses the general **principles** of termination under CISG, SGA and KLaw to expound on the mentality behind each of these legal systems on this decisive legal issue. Chapter 3 answers questions about the availability of termination when the seller **delays** delivery of the goods. Chapter 4 scrutinises cases in which the seller sends goods of a **different description** to those agreed upon. Chapter 5 examines the quality of the goods required by law and situations when the seller sends goods of **a lower quality** than the law stipulates. Finally, Chapter 6 highlights the **concluding points** with recommendations.

# 2 General Principles of Termination Under CISG, SGA and KLaw

## 2.1 Introduction

Before going into the specific provisions dealing with the issues in this book, comprehension of the general grounds of when termination of a contract is appropriate under the relevant legal systems is vital; it gives a coherent perception of the distance between or proximity of these systems. Under CISG, a fundamental breach, according to Article 25, is regarded as the main precondition for entitlement to terminate a contract.[1] A non-fundamental breach would entitle the aggrieved buyer to use less severe remedies, such as price reduction[2] and/or compensation[3] to prevent considerable unnecessary costs associated with the return and storage of goods.[4] By contrast, under SGA, termination is centred on the nature of the broken term by the seller; if such a term is a 'condition,' the buyer can resort to such a remedy, as opposed to when the broken term is a mere 'warranty.' There is a third kind of term, known as an 'intermediate term,' in which the right to terminate the contract depends on the consequences of the breach.[5] On the other hand, the main rule under KLaw is that termination as a remedy can be activated by virtue of the judiciary as the judge has discretion over whether the breach justifies termination or not.

1 Art. 49(1)(a); 64(1)(a) CISG; Ingeborg Schwenzer, 'The Danger of Domestic Preconceived Views with Respect to the Uniform Interpretation of the CISG: The Question of Avoidance in the Case of Non-Conforming Goods and Documents' (2005) 36 Vic Univ Wellington Law Rev 795, 799–801.

2 CISG Art. 50.

3 CISG Art. 74; Jianming Shen, 'Declaring the Contract Avoided: The UN Sales Convention in the Chinese Context' (1997) 10(1) NYILR 8, 11.

4 Peter Schlechtriem, *Commentary on the UN Convention on the International Sale of Goods (CISG)* (2nd edn, OUP 1998) 176.

5 Cartwright (n 114) 202; Luca Ficetola, 'Comparing Remedies for Breach of Contract in Italian and English Law' [2011] 1, 8 <;>file:///C:/Users/user1/Downloads/SSRN-id1990791.pdf>; Peel, 15th edn (n 64) 981, 982 [18–043].

DOI: 10.4324/9781003466130-2

## 2.2 Theoretical Concept of Fundamental Breach Under CISG

Article 25 permits the affected buyer to use termination when the seller fundamentally breaches the contract.[6] A breach is fundamental when: a) a non-breaching buyer suffers a *detriment* as a result of the breach, and such detriment causes a considerable *deprivation* of contractual expectations, and b) the result of the breach was foreseen by the seller or was *foreseeable* by a reasonable person in the seller's position, as illustrated in Figure 2.1:

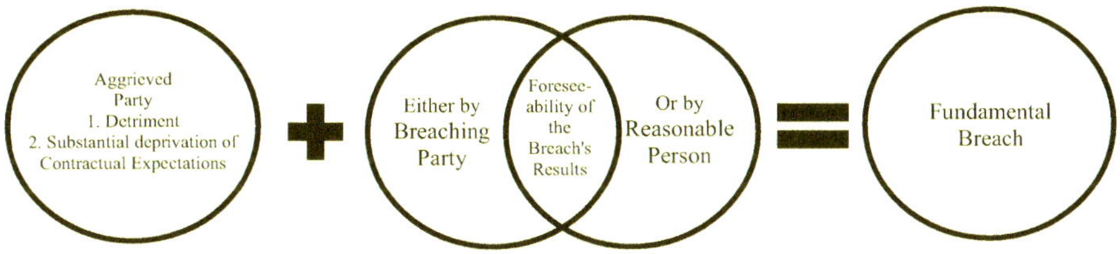


*Figure 2.1* Fundamental Breach

Under CISG, there is no automatic termination,[7] so termination will not happen by the operation of law.[8] If the stipulations of Article 25 exist, the buyer should clarify the status of the transaction and declare the contract terminated by unilateral notice of termination to the seller,[9] without the recourse to litigation, unless the breaching seller disputes the buyer's right of termination.[10] In that case, the court/arbitral tribunal cannot grant the seller a period of grace.[11]

### *2.2.1 Breach*

CISG does not include a definition of 'breach.'[12] Lubbe claims that breach encompasses all violations of any obligations of any party.[13] Some commentators

6 Schwenzer, 'The Danger of Domestic Preconceived Views' (n 129) 799–801.

7 *GMS modules case* (30/8/2007) A3/2006/79 (District Court Zug) <;https://cisgw3.law.pace.edu/cases/070830s1.html>; *Macromex Srl v Globex International Inc* (23/10/2007) 50181T 0036406 (American Arbitration Association) <;https://cisgw3.law.pace.edu/cases/071023a5.html>; Hamburg Ulrich Magnus, 'The Remedy of Avoidance of Contract under CISG: General Remarks and Special Cases' (2006) 25 JL & Com 423, 426.

8 Kröll; Mistelis; Viscasillas (n 67) 707 [7].

9 CISG Art. 26; *GMS modules* (n 135).

10 Kröll; Mistelis; Viscasillas (n 67) 356 [1].

11 CISG Art. 45(3).

12 Darren Peacock, 'Avoidance and the Notion of Fundamental Breach Under the CISG: An English Perspective' (2003) 8 ITBLA 95, 100; Saiegh (n 116) 452. See also Kröll; Mistelis; Viscasillas (n 67) 342 [15];[16].

13 Gerhard Lubbe, 'Fundamental Breach Under the GISG: A Source of Fundamentally Divergent Results' (2004) 68(3) RabelsZ 444, 449.

have attempted to determine the 'breach' by making a comparison between the defective parts of goods and whole goods.[14] Nevertheless, Article 25 measures a breach neither according to the size of a defect, the performance of a substantial number of obligations nor the performance of primary obligations.[15] It was mentioned in *FCF v Adriafil* that '[t]he importance of the breach is not determinative; only the consequences of the breach to the damaged party are determinative.'[16] Therefore, the assessment of a breach should be irrespective of whether a breach, for example, was temporal or long lasting.[17] In practice, fundamentality of a breach depends heavily on the actual obligations and factual situation. A breach could be trivial in one case and negatively affect the root of the contract in another.[18] Thus, it is impractical to include a universal definition of a breach, which would force the situation to rely on theoretical analysis, rather than practical scenarios.[19]

### *2.2.2 Substantial Deprivation of the Contractual Expectations*

The assessment of a fundamental breach depends on whether the affected buyer is *deprived of what they expect under the contract*, rather than on what the defaulting seller promises in the contract.[20]

#### *2.2.2.1 Deprivation*

In a working group at the 18th meeting of the UN Conference on Contracts for International Sale of Goods, the draft version of Article 25 stated that the innocent party should suffer a detriment that 'substantially *impair*[s] his expectations under the contract.'[21] This was substituted with the current phrase of Article 25: the detriment should 'substantially . . . *deprive* him of what he is entitled to expect under the contract.' The severity of the word 'impairment' is less than that of the word 'deprivation,' which excludes a mere weakness or reduction of the innocent buyer's contractual expectations.

14 Schwenzer, *Commentary on CISG* (n 15) 426 [16].
15 *Shen* (n 131) 11.
16 *FCF SA v Adriafil Commerciale Srl* (15/9/2000) 4C105/2000 (Bundesgericht Supreme Court) <http://cisgw3.law.pace.edu/cases/000915s2.html>.
17 *Shen* (n 131) 12.
18 Tjakie Naude; Gerhard Lubbe, 'Cancellation for Material or Fundamental Breach: A Comparative Analysis of South African Law, the UN Convention on Contracts for the International Sale of Goods (CISG) and the UNDROIT Principles of International Commercial Contracts' (2001) 12(3) StellenboschLRev 371, 393.
19 Harker (n 42) 79; Schlechtriem, *Commentary on CISG* (n 132) 176.
20 Grebler, 'Fundamental Breach' (n 48) 411.
21 UN, *Official Records of United Nations Conference on Contracts for the International Sale of Goods* (A/CONF.97/19 United Nations 1991) 12th Meeting 99 <www.uncitral.org/pdf/english/texts/sales/cisg/a-conf-97-19-ocred-e.pdf>.

#### *2.2.2.2 Expectation*

The adherence to contractual terms by the seller should meet the buyer's expectations, notwithstanding their being unrealistic.[22] Nevertheless, contractual expectations in some cases are hard to specify. Take this example: A contract was concluded to supply a buyer with standard computers of a reasonable price, but later, the seller called the buyer to inform them that such computers had sold out, offering to supply the buyer with high-tech computers for the same price. In this case, what would the buyer's expectations have been if, after all, they received the standard ones? If they were expecting to receive the high-tech computers, regarding the seller's call as an offer to modify the contract, the buyer would then have been given the opportunity to terminate the contract, despite originally requesting the standard ones. The perspective with which the court would see the expectation element could then differ. Some scholars have suggested seeing whether there is a connection between an expectation and the breach's consequences as a way of specifying contractual violation,[23] whereas Mullis relates the expectations of the aggrieved buyer to their original purpose,[24] which can be determined by recognition of the nature of a buyer's actions, whether the buyer is a dealer, a producer or the ultimate buyer of the goods.[25] In all cases, it is vital to clarify a buyer's interest in the contract in order to understand their purpose and intent[26] and then recognise their expectations, as the more the buyer explains their situation, the more they will be protected under Article 25.

#### *2.2.2.3 Substantiality of Deprivation*

At first glance, the reader of Article 25 may become confused because it defines the 'fundamentality' of a breach with 'substantiality.'[27] This 'playful tautology'[28] may return us to the starting point and leave the interpreter without a yardstick.[29] It is not always an easy task to determine the exact point at which a buyer's contractual

22 Fritz Enderlein; Dietrich Maskow, *International Sales Law: United Nations Convention on Contracts for the International Sale of Goods, Convention on the Limitation Period in the International Sale of Goods* (Oceana Publications 1992) 114.

23 Naude; Lubbe (n 146) 378.

24 Alastair Mullis, 'Avoidance for Breach Under the Vienna Convention: A Critical Analysis of Some of the Early Cases' [1998] Anglo-Swedish Studies in Law 326, 344.

25 *Packaging machine case* (18/5/2009) 4A_68/2009 (Bundesgerichtshof Federal Supreme Court) <http://cisgw3.law.pace.edu/cases/090518s1.html>.

26 Babiak (n 57) 120, 121.

27 C Bianca; Michael Bonell, *Commentary on the International Sales Law: The 1980 Vienna Sales Convention* (Giuffre 1987) 215; Enderlein; Maskow (n 150) 113; Peacock (n 140) 102; Leonardo Graffi, 'Case Law on the Concept of "Fundamental Breach" in the Vienna Sales Convention' (2003) 3 IntlBusLaw 338, 339.

28 Bianca; Bonell (n 155) 212.

29 Grebler, 'Fundamental Breach' (n 48) 409; Roy Goode; Herbert Kronke; Ewan Mckendrick, *Transnational Commercial Law: Text, Cases and Materials* (2nd edn, OUP 2015) 249, 250 [8.72].

expectations were substantially breached,[30] making it difficult to envisage at which point termination is available,[31] especially when the detriment escalates in seriousness if the breach continues.[32] There have been various attempts to identify what is meant by 'substantial' in Article 25. Some scholars find it should be a serious affliction which dispossesses the interest in performing a contract or makes an innocent buyer unsatisfied with other, less harsh remedies.[33] The problem with this proposal is that it is too subjective and relies on the aggrieved buyer's attitude and wishes. Other jurists may see that if the defects of the goods were considerable, it would be obvious that the purchaser had been deprived of their legitimate expectations.[34] Likewise, DiMatteo stated that almost full deprivation or acute derogation of contractual expectations is required.[35] However, Peacock finds that the test does not depend on the degree of the loss suffered, but rather on the significance of the loss on the injured party's compromised interests under the contract.[36] For instance, in the *Sport clothing case*, the Landshut District Court concluded that the buyer suffered substantial detriment because the clothes delivered shrunk by about 10% to 15% after their first wash. The conduct of the buyer's customers in either returning the goods or deciding not to buy them equates to the substantial deprivation of the buyer's expectations.[37]

#### 2.2.2.4 *Linkage of Expectations to the Contract*

The reliance on the affected buyer's *personal* expectations is an easy way for them to be released from the contract, especially in the case of market price fluctuation,[38] and this may impair the contract as a source of obligations.[39] However, the assessment of the deprivation of the expectations resultant from a breach should be determined by reference to the *contract*. This attachment was added as recently as 1980, just before the effective date of CISG.[40]

##### A. THE EXPECTATIONS ARE TIED TO THE CONTRACT

In the 12th meeting of the UN Conference, the Federal Republic of Germany and Portugal both suggested that the fundamentality of the breach be linked to the

30 Enderlein; Maskow (n 150) 113; Michael Bridge, 'Avoidance for Fundamental Breach of Contract Under the UN Convention on the International Sale of Goods' (2010) 59(4) ICLQ 911, 912.
31 ibid Bridge 921.
32 Enderlein; Maskow (n 150) 113.
33 Franco Ferrari, 'Fundamental Breach of Contract Under the UN Sales Convention: 25 Years of Article 25 CISG' (2006) 25 JL & Com 489, 489.
34 Martin; Snyder (n 67) 368.
35 DiMatteo et al (n 67) 472.
36 Peacock (n 140) 102, 103.
37 *Sport clothing case* (5/4/1995) 54O644/94 (Landshut District Court) <https://cisgw3.law.pace.edu/cases/950405g1.html>.
38 Bridge, 'Avoidance for Fundamental Breach' (n 158) 912.
39 Grebler, 'Fundamental Breach' (n 48) 411.
40 Bianca; Bonell (n 155) 213–215; Naude; Lubbe (n 146) 377.

content of the contract.[41] Thus, 'expectations' can be associated with economical, reputational or even ethical aspects as long as these aspects are expressed in the contract, either implicitly or explicitly, and this makes the buyer's motivations recognisable to the seller.[42] Accordingly, the buyer's hopes, desires and inner expectations would not be taken into account in order to avoid any dismay to the seller. This attachment to the contract adds an objective standard[43] as the definition of the 'expectation' is not left to the judges but tied to the contract,[44] and through the interpretation of the contract, the expectations of both parties can be revealed.[45]

B. THE EXPECTATIONS ARE TIED TO THE CONTRACTUAL CIRCUMSTANCES

At the 12th meeting of the UN Conference, the representative of the USSR indicated that not just contractual terms but all contractual circumstances should be considered in deciding the elements of fundamental breaches.[46] Thus, the phrase 'entitled to expect under the contract' in Article 25 should not be interpreted in a narrow literal sense, including only the terms and clauses of the contract. Any information relating to the contract should be considered, even if such information was not mentioned in the contract itself, such as emails and verbal promises that took place before or even after the contract concluded, showing the agreement of both parties.[47] Other circumstances should also be considered, such as previous dealings, established practices, negotiations,[48] the status of both parties and market tendencies. Through this wider meaning of the contract, the parties' expectations could be formulated and envisaged realistically.

### *2.2.3 Detriment*

As seen earlier, a fundamental breach requires the damaged party to suffer a 'detriment' which substantially deprives them of what they expected under the contract.[49] There is no definition in the Convention determining the meaning of 'detriment,'[50] so one may wonder whether the 'detriment' is an independent requirement of Article

41 Official Records (n 149) 12th Meeting 76.

42 François Dessemontet, *Convention de Vienne sur les Contrats de Vente Internationale de Marchandises* (Centre du Droit L'entreprise 1993) 213.

43 *Meat case* (28/10/1998) 4C179/1998/odi (Bundesgerich Supreme Court) <;http://cisgw3.law.pace.edu/cases/981028s1.html>; Clausson (n 80) 96; Bianca; Bonell (n 155) 213–215; Naude; Lubbe (n 146) 377; Kröll; Mistelis; Viscasillas (n 67) 341, 342 [14].

44 Bianca; Bonell (n 155) 215.

45 Ferrari, 'Fundamental Breach' (n 161) 497, 498.

46 Official Records (n 149) 12th Meeting 301.

47 *Spoldzielnia Pracy "A" in N v GmbH & Co KG in B* (11/5/2007) V CSK 456/06 (Supreme Court of Poland) <;http://cisgw3.law.pace.edu/cases/070511p1.html>; Bianca; Bonell (n 155) 213; Babiak (n 57) 120, 121; Ferrari, 'Fundamental Breach' (n 161) 497, 498.

48 CISG Art. 8(3).

49 Ferrari, 'Fundamental Breach' (n 161) 495.

50 Peacock (n 140) 101.

25 or is integrated with the 'deprivation of the promisee's contractual expectations.' For instance, if the contract stresses that the goods should be delivered *by air* through the INCOTERMS contract and delivered duty paid (DDP)[51] and the seller breaches such a condition by *shipping* the goods instead, but the goods are totally intact, and the average final consumer does not care about the delivery method, does a fundamental breach occur? Receiving the goods through the port instead of the airport could substantially deprive the buyer of their contractual expectation but may cause little harm or inconvenience to the buyer, so would the buyer be allowed to terminate the contract? One could argue that Article 25 construes the meaning of the 'detriment' to be 'deprivation of the contractual expectations,' and there is no need to *self-define* the word 'detriment' as a harm, loss or injury suffered because of a breach.[52] What reinforces this way of thinking is that Article 7.3.1 of the UPICC defines a fundamental breach similarly to CISG while completely omitting the word 'detriment.'

Nevertheless, in the commission of the diplomatic Conference, the phrase 'substantial detriment'[53] was added to the draft version of Article 25 to permit using termination, and the upshot of this is that the 'detriment' could be an independent stipulation other than the condition of 'deprivation of the contractual expectation.' The word 'detriment' in and of itself excludes cases in which a breach did not cause any injury,[54] which subsequently excludes any breach with no harmful results from being fundamental, no matter how impactful the breach is.[55] This is true especially if there is a consensus that keeping the contract afoot is one of the main principles on which the Convention is based,[56] and the terminating of a contract should only occur as *ultima ratio*, a remedy of last resort.[57] Accordingly, there may be no fundamental breach, and termination will not be activated in this scenario when there is no loss suffered by the aggrieved buyer, and the purpose of the contract is achieved even when there is a substantial deprivation of the buyer's contractual expectations. Notably, the subsequent price fall of the concerned goods would not

51 DDP is a delivery agreement through INCOTERMS in which the seller bears all responsibility, risk and cost in relation to air/ocean transportation until the destination port. INCOTERMS 2000, 'Transport Obligations, Costs and Risks' <www.thefreightrateco.com/Forms/Incoterms.pdf> accessed 8/8/2018; Robert Stein, 'Reasons Not to Use DDP' (27/8/2013) <http://mohawkglobal.com/global-news/reasons-not-to-use-ddp/> accessed 8/8/2018; Caroline Banton, 'Delivered Duty Paid (DDP)' (22/4/2019) <www.investopedia.com/terms/d/delivery-duty-paid.asp#ixzz5Pq9Hgvbq> accessed 8/8/2018.

52 Ferrari, 'Fundamental Breach' (n 161) 495, 496.

53 Proposed by the Mexican representative, Bianca; Bonell (n 155) 208.

54 ibid 211; Naude; Lubbe (n 146) 376; Kröll; Mistelis; Viscasillas (n 67) 341 [11].

55 ibid Bianca; Bonell; ibid Naude; Lubbe.

56 *Meat case* (n 171); Bruno Zeller, 'Fundamental Breach and the CISG: A Unique Treatment or Failed Experiment?' (2004) 8 VJ 81, 92; Grebler, 'Fundamental Breach' (n 48) 409, 410; Bridge, 'Avoidance for Fundamental Breach' (n 158) 921; Martin; Snyder (n 67) 367; Spagnolo (n 54) 89.

57 *Meat case* (n 171); *Globes case* (27/2/2002) 5HKO3936/00 (Landgericht District Court) <;http://cisgw3.law.pace.edu/cases/020227g1.html>; ibid Zeller 82.

constitute 'detriment'[58] as 'no possible change of market conditions can release the buyer from [the contract].'[59]

### *2.2.4 Foreseeability of the Detrimental Consequences Resulting From Breach*

It is insufficient that a breach causes a material prejudice by depriving a buyer of the contractual expectations described as fundamental, but such severe harm should be foreseeable.[60] Because foreseeability could be used as a mechanism to facilitate the breaching seller to obviate termination,[61] CISG complicates a way for this defaulting party to exonerate itself from committing a fundamental breach[62] by asking whether a reasonable person would foresee the detrimental result of a breach to the affected buyer. By adding objective criteria, the defaulting seller can excuse neither a lack of knowledge nor an incorrect assessment.[63] Therefore, unforeseeability depends objectively on a reasonable person as the minimum standard of knowledge and experience, but when the breaching seller has more experience or knowledge than a reasonable person, they should have a firm grasp of the situation in the market. This presumes their subjective foreseeability of the consequences of their breach.[64] Thus, to avoid termination by proving unforeseeability of a breach's consequences, a breaching seller should demonstrate subjective and objective unforeseeability.[65] Unfortunately, as some scholars state, the verification of unforeseeability depends on the judge/arbitrator's contentment.[66] In *Sport clothing*,[67] the court relied on the 'substantiality of the detriment' and did not analyse the 'foreseeability.' This was probably because the 'deprivation' was so substantial that it should therefore have been predictable. However, substantiality of the detriment does not automatically make such a result foreseeable.

58 Kristian Maley, 'The Limits to the Conformity of Goods in the United Nations Convention on Contracts for the International Sale of Goods (CISG)' (2009) 12 Int'lTrade & BusLRev 82, 100.

59 Unavailable name (11/6/1997) 255/1994 (Arbitration proceeding) <http://cisgw3.law.pace.edu/cases/970611r1.html>.

60 Schwenzer, *Commentary on CISG* (n 15) 419 [5].

61 Graffi (n 155) 340.

62 UN, 'Report of the UN Commission on International Trade Law on the Work of its Tenth Session' (A/32/17 Vienna 23 May -17 June 1977) 31 <http://www.uncitral.org/pdf/english/yearbooks/yb-1977-e/vol8-p11-70-e.pdf>.

63 Grebler, 'Fundamental Breach' (n 48) 409.

64 Graffi (n 155) 341.

65 CISG Art. 8(2); Bianca; Bonell (n 155) 220; *Shen* (n 131) 12; Ferrari, 'Fundamental Breach' (n 161) 499; Bridge, 'Avoidance for Fundamental Breach' (n 158) 918.

66 Bianca; Bonell (n 155) 216, 217.

67 *Sport clothing case* (n 165).

## 2.3 Conditionality and Termination Under SGA

There are three types of contractual terms: 'condition,' 'warranty' and 'intermediate term.' Only breaching a 'condition' affords an automatic right to terminate the contract, as illustrated in Figure 2.2:

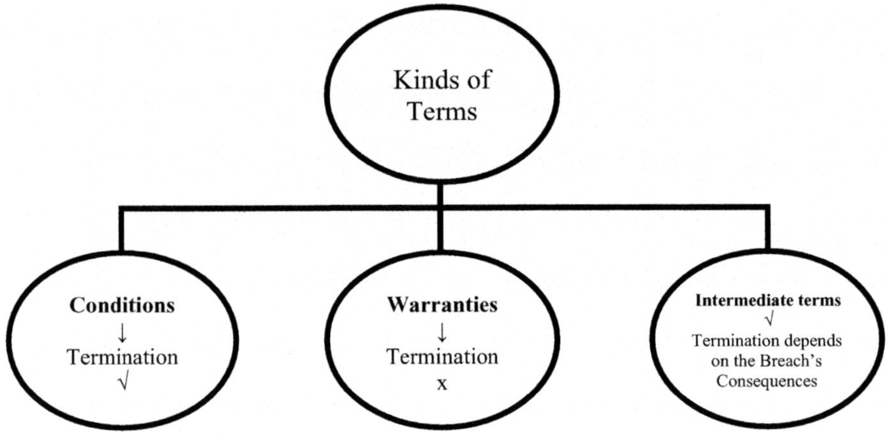


*Figure 2.2:* Kinds of Terms Under SGA

### *2.3.1 Classification of the Breached Term*

#### *2.3.1.1 Conditions*

'Conditionality' of the term permits an innocent buyer to terminate a contract when such a term is breached 'without regard to the magnitude of the breach' and its consequences.[68] This means that the injured buyer is able to 'undo' the deal, be released from further obligations, reject the defective goods if delivered and sue for price retrieval.[69] The status of a term of being a 'condition' is derived either from SGA or from the contract.[70]

A. CONDITIONS IN SGA

Express terms written in the contract are usually not comprehensive; even the most sophisticated contracts do not prognosticate all future issues. These gaps will often be filled by implied terms[71] mentioned in SGA, which are mostly

68 *Lombard North Central Plc v Butterworth* [1987] QB 527, 535. See also Paul Davies, *JC Smith's the Law of Contract* (3rd edn, OUP 2021) 380 [25.3.1]; Chen-Wishart (n 77) 477 [12.2.3].

69 Peel, 15th edn (n 64) 955, 956 [18–001].

70 *L Schuler AG v Wickman Machine Tool Sales Ltd* [1974] AC 235; Cartwright (n 114) 282; Stephen Smith, *Atiyah's Introduction to the Law of Contract* (6th edn, OUP 2005) 196.

71 ibid Cartwright 202.

classified as conditions, associated, for instance, with the correspondence on description and satisfactory quality. The implied term of compliance with the contractual description may not provide great protection as the contract may not describe the goods in detail but only name the goods as, for instance, potatoes; thus, the goods should be of satisfactory quality.[72] The buyer is secured by substantial protection[73] as these implied terms will be applied even if the parties have not included them in their contract.[74] In case of a breach of an implied term, SGA allows the buyer to find exactly what they want from another supplier, allowing the seller to resell the unwanted goods to somebody else at a good price.[75]

### B. CONDITION PRECEDENT

SGA embodies 'an ethos of individualism, whereby the parties are free to pursue their own self-interest . . . in performing contracts provided they do not act in breach of a term of the contract.'[76] Therefore, parties are at liberty to classify in advance a term as a condition making *any* failure to perform that term a breach going to the root of the contract.[77] This is even if such a term per se is not an important one and will not entitle the innocent buyer to terminate the contract.[78] Mustill LJ in *Lombard* stated that '[a] provision in the contract [could make] a term a condition even if it would not be so in the absence of such a provision.'[79] Blackburn J in *Bettini v Gye* also affirmed that '[p]arties may think some matters, apparently of very little importance, essential; and if they sufficiently express an intention to make the literal fulfilment of such a thing a condition precedent, it will be one.'[80] However, in contrast to regarding a term as a condition by law, which is largely straightforward, considering a term as a condition precedent could be unclear, depending on the interpretation of the contract[81] in light of surrounding circumstances[82] which reflect the parties' intentions in the eyes of the court.[83]

72 Twigg-Flesner; Canavan (n 30) 115.
73 ibid.
74 Ewan McKendrick, *Sale of Goods* (LLP 2000) 485, 486.
75 ibid 341, 342.
76 Leggatt J in *Yam Seng Pte Ltd v International Trade Corp Ltd* [2013] EWHC 111 (QB) [123].
77 *Lombard* (n 196) 535; Bridge, *The Sale of Goods* (n 28) [10.05].
78 *Photo Production Ltd v Securicor Transport Ltd* [1980] AC 827, 847; Smith, *Atiyah's* (n 198) 193, 197; Chen-Wishart (n 77) 479 [12.2.3.2]; Ewan McKendrick, *Contract Law: Text, Cases, and Materials* (9th edn, OUP 2020) 774.
79 *Lombard* (n 196) 528.
80 *Bettini v Gye* (1876) 1 QBD 183, 187.
81 *Schuler* (n 198) 256; Chen-Wishart (n 77) 479, 480 [12.2.3.2.]; McKendrick, *Contract Law* (n 206) 742, 743.
82 *Bentsen v Taylor Sons* (No.2) [1893] 2 QB 274, 281.
83 Bridge, *Benjamin's* (n 28) [10–027].

#### *2.3.1.2 Warranty*

If the broken term is classified by SGA as a 'warranty' rather than a 'condition' or it is of minimal importance, depending on the construction of the contract,[84] the termination will not be activated.[85] A breach will then only entitle an innocent buyer to claim damages.[86]

#### *2.3.1.3 Intermediate Term*

In addition to the condition-warranty dichotomy, a third categorisation was created through English case law, regarded as *tertium quid* to the traditional classification.[87] According to *Cehave v Bremer*, if it is difficult to categorise a breached term as a 'condition' or 'warranty,' such a term will be considered an 'intermediate term'[88] when the outcomes of a breach could range from minor to severe.[89] Thus, the seriousness of the consequences of a breach, rather than the nature of the breached term, determines the availability of termination.[90] Such an 'intermediate term' authorises termination only if the breach's consequences are so great that they 'deprive [the buyer] . . . of substantially the whole benefit which it was the intention of the parties as expressed in the contract.'[91] It might be seen that case law clashes with the language of s.11(3) SGA, which intimates that there is only binary classification of 'condition' and 'warranty,'[92] but SGA refers in s.62(2) to the common law rules,[93] permitting the *Cehave* attempt to conciliate the schism between SGA and general contract law.

### *2.3.2 Restrictions on Terminating a Contract According to S.15A*

Unless otherwise agreed, s.15A prevents a buyer from terminating a contract when the breach is 'so slight' that it would be unreasonable for the buyer to reject the goods and terminate the contract, even if the breached term was a 'condition.' In this case, the breached 'condition' would convert to a 'warranty,' entitling damages only.[94] This provision was promulgated to reduce over-technicality in resorting to

84 SGA s.11(3).
85 SGA s.61(1); H Beale, *Chitty on Contracts Volume II: Specific Contracts* (29th edn, Sweet & Maxwell 2004) 1309 [43–044].
86 Stone; Devenney (n 64) 646; McKendrick, *Contract Law* (n 206) 757.
87 *Cehave* (n 126) 52.
88 ibid 51.
89 Ficetola (n 133) 8; Bridge, *The Sale of Goods* (n 28) [10.30].
90 John Adams; Roger Brownsword, *Understanding Contract Law* (5th edn, Sweet & Maxwell 2007) 167, 168; Twigg-Flesner; Canavan (n 30) 116, 117; Bridge, *Benjamin's* (n 28) [10–033].
91 Diplock LJ in *Hong Kong Fir Shipping Co Ltd v Kawasaki Kisen Kaisha Ltd* [1962] 2 QB 26, 66.
92 See Bridge, *The Sale of Goods* (n 28) [10.35]; [10.36].
93 *Cehave* (n 126) 83.
94 SGA s.15A(b).

termination[95] and to avoid escape from contracts motivated by caprice or adverse movements in the market.

According to s.30(2A) and 15(A), the sphere of slight breaches is limited to non-consumer contracts[96] and applies only to breaches of specific implied terms associated with descriptions, quality, quantity, fitness for the purpose and compliance with the sample.[97] From this confined sphere of slight breaches, other contractual conditions such as time stipulations[98] will entitle the buyer to terminate the contract even if it is unreasonable to reject the goods and even if the motive for such a termination is obviation of loss due to market fluctuations.[99]

#### *2.3.2.1 Emphasis on Slightness*

It was stated in Atiyah that '[i]n the past . . . even the most trivial breach of a statutorily implied condition might give the right to terminate. For example, if goods deviated in even the slightest respect from their description the buyer could reject them.'[100] In this statement, intensified words such as 'the most trivial' and 'the slightest' were used, which means s.15A limits the prevention of termination to extreme slight breaches,[101] making its threshold very high and rarely reachable. The Law Com No. 160 states that s.15A is 'not intended as a major alteration in the law.'[102] Thus, s.15A has a 'very limited effect and has made little difference in practice'[103] as there is no single legal order regarding this section that has been reported since its enactment.[104]

The problematic issue is that it is unclear what a slight breach is equivalent to,[105] which means its interpretation depends on the court. In *Millars v Turpie*, it was found that a slight breach could have occurred when the defect could have been rectified with great ease and at a negligible charge.[106]

95 Neil Andrews, *Contract Law* (2nd edn, CUP 2015) 457.

96 Bridge, *The Sale of Goods* (n 28) [10.29].

97 SGA s.15A(1)(a).

98 Alastair Mullis, 'Termination for breach of Contract in C.I.F. Contracts under the Vienna Convention and English law; Is there a Substantial Difference?' in Guest, *Contemporary Issues in Commercial Law* (Sweet & Maxwell 1997) 152; Bridge, *Benjamin's* (n 28) [12–25].

99 Bridge, *The Sale of Goods* (n 28) [10.25].

100 Smith, *Atiyah's* (n 198) 197.

101 Mullis, 'Termination for Breach of Contract' in Guest (n 226) 141.

102 The Law Commission and The Scottish Law Commission, *Report on a Reference Under Section 3(1)(e) of the Law Commissions Act 1965* (Law Com No 160 Scot Law Com No 104 1987) [4.21] 41 <https://s3-eu-west-2.amazonaws.com/lawcom-prod-storage-11jsxou24uy7q/uploads/2016/07/LC.-160-SC.-104-REPORT-ON-A-REFERENCE-UNDER-SECTION-3le-OF-THE-LAW-COMMISSIONS-ACT-1965-SALE-AND-SUPPLY-OF-GOODS-1.pdf>.

103 Bridge, *Benjamin's* (n 28) [12–026].

104 ibid.

105 Burrows, *Principles of English Commercial Law* (n 28) 77, 78; Chen-Wishart (n 77) 479 [12.2.3.1].

106 *Millars of Falkirk Ltd v Turpie* 1976 SLT (Notes) 66, 67.

#### *2.3.2.2 Slightness and Reasonableness*

S.15A states that when a buyer has the right to reject the goods but the breach is 'so slight' that it makes the rejection unreasonable, termination cannot be used. Then the question arises whether 'slightness' and 'unreasonable rejection' are two separate requirements or not.

##### A. TWO SEPARATE REQUIREMENTS

To prevent a buyer from terminating the contract, some scholars assert that the 'slightness of the breach' and 'unreasonable rejection' are two separate stipulations.[107] Accordingly, if a seller's breach of a 'condition' is 'so slight' but it remains 'reasonable' to reject the goods, this 'condition' will not be turned into a 'warranty' because the second stipulation of 'unreasonableness' does not exist and vice versa. One interpretation of 'unreasonableness' can occur when the seller substantially fulfils the contract.[108] Another interpretation is that the 'unreasonableness' can occur when a slight breach does not affect the buyer's needs, especially when damages would be adequate compensation for the breach.[109]

##### B. UNREASONABLE REJECTION IS CONNECTED TO SLIGHT BREACHES

S.15A indicates that the buyer loses the right to termination when the breach is 'so slight' that it makes the rejection unreasonable, which may connect the 'unreasonableness' to the 'breach's slightness.' When the 'unreasonableness' is a separate stipulation from the 'slightness of a breach,' external factors will be taken into account. For instance, the seller's willingness to rectify the slight breach[110] may make the buyer's rejection of the goods unreasonable. However, there is no obligation on the buyer to accept the seller's repair of the defective goods, and the buyer should not be prevented from terminating the contract when they unreasonably refuse the seller's offer to rectify the defects.[111]

#### *2.3.2.3 Consequences Versus Breach*

A question now arises regarding whether the 'slightness' benchmark could be applied over a 'breach' or its 'consequences.'

##### A. SLIGHTNESS IS ATTACHED TO A BREACH

Through literal scrutiny of s.15A, it appears that the assessment of the 'slightness' and 'unreasonableness' test is on the breach itself rather than its consequences, in

107 Stone; Devenney (n 64) 631.
108 *H Dakin & Co v Lee* [1916] 1 KB 566, 576.
109 McKendrick, *Sale of Goods* (n 202) 300, 301. See Bridge, *Benjamin's* (n 28) [8–044] (regarding quantity).
110 Bridge, *The Sale of Goods* (n 28) [6.43].
111 ibid [10.27].

contrast to CISG. It was pointed out in the Law Com No 160 that 'it would be better not to refer to "the consequences" of the breach.'[112] Thus, when a breach is 'so slight' it makes rejection of the goods unreasonable but the consequences hinder the buyer, they might be prevented from terminating the contract.

B. CONSEQUENCES ARE THE CORE

Some scholars apply the slightness criterion to the consequences of breaching a 'condition.'[113] When the consequences of a breach are 'so slight,' it will be deemed unreasonable to terminate the contract.[114] Burrows[115] and Peel[116] find that s.15A has the same policy of an intermediate term, but it should not mean the term that is slightly breached can be converted to an intermediate term. However, when the slightness norm is applied to the consequences, the breached 'condition' will automatically convert to an 'intermediate term.' Sending goods in a different size to that agreed, for instance, may not be a slight breach (and may, in fact, be a considerable breach) but may make no difference to the buyer, and, accordingly, they would not be entitled to terminate the contract. Nonetheless, this would make the test unpredictable and subjective, depending on the consequences suffered by the buyer. As Buckley LJ stated in *Gillespie v Roy*, it is not the function of a court to fashion a condition or a condition precedent according to the meaning of fairness or reasonableness.[117]

It could rightly be said that 'slightness' might be attached to a breach itself, and 'unreasonableness' may be linked to the breach's consequences. However, s.15A does not confine the reasonableness of rejecting goods to 'normal' or 'expected' consequences, similar to CISG's approach. This may permit the consideration of a buyer's personal position, such as their reputation in the market, to assess the 'reasonableness.'[118] This is true, especially as s.15A states that a buyer cannot terminate a contract when a 'breach is so slight that it would be unreasonable *for him* to reject' the goods. A small scratch can be regarded as slight, but the consequence of this defect may result in the buyer's inability to resell the goods, making rejection of the goods reasonable, even if the buyer's personal circumstances and desires are not explained to the seller.

### *2.3.3 Termination Is a Self-Remedy*

Similar to CISG, termination is not automatic,[119] even where a breach is repudiatory,[120] but sovereignty is granted by law to the aggrieved buyer to choose

112 The Law Commission (n 230) footnote 23, 41.
113 McKendrick, *Sale of Goods* (n 202) 487.
114 Adams; Brownsword (n 218) 166, 167; Burrows, *Principles of English Commercial Law* (n 28) 77, 78; Bridge, *The Sale of Goods* (n 28) [10.27].
115 Burrows, *Principles of English Commercial Law* (n 28) 77, 78 footnote 263.
116 Peel, 15th edn (n 64) 996 [18–060].
117 *Gillespie Bros & Co Ltd v Roy Bowles Transport Ltd* [1973] QB 400, 421.
118 Twigg-Flesner; Canavan (n 30) 418.
119 *Heyman v Darwins Ltd* [1942] AC 356, 361; *Paribas* (n 78) [40]; Cartwright (n 114) 283; Jack Beatson; Andrew Burrows; John Cartwright, *Anson's Law of Contract* (30th edn, OUP 2016) 534.
120 Stone; Devenney (n 64) 644.

it[121] by rejecting the goods and demanding recovery of the price.[122] This is without the need to obtain a court order,[123] avoiding expenses, wasted time and inconvenience.[124] The breaching seller is the one who should go to court to challenge the termination.[125]

## 2.4 Termination Is Judicial Under KLaw[126]

The main stipulation to activate a judicial termination under KLaw is that a seller has failed to perform their contractual obligation,[127] without specifying the degree of such a breach. The buyer shall request termination of the contract through the court[128] as only by the ruling of the judge can termination be authorised.[129] The statute of limitations for legal proceedings to claim termination of a commercial contract (extinctive prescription) is ten years from the date on which the obligation should have been fulfilled or from the date a breaching seller is advised to perform their obligations, unless the law provides a shorter period.[130]

The ruling of a termination relies heavily on the judge's discretion.[131] The trial court has full authority to determine the reality of a case and to assess the evidence and documents submitted to it.[132] The court may accept some pieces of evidence but ignore others.[133] Establishing the reasons for termination or refusing it is one of the matters in which the judge of a case is unaffiliated and is not presided over by the court of cassation if the judgement was based on convincing reasons.[134] Any

121 *Alghussein Establishment v Eton College* [1988] 1 WLR 587; Morris Cohen, 'The Basis of Contract' (1933) 46(4) HarvLRev 553, 586.

122 Chitty (n 64) [24–001]; McKendrick, *Sale of Goods* (n 202) 485, 486; Burrows, *A Casebook on Contract* (n 43) 353.

123 McKendrick, *Contract Law* (n 206) 741.

124 Chen-Wishart (n 77) 471 [12.2.1].

125 ibid.

126 This type of termination applies to contracts, regardless of the nature of the contract of sale, either civil or commercial. Kaled Al-Defery; Yaser Al-Sayrafy, Sale Contract in Kuwaiti Civil Law (Kuwait University 2010) 367.

127 KCIC Art. 209(1); The Egyptian Supreme Court (8/6/1944) 44/17Q reproduced in Assayed Muhammad, *Sale Contract* (Dar AlFeker 1999) 785; Ateya (n 50) 155.

128 KCIC Art. 209(1).

129 Muhammad AboSaad, *Sale Contract* (Dar AlFeker 2000) 44; Abdulrasool Abdulreda; Jamal Al-Nakas, *Sources of Commitment and Proof* (Dar AlKotob 2015) 196.

130 KCOC Art. 118; Huneidi (n 39) 406; Ibrahim Abulil, *The Contract and the Unilateral Will* (Dar AlKotob 1998) 417, 418; Yaqob Sarko, *Commercial Contracts in Kuwaiti Commercial Law* (Kuwait University 1998) 31; H Shaaban, 'Commercial Transactions in the Middle East: What Law Governs?' (1999) 31(1) Law & Pol'y Int'l Bus 157, 164, 165.

131 KCIC Art. 209(1); Case 6/11/1998 Court of Cassation/Commercial 85 in Ministry of Justice, *The Legal Principles Decided by the Court of Cassation During Forty Years in Commercial Provisions volume 9* (2016) 412; Abdulreda; Al-Nakas (n 257) 194.

132 Case 29/12/2009 Court of Cassation/Commercial 768/2007 781/2007 p. 10.

133 Case 20/5/1998 (n 43) 5; Case 15/10/2006 Court of Cassation/Commercial 1250/2004, 1157/2004 p. 6.

134 ibid; Egyptian Supreme Court (15/10/1990) 2271 Y 58 reproduced in Ateya (n 50) 164.

party may challenge the judgement when it violates the law, when it is in error in its application or interpretation, or when the judgement's reasoning and inference are invalid.[135]

There is procedural limitation on a judge's power to rule for termination not mentioned in law: A seller has the right[136] to obviate the judgement of termination by carrying out their default obligation until the hearing in which the final judgement will be rendered is closed in court.[137] In such cases, the judge will only have the right to award damages if they are required.[138] However, in one case, the judge's decision to terminate the contract occurred despite the fact that the debtor had performed their obligation before the decision of termination was made.[139] This indicates that even in the event of a seller's late performance, judges still possess their discretionary authority to decide if this performance prevents termination.

### *2.4.1 Rejecting Termination Due to the Insignificancy of the Breach*

According to Article 209(2) KCIC, it is permissible for a judge to reject a termination request if the seller's failure to perform is of 'little importance' in comparison to their fulfilled obligations as a whole. By using the word 'permissible' in Article 209(2) and by means of *contrario* reasoning, the judge can rule for termination even if the unfulfilled obligation is of little importance when the judgement is based on justified reasons. Ateya states that if a performance is partial, the buyer is entitled to terminate the contract unless the judge deems the remaining part insignificant.[140] Al-Jarmy states that the main rule is the inadmissibility of the refusal of the termination because the option is decided on by the buyer, and the rejection of termination is exceptional.[141] Thus, the suggestive nature of this provision is presented in a way that can be considered a guideline rather than a mandatory legal rule, depending on the judiciary.

Furthermore, the 'insignificance of a breach' does not provide clear guidance, and the word 'little' does not determine the boundaries of a rejection, which can be interpreted in multiple ways. The judge may reject a termination request if the unfulfilled obligation is small in comparison with the *fulfilled obligations in their entirety*. Alternatively, a judge may refuse termination if the unfulfilled part of a

135 Case 6/2/2001 Appellate Court/Commercial 2134, 2135/1998 p. 7; Case 20/3/2005 Appellate Court/Commercial 2982/2005 p. 10; Case 7/2/2012 Court of Cassation/Commercial 188, 225, 237/2010 p. 4–7.

136 Mustafa Al-Jarmy, *Termination of Contract: Comparative Study on Egyptian and French Law* (Dar AlNahda 1988) 106.

137 Case 29/4/2006 Court of Cassation/Commercial 1289/2004 p. 9; Case 2/11/2010 Court of Cassation/Commercial 1175/2008 p. 5.

138 Egyptian Supreme Court (2/6/1981) 403S22S Y48P 1682 reproduced in Ateya (n 50) 160; Abdulhameed Al-Shawarby, *Termination of Contract* (Manshat AlMaaref 1990) 63; Abulil (n 258) 418; AboSaad (n 257) 441; Abdulreda; Al-Nakas (n 257) 196.

139 Egyptian Supreme Court (24/3/2004) 1535 Y 67 reproduced in Ateya (n 50) 164.

140 ibid 173.

141 Al-Jarmy (n 264) 96.

seller's obligation has insignificant importance compared to the *breached obligation*. In other situations, a termination request could be rejected if the breach does not frustrate the *purpose of the contract*.[142] However, in one case, the court considered the seller's genuine willingness to meet the required terms sufficient to reject the termination request.[143] Nevertheless, Al-Jarmy suggests that the law should be read in the opposite sense as follows: The judge may not refuse termination if the unfulfilled part is significant for the contract as a whole.[144] More problematically, 'little' can be construed under the personal perspective of the judge without resorting to any of the various criteria mentioned here.

### *2.4.2 Granting an Additional Period to Perform*

According to Article 109 KCOC, only in cases of 'utmost necessity' may a judge afford a seller an additional period of time to perform their contractual obligations. This term does not merely entail 'necessity' but requires this necessity to be 'utmost,' and this eliminates the option of granting an additional period, which lessens the recourse to termination.[145] Furthermore, the law uses the phrase 'utmost necessity' without rendering the guidelines for good application, or at least examples, in EMKCIC. This vague approach leads to courts reaching a range of different rulings as this phrase can be employed according to the judge's doctrine, whether it is associated with the seller's situation or the contractual circumstances. One interpretation of 'utmost necessity' is that granting the seller additional time should not cause serious harm to the buyer.[146] Another interpretation is that it is not permissible to grant an additional period except at the request of the breaching seller as this request indicates the seller's willingness to properly execute their obligation.[147] However, there might be cases in which the seller requests an additional period without reflecting the reasons of 'utmost necessity' and vice versa. This exemplifies how general phrases can lead to convoluted results.

### *2.4.3 Ruling Termination of the Contract*

With the lack of legal guidelines in KLaw, different judges might adopt different criteria to rule termination, as follows:

142 Egyptian Supreme Court (9/6/1987) 458 Y 54 Q reproduced in Muhammad (n 255) 800.
143 Egyptian Supreme Court (9/12/1948) Y 17 Q 121 reproduced in ibid 475.
144 Al-Jarmy (n 264) 96.
145 Many other civil law countries resort to an additional period as the main rule and specifically determine the exception to this rule to minimise resorting to termination. For example, according to German Civil Code 2002 s.323(1), an additional period for performance or cure should be granted unless 1) there are special circumstances that *justify* immediate termination; 2) the seller *refuses* performance; or 3) the seller does not render performance by a date specified in the contract, which is of *essential importance* to the buyer.
146 Al-Jarmy (n 264) 105.
147 ibid.

#### 2.4.3.1 *A Seller's Unwillingness to Perform*

A court may find from its assessment of all the evidence that there is little chance that the breaching seller will perform shortly. Thus, as Abolil states,[148] termination should be ruled where it is apparent that the seller cannot/will not perform their obligation.[149]

#### 2.4.3.2 *Harmful Effects of the Refusal of Termination on the Buyer*

It could be said that when refusal of a termination request harms the buyer, the court should rule in favour of termination.[150] However, it might be illogical to assess the detriment of the *refusal* of a remedy, rather than assessing the detriment of the *cause* (the breach).

#### 2.4.3.3 *Negligence and Deliberate Non-Performance*

A judge could rule termination if it is clear that the seller *deliberately* fails to implement their obligation or if they have neglected to properly perform their obligation despite notification from the buyer.[151] Nevertheless, finding out the cause of the breach and the seller's intention is too subjective and difficult to prove, and it may be irrelevant to the contractual relationship. The consequences of this negligence should be scrutinised, as should deliberate refusal to perform and its effects on the buyer, especially when the breach is partial. However, a similar approach is adopted by Article 7.3.1.(c) UPICC when assessing the fundamentality of a breach, in which regard shall be given to whether the seller has intentionally or recklessly failed to perform their obligations.

#### 2.4.3.4 *The Nature of Certain Obligations and Partial Fulfilment*

Al-Jarmy states that the nature of some obligations excludes discretionary authority and requires termination no matter how small the breach is, unless the termination can be partial.[152] However, according to Article 406 KCIC, a seller may not compel the buyer to accept partial fulfilment,[153] and this increases the likelihood of termination of the whole contract.

148 Case 27/11/1996 Appellate Court/Civil 439/1996 p. 5.

149 Abulil (n 258) 418.

150 ibid.

151 Abdulrazaq Al-Sanhory, *The Sources of Commitments* (Dar Alnahda 1964) 799.

152 Al-Jarmy (n 264) 97.

153 KCIC Art. 406; EzEdeen Al-Danasory; Abdulhameed Al-Shawarbee, *Practical Problems, Claims and Defences in the Contract of Sale* (Manshaat AlMaaref 2002) 70.

## 2.5 Comparative Analysis and Conclusion

### *2.5.1 Hypothetical Scenario*

Different outcomes will be clarified under the three legal systems, depending on their general requirements for termination, using the following hypothetical scenario:

Instead of low-fat milk, a shipment of whole-fat milk is dispatched to a buyer, and the milk spoils several hours after its receipt as it is not refrigerated.

Under **CISG**, termination is not an option because there is no substantial foreseeable detriment, as the buyer could not allege that delivering whole-fat milk plays a significant role in its quick putridity. It is unlikely that any reasonable person would have been able to predict the relationship between the seller's breach and damage of this kind. Under **SGA**, the conditionality of the term is the focus, and sending whole-fat milk instead of low-fat milk is not regarded 'so slight' as under s.15A, which permits termination. Under **KLaw**, the buyer can request termination even if they suffered no harm, but it is unclear whether the difference in goods can be regarded as of 'little importance' or not; it will depend on the judiciary's interpretation and perspective, irrespective of the causative relationship between the breach and the detriment.

### *2.5.2 Preserving the Contract and Clarity of Legal Outcomes*

Under **CISG**, it could be rightly argued that Article 25 is controversial because of its open-textured nature, which may lead to indecision as to what constitutes a fundamental breach. As stated in the *Shoe leather case*, Article 25 'includes numerous undefined terms.'[154] However, Article 25 plays a great positive role because:

**First**, it tightens the definition of the detriment caused by the breach by confining it to cases in which the affected buyer is prevented from acquiring their contractual expectations. **Secondly**, the 'substantiality' of the deprivation of contractual expectations is a significant factor that indicates CISG's approach in preserving the contract. **Thirdly**, a foreseeability factor encourages the parties to inform each other about all the aspects, considerations and purposes of the contract to clarify the full picture of the situation. **Fourthly**, resorting to the criteria of 'expectations' and 'foreseeability' attains legal consistency by attempting to prevent the adjudicator from having to put themselves in the place of either party. **Fifthly**, setting a high threshold from which to claim termination in Article 25 has financial advantages: decreasing costs and minimising the wastage of goods.[155] **Finally**, as stated in the *Packaging machine* case, in case of scepticism of the qualification of a breach as fundamental, there should be an assumption that there is no fundamental breach.[156]

154 *Shoe leather case* (11/5/2007) V CSK 456/06 (Supreme Court of Poland).
155 Spagnolo (n 54) 52.
156 *Packaging machine case* 18/5/2009 (n 153). See also *FCF v Adriafil* (n 144).

Termination under **SGA** is contingent primarily on the conditionality of the breached term, regardless of the seriousness of the breach.[157] The justification of the English attitude towards termination is that transactions in the realm of trading commodities are dynamic, volatile and stratified, which necessitates strictness in the application of contractual agreements.[158] Thus, buyers will know when they are authorised to reject goods, and sellers will anticipate buyers' recourse to termination as a remedy. SGA reduces the intensity of the conditionality by adopting s.15A, which could be similar to Article 25's approach of CISG, but the latter gives great attention to the breach's consequences rather than the slightness of the breach itself. Additionally, Article 25 CISG articulates cases in which termination is applicable, but s.15A SGA states the cases in which termination is inapplicable, which could indicate that termination is an exception under CISG but a rule under SGA. Nevertheless, assessing the breach under s.15 could be more apparent and objective[159] than estimating its consequences under Article 25. Thus, CISG tries to 'objectify' its test by comparing the consequences to those expected under the contract. Adopting the theory of an 'intermediate term' in SGA adds flexibility resembling CISG's methods, but this approach is still inapplicable to 'conditions.'

**KLaw**, on the other hand, regulates termination from a different angle as it organises the subject from a more procedural aspect, whereas CISG and SGA are characterised by substantive law. KLaw necessitates recourse to the court, and the judge has discretionary authority to decide on termination. The judge may grant the breaching seller an additional period within which to perform their obligation (the judge does not have this facility under either CISG or SGA), but it is confined to 'utmost necessity,' leaving its interpretation to the court. Substantively, termination depends merely on the seller's breach, and this does not base termination on the assessment of the breach's essentiality or on the injury of the aggrieved buyer, as outlined in CISG. The absence of a general legal threshold upon which to determine cases in which contracts can be terminated is the problem, leading to the arbitrary termination of contracts according to what is most beneficial for the buyer. There is no concrete definition of the 'insignificance of a breach' required to reject termination, and it is unclear whether the 'insignificance' is based on the breach itself or on its consequences to the buyer. More problematically, the dependence on the judge's view leads to subjective decision-making, even if the remaining unfulfilled part of the contract is of little importance,[160] as long as they cite justified reasons in the judgement. This contradicts the notion that predictability is essential, and there must be no discretionary power exercised by the judge

157 McKendrick, *Contract Law* (n 206) 737.
158 Bridge, *The Sale of Goods* (n 28) [7.29].
159 McKendrick, *Sale of Goods* (n 202) 338.
160 See Al-Jarmy (n 264) 96.

when the breach is of 'little importance,' as is the case under Article 25 CISG and s.15A SGA.[161]

These comparisons show the main regulations for resorting to termination; there are other requirements pertinent to specific obligations, which will be discussed in the upcoming chapters.

161 It is also contrary to most civil laws of other countries as they necessitate a threshold to terminate the contract: e.g., German Civil Code 2002 s.323(5), which states that if the seller has not performed pursuant to the contract, the buyer may not terminate the contract if the breach is trivial. Furthermore, French Civil Code 2016 Article 1224 permits termination of the contract when the breach is 'sufficiently serious.'

# 3 Terminating a Contract Due to the Seller's Non-Delivery/Delay in Delivering the Goods

## 3.1 Introduction

The physical transfer of goods by a seller to a buyer is the most common method of delivery.[1] The seller should deliver the goods to the agreed place on the agreed date or within the period agreed in the contract by conveying the possession of the goods to the buyer and yielding effectual control over them.[2] This duty is absolute, which means when the seller fails to deliver, they cannot plead that they have not caused a fault in dispatching the goods or have taken all the reasonable care for proper delivery.[3] On the other hand, delay is common and likely to happen, and the prevailing circumstances at the delivery time and place can have an impact on the ability to perform on time.[4] Transferring goods from a distant location at immense cost only for them to be rejected by the buyer because the delivery was not congruent with the agreed date is likely to cause the seller hardship. This chapter examines in which where delay can lead to termination, assuming that the place of delivery is agreed in the contract, and the contract involves either carriage of goods to that place by the seller[5] or the buyer collecting the goods from the agreed place at a specific time.

## 3.2 Time Is Specified Without Emphasis

This section assumes that the date/period for delivery is merely specified in the contract without any emphasis.

### *3.2.1 CISG*

Article 31 stresses that the seller performs their obligation of delivery when the goods are delivered to the agreed location at the agreed time. If the parties are

1 McKendrick, *Sale of Goods* (n 202) 291.

2 SGA s.61(1); Al-Defery; Al-Sayrafy (n 254) 201; Bridge, *The Sale of Goods* (n 28) [6.02];[6.03]; Sameer Tnago, *Sale Contract* (Manshaat ALMaaref) 318.

3 Twigg-Flesner; Canavan (n 30) 95.

4 ibid 102.

5 CISG Art. 80.

DOI: 10.4324/9781003466130-3

aware at the time of the contract conclusion of the collection location, delivery is considered fulfilled when the goods are placed at the buyer's disposal (either at the factory, a farm or a warehouse)[6] at the agreed time.[7] The seller should ensure the goods are packaged and available[8] on the agreed date. Otherwise, the obligation of delivery is not performed.[9]

In cases in which a delay arises, the buyer can resort to termination according to either Article 49(1)(a) or Article 49(1)(b), as discussed next.

#### *3.2.1.1 Non-Delivery/Delay Amounts to Fundamental Breach According to Article 49(1)(a)*

According to Article 49(1)(a), the buyer can terminate the contract in relation to *any* defaulting obligation by the seller once the stipulations of Article 25 exist,[10] which could embrace the breach of non-delivery/delay[11] when, for example, this breach is objectively serious, affecting the buyer's contractual interests.[12] This is what was pursued in the *Chemical fertilizer case*, in which Article 49(1)(a) was applied to a delay.[13]

The sole fact that a precise delivery/collection time was agreed on does not in itself make non-compliance to this time a fundamental breach.[14] As stated in the *Memory module case*, the 'mere agreement on a firm time for delivery in itself is insufficient in order to establish a firm deal.'[15]

##### 3.2.1.1.1 CASES IN WHICH NON-DELIVERY CONSTITUTES FUNDAMENTAL BREACH

There is controversy over when non-delivery/delay can be considered a fundamental breach, as discussed next.

6 CISG Art. 31.
7 Schwenzer, *Commentary on CISG* (n 15) 534 [43].
8 *Machine case* (10/3/2003) Proz Nr 433/02 (Cantonal Court Appenzell Auserrhoden) <https://cisgw3.law.pace.edu/cases/030310s1.html>.
9 See Schwenzer, *Commentary on CISG* (n 15) 535–536.
10 Bianca; Bonell (n 155) 346.
11 *Italdecor v Yiu's Industries* (20/3/1998) (Appellate Court Milan) <https://cisgw3.law.pace.edu/cases/980320i3.html>.
12 Schwenzer, *Commentary on CISG* (n 15) 768, 769 [15].
13 *Chemical fertilizer case* (1995) 8128 (Court of Arbitration of the International Chamber of Commerce) <http://cisgw3.law.pace.edu/cases/958128i1.html>.
14 *Shoes case* (24/4/1997) 6 U 87/96 (Düsseldorf Appellate Court) <;http://cisgw3.law.pace.edu/cases/970424g1.html>; *Furniture case* (6/4/2000) 12 HKO 4174/99 (District Court München) <;https://cisgw3.law.pace.edu/cases/000406g1.html>; *Memory module case* (12/11/2001) 13 U 102/01 (Appellate Court Hamm) <;http://cisgw3.law.pace.edu/cases/011112g1.html>; Bianca; Bonell (n 155) 343; Ferrari, 'Fundamental Breach' (n 161) 504; Schwenzer, *Commentary on CISG* (n 15) 777 [5]; Kröll; Mistelis; Viscasillas (n 67) 711 [29].
15 ibid *Memory module case*.

*a. Long Postponement* A short delay might not be considered a fundamental breach as such. In *Valero v Greeni*, a two-day delay was not fundamental as the buyer did not incur any damages due to the delay.[16] Conversely, and as stressed in the *Chemical fertilizer case*,[17] the *mobile shear baler case*[18] and the *LDPE film case*,[19] the seller's procrastination and continuous requests for further extensions to the delivery date may entitle the buyer to terminate the contract 'even in the absence of an explicit agreement [to make the delivery time essential).'[20] Not sending the truck for more than two months in *Steinbock-Bjonustan v Duma* constituted a breach under Article 49(1)(a).[21] Similarly, in the *Television sets case*, a more than two-week delay in delivering television sets caused the buyer to incur additional costs to their customers to avoid imminent penalties, and this was considered by the court when assessing the breach.[22] Additionally, in *Arens Sondermaschinen v Smit Draad/Draad Nijmegent*, when the seller exceeded the agreed timeframe and promised to deliver the goods on a new date but without fulfilment, termination was activated.[23]

Long delay per se may permit termination; this happens when it is impossible to perform on the agreed date or at a time close to it. In the *Canned oranges case*, a contract for 42,000 cartons of canned orange was terminated because the postponement of performance was not short, causing damage to the buyer. Termination was permitted even though there was a decrease in orange production and an increase in their price, and, simultaneously, the price of sugar and cans saw rises after concluding the contract.[24]

16 *Valero Marketing & Supply Company v Greeni Trading Oy* (19/7/2007) 06–3390/06–3525 (Federal Court of Appeals) <https://cisgw3.law.pace.edu/cases/070719u2.html>. See also *Valero Marketing v Greeni Oy* (4/4/2006) Civ. 01–5254 (Federal District Court) <https://cisgw3.law.pace.edu/cases/060404u1.html>.

17 *Chemical fertilizer case* (n 302).

18 *Mobile Shear Baler case* (31/5/2010) T-10/09 (Foreign Trade Court) <https://cisgw3.law.pace.edu/cases/100531sb.html>.

19 *LDPE film case* (2006) CISG/2006/18 (CIETAC arbitration proceeding) <https://cisgw3.law.pace.edu/cases/060500c2.html>.

20 *Mobile car phones case* (21/4/2004) 15U88/03 (Appellate Court Düsseldorf) <https://cisgw3.law.pace.edu/cases/040421g3.html>.

21 *Steinbock-Bjonustan EHF v NV Duma* (4/6/2004) AR21–36/2003 (District Court Kortrijk) <https://cisgw3.law.pace.edu/cases/040604b1.html>. See also *Foliopack v Daniplast* (24/11/1989) 77/89 (Pretura Circondariale Court of First Instance) <;http://cisgw3.law.pace.edu/cases/891124i3.html>; *Automobile case* (31/3/2008) 6U220/07 (Appellate Court Stuttgart) <http://cisgw3.law.pace.edu/cases/080331g1.html>.

22 *Television sets case* (28/5/2004) I-17 U 20/02 (Appellate Court Düsseldorf) <https://cisgw3.law.pace.edu/cases/040528g1.html>.

23 *Arens Sondermaschinen GmbH v Smit Draad/Draad Nijmegent B.V.* (7/10/2008) 104.003.479 (Gerechtshof Appellate Court) <https://cisgw3.law.pace.edu/cases/081007n1.html>.

24 *Canned oranges case* (2006) CISG/2006/06 (CIETAC arbitration proceeding) <https://cisgw3.law.pace.edu/cases/060500c1.html>.

*b. Seller's Refusal* When the seller refuses to deliver the goods, non-delivery is fundamental, permitting termination.[25] However, the seller's mere inability to deliver the goods on time might not be equivalent to a refusal, which should be serious and final.[26] Refusal can be deduced when the seller demands new stipulations other than those agreed,[27] such as demanding a higher purchase price for delivery,[28] asking for payment before delivery[29] or, as happened in the *Iron molybdenum case*, demanding an adjusted price and threatening delivery of lower-quality goods.[30]

*c. Nature of the Goods* When the goods are subject to sharp fluctuations in cost, delay could be fundamental.[31] According to the *Clothes case*, exceeding the agreed delivery date by two days did not make the seller responsible for a fundamental breach because the 'goods did not lose any of their value by virtue of the delay,'[32] and claiming that the goods became 'useless' was not supported by realistic evidence.[33]

Nevertheless, according to *Memory module*, the sole fact that the goods were exposed to the 'running market price which was undergoing strong fluctuations' would not make the delay fundamental per se as there was an equivalent possibility of the goods' marketability increasing in the event of a delay of loss.[34] Likewise, in *Valero v Greeni*, the court denied the buyer's defence, citing that the delay was fundamental based on the buyer's market.[35] Furthermore, in *Printed materials*, the court found that delayed goods could still be used, and any reduction of their market value could be compensated for through damages or price reduction.[36]

*d. Economic Loss* Opinions are divided as to whether the detriment of the delay/non-delivery should have to lead to economic loss by the buyer in order to be considered fundamental. **One viewpoint** is that the detriment caused by the delay should be represented as financial harm in order to assess its fundamentality, rather

25 Schwenzer, *Commentary on CISG* (n 15) 778 [6]; Kröll; Mistelis; Viscasillas (n 67) 711 [26]; 713 [33].
26 *Shoes case* 24/4/1997 (n 303).
27 Schwenzer, *Commentary on CISG* (n 15) 778, 779 [6]; 785 [20].
28 *Machines case*) 20/12/2006) 4C.314/2006 (Federal Supreme Court) <https://cisgw3.law.pace.edu/cases/061220s1.html>.
29 *Italdecor v Yiu's Industries* (n 300).
30 *Iron molybdenum case* (28/2/1997) 1U167/95 (Appellate Court Hamburg) <http://cisgw3.law.pace.edu/cases/970228g1.html>.
31 John Honnold, *Uniform Law for International Sales Under the 1980 United Nations Convention* (4th edn, Turpin Distribution Services 2009) 437 [305].
32 *Clothes case* (21/12/1990) 4C549/90 (Lower Court Ludwigsburg) <. https://cisgw3.law.pace.edu/cases/901221g1.html>.
33 ibid.
34 *Memory module case* (n 303).
35 *Valero Marketing v Greeni Oy* (15/6/2005) CIV.01–5254(DRD) (Federal District Court) <http://cisgw3.law.pace.edu/cases/050615u1.html>.
36 *Printed materials case* (25/6/2007) HG050430/U/ei (Commercial Court Zürich) <http://cisgw3.law.pace.edu/cases/070625s1.html>.

than sticking to the literal implementation of the agreed time.[37] In a *Case involving machine for repair of bricks*, it was stated that 'CISG distinguishes a fundamental breach of contract from a breach that is ancillary or supplementary, by which the non-breaching party could still obtain the economic result that it expected from the contract.'[38] Accordingly, the fact that the delay badly affected the buyer's production process in the *Rolled steel case* entitled the buyer to terminate the contract.[39]

The **second viewpoint** is that economic detriment is not required to render the delay a fundamental breach;[40] the Czechoslovakian delegation in one CISG Conference stated that it was doubtful in determining whether termination was dependent on economic loss.[41] Per the wording of Article 25, a fundamental breach depends on the substantiality of the deprivation of the non-breaching buyer's contractual interest, regardless of the pecuniary loss.[42] The detriment might embrace all actual and future negative consequences and includes any kind of deplorable results of a breach,[43] with the exclusion of 'death or personal injury caused by the goods to any person,'[44] which is outside CISG's sphere.

One may argue that Article 74 can be resorted to to fill this gap as it articulates 'loss' and 'loss of profit,' so a breach in relation to intangible damage cannot be seen as a detriment. Even with this in mind, damage to a reputation of punctuality, inconvenience or disappointment[45] could be considered an illustration of loss, as it could have an indirect impact on the buyer's financial interests.[46]

*e. Adequacy of Using Other Remedies for the Delay* This view sees that CISG provides easy access to less harsh remedies than termination,[47] such as a price reduction or damages, and if such remedies render an adequate solution to delay, they may make delay non-fundamental.[48] In one CISG drafting conference, the UK

37 For a similar view, see Enderlein; Maskow (n 150) 113.

38 *Case involving machine for repair of bricks* (27/12/2007) (Appellate Court Navarra) <https://cisgw3.law.pace.edu/cases/071227s4.html>.

39 *Rolled steel case* (3/11/1997) 729/96-B (Appellate Court Barcelona) <https://cisgw3.law.pace.edu/cases/971103s4.html>.

40 Schwenzer, *Commentary on CISG* (n 15) 428 [22].

41 Comments by Governments and International Organizations on the Draft Convention on the International Sale of Goods, *Yearbook of the UN Commission on International Trade Law 1977 Volume VIII* 1 1978 (A/CN.9/125 and A/CN.9/125/add.1 to 3) 113 & <https://www.uncitral.org/pdf/english/yearbooks/yb-1977-e/yb_1977_e.pdfhttp://dag.un.org/bitstream/handle/11176/262648/A_CN.9_125-EN.pdf?sequence=1&isAllowed=y>&<https://www.uncitral.org/pdf/english/yearbooks/yb-1977-e/yb_1977_e.pdf >.

42 Dessemontet (n 170) 215; Goode; Kronke; Mckendrick (n 157) 2015 edn, 249, 250 [8.72].

43 Ferrari, 'Fundamental Breach' (n 161) 495. This conclusion is equivalent to the wording of Art.74; Bridge, 'Avoidance for Fundamental Breach' (n 158) 918, 919.

44 CISG Art. 5.

45 Bridge, 'Avoidance for Fundamental Breach' (n 158) 918, 919.

46 Kröll; Mistelis; Viscasillas (n 67) 341 [12].

47 Spagnolo (n 54) 90.

48 Peacock (n 140) 102; Zeller, 'Fundamental Breach' (n 184) 82; Ferrari, 'Fundamental Breach' (n 161) 496, 497; Grebler, 'Fundamental Breach' (n 48) 409, 410; Honnold, *Uniform Law* (n 320) 291,

representative established a link between the fundamentality of the breach and an inability to cure it by damages, stating '[a] breach does not result in substantial detriment to the other party if damages would be an adequate remedy for him.'[49] Therefore, according to the *Meat case*, before resorting to termination, the buyer should make use of other remedies[50] which are likely to be economically more efficient in international contracts[51] and are compatible with the 'reasonableness' principle on which CISG is based.[52]

#### 3.2.1.1.2 DEPENDENCY OF FUNDAMENTALITY ON CURABILITY?

Article 48(1) enables the seller to cure 'any failure' of performance, unilaterally and independently of the buyer's actions towards the breach,[53] and this right to cure may include non-fundamental as well as fundamental breaches.[54] There are two perspectives on the relationship between the seller's right to cure the non-delivery and fundamental breach. The **first** perspective sees that fundamentality of non-delivery depends on the curability right as, at the 38th meeting of the diplomatic conformance on 7 April 1980, the phrase: 'the seller may, even after the date for delivery . . . remedy . . . any failure to perform his obligations . . .' was adopted, but the phrase '[u]nless the buyer has declared the contract avoided' was deleted.[55] It can be understood from this deletion and the wording of Article 49(2), as stated in the *Inflatable triumphal arch case*, that there is 'priority of the entitlement to subsequent cure or remedy over the entitlement of contract avoidance that forms the basis of the UN Sales Law, even in the case of an objective fundamental [breach].'[56] The seller's reasonable cure might remove any possibility of definite risk to the buyer's essential interests.[57] In the *Cloth case*, the court found that the buyer was only entitled to terminate the contract after giving the seller an opportunity to cure their performance.[58] In *Key press*, too, the court found that when the delivery was 'objectively possible' and the seller was willing

292 [193]; Bridge, 'Avoidance for Fundamental Breach' (n 158) 921; Martin; Snyder (n 67) 367; Kröll; Mistelis; Viscasillas (n 67) 341 [13].

49 Official Records (n 149) 1st Committee 99; *Shen* (n 131) footnote 25.

50 *Meat case* (n 171).

51 Spagnolo (n 54) 89.

52 Saiegh (n 116) 448.

53 Jonathan Yovel, 'The Seller's Right to Cure a Failure to Perform: An Analytic Comparison of the Respective Provisions of the CISG and the PECL' (2005) 1 Nord J Commer Law 1, 3, 4. See also *Arens Sondermaschinen v Smit Draad/Draad* (n 312).

54 ibid Jonathan Yove l5.

55 John Honnold, *Documentary History of the Uniform Law for International Sales* (Kluwer Law and Taxation Publishers 1989) 686, 687.

56 *Inflatable triumphal arch case* (5/11/2002) OR.2001.00029 (Commercial Court of the Canton of Aargau) <http://cisgw3.law.pace.edu/cases/021105s1.html>.

57 ibid.

58 *Cloth case* (24/9/1998) 6O107/98 (District Court Regensburg). <http://cisgw3.law.pace.edu/cases/980924g1.html>.

to cure the non-delivery of the goods, this might affect categorising the breach as fundamental,[59] thwarting hasty termination.[60] It was also stated in the *Acrylic blankets case* that 'regard must be had not only to the gravity of the breach, but also to the willingness of the seller to cure the defect,'[61] and, subsequently, 'there is no fundamental breach if there is a serious offer to cure the defect.'[62] In parallel, it was stated in the *Designer clothes case* that

> not only the weight of the defect, but also the preparedness of the seller to cure the defect without unacceptable delay and burden to the buyer is of importance. Even a serious defect is not a fundamental breach of contract if the seller is prepared to [deliver] the goods without unacceptable burden to the buyer.[63]

According to the *Inflatable triumphal arch case*, in case of doubt about whether the late delivery would remove the detriment suffered by the buyer, the contract will still be upheld.[64]

On the contrary, the **second** view advocates that the fundamentality of non-delivery according to Article 49(1)(a) does not depend on the seller's subsequent performance. The focus should be on foreseeable substantial deprivation of the contractual expectations resulting from the delay, making any subsequent execution useless.[65] The phrase 'subject to Article 49' found in Article 48(1) could signify that the seller's curability right can be interrupted (when it has not been exercised yet) by the buyer's declaration of termination when the non-delivery itself is considered fundamental. This indicates that fundamentality should be established objectively without consideration to curability rights,[66] and the seller cannot thwart the buyer's termination right by late delivery.[67] Hence, Bianca and Bonell state that the buyer's termination right has precedence over the seller's right to cure,[68] and, as Peacock finds, the seller's curability right (even if it is reasonable)

59 *Key press case* (18/11/1993) 6U228/92 (Appellate Court Düsseldorf) <http://cisgw3.law.pace.edu/cases/931118g1.html>.

60 Ahmad Azzouni, 'The Adoption of the 1980 Convention on the International Sale of Goods by the United Kingdom' [2002] 10 <;http://www.cisg.law.pace.edu/cisg/biblio/azzouni.html>; Peter Schlechtriem, 'Subsequent Performance and Delivery Deadlines- Avoidance of CISG Sales Contracts due to Non-Conformity of the Goods' (2006) 18(1) Pace Int Law Rev 83, 89; Honnold, *Uniform Law* (n 320) 426, 427 [296].

61 *Acrylic blankets case* (31/1/1997) 2U31/96 Appellate Court Koblenz <http://cisgw3.law.pace.edu/cases/970131g1.html>.

62 ibid.

63 *Designer clothes case* (14/10/2002) 16U77/01 (Appellate Court Köln) <http://cisgw3.law.pace.edu/cases/021014g1.html>.

64 *Inflatable triumphal arch case* (n 345).

65 Dessemontet (n 170) 215.

66 Peacock (n 140) 119, 120. See also Yovel (n 342) 6; Schlechtriem, 'Subsequent Performance' (n 349) 88.

67 Schwenzer, *Commentary on CISG* (n 15) 770 [17].

68 Bianca; Bonell (n 155) 362.

does not exclude the termination, unless the breach is not fundamental.[69] Other scholars have found a hierarchy between the termination right and the curability right, and the latter is only available when the former is not correctly exercised.[70]

### 3.2.1.2 *Additional Period Procedure (*Nachfrist*) According to Article 49(1)(b)*

If non-delivery does not amount to a fundamental breach as to permit immediate termination[71] or there is uncertainty over whether or not the non-delivery qualifies as a fundamental breach,[72] the buyer may grant the seller a cut-off period of reasonable length (*Nachfrist*)[73] to deliver the goods,[74] within which the delivery should be received.[75] Pursuant to Article 27, if the buyer sends a notice of *Nachfrist* to the seller, it is effective on its dispatch date, so the buyer does not bear the risk of its transmission to reach the seller. Upon the expiration of *Nachfrist* without the seller's success in sending the goods or when the seller refuses to deliver the goods during such a period, the buyer is released from the burden of proving the fundamentality of the non-delivery[76] and can declare the contract terminated directly after the expiration of such a period or directly after the seller's refusal,[77] irrespective of Article 25's conditions.[78]

#### 3.2.1.2.1 PHRASING *NACHFRIST* NOTICE AND ITS REASONABLE LENGTH

The important issue to consider with a *Nachfrist* notice is its contents; it should have a warning clause specifying a final deadline[79] within which the goods should be delivered.[80] Over-politeness in stating phrasing[81] (by saying, for instance, 'I hope you deliver the goods by 30/8' or using ambiguous phrases such as 'promptly'[82] or 'without delay') would not be considered *Nachfrist*.[83] It is sufficient for

69 Peacock (n 140) 119, 120.
70 Yovel (n 342) 10.
71 Chengwei Liu, 'Additional Period (*Nachfrist*) for Late Performance: Perspectives from the CISG, UNIDROIT Principles, PECL and Case Law' (2005) 4 <;http://cisgw3.law.pace.edu/cisg/biblio/liu4.html>; Kröll; Mistelis; Viscasillas (n 67) 718 [52].
72 ibid Kröll; Mistelis; Viscasillas 718 [52].
73 It could be specified orally. See the *Chemical fertilizer case* (n 302); Graffi (n 155) 341.
74 This period is based on German law, Azzouni (n 349) 10.
75 *Printed materials case* (n 325).
76 Schwenzer, *Commentary on CISG* (n 15) 783 [15].
77 CISG Art. 47(2); 492(b)(ii).
78 *Packaging machine case* (8/11/2006) P-2004–152 (Civil Court Basil-Stadt) <https://cisgw3.law.pace.edu/cases/061108s1.html>.
79 Kröll; Mistelis; Viscasillas (n 67) 689 [13].
80 *Shoes case* 24/4/1997 (n 303); Honnold, *Uniform Law* (n 320) 420 [289].
81 Bianca; Bonell (n 155) 345; Schwenzer, *Commentary on CISG* (n 15) 757 [4];[5]. CISG Art. 49(2).
82 *Shoes case* 24/4/1997 (n 303).
83 Bianca; Bonell (n 155) 345; Honnold, *Uniform Law* (n 320) 420 [289]. CISG Art. 49(2); Tobias Plate, 'The Buyer's Remedy of Avoidance Under the CISG: Acceptable From a Common Law Perspective?' (2002) 6 VJ 57, 69–71.

the buyer to state, for example, 'You have until 31/10 to deliver the goods.'[84] Both sending a letter to the seller instructing them to perform within a specific period or the buyer will request a refund[85] and granting more than one period for delivery[86] have qualified as *Nachfrist*. However, in the *Memory module case*, demanding over the phone that the goods be available on a particular date did not constitute a proper specification of *Nachfrist*.[87]

A notice of *Nachfrist* should be of reasonable length, and its reasonability depends on the circumstances of each case.[88] Instant termination after the expiration of insufficient *Nachfrist* makes the declaration of termination ineffective and outside the reasonable time specification of Article 49(2).[89] In the *Used printing press case*, termination was declared seven weeks after fixing *Nachfrist*, making a short *Nachfrist* (two weeks) reasonable.[90]

##### 3.2.1.2.2 SELLER'S CURABILITY RIGHT[91] VERSUS *NACHFRIST*

The question arises as to whether the seller may use the curability right after the expiration of *Nachfrist*, as discussed next.

*a. Curability Period Is Longer Than* Nachfrist The buyer can fix a *Nachfrist* of reasonable length, and then the seller can notify the buyer of their right to perform within a longer period of time. The buyer who intends to terminate the contract should object to this period of time even if conditional termination is declared in *Nachfrist* upon its expiration without success.[92] Take this example: The contract specifies the delivery time to be on 1 March. On 2 March, the buyer specifies *Nachfrist* to have the goods delivered by 10 March at the latest; otherwise, the contract will be terminated. The seller replies on the same day, with the intention of delivering the goods by 30 March instead. Not rejecting the seller's proposal within a reasonable time[93] means it will prevail over the buyer's *Nachfrist*.[94]

*b. Curability After the Expiration of* Nachfrist When *Nachfrist* expires (if it does not state that termination is conditional upon its expiration) but before the buyer

84 Schwenzer, *Commentary on CISG* (n 15) 757 [4];[5].
85 *Rolled steel case* (n 328).
86 Unavailable Name (1/3/2006) 101/2005 (Tribunal of International Commercial Arbitration) <https://cisgw3.law.pace.edu/cases/060301r1.html>.
87 *Memory module case* (n 303).
88 *Packaging machine case* 18/5/2009 (n 153); Bianca; Bonell (n 155) 345.
89 See also UPICC Art. 7.1.5.(3).
90 *Used printing press case* (24/5/1995) 20U76/94 (Appellate Court Celle) <http://cisgw3.law.pace.edu/cases/950524g1.html>. A similar conclusion was reached in the *Automobile case* (27/4/1999) 9U146/98 (Appellate Court Naumburg) <https://cisgw3.law.pace.edu/cases/990427g1.html>.
91 This right can be used for any breach, not just for non-delivery.
92 Kröll; Mistelis; Viscasillas (n 67) 702, 703 [33].
93 CISG Art. 48(2).
94 Kröll; Mistelis; Viscasillas (n 67) 720 [61].

declares termination and the seller clarifies their willingness to perform for another period, the buyer should act immediately, objecting to the seller's request for late delivery and declaring the contract terminated.[95] As stated in the *Designer clothes case*, the buyer does not have to accept the seller's willingness to deliver the goods after the agreed time[96] or after *Nachfrist*, making the buyer's reaction to the seller's request decisive.[97] In *Scaffold fittings*, the tribunal also stated that the seller was not permitted to subsequently perform after the agreed delivery date without the buyer's approval.[98]

Upon the buyer's failure to object and according to Article 48(2), the seller can perform until the last day specified in the seller's notification for the subsequent delivery.[99] However, using an ambiguous and indefinite term in this notification, such as 'as soon as possible'[100] or 'try to deliver the goods,' could have a negative impact on its effectiveness.[101]

According to Article 7.1.5. (3) and (4) UPICC, when *Nachfrist*'s notice has mentioned that the contract shall be terminated *automatically* after its expiration without success, the seller might not be permitted to specify a supplementary period according to their curability right.[102] This is unless the undelivered goods are minor parts of the contractual obligation of the seller. However, when *Nachfrist* is not of a reasonable length pursuant to Article 47, the seller can perform beyond this time limit (even in the case of the buyer's objection) but within a reasonable time frame when they make it clear that they refuse the performance only with regards to such a short period.[103]

### *3.2.2 SGA*

The seller is under an obligation to ensure the goods are in a 'deliverable state' in order to be collected by the buyer from the agreed place at the agreed time. Although 'deliverable state' is defined in neither s.29(6) nor s.61(5), this term could be interpreted by reference to the goods' physical movability,[104] enabling the buyer to collect them.[105] When an engine was bolted to concrete flooring in *Underwood*[106] and the goods were sent in heavy bales not laid by the seller as agreed in

95 Yovel (n 342) 14; ibid 703 [38].
96 *Designer clothes case* (n 352).
97 Yovel (n 342) 10.
98 *Scaffold fittings case* (1994) 7531 (Court of Arbitration of the International Chamber of Commerce) <http://cisgw3.law.pace.edu/cases/947531i1.html>.
99 Schwenzer, *Commentary on CISG* (n 15) 786 [21].
100 *Designer clothes case* (n 352).
101 ibid.
102 Schwenzer, *Commentary on CISG* (n 15) 768 [14].
103 Kröll; Mistelis; Viscasillas (n 67) 721 [63].
104 Twigg-Flesner; Canavan (n 30) 234.
105 McKendrick, *Sale of Goods* (n 202) 294.
106 *Underwood Ltd v Burgh Castle Brick & Cement Syndicate* [1922] 1 KB 343, 343, 344.

*Philip v Showfronts*,[107] the goods were considered not to be in a deliverable state. In *Kulkarni v Manor*, however, 'deliverable state' was interpreted to mean legal movability. Thus, not attaching registration plates to cars meant they were not in a deliverable state.[108]

Under this obligation and one in which the seller delivers the goods to a specific place at a specific time, there is nothing in SGA that confirms that a delivery time clause is a 'condition.' Instead, SGA refers to the contractual terms to deduce whether time is of the essence or not.[109] This failure to precisely state what the legal consequences of late performance are could make time stipulation an 'intermediate term.' However, most courts have considered delivery time a 'condition' in commercial contracts.

#### *3.2.2.1 Conditionality of Delivery Time*

In *Bunge v Tradax*, it was stressed that in commercial contracts, time should be considered a 'condition'[110] since certainty has been the most crucial element of these contracts.[111] Thus, a breach of delivery time, no matter how slight,[112] entitles the innocent buyer to terminate the contract,[113] and the 'gravity of the breach,' according to *Hong Kong*, would be improper to apply.[114] This is trueeven if there is no indication in the contract that the delivery time is of the essence.[115] It is true that breaching a time stipulation greatly varies in its effects,[116] but, as accentuated in *Union Eagle v Golden Achievement*, the duration of the delay is irrelevant, whether it is ten minutes or one month.[117]

The seller subsequently has the right to perform until the last day of the agreed period, and if the last day is a non-working day, such as a bank holiday, the period will not be extended to the day after.[118] Sending the goods beyond this limit justifies rejecting the whole shipment[119] as the buyer may be unable to take/receive the

107 *Philip Head & Sons Ltd v Showfronts Ltd* [1970] 1 Lloyd's Rep 140.

108 *Kulkarni v Manor Credit (Davenham) Ltd* [2010] EWCA Civ 69.

109 SGA s.10(2).

110 See also *McDougall v Aeromarine of Emsworth* [1958] 1 WLR 1126; *Wimshurst v Deeley* 135 ER 942 [7].

111 *United Scientific Holdings Ltd v Burnley BC* [1978] AC 904, 924; *Bunge Corp v Tradax Export SA* [1981] 1 WLR 711, 712, 715.

112 Peel, 15th edn (n 64) 1025 [18–114].

113 Beale (n 213) 1408 [43–271].

114 *Bunge v Tradax* (n 400) 716. The same conclusion was reached in *Gill & Duffus SA v Societe pour l'Exportation des Sucres SA* [1986] 1 Lloyd's Rep 322. It was stated that the time would generally be treated as a condition.

115 *Coddington v Paleologo* (1866–67) LR 2 Ex 193, 197; *Bowes v Shand* (1877) 2 App Cas 455, 458; *Maredelanto* (n 78) 164; Blair (n 25) 12; Bridge, *The Sale of Goods* (n 28) [10.39].

116 John Stannard, 'So What if Time is of the Essence?' [2005] Sing J Legal Stud 114; Davies (n 196) 3rd edn 382 [25.3.3].

117 *Union Eagle Ltd v Golden Achievement Ltd* [1997] AC 514.

118 *Jacobson van den Berg & Co (UK) v Biba* [1977] 1 WLUK 254.

119 Smith, *Atiyah's* (n 198) 200.

goods at a later time, which could affect the goods' quality.[120] The buyer should only intimate to the seller within reasonable time about this rejection.[121]

This is true unless the parties have agreed otherwise,[122] making time an 'intermediate term'[123] by saying, for example, 'It is preferable/if it is possible to send the goods on the agreed date,'[124] or 'The seller will use their best endeavours to deliver on the agreed date.' In *Cie Commerciale Sucres v Czarnikow*, in which the contract mentioned a period of time for the performance, after fulfilling another commitment, the time limit was not essential.[125] Similarly, in *Raffinerie v Chevron*, it was held that the agreed delivery period was not a condition due to the effect of demurrage and laycan on the timely delivery, giving the obligation a degree of flexibility.[126]

#### 3.2.2.1.1 TECHNICAL TERMINATION

The collapse of the goods' market after concluding the contract may encourage the buyer to reject the goods,[127] claiming that the reason for rejection is the failure to comply with contractual terms.[128] Some courts may hold that termination is not permitted when the real motive is not avoiding the prejudice resulting from the breach.[129] Roskill LJ in *Cehave* stated that 'contracts are made to be performed and not to be avoided according to the whims of market fluctuation.'[130] Lord Denning also mentioned that it could be unfair to permit rejecting the whole consignment when the aim is to evade falling prices of the goods sold after concluding the contract.[131] Thus, the decline in the market price was scrutinised in *Tradax Internacional* to assess the buyer's termination right.[132]

However, when considering the majority of opinions, goods' merchantability constitutes an irrelevant factor under s.13(1);[133] courts[134] may be aware that SGA

120 See Bridge, *The Sale of Goods* (n 28) [6.30].
121 SGAs.35(4); s.36(1).
122 *Bunge v Tradax* (n 400) 716.
123 *Scandinavian Trading Co A/B v Zodiac Petroleum SA (The Al Hofuf)* [1981] 1 Lloyd's Rep 81; *Bunge v Tradax* (n 400) 714, 721. The duty in this case was to give notice of probable readiness of the vessel by the buyer. Although the duty was not about timely delivery, the rule can be applied to such a duty by analogy. See also *Bentsen* (n 210) 281; *Raineri v Miles* [1981] AC 1050, 1051; *Thunderbird Industries LLC v Simoco Digital UK Ltd* [2004] EWHC 209 [10]; *Soufflet Negoce SA v Bunge SA* [2010] EWCA Civ 1102 [11]; Andrews, *Contractual Duties* (n 78) 219.
124 ibid *Raineri v Miles*.
125 *Cie Commerciale Sucres* (n 78) 1339–1340.
126 *Raffinerie* (n 73) 808.
127 Adams; Brownsword (n 218) 169–171.
128 *Reardon Smith Line Ltd v Hansen-Tangen (The Diana Prosperity)* [1976] 1 WLR 989, 989–991.
129 Peel, 15th edn (n 64) 977 [18–037].
130 *Cehave* (n 126) 71.
131 ibid 63.
132 *Tradax Internacional SA v Goldschmidt SA* [1977] 2 Lloyd's Rep 604, 604, 605, 614.
133 *Arcos Ltd v EA Ronaasen & Son* [1933] AC 470; *Rapalli v KL Take* [1958] 2 Lloyd's Rep 469; *Tradax Export SA v European Grain & Shipping Ltd* [1983] 2 Lloyd's Rep 100, 104, 105; Beale (n 213) 1324 [43–076].
134 See *Bowes v Shand* (n 404) 455.

can technically be used to escape from a bad transaction,[135] and 'in a falling market [the] buyers are often as eager to insist on their legal rights.'[136] Nonetheless, conjecture around the reason for termination is unrelated because promotion of certainty prevails over any considerations,[137] and '[c]ourts . . . are ready to maintain' buyer's rights.[138]

Permitting a seller to contest a buyer using a technical breach to escape from a declining market would lead to inextricable disputes,[139] paving the way for the breaching seller to prioritise self-interest.[140] The seller could easily breach the contract because they knew the buyer could not terminate the contract if the market price of the goods fell dramatically. Therefore, in *Bowes v Shand*, when the sellers delivered some of the agreed quantity of rice in a different month instead of the agreed months of 'March and/or April,' the buyer was entitled to reject the whole cargo without showing any particular damage suffered because of untimely delivery.[141] This was true even though there was no difference in sending the goods in the delivered month and the agreed months.[142] Lord O'Hagan stated there was no liberty to speculate the motives in specifying that particular time for delivery, and there was no consideration of the comparative benefit of sending the goods at a time other than that mentioned in the contract.[143]

#### 3.2.2.1.2 THE BASIS OF CONSIDERING TIME A CONDITION

The reasons courts are keen to consider time a condition in mercantile contracts[144] can be different. Some reasons from case law and scholarly opinions are as follows:

*a. Delivery Time Is a Part of Description* Timely delivery has been held in some cases to be part of contractual descriptions.[145] In *Bowes v Shand*, Lord Blackburn[146] stated that the buyer was not obliged to accept peas instead of beans, and similarly, 'a February shipment . . . cannot be a March shipment,'[147] and the buyer was

135 Adams; Brownsword (n 218) 169, 170; Peel, 15th edn (n 64) 987, 988 [18–050].

136 Lord Atkin in *Arcos v Ronaasen* (n 422) 480.

137 Smith, *Atiyah's* (n 198) 200.

138 Lord Atkin in *Arcos v Ronaasen* (n 422) 480.

139 Twigg-Flesner; Canavan (n 30) 103.

140 James Fisher, 'Uncertainty, Opportunism and the Intermediate Term: The Hong Kong Fir Principle in English and Irish Contract Law' (2015) 14 Hibernian Law J 96, 108; Bridge, *The Sale of Goods* (n 28) [6.28].

141 *Bowes v Shand* (n 404) 467.

142 ibid 475–479.

143 ibid 479.

144 ibid 479, 480; *Reuter Hufeland v Sala* (1879) 4 C.P.D. 239, 249; *Bunge v Tradax* (n 400) 712; *Gill v Societe pour l'Exportation des Sucres* (n 403) 322; *Cie Commerciale Sucres* (n 78) 1338.

145 McCardie J in *Hartley v Hymans* [1920] 3 KB 475, 483; *Phibro Energy Inc v Coastal (Bermuda) Ltd* [1987] 4 WLUK 158.

146 *Bowes v Shand* (n 404) 461.

147 ibid 483.

not bound to take the goods on another date.[148] Moreover, in *Aron v Comptoir Wegimont*, McCardie J stated that 'a contract requirement that goods are to be shipped at a given time is far more than a mere description of the goods. . . . [I]t is a condition precedent.'[149]

*b. Fluctuation of Goods' Price* The rapid fluctuation of the goods' value in the market has specific risk in commercial contracts, and this places delay under a zero-tolerance policy, construing the courts' readiness to consider delivery time a condition.[150] Bridge indicates that time is an intermediate term in consumer contracts because it is less important than in commercial contracts.[151] This tendency is probably because the consumer is normally not affected by and does not care about the price fluctuation of the bought goods, as opposed to the merchant, who intends to resell the goods and may be significantly affected by late delivery because of the adverse change in prices.

*c. Respecting the Contract* According to *Gill v Societe pour l'Exportation des Sucres*, not treating a time clause as a condition may be considered unjustifiable interference with the parties' determination of the time in the contract and would extend the time of performance for the seller, which could affect the buyer considerably.[152] Any criticism of this approach of being supportive to the buyer can be countered with the argument that the contractual obligations are interchangeable.[153] However, this might not be the case as the payment time is not a 'condition,'[154] but it may be considered so when it comes to delivery time.

*d. Time Is a Condition Mentioned Implicitly in SGA* As McCardie J stated in *Hartley v Hymans*, the courts support the idea that '[i]n ordinary commercial contracts for the sale of goods the rule clearly is that time is *prima facie* of the essence with respect to delivery.'[155] This could be based on the implicit importance attached to time in SGA. For instance, s.29(5) mentions that the delivery should be at a reasonable hour (although without regarding it as a 'condition'), indicating the necessity of the precision of the delivery time. Conclusions regarding the importance of time can also be reached through s.10, which states that payment time is not of the essence in sale contracts, and this supports the understanding that any time clause, other than timely payment, is of the essence.

148 ibid 480, 481.
149 J Aron & Co Inc v Comptoir Wegimont SA [1921] 3 K.B. 435, 441.
150 Peel, 15th edn (n 64) 992, 993 [18–056].
151 Bridge, *The Sale of Goods* (n 28) [10.40].
152 *Gill v Societe pour l'Exportation des Sucres* (n 403) 322.
153 Bridge, *The Sale of Goods* (n 28) [6.30].
154 SGA s.10(1).
155 Mccardie J in *Hartley v Hymans* (n 434) 484.

*e. Avoiding Protracted Litigation* There is great discrepancy regarding time; in some circumstances, a one-day delay is extremely detrimental, whereas in other cases, a one-month delay does not cause any harmful effect.[156] To fix this divergence, time is generally of the essence, and breaching it would bring the contract to an end,[157] obviating the risk of unlawful and premature termination.[158] Lord Wilberforce in *Bunge v Tradax* stated that the test of the 'intermediate term' would be commercially undesirable as it could encourage the seller to delay in performing their duties in the hope of a ruling for damages.[159] Thus, treating time as a 'condition' would avoid a 'large increase in arbitrations' and protracted trials, which consume time and money and are cumbersome processes to assess both the prejudice of breaching time leading to termination and damages.[160]

### 3.2.2.2 *Merely Specifying Time in the Contract May Make It Intermediate Term*

Despite the fact that the general rule in case law regards delivery time in commercial contracts as a condition,[161] 'time is not of the essence as regards the performance of contractual obligations, but exceptions overshadow the general rule.'[162]

#### 3.2.2.2.1 COULD DELIVERY TIME BE AN INTERMEDIATE TERM?

A small number of cases did not consider the sole indication of time being of the essence, although they were associated with the international sale of goods,[163] as s.10(2) refers to the contract to find out whether the delivery time is a 'condition precedent.' A time clause could be an intermediate term according to the following considerations:

*a. Rules of Common Law of Contract* According to the common law of contracts (other than sale of goods contracts) and cases of sale of goods contracts which deal with delay not associated with delivery, there is flexibility in regarding time as an 'intermediate term' rather than an absolute 'condition.' It can be argued that these cases might be resorted to by analogy to be applied in relation to delayed delivery, especially, as stated in *Cehave*, when there is no reason not to apply common law rules, particularly *Hong Kong*'s rule of 'intermediate term,' to contracts concerning the sale of goods.[164]

156 Furmston (n 30) 689.
157 ibid 690.
158 Bridge, *The Sale of Goods* (n 28) [6.30].
159 *Bunge v Tradax* (n 400) 715.
160 ibid.
161 Mullis, 'Termination for Breach of Contract' in Guest (n 226) 142; Stannard (n 405) 115.
162 Malcolm Clarke, 'Time and the Essence of Mercantile Contracts: The Law Loses Its Way' (1991) 50(1) CLJ 29, 31. See also Paul Davies, *JC Smith's the Law of Contract* (OUP 2016) 370.
163 *Phibro Energy AG v Nissho Iwai Corp (The Honam Jade)* [1991] 1 Lloyd's Rep 38.
164 *Cehave* (n 126) 49, 60.

When the contract fixes the delivery time without specifying its being of the essence, regarding it as an 'intermediate term' would not contradict the parties' intentions and would be compatible with s.10(2).[165] In *Torvald v Arni*, the House of Lords held that a time clause in a mercantile transaction was not a 'condition' but an 'intermediate term,' and, as long as the delay was short, termination was unjustified.[166] Hence, only when the consequences of the delay cause frustration[167] to the commercial purpose of the contract[168] and, as stated in *Suisse Atlantique*,[169] deprive the buyer of profit[170] is termination authorised.[171]

*b. Equity Rules* Although it was stated in *Parkin v Thorold*[172] that time has always been of the essence when fixed in the contract, it was recommended that contracts be construed in correspondence with law and equity. Pursuant to equity rules, time could be an 'intermediate term,'[173] unless the parties 'introduce a clause expressly stating that time is to be of the essence of the contract,' or it could be so, deriving from the circumstances of the case.[174] Otherwise, as Mr Justice Christopher Clarke in *Paribas v Wockhardt* asserted, time can be made 'of the essence' by notifying the defaulting seller, stating clearly the need for performance to be fulfilled within a reasonable time and that the failure to do so will permit the buyer to terminate the contract.[175] However, as emphasised by Cotton LJ in *Reuter Hufeland v Sala*,[176] the time fixed in the contract is a 'condition' without applying the equity principle, and not treating it as such in relation to mercantile contracts would be unreasonable and dangerous.

*c. Jurists' Opinions* Time might not be a 'condition' in all cases, as Lord Wilberforce in *Bunge v Tradax* stated that 'the courts should not be too ready to interpret contractual clauses as conditions,'[177] and, as Roskill LJ asserted in *Cehave*, 'where there is a free choice between two possible constructions . . . the court should tend to prefer that construction which will ensure performance and not

165 See Beale (n 213) 1408 [43–271]; Bridge, *Benjamin's* (n 28) [8–025].
166 *Torvald Klaveness A/S v Arni Maritime Corp (The Gregos)* [1994] 1 WLR 1465, 1475.
167 Adams; Brownsword (n 218) 167–169; Bridge, *Benjamin's* (n 28) [10–033]; Twigg-Flesner; Canavan (n 30) 116, 117.
168 *Hong Kong* (n 219) 27; *Suisse Atlantique Societe d'Armement SA v NV Rotterdamsche Kolen Centrale* [1967] 1 AC 361, 435.
169 ibid *Suisse Atlantique* 370, 371, 374.
170 ibid 374, 379.
171 *Universal Cargo Carriers Corp v Citati (No.2)* [1958] 2 QB 254, 257.
172 *Parkin* (n 76) 701.
173 *United Scientific Holdings v Burnley* (n 400) 927; *Peregrine Systems Ltd v Steria Ltd* [2005] EWCA Civ 239 [15]; *Shawton Engineering Ltd v DGP International Ltd (t/a Design Group Partnership)* [2005] EWCA Civ 1359 [32]. See also *Parkin* (n 76) 698.
174 *Parkin* (n 76) 701. See also *Paribas* (n 78) [34].
175 *ibid Paribas* [40].
176 *Reuter v Sala* (n 433) 248, 249.
177 *Bunge v Tradax* (n 400) 715.

encourage avoidance of contractual obligations.'[178] This is especially the case, as Lord Lowry stated in *Bunge v Tradax*, when treating time in mercantile contracts as a 'condition' is not justifiable by a rule of law or presumption of fact but by being a practical expedient dictated by business experience.[179] McCardie J in *Hartley v Hymans* pointed out that in ordinary sale of goods contracts, time is *prima facie* of the essence in delivering the goods,[180] and in *Bunge v Tradax*, it was stated that '*[b]roadly speaking* time will be considered of the essence in "mercantile" contracts'[181] (emphasis added). Using the phrases '*prima facie*' and 'broadly speaking' gives the impression that this rule is not comprehensive for all cases.

#### 3.2.2.2.2 INCONSISTENCY IN DETERMINING TERMINATION'S AVAILABILITY WHEN CONSIDERING TIME AN INTERMEDIATE TERM

If time is deemed an 'intermediate term,' the gravity of consequences can be assessed through many different approaches. Some jurists find that it depends on the seriousness of the breach,[182] its fundamentality[183] or the ease of rectification.[184] Other approaches from case law are as follows:

*a.* Ampurius v Telford *Approach* The core of assessing the consequences of delay was contemplating all the parties' circumstances. As Lord Justice Lewis stated, the important issue to consider was 'what benefit the injured party intended to obtain from performance of the contract,'[185] 'the effect of the breach on the injured party' and

> What financial loss has it caused? How much of the intended benefit under the contract has the injured party already received? Can the injured party be adequately compensated by an award of damages? Is the breach likely to be repeated? Will the guilty party resume compliance with his obligations? Has the breach fundamentally changed the value of future performance of the guilty party's outstanding obligations?[186]

However, this assessment could be too subjective and protracted.

*b.* Bettini v Gye *Approach* Termination was available when the breach went to 'the root of the matter,' which depended on the breach's effect on the foundation

178 *Cehave* (n 126) 71.
179 *Bunge v Tradax* (n 400) 719.
180 *Hartley v Hymans* (n 434) 484; Donaldson J in *Aruna Mills Ltd v Dhanrajmal Gobindram* [1968] 1 QB 655, 665.
181 *Bunge v Tradax* (n 400) 715.
182 *Suisse Atlantique v Rotterdamsche* (n 457) 363; Stone; Devenney (n 64) 645.
183 ibid *Suisse Atlantique*.
184 *Lowe & anr v W Machell Joinery Limited* [2011] EWCA Civ 794 [3].
185 *Ampurius Nu Homes Holdings Ltd v Telford Homes (Creekside)* Ltd [2013] EWCA civ 577 [51].
186 ibid [52].

of the intended purpose under the contract,[187] rendering the performance different from what had been stipulated.[188] A similar approach was employed in *Bentsen v Taylor*, where Bowen LJ stated that this depended on whether the breach went to the heart of the substantive part of the contract.[189] Only this breach, as affirmed in *Davidson v Gwynne*, could discharge the innocent buyer from further liability.[190]

However, this test can be vague and can be used either objectively or subjectively, minimising predictability. Moreover, as Lord Sumner emphasised in *Bank Line v Arthur Capel*, going to 'the root of the contract' is a metaphor, and 'like most metaphors it is not nearly so clear as it seems,'[191] not providing a solution but rather 'picturesque language.'[192] Therefore, if a time clause is considered an 'intermediate term,' determining whether delay goes to the root of the contract can be done in different ways, as assembled from case law in the following examples:

i) Effect of Delay on the Whole Contract In *Wallis v Pratt*, Fletcher Moulton LJ stated that there were some breaches that went so directly to the substance of the contract which may have reasonably been considered by the innocent buyer as a substantial failure to perform the contract.[193] According to Upjohn LJ in *Hong Kong v Kawasaki*, this made further performance impossible, rendering the whole contract frustrated.[194]

ii) Delay Frustrates Commercial Purpose According to *Cehave*,[195] *Macandrew v Chapple* and *Stanton v Richardson*,[196] a breach of an 'intermediate term' does not go to the root of the contract, and the innocent buyer is not entitled to terminate the contract when the delayed goods can be used for their intended commercial purpose.

iii) The Responsibility of Judges and Arbitrators According to Sachs LJ in *Decro-Wall v Practitioners in Marketing*, the question of whether a breach goes to the root of a contract is left to the court, depending on the facts of each case.[197]

187 Bowen LJ in *Bentsen* (n 210) 281. This approach was also used in *Davidson v Gwynne* (1810) 104 E.R. 149, 153; *Macandrew v Chapple* (1865–66) LR 1 CP 643, 648; *Poussard v Speirs & Pond* (1876) 1 QBD 410; *Honck v Muller* (1881) 7 QBD 92, 100; *Mersey Steel & Iron Co Ltd v Naylor Benzon & Co* (1884) 9 App Cas 434, 443, 444; *Guy-Pell v Foster* [1930] 2 Ch 169, 170; and *Heyman v Darwins* (n 247) 359.

188 Blackburn J in *Bettini* (n 208) 188.

189 Bowen LJ in *Bentsen* (n 210) 279.

190 *Davidson v Gwynne* (n 476) 152.

191 Lord Sumner in *Bank Line Ltd v Arthur Capel & Co* [1919] AC 435, 459.

192 Furmston (n 30) 676.

193 *Wallis, Son & Wells v Pratt & Haynes* [1910] 2 KB 1003, 1012.

194 Upjohn LJ in *Hong Kong* (n 219) 63.

195 *Cehave* (n 126) 45.

196 *Macandrew v Chapple* (n 476) 646; *Stanton v Richardson* (1873–74) LR 9 CP 390.

197 Sachs LJ in *Decro-Wall International SA v Practitioners in Marketing* [1971] 1 WLR 361, 374.

*c.* Hong Kong v Kawasaki *Approach* Permission to resort to termination depended heavily on the foreseeable consequences of the breach[198] and whether the innocent buyer was substantially deprived of the whole benefit intended by the parties under the contract.[199] Notably, the test used in this case was applied in many other cases,[200] but in different ways:

i) *Decro-wall v Practitioners*
Termination for breaching an 'intermediate term' depended on the deprivation of a 'substantial part of the benefit to which [the injured buyer] was entitled under the contract.'[201] This could make the assessment of deprivation dependent on a single term of the contract, whereas deprivation in *Hong Kong* was associated with the contract as a whole. It was also affirmed in *Decro-wall* that termination could occur when a remedy for damages was insufficient, and it would have been unfair to the injured buyer to maintain the contract.[202]

ii) *Photo Production v Securicor Transport*
Termination was available when the seller's failure caused a substantial deprivation of the whole intended benefit which should have been obtained from the contract[203] without stipulating its foreseeability, as in the case of *Hong Kong*.

iii) *Maple Flock v Universal Furniture*
Substantiality of deprivation was assessed through the quantitative ratio of the failure in comparison to the contract as a whole.[204]

### *3.2.3 KLaw*

KLaw looms large in delivery time because it sees that the seller's failure to deliver the goods on the agreed date is an obstruction to attaining the promised result,[205] allowing the buyer to exercise the owner's rights.[206] Additionally, the passage of risk is linked to the delivery time, and this assists the parties in determining

198 *Hong Kong* (n 219) 27, 28.
199 ibid 72.
200 *Macandrew v Chapple* (n 476) 648; *Decro-Wall v Practitioners in Marketing* (n 468) 380; *Cehave* (n 126) 71.
201 Buckley LJ in ibid *Decro-Wall*.
202 ibid.
203 *Photo Production* (n 206) 849.
204 Lord Hewart CJ in *Maple Flock Co Ltd v Universal Furniture Products (Wembley) Ltd* [1934] 1 KB 148, 157.
205 Suleiman Ayob, *The Concept of Fault in Contractual Liability* (Lebanese University 1996) 155.
206 Case 28/6/1993 Court of Cassation/Commercial 222–232/93 in Ministry of Justice, *Civil Provisions* (n 955) 293; Case 15/4/1996 Appellate Court/Commercial-2 1346/1995; Case 6/3/2003 Court of Cassation/Commercial 549/2003 in Ministry of Justice, *Civil Provisions* (n 955) 294; Jaafer Al-Fadly, *Synopsis in Civil Contracts* (Dar Althaqafa 1997) 91.

at which point the liability for loss is transferred from the seller to the buyer.[207] Timely delivery of the goods also protects the first buyer and prevents the seller from reselling the goods to a different buyer. As is the case when reselling the goods, the transferal of possession to the second buyer is considered a title deed.[208] Furthermore, when it is stipulated that the agreed price is the prevailing price at the delivery time, the seller's delay in delivery could result in a higher selling price.[209]

KCOC mentioned a case in which the seller fails to deliver the goods on the agreed date, whereas KCIC mentioned a case in which the seller fails to prepare the goods specified in kind on the agreed date.

#### *3.2.3.1 Failure to Deliver the Goods on the Agreed Date Leads to Termination*

According to Article 131(1) KCOC, if the seller fails to deliver the goods on the agreed date, the contract shall be deemed *terminated* without the need for notification, unless the buyer notified the seller of their adherence to the execution of the contract within three days from the agreed date.[210] As a result of such a termination, the buyer shall be entitled to retrieve the price of the whole sale,[211] without prior notice or judgement, by refusing all the delayed goods, even if the non-delivery was partial.[212] Nonetheless, some contractual phrases on delivery time may reduce its legal importance and then affect the availability of termination, when, for instance, it is stated in the contract that unless the goods are delivered on a specific delivery date, compensation for the delay must be paid.[213]

##### 3.2.3.1.1 TERMINATION WITHOUT THE NEED FOR THE JUDICIARY

From the wording of Article 131(1) KCOC, non-delivery on the agreed date/during the agreed period leads to automatic termination without the need to resort to the judiciary to assess the delay. A ruling issued by a judge terminating a contract would be considered a revealing decision, not an establishing decision. In one case, when the delivery did not take place despite the buyer's paying most of the price and warning the seller, the contract was terminated.[214] In another case, the seller claimed that the delivery date of a water tanker should have been within 15 days of concluding the contract, as long as there was a technical obligation upon them to install a new water tank which needed such a period, and both parties agreed that

207 Case 6/3/2004 Court of Cassation/Commercial 549/2003 in Ministry of Justice, *Civil Provisions* (n 955) 294.
208 KCIC Art. 937; Husam Al-Ahwany, *Sale Contract* (That AlSalasel 1989) 337, 338.
209 ibid Al-Ahwany 387.
210 See Case 14/6/1993 Court of Cassation/Commercial 212/92 in Ministry of Justice, *Civil Provisions* (n 955) 293.
211 See Case 29/4/2007 Appellate Court/Civil-2 629/647/650–2007.
212 Case 4/6/1996 Appellate Court/Commercial 933/1995, 2–3.
213 See Case 19/3/2007 Court of Cassation/Civil-2 875–879/2005.
214 Case 29/3/2006 Appellate Court/Commercial-10 235/295/2005.

the cheque was due after the aforementioned date. The seller also claimed that the buyer closed their bank account to prevent the cheque from being cashed after the seller had actually fulfilled their technical obligation. The court stated that closing the account was the buyer's right of retention after it turned out that the vehicle was registered in a third party's name, and this fact might hinder delivery on the agreed date, so the contract was terminated. Surprisingly, in one case,[215] the trial court appointed an expert to determine the detriment caused by the delay, although there was no legal requirement to assess it.[216]

In practice, there can be an assumption of receiving the goods, even if the buyer alleges otherwise when they fail to bring a lawsuit for a significant period after the agreed date of delivery, and most of the price has been paid. The buyer's receipt might be reinforced, especially if the buyer filed their claim of non-delivery only when the seller demanded the buyer pay the remainder of the price.[217] In one case,[218] when the buyer brought a lawsuit to terminate the contract due to the non-arrival of heaters from Iran, the trial court stated that the buyer did not take any legal action regarding the non-delivery except sending a late warning to the seller. They neglected to file a lawsuit for many years without justification, which provoked doubts about whether the buyer actually did not receive the goods.[219] Likewise, another case mentioned that it was unimaginable that the plaintiff bought the cars and paid the greater part of their price without receiving them, especially as they did not resort to legal action for over five years. The court, therefore, concluded that the plaintiff waited for this period to evade their commitment to pay the rest of the price.[220]

In contrast, in a different case, the court decided on termination and refunding the price because a significant time had elapsed without the seller fulfilling obligation of delivery. In another case, too,[221] the court rejected the defence that the buyer could not claim termination because the statute of limitations for termination due to non-delivery was one year[222] and applied the general rule of the statute of limitations for commercial disputes, which was ten years from the date on which the obligation should have been fulfilled.[223] This long period of time could be problematic as the contract is terminated autonomously once the seller delays sending the goods, and the seller should return the money accordingly. Otherwise, the buyer can be silent after the automatic termination, demanding a refund later, and this permits them to speculate with such an amount to make a profit, depending on currency rates, the market price of the goods and moratory interests.

215 Case 20/5/1998 (n 43).
216 Case 6/2/1996 Appellate Court/Commercial 932/1995 p. 1.
217 By analogy to Case 15/10/1996 Appellate Court/Commercial 406/1996 p. 3.
218 Case 6/2/1996 (n 505) 1.
219 ibid 2–5.
220 Case 2/1/2005 Appellate Court/Commercial-3 1349/2004.
221 By analogy to Case 19/5/2003 Court of Cassation/Civil-1 355/2002.
222 Case 25/3/96 Appellate Court/Commercial 357/1995 p. 1, 4, 5.
223 KCOC Art. 118.

#### 3.2.3.1.2 NO NEED OF NOTIFICATION FOR TERMINATION BUT FOR CONTRACT ACTIVATION

The contract is deemed terminated based on non-delivery/delay without notification[224] unless the buyer activates the contract by notifying the seller of their willingness to execute the contract within three days after assuming it terminated. However, in one case, when a number of cars were sold but not delivered by the agreed time, the buyer demanded to implement the obligation of delivery under the lawsuit. The court stated that because the seller did not fulfil their commitment until the time of hearing about the lawsuit, and they did not provide a justification for this mal-performance, the contract was terminated, and the parties should be returned to the state they were in before concluding the contract pursuant to Article 211(1) KCIC.[225] In this case, the court did not examine the legal aspect of whether the buyer's demand for delivery was within or after the three-day limit.[226]

#### 3.2.3.1.3 REFUSAL TO ACCEPT DELAYED GOODS

Article 211(1) KCIC stipulates automatic termination once the goods are delayed to clarify both parties knowing beforehand where they stand when the seller breaches the agreed date. Although this is theoretically true, according to case law, it is not practically true; the seller can send the delayed goods at any time after the agreed time with the hope that the buyer will accept the goods after the automatic termination of the contract. Therefore, when a buyer signed documents of receipt, the obligation of delivery was fulfilled, and the concrete was received, even though the delivery was late.[227] When the seller delivered the delayed shipment to the buyer, who did not object, the goods' value should have been paid.[228]

Similarly, in one case,[229] a buyer claimed they had not received the cars they ordered. Nevertheless, the expert appointed by the court affirmed that the cars were handed over but on a different date to the one agreed on to someone working for the buyer who signed the receipt documents. This served as proof of the buyer's approval of the goods being delivered at a different time. The court refused the buyer's two claims that the person who signed was not authorised to receive the cars, and the agreed delivery date should have been interpreted according to the buyer's interest, not the seller's. The court ruled that delivery had been fulfilled, and the price had to be paid.[230]

However, one may wonder about the legal basis of the buyer's activation of the terminated contract by accepting the delayed goods after the three-day limit mentioned in law: Is it a new contract? Is it an implicit modification of the contractual date? Or is the contract subject to a conditional termination term: i.e. the contract

224 Case 4/6/1996 (n 501) 2, 3.
225 Case 25/3/96 (n 511) 1, 4, 5.
226 The same applies to Case 4/6/1996 (n 501) 2, 3.
227 Case 4/1/1997 Appellate Court/Commercial-4 658/96.
228 Case 17/4/1995 Appellate Court/Commercial-1 293/1995 p. 1.
229 Case 15/10/1996 (n 506) 1, 3. See also Case 4/6/1996 (n 501) 2, 3.
230 ibid.

will not be terminated unless the buyer refuses to take the delayed goods? These interpretations may contradict the phrasing of Article 131(1) and make the situation unclear. Sending the goods after the delivery date would be perilous because of the dependence on the buyer's attitude unless the seller obtains written consent from the buyer for late delivery.

#### *3.2.3.2 Special Provision: Failure to Prepare the Goods (Specified in Kind) on the Agreed Date*

When the delivery location is at the seller's premises but the seller fails to prepare the goods on the agreed date, will the contract be automatically terminated?

##### 3.2.3.2.1 UNPREPARED GOODS ON THE AGREED DATE

According to Article 285 KCIC, if the goods sold are of kind and the seller did not ready the goods for collection, the buyer may obtain goods of the same kind at the seller's expense. In ordinary cases, this alternative transaction could be concluded after the permission of the judge. Another option for the buyer is to claim the value of the unprepared goods.[231] This provision solves many different situations, and the punishment for the seller is the same. When, at the time of collection, the goods are not manufactured, the goods are in the warehouse but not packaged, the goods are boxed but not in the warehouse, or the goods are about to be boxed, the buyer, in theory, has the right to demand purchase of alternative goods of the same kind at the seller's expense or a refund in all these cases.

##### 3.2.3.2.2 THE SITUATION IS IN THE BUYER'S HANDS

The seller's failure to prepare the goods does not lead to automatic termination; the buyer can either wait for the non-prepared goods or request termination immediately after finding that the goods are not prepared by obtaining judicial permission to buy alternative goods at the seller's expense, even if the delay causes no harmful effects to the buyer. The law does not specify the modality through which the buyer can conclude the alternative transaction; the buyer can buy substitute goods of the same price as the original goods or even more expensive goods, possessing the same or superior level of quality, especially if no goods similar to those which were agreed on could be found on the market.

##### 3.2.3.2.3 DOUBTFULNESS OF APPLYING ARTICLE 285 KCIC IN COMMERCIAL CONTRACTS

Judges may not apply this provision on the basis that it is in KCIC, and there is no need to apply it as long as KCOC has a general provision. However, pursuant to the principle of *lex specialis derogat generali*, other judges may regard the failure of preparation of the goods specified in kind as a specific case overriding the general

231 KCIC Art. 285.

rule mentioned in Article 131(1) KCOC. The reference to both KCIC and KCOC, depending heavily on the judge and their legal characterisation of the case, can undoubtedly be confusing.

### *3.2.4 Comparative Analysis*

#### *3.2.4.1 Possible Outcomes Under the Three Legal Systems*

A) FIRST SCENARIO: THE AGREED DELIVERY DATE IS 2 FEBRUARY, BUT THE GOODS ARE NOT DELIVERED/NOT PREPARED FOR COLLECTION AT THAT TIME

**Under CISG**, there are two cases: **First**, if non-delivery of the goods on 2 February causes substantial detriment to the buyer foreseeable to the seller under the contract, termination of the contract can be declared immediately without the need to fix *Nachfrist*. This is unless the adjudicator finds the fundamentality of the non-delivery should be assessed after giving the seller a chance to cure their performance if the seller is willing to perform their obligation of delivery within a reasonable timeframe and without causing considerable burden to the buyer. **Secondly**, if the non-delivery/non-preparation of the goods for collection on the agreed date is not a fundamental breach under Article 25, immediate termination is not an option. The buyer should fix *Nachfrist* of reasonable length, warning the seller to send the delivery, for example, on 2 March at the latest. If the seller sends another notice on 15 February to send the goods on 15 March instead, the latter date will be effective, extending *Nachfrist* if the buyer fails to object to the notice promptly. However, if the buyer objects to the seller's notice and the seller fails to send the goods on 2 March, the buyer could declare termination on 3 March. If the buyer does not declare the contract terminated on 3 March but receives another notice from the seller stating that they will send the goods on 15 March, and the buyer does not object to this notice until, for instance, 7 March and declares the contract terminated, termination might not be activated, and the curability period could be valid. This is despite the fact that other jurists might see that according to 49(1)(b), the termination right took precedence over the seller's curability right.

**Under SGA**, when the buyer collects the goods, they should be in a deliverable state, enabling the buyer to take them physically and legally. If they are not in a deliverable state or not delivered on 2 February as agreed, there are two perspectives:

**First**, according to the majority view, sending the goods on 2 February is a 'condition' as long as the contract is commercial, unless otherwise stated. This permits termination when the buyer, according to s.35(1)(a) and s.36(1), intimates to the seller that they refuse the goods. **Secondly**, even if it is less likely, delivery time might be considered an 'intermediate term' according to the wording of s.10(2), which refers to contractual terms to deduce its categorisation. In this case, only when the consequences for non-delivery on 2 February are grave can termination be permitted.

**Under KLaw**, theoretically, failure to deliver the goods on 2 February leads to automatic termination according to Article 131 KCOC, without an obligation on the buyer to notify the seller of a last chance to perform or even of termination. Practically, it is advisable for the buyer to resort to legal action in order to obtain a ruling as soon as possible if they intend to terminate the contract. Otherwise, negligence in filing the lawsuit without justification would raise doubts about the non-delivery of the goods, especially when the buyer has paid most of the price. Failure to prepare the goods for collection at the agreed time might have the same legal rule of Article 131 KCOC, or the adjudicator might see that Article 285 KCIC is more suitable. Under Article 285 KCIC, the buyer might obtain goods of the same kind as the unprepared goods agreed on at the seller's expense, or they may claim a refund after gaining judicial permission. The buyer could explain that even the goods being merely unboxed at the agreed time would be detrimental, and the judge, at their discretion, might permit the buyer to resort to an alternative transaction.

#### B) SECOND SCENARIO: THE AGREED DELIVERY DATE IS 2 FEBRUARY, BUT THE SELLER DELIVERS THE GOODS ON 3 FEBRUARY, AND THEY ARE REFUSED BY THE BUYER

**Under CISG**, a one-day delay would not generally cause substantial deprivation of contractual expectations foreseeable under the contract, especially if the time is not emphasised in the contract. Consequently, termination is not an option. **Under SGA**, according to the majority opinion, any failure to conform to timely delivery could raise the right to terminate the whole contract, even if the one-day delay is trivial, does not cause problems for the buyer and does not affect the goods' value, even if time is not of the essence in the contract and regardless of the buyer's intention to escape from an unsatisfactory transaction. There is no place to apply the slight breach rule to time stipulations[232] as the sphere of s.15(A) is limited, applicable only when breaching specific implied terms, not including time clauses.[233] Thus, a slight breach of time entitles the buyer to terminate the contract even if it is unreasonable to reject the goods due to a one-day delay. Nevertheless, if time is considered an 'intermediate term' (although doubtful), the gravity of the consequences of the one-day delay will be scrutinised, and it will be unlikely to be considered a frustrating delay leading to termination of the whole contract. **Under KLaw**, as long as the buyer/their representatives refuse to take the delayed goods on 3 February, the contract will be deemed terminated. The buyer should ask for a refund if the price is paid, and if the seller disputes this matter, the buyer should resort to court as soon as possible. The law does not stipulate assessing the

232 Mullis, 'Termination for Breach of Contract' in Guest (n 226) 152; Bridge, *Benjamin's* (n 28) [12–025].
233 SGA s.15A(1)(a).

detrimental result of the delay for the buyer despite the fact that, in one case,[234] the court appointed an expert to assess this result.

### *3.2.4.2 Certainty of Using Termination Due to Non-Delivery/Delay*

**Under CISG**, certainty of the legal outcome might be lessened for two reasons:

**First**, the fundamentality of non-delivery permitting immediate termination may vary according to the circumstances of the case and the adjudicator's perspective, depending, inter alia, on: 1) the seller's attitude; 2) sufficiency of remedies for delay other than termination; 3) the length of the deferment, although deciding whether the delay is short or long is not straightforward; 4) fluctuation of the goods' prices, although some commentators may object to this recourse; and **5)** causing foreseeable economic loss; however, it could be argued that Article 25 does not confine substantial deprivation as a result of delay to financial harm. **Secondly**, there are divided opinions on the impact of the seller' curability right on the fundamentality of non-delivery. The first perspective finds that fundamentality should be assessed not only according to the gravity of the breach's repercussions but also according to the seller's willingness to reasonably cure their performance. The second opinion finds that non-delivery in itself, according to Article 25, could objectively be regarded as fundamental, permitting termination without considering the seller's curability right.

Conversely, the *Nachfrist* system removes both the uncertainty as to when the delivery will happen and the uncertainty as to whether the delay amounts to a fundamental breach. Its warning phrasing also encourages the seller to understand what type of notice it is and clarifies the buyer's intention to terminate the contract. Despite this clear certainty, this facility leaves the buyer unsure about *Nachfrist*'s reasonable length,[235] which depends on endless factors, and this may make the buyer believe the *Nachfrist* length they specified is reasonable, whereas the seller might not. Furthermore, termination should be declared within reasonable time after the expiration of *Nachfrist*, and postponing it in order to stretch an insufficient *Nachfrist*, as has happened in some cases,[236] may take termination outside the reasonable time limit, preventing the buyer from terminating the contract. Moreover, as stated in the *Packaging machine case*, the buyer

> may wait for as long as he wishes before he actually exercises the right to avoid the contract. This rule applies irrespective of whether the avoidance is based on a fundamental breach or on the fact that [*Nachfrist*] has expired.[237]

234 Case 6/2/1996 (n 505) 1.

235 Bianca; Bonell (n 155) 344.

236 *Used printing press case* (n 379). A similar conclusion was reached in the *Automobile case* 27/4/1999 (n 379).

237 *Packaging machine case* 8/11/2006 (n 367).

This may lessen certainty and make the buyer speculate at the seller's expense according to the marketability of the goods.

**Under SGA**, '[t]ime will be of the essence in mercantile contracts, [due to] the power of precedent.'[238] This means once the parties have articulated the delivery time, it will be regarded as a 'condition,' and the situation will be straightforward as there is no need for 1) assessing the detriment resulting from untimely delivery, 2) assessing the market price to find out whether the buyer intends to escape from the contract or 3) calculating damages. This approach gives clear visibility to the existence of a termination and facilitates consistency in results. Nonetheless, regarding time in all contracts as a 'condition,' whatever the degree of the breach and the detriment are, could result in criticisms of rigidity, preventing change and flexibility according to the situation and preventing a fairer outcome.

Conversely and less likely, regarding delivery time as an 'intermediate term' will reduce clarity[239] as there is no uniform norm with which to assess the gravity of the delay/non-delivery. The contrasting approaches and the abstraction of the metaphorical concepts used to assess the consequences of the 'intermediate term' provide impreciseness[240] and support judicial intervention.[241] Not only will this render decisions unpredictable, but it will also encourage various legal orders. This situation makes the idea of considering time an 'intermediate term' less attractive when applied to commercial contracts, which necessitate rapid and clear legal solutions.

**Under KLaw**, because of automatic termination in the case of an untimely delivery, the law in codes is rigorous, attaining a high degree of certainty without allowing the availability of termination to be shaped according to the degree of the breach or detriment. However, this is not the case in practice as in some cases, the situation was assessed according to the payment and according to when the buyer judicially asked for the refund.

Additionally, activating the contract after it is deemed terminated positions the seller in an undecided status for three days as they cannot deliver the goods one day after delivery date for fear that the contract is considered terminated, and the buyer may not intend to uphold it by notification. Even if the buyer determines a new deadline for the delivery within the three-day limit, if the seller still fails to deliver the goods, there is uncertainty as to whether the contract will be deemed terminated by itself or if the buyer should judicially ask for termination. The law neither specifies the period within which the buyer may request termination nor requires a reasonable period. The matter is in the hands of the adjudicators, who may depend primarily on the aggrieved buyer's situation, even if it is unknown to the seller. On the other hand, if the buyer's demand to deliver the goods occurs after the expiration of the three-day limit, the contract is terminated, and upholding it is futile. In practice, however, the courts have not been anxious to examine the three-day

238 Clarke (n 451) 31.

239 *Mansel Oil Ltd v Troon Storage Tankers SA* [2009] EWCA Civ 425 [1].

240 *Ampurius v Telford* (n 474) [50].

241 Bridge, *The Sale of Goods* (n 28) [10.51].

limit, meaning that the situation is left to the buyer even after this limit. This clash between law in codes and law in courts makes the legal outcome difficult to predict.

### *3.2.4.3 Preserving the Contract in Case of Non-Delivery/Delay*

**Under CISG**, termination is not permitted unless non-delivery/delay reflects a fundamental breach, and in case of doubt, in considering such a breach fundamental, the contract shall be preserved.[242] This rigidity explains the tendency of some commentators to regard the curability right as prevailing over the termination right. This makes termination unavailable unless the seller is given an opportunity to rectify their performance. With this strict definition of fundamental breach, the buyer may set *Nachfrist*, which also aims to preserve the contract because it offers another opportunity to the seller to perform the obligation of delivery within a reasonable period.

**Under SGA**, because most of the adjudicators have seen the delivery time in mercantile contracts as a 'condition,'[243] a less-than-perfect performance entitles the buyer to terminate the contract.[244] This is true even if there is no prejudice suffered by the buyer in any respect, enticing disadvantaged buyers to abandon contracts in cases of potential fluctuation in the price of commodities.[245] However, the buyer should let the seller know that the delayed goods are rejected, meaning that termination is not automatic. The seller does not have the right to deliver the goods after the delivery time has passed[246] as the Law Commission previously rejected calls to establish cure provisions in relation to commercial contracts. This rejection aimed to obviate complexity and impracticability,[247] but, in fact, it minimises the degree of contract preservation. Goode regrets that

> opportunity has not been taken to modernise the Sale of Goods Act by including express provisions as to the right of cure, a right which mitigates the impact of an improperly motivated rejection by the buyer while at the same time tending to avoid economic waste.[248]

Conversely, when the parties use flexible terms in formulating time clauses, time is likely to be regarded as an 'intermediate term,' and then the test of *Hong Kong* will be applied, by which termination requires a foreseeable substantial deprivation on non-delivery/delay, similar to Article 25 CISG. This attains a higher level in preserving the contract according to the parties' will.

242 *Meat case* (n 171).
243 Peter Piliounis, 'The Remedies of Specific Performance, Price Reduction and Additional Time (*Nachfrist*) Under the CISG: Are These Worthwhile Changes or Additions to English Sales Law?' (2000) 12(1) Pace Int Law Rev 1, 25.
244 Furmston (n 30) 661.
245 Peacock (n 140) 106; Peel, 15th edn (n 64) 977 [18–037].
246 Azzouni (n 349) 10.
247 Peacock (n 140) 121, 122.
248 Ewan McKendrick, *Goode on Commercial Law* (5th edn, Penguin Books 2016) 368, 369.

**Under KLaw**, termination is the first option in relation to non-delivery/delay as the contract is automatically terminated once the delivery time has passed.

The judge might not have discretion (as mentioned in the general rules) over whether the delay justifies termination, although, in practice, the situation might be different. It may be argued that commercial customs do not accept termination in case of exiguity of the detriment caused by non-performance,[249] and a short delay could be considered insignificant and harmless. However, Article 131 KCOC does not originally depend on detriment, and realistically, the judge relies on text more than custom, which could be unfamiliar to the judge and must be proven by the breaching seller. Additionally, the buyer can claim that a specific date should be adhered to because the agreement is in a legal degree above that of custom. On the other hand, the restriction of a three-day limit in demanding specific performance treats termination as a general rule and implementation of the contract as an exception. The seller is not supposed to send anything in case they fail to deliver on the day specified in the contract unless the buyer notifies them, although the buyer's silence could be construed by the seller to mean the buyer is not in a rush. The buyer's notification on the fourth day onwards to implement the contract would not, theoretically, be considered. Nevertheless, in practice, the decision on whether to accept or refuse the delayed goods even after the three-day limit is in the buyer's hands. This situation does not encourage preserving the contract.

## 3.3 Attaching Emphasis to Time

When time is highlighted in the contract by stressing the importance of timely delivery, the question arises as to whether this prominence changes the availability of termination from that when time is specified in the contract without emphasis.

### *3.3.1 CISG*

There are three views regarding delivery time emphasised in the contract. The **first** view, pursued in *Diversitel v Glacier*, finds that the parties' conduct and communications can formulate that time is of the essence, making untimely performance a fundamental breach.[250] The **second** view, followed in the *Memory module case*, finds that concluding a firm deal with a delivery time might not permit termination as such, except where the existence of a particular interest in timely fulfilment to the buyer is known by the seller.[251] The **third** opinion finds that even if the time was firmly articulated in the contract and the reason for its essentiality was revealed to the seller, termination is only permitted when Article 25's requirements are met. These views are discussed next.

249 Husny Al-Masry, *Commercial Contracts in Kuwaiti Law, Egyptian Law and Comparative Law* (AlSafar Bookstore 1990) 78.

250 *Diversitel v Glacier* (6/10/2003) 03-CV-23776 SR (Superior Court of Justice) <https://cisgw3.law.pace.edu/cases/031006c4.html>.

251 *Memory module case* (n 303).

### 3.3.1.1 *Attaching Emphasis to Time Permits Termination Pursuant to Party Autonomy Principle*

Designating time as essential by fixing a firm delivery date in a contract activates a termination upon its breach.[252] Time can be crucial[253] when stating that delivery must be fulfilled on a specific date or through simply stating that 'time is of the essence.'[254] This is what was asserted at one CISG conference as the delegation from the Federal Republic of Germany stated that the fundamentality of a breach depended heavily on the contractual terms and could not be defined in abstract. The delegation gave an example, saying that the delivery date could be of the essence to a contract, and the failure to deliver the goods on that date would amount to a fundamental breach, despite the fact that not delivering the goods on that date under another contract which did not emphasise the importance of the delivery time would be unlikely to amount to a fundamental breach.[255] His delegation emphasised that it is advisable to determine, either expressly or implicitly, which terms in the contract would result in a fundamental breach in case of violation.[256] In parallel, in the *Shoes case*, it was stated that 'the particular importance of the date of delivery [to be of the essence] can result from the contract itself.'[257] Because the essentiality of the time was not accentuated[258] in the *Cobalt sulphate case* and the delayed goods could still be resold, there was no fundamental breach. Likewise not agreeing, in the *Memory module case*, 'compliance with a time limit for delivery be crucial for the existence of the contract as a whole'[259] would not make breaching delivery time fundamental. However, when the seller was made aware at the contract conclusion that 'the buyer would prefer no delivery at all to a delayed delivery,'[260] breaching this agreement was likely to activate a termination.

#### 3.3.1.1.1 NO NEED TO MENTION THE REASON FOR TIME'S ESSENTIALITY

Immediate termination based on almost any delay can be justified when it is apparent in the contract that time is essential,[261] irrespective of the reason indicating such

252 Art. 6; Joseph Lookofsky; Herbert Bernstein, *Understanding the CISG in Europe* (2nd edn, Kluwer Law International 2003) 126; Schwenzer, *Commentary on CISG* (n 15) 789, 790 [27];[28].

253 Graffi (n 155) 341.

254 Naude; Lubbe (n 146) 377, 378; Schwenzer, *Commentary on CISG* (n 15) 429 [23].

255 Official Records (n 149) 12th Meeting 300.

256 ibid.

257 *Shoes case* 24/4/1997 (n 303).

258 *Cobalt sulphate case* (3/4/1996) VIIIZR51/95 (Bundesgerichtshof Supreme Court) <https://cisgw3.law.pace.edu/cases/960403g1.html>.

259 *Memory module case* (n 303).

260 ibid. A very similar sentence is found in the *Shoes case* 24/4/1997 (n 303).

261 Schlechtriem, *Commentary on CISG* (n 4) 147; Harry Flechtner, 'Transcript of a Workshop on the Sales Convention: Leading CISG Scholars Discuss Contract Formation, Validity, Excuse for Hardship, Avoidance, Nachfrist, Contract Interpretation, Parol Evidence, Analogical Application, and Much More' (1999) 18(2) JL & Com 191, 254; Ferrari, 'Fundamental Breach' (n 161) 498; Schwenzer, *Commentary on CISG* (n 15) 419 [4]; 431 [27]; 778 [5].

importance[262] and even if the reason of essentiality was not conveyed to the seller. This approach could be influenced by Article 7.3.1 UPICC, which clearly states that a breach is considered a fundamental breach when 'strict compliance with the obligation which has not been performed is of the essence under the contract.' As affirmed in the *Printed work case*, the mere stating in the contract that the delivery date is a 'fixed commercial date' may make breaching it fundamental.[263] In the *Printed materials case*, it was held that if time was of the essence, reflecting the meaning of a fixed term, there was no obligation on the buyer to set an additional period before declaring termination.[264] More explicitly, in the *Memory module case*, it was stated that in order to consider the delivery time essential, the buyer 'could have easily documented the importance of delivery in time for the performance of the contract as a whole.'[265] Similarly, in the *Shoes case*, the court held that the mere non-compliance with the agreed delivery time did not constitute a fundamental breach unless the affected party stated firmly, even without manifesting the interest, that the delivery date should be respected; otherwise, it was preferable for the goods not to be delivered at all.[266] Hence, if the buyer agreed to delivery of the goods exclusively on a specific date, the seller should adhere to this obligation, regardless of their knowledge of the buyer's commitments towards their customers on that date.[267]

#### 3.3.1.1.2 PRESUMED FORESEEABILITY AND DETRIMENT

Some scholars find that foreseeability can be raised only in relation to those terms not adequately designated as the core of the contract.[268] This means when the time clause is emphasised in the contract, breaching it permits termination as there is presumable foreseeability of the result of the delay.[269] Van Reesch asserts that 'it is difficult to establish that consequences were unforeseen when the terms of a contract are clear and unequivocal [thus] the consequences [of delay] must have been foreseen [even in case of proving otherwise].'[270] Additionally, the seller's demonstration that breaching essential delivery time caused insubstantial detriment may not be considered. The importance of time depends primarily on the parties' attribution rather than assessing the detriment or objective loss.[271]

262 Schwenzer, *Commentary on CISG* (n 15) 432 [28]; Kröll; Mistelis; Viscasillas (n 67) 710 [23].
263 *Printed work case* (29/5/2012) 88O57/11 District Court <https://cisgw3.law.pace.edu/cases/120529g1.html>.
264 *Printed materials case* (n 325).
265 *Memory module case* (n 303).
266 *Shoes case* 24/4/1997 (n 303). See also ibid.
267 Schwenzer, *Commentary on CISG* (n 15) 432 [28].
268 Naude; Lubbe (n 146) 379; Kröll; Mistelis; Viscasillas (n 67) 344 [23].
269 Schwenzer, *Commentary on CISG* (n 15) 436 [36].
270 Zeller, 'Fundamental Breach' (n 184) 90, 91.
271 Schwenzer, *Commentary on CISG* (n 15) 434, 435 [33].

#### 3.3.1.2 *Mentioning the Reason for the Essentiality of Time Is Prerequisite for Immediate Termination*

Explaining the significance of having the goods on a specific date and the reason underpinning this importance, either implicitly or explicitly,[272] is vital to regarding its breach as fundamental. In the *Printed work case*, it was stated that the default of the delivery date constituted a fundamental breach 'if the delivery date was evidently of centrality and the [Buyer] had no or little interest in later delivery [which] had to be evident for the [Seller] at contract conclusion.'[273] More expressly, in the *Iron molybdenum case,* the court stated that fundamentality of the non-delivery/delay could only exist when the buyer had a special interest in precise compliance with the agreed date, and this was recognised by the seller at the contract conclusion.[274] Similarly, in the *Shoes case*, when the buyer had a specific interest in precisely complying with the delivery date and delayed goods were 'no longer of any value to the buyer' who had 'no more interest in the contract,'[275] delay was fundamental.

In the 12th meeting of the UN Conference, a Swedish representative stressed that if the seller was unaware that the goods were bought to be resold – for example, at Christmas – a delay of one, two or even three days after the agreed delivery date was unlikely to constitute a fundamental breach. Conversely, a delay of only one day would likely constitute a fundamental breach if the buyer informed the seller that the goods would be resold at Christmas.[276] Thus, time will be essential if the seller knows that the goods are sold for production purposes which necessitate the arrival of the goods just in tim,[277] or when the buyer explains that they need a timely delivery before their end-of-year sales, even if the agreed delivery time is extremely short.[278]

The reason for the essentiality of time could be implicit when both parties were aware that 'the existence of the contract imperatively [depended] on timely delivery.'[279] When the goods are of a seasonal nature, they may not bear 'flexibility in the delivery date'[280] as sending them after the end of the season would cause a total loss of their marketability.[281] In the *Designer clothes case*, it was concluded that sending fashion products after the summer season, when prices are at their peak, made their salability only possible when the price was discounted, which

272 Kröll; Mistelis; Viscasillas (n 67) 342, 343 [17].
273 *Printed work case* (n 552).
274 *Iron molybdenum case* (n 319).
275 *Shoes case* (17/9/1991) 5U164/90 (Oberlandesgericht Appellate Court Frankfurt) <http://cisgw3.law.pace.edu/cases/910917g1.html>.
276 Official Records (n 149) 12th Meeting 297.
277 Kröll; Mistelis; Viscasillas (n 67) 710 [23].
278 *Italdecor v Yiu's Industries* (n 300).
279 *Mobile car phones case* (n 309).
280 *Macromex* (n 135); Graffi (n 155) 341; Schwenzer, *Commentary on CISG* (n 15) 777, 778 [5].
281 *Shoes case* 24/4/1997 (n 303); *Memory module case* (n 303).

rendered time essential[282] and made breaching it fundamental.[283] However, Kroll *et al* find that the mere fact that goods are seasonal does not suffice to deem time essential.[284]

The reason for time's essentiality can be discussed either in the contract and preceding negotiations or perhaps even in subsequent talks between the parties.[285] At the 12th meeting of the UN Conference, the British delegation asserted that it was difficult to support the idea of the confinement of the meaning of 'expectations' to the express and implied terms of the contract.[286] Thus, as the official records indicated, any information provided following the contract conclusion could modify the meaning of the 'detriment' and 'foresight.'[287] Because the later information emphasising the importance of the time specified in the contract does not genuinely modify the contract, it is considered, according to Article 27, a notice. This notice is effective on its mere dispatch,[288] when the buyer uses reasonable means and time to communicate the information to the seller. Then, violating the time limit is fundamental,[289] even if this notice does not reach the seller. Nonetheless, when this communication is too late, there is not sufficient opportunity to foresee the consequences of breaching the new terms.[290] However, in *Chemical fertilizer*, it was stated that time could be of the essence; any delay may be considered fundamental, even if the letter emphasising the importance of the delivery date because of contractual penalties to the buyer's client[291] was sent around the delivery time.[292] Despite this, some jurists find that sending later information emphasising the importance of the delivery time, which in normal cases is insignificant, might not count.[293]

### *3.3.1.3 Breaching Emphasised Delivery Time May Not Constitute Fundamental Breach*

The court may not depend on the technical phraseology of the essentiality of the delivery time.[294] Even if the time clause was emphasised and the reason for this emphasis was mentioned in the contract, breaching it might not meet the

282 *Designer clothes case* (n 352).
283 *Fashion textiles case* (24/4/1990) 5C73/89 (Lower Court Oldenburg) <http://cisgw3.law.pace.edu/cases/900424g1.html>.
284 Kröll; Mistelis; Viscasillas (n 67) 712 [31].
285 Naude; Lubbe (n 146) 379.
286 Official Records (n 149) 12th Meeting 300, 301.
287 ibid 1st Committee, 302.
288 CISG Art.27 ; Art. 8(3).
289 Enderlein; Maskow (n 150) 116.
290 Honnold, *Uniform Law* (n 320) 277 [183]. See also John Honnald, *Documentary History* (n 344) 258; Babiak (n 57) 115; *Shen* (n 131) 13.
291 *Chemical fertilizer case* (n 302). See also *Iron molybdenum case* (n 319).
292 ibid *Chemical fertilizer case*.
293 Bianca; Bonell (n 155) 221.
294 See Peacock (n 140) 103.

'deprivation' criterion mentioned in Article 25.[295] For instance, this could happen when the goods are intended to be displayed at an exhibition, making the delivery time essential, but if the exhibition is later cancelled, then time is no longer important. Thus, as Zeller asserts, '[e]ven severe [breaches], which are in essence amounting to a fundamental breach, do not guarantee that avoidance will be allowed by the courts.'[296]

It could be argued that Article 6 supports the party autonomy principle and that the parties aimed to implicitly exclude Article 25 by emphasising the time. However, the judge/arbitrator may have other considerations associated with preserving the contract and with the good faith accentuated in Article 7,[297] opposing arbitrary acts, which makes attaching[298] the word 'important' to a time clause an inadequate exclusion of Article 25. The court might assess the fundamentality of the delay/non-delivery by finding out whether the 'buyer is better off without the delivery than with a delayed delivery.'[299] In the *Clothes case*, although the clothes should have been displayed at the beginning of the summer season and the buyer explained to the seller during the negotiations about the repercussions of the delayed delivery, it was held that exceeding the delivery by a few days had 'only a minor bearing on [Buyer]'s interests'; thus, termination was not an option.[300] Moreover, in *Cobalt Sulphate*, it was stated that 'it needs to be ascertained whether a different method of processing or sale of the [delayed] goods was possible and reasonable in the normal course of business,'[301] although at a lower price,[302] and 'it has to be considered whether it can be expected for the buyer to put the [delayed] goods to another reasonable use.'[303] If reselling/reusing the goods is possible, the buyer may not be allowed to terminate the contract,[304] even if the delivery time was emphasised in the contract.

### *3.3.2 SGA*

It is true that, in most cases, the mere agreement on a specific delivery date constitutes a 'condition,' but, as stated in *Charles Rickards v Oppenheim*:

> The question arises . . . whether the defendant's letter of June 29, 1948, threatening to cancel the contract if the work were not completed by July 25,

295 See *Valero Marketing & Supply Company v Greeni Trading Oy* (n 305). See also *Valero Marketing v Greeni Oy* 4/4/2006 (n 305); *Canned oranges case* (n 313).
296 Zeller, 'Fundamental Breach' (n 184) 92.
297 Peacock (n 140) 103.
298 Naude; Lubbe (n 146) 378.
299 Kröll; Mistelis; Viscasillas (n 67) 712 [32].
300 *Clothes case* 21/12/1990 (n 321).
301 *Cobalt sulphate case* 3/4/1996 (n 547).
302 Kröll; Mistelis; Viscasillas (n 67) 711 [28].
303 *Cobalt sulphate case* 3/4/1996 (n 547).
304 Kröll; Mistelis; Viscasillas (n 67) 711 [28].

> 1948. . . made time of the essence of the contract. In certain circumstances there is such a rule in the case of a contract for the sale of goods.[305]

Using the phrase 'certain circumstances' gives the impression that not all terms of delivery time are of the essence as such. The parties may degrade the 'conditionality' of time in their previous dealings; determining whether delivery time is of the essence in the current dealing depends, according to the wording of s.10(2), on the terms of the contract. More importantly, the judge might not follow the majority opinion in case law, which considers time a condition but finds that SGA, as a substantive law, should prevail over the case law. As stated in *The State Trading Corporation v Golodetz*, the status of time stipulation is not unalterable,[306] and, as Blackburn J stated in *Bettini v Gye*, time may depend on the 'true construction of the contract taken as a whole'[307] or on essential implications of contractual circumstances.[308]

If time is of the essence in the contract, the buyer can terminate the contract if the seller breaches such a term,[309] and there is no place to apply the 'intermediate term' theory. Making time of the essence in the contract can be deduced in three ways:

**First**, time should be of the essence if the parties' real intention, either implicitly or explicitly, is making time important.[310] In *Schuler v Wickman*, Lord Reid pointed out that 'a breach of a term gives [termination] option to the aggrieved party because . . . the parties have chosen to stipulate that it shall have that effect.'[311] However, in *Hudson v Temple*, it was concluded that time could not be of the essence unless it was articulated in the contract that the time shall be so *explicitly*.[312] Similarly, in *Photo Production v Securicor Transport*, Lord Diplock stressed that a 'condition' should be restricted to circumstances

> [w]here the contracting parties have agreed, whether by express words or by implication of law, that *any* failure . . . to perform a particular primary obligation . . . . irrespective of the gravity of the event that has in fact resulted from the breach, shall entitle the other party to elect to put an end to [the contract].[313]

Likewise, as stated in *Mansel Oil*, if the seller failed to deliver the goods on time, which was expressed as a 'terminating clause' in the contract, the buyer was not

305 See ibid.

306 *The State Trading Corporation of India Limited v M. Golodetz Limited* [1989] 7 WLUK 93.

307 Blackburn J in *Bettini* (n 208) 187.

308 *Paribas* (n 78) [34]; Andrews, *Contractual Duties* (n 78) 218. See also Furmston (n 30) 208.

309 Mustill LJ affirmed in *Lombard* (n 196) 535, 536, 542.

310 *Maredelanto* (n 78) 175; Furmston (n 30) 690, 691.

311 *Schuler* (n 198) 251.

312 *Hudson v Temple* 54 ER 735, 738; McCardie J in *Hartley v Hymans* (n 434) 483.

313 *Photo Production* (n 206) 849.

bound to wait longer for the shipment.[314] In *Steedman v Drinkle*, too, it was stressed that time could ideally be of the essence by express agreement in the contract.[315] This can be done by stating, for instance, that 'if [a party] commits a breach of [delivery time]'[316] breaching it would lead to termination or by classifying a term as a 'condition' in the contract.[317] This remains true even when the word 'condition' might not be conclusive[318] as it might be synonymous with 'clause' or 'term'[319] without having any technical sense. As Treitel stated, '[o]ne of the most notorious sources of difficulty in the law of contract is the variety of senses in which it uses the expression "condition."'[320] More strictly, Lord Reid in *Schuler v Wickman* stressed the significance of defining the reason for considering a term a 'condition' in the contract.[321]

**Secondly**, as stated in *Hartley v Hymans*, the nature of both the contract and the goods could be the main factor in determining whether time was of the essence.[322] Thus, according to *Lock v Bell*, the goods' nature being speculative, fluctuating in value and exposed to daily variation necessitates performance being precisely on the agreed date without the need to express so in the contract.[323]

**Thirdly**, according to *Charles Rickards v Oppenheim*, when the agreed delivery time is after a sufficient period in which the seller can prepare for performance, time is considered of the essence,[324] permitting immediate termination if the seller fails to perform on the agreed date.[325]

### *3.3.3 KLaw*

Termination may occur on its own by the force of law as soon as the seller violates the delivery time, and if the seller disputes and refuses to refund, the buyer can resort to court to decide termination.[326] This makes delivery an obligation to achieve the result[327] of sending the goods on time. The law sees that once the delivery date has passed, it is deemed impossible to implement the obligation as agreed, the damage is absolute to the buyer, and any implementation after the deadline does

314 *Mansel v Troon* (n 528) [1].

315 *Steedman v Drinkle* [1916] 1 AC 275; *Country & Metropolitan Homes Surrey Ltd v Topclaim Ltd* [1996] Ch 307. See also *Parkin* (n 76) 701.

316 *Rice (t/a Garden Guardian) v Great Yarmouth BC* [2000] 6 WLUK 829 [15].

317 *London Guarantie Co v Fearnley* (1880) 5 App Cas 911, 917; *Thomson v Weems* (1884) 9 App Cas 671, 684; *Dawsons Ltd v Bonnin* [1922] 2 AC 413, 424; McKendrick, *Contract Law* (n 206) 745.

318 *Schuler* (n 198) 251.

319 Smith, *Atiyah's* (n 198) 193; Chen-Wishart (n 77) 479, 480 [12.2.3.2.].

320 G Treitel, "'Conditions" and "Conditions Precedent"' (1990) 106 (Apr) LQR 185.

321 *Schuler* (n 198) 250.

322 McCardie J in *Hartley v Hymans* (n 434) 483.

323 *Lock v Bell* [1931] 1 Ch 35, 35, 43; *Hare v Nicoll* [1966] 2 QB 130, 142.

324 *Charles Rickards Ltd v Oppenheim* [1950] 1 KB 616, 621, 622.

325 H Beale; W Bishop; M Furmston, *Contract: Cases and Materials* (5th edn, OUP 2006) 574.

326 Case 12/1/2004 Egyptian Supreme Court 1116S64Q reproduced in Ateya (n 50) *255*.

327 Case 10/5/1993 Court of Cassation/Commercial 194/92 in Ministry of Justice, *Civil Provisions* (n 955) 293.

not fulfil the intended purpose of the contract. This is even though KLaw does not require the buyer to make their interests known to the seller in order to receive the goods on a specific date. Delivering goods the day after the agreed date theoretically renders the delivery unfulfilled, even if the buyer does not need the goods on the agreed date, and there is no deprivation of benefits and no detriment suffered by the buyer, unless the buyer accepts the delayed goods. Surprisingly, in one case, when the seller did not supply iron sheets within the agreed period, it was concluded that nothing was shown regarding the buyer disclosing their will to request *autonomous termination agreed* in the contract.[328] Not activating the agreement of the autonomous termination by the buyer in this case would activate the law, which has the same effect as the parties' agreement.

The court has no discretionary authority to determine the availability of termination according to the emphasised formulation of the time clause, the importance of the time to the buyer or according to the contract's original purpose. The mere fact of determining the delivery date accurately in the contract makes it of the essence, and termination can be decided upon when proving the seller's failure to fulfil their delivery obligation.[329] Some phrases in the contract could emphasise the importance of timely delivery without changing the legal outcome. When it was agreed that the delivery should be *no later* than 15 June 1999 and the buyer paid the instalments but the seller did not fulfil the obligation of delivery despite the buyer's warning, the court ruled for termination[330] and would have ruled for termination even without the emphasis on timely delivery. The purpose of this fastidiousness could be urging the seller to deliver the goods on time so as to avoid speculation by either the seller or the buyer, especially in relation to those products which are subject to variable pricing.[331] This autonomous termination, however, can facilitate fluctuation, especially when the seller finds a more profitable transaction, as they need to do nothing more than refrain from delivering the goods on time.[332]

As mentioned previously and according to Article 285 KCIC, when the seller fails to prepare the goods specified in kind on the agreed date, the buyer may obtain goods of the same kind at the seller's expense. Problematically, in cases of urgency, after discovering that the goods are not prepared, the buyer is entitled to buy alternative goods without obtaining judicial permission. This emphasis on 'urgency' by law does not specify on what grounds the buyer is allowed to claim it and does not require the seller's knowledge of its possibility, permitting fabrication of this urgency by the buyer. Urgency could vary, depending on the buyer's situation, a standard person's situation or the market status. If the buyer's situation is the focus, different scenarios can be rendered as the urgency could depend on the buyer's actual loss, possible harm or the loss of a significant opportunity to resell the goods for a good price.

328 It was agreed in the contract that autonomous termination would occur in case of delay. Case 13/5/2001 Court of Cassation/Commercial-2 660/2000 p. 2–6.

329 Case 12/12/2007 Court of Cassation/Civil-3 327/2006.

330 By analogy to Case 31/5/2004 Appellate Court/Commercial 318/2002.

331 Al-Ahwany (n 497) 385, 386, 417.

332 ibid 416, 417.

### *3.3.4 Comparative Analysis*

#### *3.3.4.1 Possible Outcomes Under the Three Legal Systems*

**a) First Scenario**: Three flower shipments are ordered by three different buyers. The first buyer mentions in the contract that 'time is *of the essence*,' the second buyer states that 'the delivery time is important because the flowers will be resold on *Mother's Day*,' and the third buyer mentions that 'it is *preferable* to deliver the goods on the agreed date.' If the delivery date associated with each shipment passes without delivery, the question arises: Which buyer can terminate the contract?

**Under CISG**, some jurists may find that the phrase *time is of the essence* permits immediate termination in case of breaching time clauses, owing to the party autonomy principle. However, others might not consider this statement an exclusion of Article 25 and might not find that it strongly indicates that foreseeable substantial detriment to the buyer would occur in case of its breach. This is especially true when the delayed goods were suitable to be used for a purpose other than the one intended by the buyer, or they were resalable in the ordinary course of business, even at a lower price. Hence, immediate termination might not be an option, and *Nachfrist* should be set. Stating the reason for the essentiality of the delivery time (flowers to be resold on Mother's Day) would tick the seller's foreseeability box as the seller and any reasonable person in their place should anticipate material prejudice if delivery is not on time. This would permit the buyer to immediately terminate the contract after non-delivery on the agreed date. The third buyer would not be able to immediately terminate the contract, and the situation would be resolved either by the buyer's setting *Nachfrist* or by treating the delivery date as not agreed at all, as clarified in the next section.

**Under SGA**, according to both the majority school advocating 'conditionality' of delivery time and 'intermediate term' theory, the statements of the first and second buyer make delivery time a 'condition.' Under 'conditionality' of delivery time, emphasising the delivery time either with or without mentioning the buyer's interest in having the goods on a specific date does not change the situation, as the delivery time in mercantile contracts is considered a 'condition,' permitting immediate termination when it is breached. According to 'intermediate term' theory, delivery times for these cases could be considered 'conditions precedent,' as the court/tribunal would likely give significant consideration to the expression of the contract. Even according to the 'conditionality' of the delivery time, the third buyer's statement demotes the 'conditionality' of time to an 'intermediate term,' so termination will not be available unless the delay frustrates the contractual purpose.

**Under KLaw**, the contract shall be terminated when the contractual terms are not fulfilled,[333] especially those associated with timely delivery, irrespective of the way they may be emphasised in a contract. Therefore, the phrasing in the first two

333 Ayob (n 494) 49.

cases does not change the situation as non-delivery on the agreed date permits termination on its own, and the mere agreement on time makes it of the essence. Nevertheless, the third case might place the delivery time under the general rule of judicial termination, and the court may retrieve its discretionary authority, as discussed in Chapter 2.

**b) Second Scenario:** On 1 February, it is agreed that goods delivery will be on 1 March, without emphasis. On 15 February, the buyer sends a letter stating that 'the goods must be delivered on time, otherwise do not deliver the goods at all. The goods will be resold on Mother's Day.' (In this year, Mother's Day falls on 14 March). The question arises: Could the buyer terminate the contract if the seller sends the goods on 10 March?

**Under CISG**, the letter is effective on its dispatch, which might make *time of the essence*, especially when it is sent in reasonable time and by reasonable means. However, as long as the buyer does not declare the contract terminated immediately after the non-delivery, the delay might be assessed according to Article 25, even in a case in which the time's importance is emphasised, and its reason is mentioned in the contract. There might not be a detriment conceived under the contract as the buyer could still resell the goods on Mother's Day; thus, termination might not be an option. **Under SGA**, the buyer can advise the seller within a reasonable period from the time the delayed goods are receiv thaedt the goods are refused as delivery time is largely considered a 'condition.' If time is considered an 'intermediate term,' details mentioned outside the contract may not affect the status of time and may not play a role in contractual interpretation.[334] Thus, termination is available only when such a delay is frustrating, which might not be the case in this scenario. **Under KLaw**, the contract might be considered terminated on 1 March, even without sending the later letter unless the delayed goods are accepted by the buyer.

#### *3.3.4.2 Certainty of Using Termination Based on Non-Delivery/Delay*

**Under CISG**, reliance on 'foreseeability' to determine the fundamentality of non-delivery/delay encourages the buyer to reveal all the aspects, considerations and purposes of the contract to the seller to provide a clear picture of the situation. However, it is not always straightforward when time is important, permitting termination upon its breach. Some jurists may find that the facility of immediate termination might be used when breaching time as its essentiality is *expressly* articulated in the contract; others may go further and find that this essentiality can be indicated *implicitly* under the contractual circumstances. This is true even without conveying the reason of this essentiality to the seller. Nevertheless, others may find that the *special interest* of the precise compliance with delivery time should be mentioned in the contract by stating, for instance, that 'the goods would be used for a wedding theme.' An alternative view may be to ignore the contract's phraseology and

334 See *Investors Compensation Scheme Ltd v West Bromwich Building Society (No. 1)* [1998] 1 WLR 896, 897.

concentrate on the elements of Article 25 to terminate the contract. These different interpretations of immediate termination may reduce the predictability of the legal outcome.

**Under SGA**, the court may be inclined to avoid excessive aberrant outcomes in the commercial sphere[335] and might be least keen to regard delivery time as an 'intermediate term' unless the parties clearly agree to downgrade time's 'conditionality.' This is true even if the time is not emphasised. SGA's over-simplistic system[336] may have a positive impact on certainty, facilitating prediction[337] and, subsequently, stimulating confidence in business, as the parties will know the legal consequences of their actions.[338] Under the 'intermediate term' school of thought, if the time is emphasised expressly or implicitly, the time is a 'condition,' and there is no need to assess the consequences of delay, achieving a high degree of clarity. Nevertheless, stating in the contract that any breach of any term permits termination may not convert all the terms to 'conditions.'[339]

**KLaw** sees the failure of traders to timely fulfil their obligations as a disruption to commercial life, requiring the adoption of penalties to urge the parties to fulfil their obligation in terms of due dates to maintain the stability of legal centres. Theoretically, the court's discretionary authority is less apparent in assessing the importance of time, as the mere mention of a delivery date in the contract is equivalent to emphasis of its importance, which enables the law to establish certainty. However, Article 285 KCIC does not stipulate the obviousness of the 'urgency' under the contractual circumstances, making it dependent on the buyer's situation. This not only reduces clarity but also disturbs the contractual balance between the parties.

### *3.3.4.3 Preserving the Contract in Case of Non-Delivery/Delay*

**Under CISG**, a one-day delay in delivery may not constitute a fundamental breach as such, even if the time is emphasised in the contract, similar to what occurred in the *Clothes case*,[340] but it could be so if the seller is made aware at the contract conclusion that the buyer wants to display the goods for an exhibition on a specific day[341] and foresees the harm in the delay. This assessment of the non-delivery/delay according to the contractual circumstances, through an economic lens and according to the benefits of both parties, takes clear steps to achieve contract preservation in order to reduce waste, attain time efficiency and maintain the goods.

**Under SGA**, when the delivery time is emphasised, immediate termination is allowed, regardless of whether the time is considered a 'condition' or an 'intermediate term,' and there is no need for any assessment of the consequences of the

335 *Rice v Great Yarmouth* (n 605) [18].
336 Piliounis (n 532) 23.
337 Bridge, *The Sale of Goods* (n 28) [10.38].
338 *PT Berlian Laju Tanker TBK v Nuse Shipping Ltd* [2008] EWHC 1330 (Comm) [66].
339 *Antaios Compania Naviera SA v Salen Rederierna AB (The Antaios)* [1985] AC 191, 194.
340 *Clothes case* 21/12/1990 (n 321).
341 Shafiq (n 50) 120.

breach. This can be true even if the reason for this emphasis is not mentioned in the contract, providing a lower degree of preserving the contract than CISG.

**Under KLaw**, termination for non-delivery/delay is active without much assessment of the contractual circumstances, without entailing any subjective or objective elaboration of the parties' intentions, without scrutinising the detriment caused by the delay and without resorting to an ordinary person's view to determine if time is important. This is true even though Article 213 KCIC, for example, which deals with the particular successor of each party, adopts the principle of the ordinary person.[342] This harsh application of time converts any breach, however trivial, to one leading to termination, without the need to mention the interest in choosing the agreed delivery date.

## 3.4 Delivery Time Is Not Specified/Specified Vaguely in the Contract

When the delivery date is not specified or vaguely specified in the contract, how long is the buyer required to wait before termination becomes available?

### *3.4.1 CISG*

When the contract is silent about the delivery date/period or it is unclearly fixed,[343] the seller, according to Article 33(c), should deliver the goods within a reasonable time after concluding the contract.[344] Delivering subsequent replacement parts should also be within such a reasonable period.[345] In *Norfolk Southern Railway Company v Power Source Supply*, the court did not consider the allegation that the delivery date was agreed upon before the final conclusion of the contract and demanded the seller deliver the locomotives within the reasonable time.[346] According to the *Automobile case*, when contracts do not specify the delivery date, buyers can fix *Nachfrist*, and, upon non-delivery, termination is permitted.[347] Notably, as happened in the *Dye for clothes case*, accepting the goods without protest at the actual delivery presumed that the goods were sent within the reasonable time, and this conclusion was not affected by the fact that the goods were of a seasonal nature.[348]

342 Case 10/5/2010 Court of Cassation/Civil-2 p. 3.

343 *Sports clothing case* (29/6/1998) C197–288 (Appellate Court Valais) <https://cisgw3.law.pace.edu/cases/980629s1.html>.

344 See *Electric heaters case* (30/3/1999) CISG/1999/15 (CIETAC arbitration) <https://cisgw3.law.pace.edu/cases/990330c3.html>.

345 *Industrial equipment case* (23/1/1997) 8611/HV/JK (ICC arbitration) <https://cisgw3.law.pace.edu/cases/978611i1.html>.

346 *Norfolk Southern Railway Company v Power Source Supply Inc.* (25/7/2008) 07–140-JJf (Federal District Court) <https://cisgw3.law.pace.edu/cases/080725u1.html>.

347 *Automobile case* 27/4/1999 (n 379).

348 *Dye for clothes case* (20/6/1997) 755/95-C (Appellate Court Barcelona) <https://cisgw3.law.pace.edu/cases/970620s4.html>. See also the *Clothes case* (18/4/1995) CISG/1995/06 (CIETAC arbitration proceeding) <https://cisgw3.law.pace.edu/cases/950418c1.html>.

#### 3.4.1.1 Ambiguous Phrases in Determining Delivery Time

Contractual undeterminable phrases, such as 'immediately' and 'as soon as possible'[349] may not make the delivery time a firm deal; thus, the seller should deliver the goods within a reasonable time.[350] In the *Technical equipment case*, although there was an 'urgent' clause in the contract, sending the goods two months after the agreed date did not constitute a breach.[351] Likewise, in the *Fashion textiles case*, the phrase 'to be delivered July, August, September +-' did not precisely specify the delivery time to entitle the buyer to immediately terminate the contract.[352] In the *Stones case*, too, when only 'estimated' dates were given for delivery, these dates could be used only to frame the length of the reasonable time.[353]

However, vague phrases with determinable times can be taken into consideration. In the *Memory module case*, the phrase 'at the latest' was deemed an adequate indication that the delivery time was a firm deal.[354] Additionally, in the *Mobile car phones case*, when it was agreed to deliver the mobile phones immediately after receiving 20% of the purchase price, the contract required prompt delivery, '[e]ven if the parties did not expressly agree on an exact delivery date' and irrespective of the seller's knowledge that the buyer resold the goods to their customer.[355] The payment of 20% of the purchase price was made on 29 June 2000, but the seller sent an email on 30 June 2000, apologising for the delay, and the goods were delivered on 3 July 2000. It was concluded that the seller committed a fundamental breach, even if such a breach was not of 'utmost importance to the contract,'[356] since the seller knew that prompt delivery was important for the buyer, and the seller admitted the delay in their email.[357]

#### 3.4.1.2 Delimiting Reasonable Time

A reasonable time 'depends on what constitutes acceptable commercial conduct in the circumstances of the case.'[358] In some cases, it could be 'two to three months after a call for delivery'[359] or two weeks after the payment,[360] but, in other cases,

349 *Memory module case* (n 303).
350 Bianca; Bonell (n 155) 263; Schwenzer, *Commentary on CISG* (n 15) 574 [7].
351 *Technical equipment case* (26/10/2004) 02/00109 (Appellate Court Poitiers) <http://cisgw3.law.pace.edu/cases/041026f1.html>.
352 *Fashion textiles case* (n 572).
353 *Stones case* (21/11/2001) 419O48/01 (District Court Hamburg) <https://cisgw3.law.pace.edu/cases/011221g1.html>.
354 *Memory module case* (n 303).
355 *Mobile car phones case* (n 309).
356 ibid.
357 ibid.
358 Secretariat Commentary, *Commentary on the Draft Convention on Contracts for the International Sale of Goods* (UN DOC A/CONF 97/5 1978) 31 <http://www.cisg-online.ch/index.cfm?pageID=644#Article%2033>.
359 *Stones case* (n 642); Unavailable name (3/4/2006) 105/2005 (Arbitration proceeding) <https://cisgw3.law.pace.edu/cases/060413r1.html>.
360 *Second-hand bulldozer case* (28/10/1997) C1/97/167 (Appellate Court Valais) <http://cisgw3.law.pace.edu/cases/971028s1.html>.

sending the goods more than three months late could exceed the reasonable period.[361] As stated in the *Plastic ketchup bottles case*, only circumstances which the seller 'foresaw or could have foreseen . . . at the time of contract conclusion' should be considered in determining a reasonable length of time.[362] In this case, the buyer changing the bottle design extended the reasonable time, especially since the seller regularly informed the buyer about the delivery situation.[363] In the *Machine case*, an email sent by the seller stating that the machine was still in operation until a specific month was taken into account to determine a reasonable length of time and made the delivery time of 45 days reasonable.[364] In the *Automobile case*, merely mentioning the delivery date in the buyer's offer was not binding on the seller but could be considered in determining a reasonable time for delivery, especially when that date was important to the buyer.[365] Subsequently, delivering vehicles two months later than the time specified in the buyer's offer exceeded the reasonable time, even if a two-to four-week delay was common in the international sale of vehicles.[366] Moreover, in *Alpha v Holland Loader*, the fact that both parties agreed to refurbish the loader purchased in July 2008, which took about 180 days and the buyer indicated they did not have immediate need for the loader resulted in delivery taking place within a reasonable time, even when delivery occurred after May 2009.[367]

#### *3.4.1.3 Termination Notice Versus Cure Notice*

When the goods are not delivered within a reasonable time, the buyer may declare the contract terminated.[368] Termination should be expressed clearly and explicitly in the notice,[369] without the requirement of specific terms[370] indicating whether the buyer is unwilling to adhere to the contract because of non-delivery/delay[371] or will not accept the late delivery.[372] Stating in the notice that the goods should be delivered on the agreed date/within a reasonable time does not justify termination.[373] However, in the *GMS modules case*, it was stated that termination 'may be declared orally and even impliedly through the buyer's conduct, where such conduct is sufficiently clear.'[374]

361 *Machine case* 10/3/2003 (n 297).

362 *Plastic ketchup bottles case* (15/9/2003) 3U19/03 (Appellate Court Rostock) <https://cisgw3.law.pace.edu/cases/030915g1.html>.

363 ibid.

364 *Machine case*10/3/2003 (n 297)

365 *Automobile case* 27/4/1999 (n 379).

366 ibid.

367 *Alpha Prime Development Corporation, Plaintiff v Holland Loader* (6/7/2010) (District Court) <https://cisgw3.law.pace.edu/cases/100706u1.html>.

368 This applies to any type of fundamental breach.

369 *Designer clothes case* (n 352); *Macromex Srl v Globex International Inc* (23/10/2007) 50181T 0036406 (American Arbitration Association) <https://cisgw3.law.pace.edu/cases/071023a5.html>.

370 *GMS modules* (n 135).

371 *Plastic ketchup bottles case* (n 651).

372 ibid.

373 ibid.

374 *GMS modules* (n 135).

Premature termination permits the seller to reasonably cure their default for delivery[375] without causing unreasonable inconvenience to the buyer[376] by either sending the goods after the reasonable time elapses or sending a request for subsequent performance. When the buyer has been silent[377] for a reasonable time following the receipt of the seller's inquiry,[378] the seller's notification might be effective,[379] obliging the buyer to accept the subsequent performance[380] and preventing them from resorting to termination within the seller's curative period.[381] This case could be an exception to both Article 29(1), which requires the agreement of both parties to amend any contractual term, and Article 18(1), which states that 'silence or inactivity does not in itself amount to acceptance.'

Termination should be declared within a reasonable time[382] after the buyer's refusal to accept buyer's curability,[383] after the buyer's awareness of late delivery[384] (when the delay itself constitutes a fundamental breach) or after the expiration of the reasonable time for delivery. Termination time 'has to be determined according to all circumstances of the case.'[385] In the *Rolled steel case*, termination was effective because it was declared within 48 hours of the late delivery.[386] However, the buyer 'is not entitled to wait for more than one year following the identification of the [breach to] inform the seller that it did not want to adhere to the contract'[387] as the termination right had been forfeited.[388] In the *Minibus case*, the court did not scrutinise the two-day delay in delivering the minibuses to decide whether it constituted a fundamental breach or not; the court merely stated that the buyer relinquished their termination right because they did not complain about the late delivery within a reasonable time after the delivery.[389] In the *Clothes case*, the buyer lost their termination right when they implicitly declared it six weeks after receiving the goods. This was because the goods were summer clothes, and the late

375 Yovel (n 342) 3, 4; Kröll; Mistelis; Viscasillas (n 67) 711 [26].
376 ibid Kröll; Mistelis; Viscasillas 698 [9].
377 CISG Art. 48(2).
378 *NV Boco v S.r.l. Lenzi Egisto* (8/11/2004) 2001/AR/1982 (Hof van Beroep Appellate Court Gent) <http://cisgw3.law.pace.edu/cases/041108b1.html>.
379 CISG Art. 48(2);(4).
380 *Inflatable triumphal arch case* (n 345).
381 CISG Art. 48(1)&(2).
382 A reasonable time would be after the elapse of the buyer's *Nachfrist* or after the seller's refusal to perform within such a period (CISG Art. 49(2)(b)(ii)).
383 CISG Art. 49(2)(b)(iii)
384 CISG Art. 49(2)(a). A similar meaning is found in UPICC 7.3.2.(2); *Shoes case* (14/6/1994) 3C75/94 (Lower Court Nordhorn) <https://cisgw3.law.pace.edu/cases/940614g1.html>.
385 *Automobile case* 31/3/2008 (n 310).
386 *Rolled steel case* (n 328).
387 *GMS modules* (n 135).
388 *Packaging machine case* (26/9/2008) 16/2007/MEM/chi (Appellationsgericht Basel-Stadt) <http://cisgw3.law.pace.edu/cases/080926s1.html>.
389 *Minibus case* (29/7/2009) (District Court Arnhem) LJN BJ4645; 172927/HA ZA 08–1230 <https://cisgw3.law.pace.edu/cases/090729n1.html>.

declaration diminished 'the seller's opportunities to sell the goods in question to other buyers.'[390]

Problematically, there is friction between a termination notice and a curability notice, each of which has a different procedural rule. The seller's notice for later delivery is not effective unless it *reaches* the buyer;[391] as stated in the *Canned food case*, the seller bears the transmission's risk of loss/error of their request to cure.[392] Conversely, the buyer's declaration of termination is effective, according to Article 27, upon its *dispatch* (the same applies to the buyer's reply to accept or object to curability), regardless of whether it reaches the seller or not[393] as long as it is sent by appropriate means.[394] Nevertheless, curability may be exercised by dispatching the goods without notifying the buyer,[395] and in this case, the comparison is between the time of the goods' receipt by the buyer and the time of the dispatch of the termination notice. If the goods are delivered before dispatch of the termination declaration, the buyer can only terminate the contract based on a fundamental breach of the delayed goods rather than non-delivery. This is despite the fact that it was stated in the *GMS modules case* that 'in cases where the seller has delivered the goods, the buyer loses the right to declare the contract avoided' with respect to late delivery.[396] If the goods are dispatched but still not received by the buyer, the dispatched termination notice is effective.[397]

### *3.4.2 SGA*

When the contract does not fix a delivery time, s.29(3) obliges the seller to deliver the goods within a reasonable time,[398] without categorising such a duty as a 'condition' or a 'warranty.' Atiyah finds that the seller's failure to deliver the goods within a reasonable time is a breach of a 'condition.'[399] Likewise, in *McDougall*, the delivery date was 1 May, but the contract stated that 'owing to the effect of delays and shortages, such delivery date cannot be guaranteed.' The seller provided defective goods within a reasonable time from 1 May and could not deliver the required goods within such a timeframe. The court held that the

390 *Clothes case* 21/12/1990 (n 321).

391 CISG Art. 48(4); Yovel (n 342) 18.

392 *Canned food case* (12/11/1997) S 97/324 (Turku Court of Appeal) <http://cisgw3.law.pace.edu/cases/971112f5.html>.

393 ibid.

394 This occurs when the declaration is between absentees; when the declaration is oral (in person or via telephonic communication), there is no difference between the dispatch of the notice and its receipt, although this is difficult to prove. Bianca; Bonell (n 155) 362; Yovel (n 342) 18; Kröll; Mistelis; Viscasillas (n 67) 367 [15]; 368 [20].

395 Yovel (n 342) 18.

396 *GMS modules* (n 135).

397 *Printed materials case* (n 325).

398 SGA s.29(3); *Postlethwaite v Freeland* (1880) 5 App Cas 599; *Hick v Raymond & Reid* [1893] AC 22.

399 Twigg-Flesner; Canavan (n 30) 102.

failure to deliver the ordered goods within a reasonable time was a breach of 'condition,' entitling the buyer to reject the goods and end the contract.[400] As Diplock J pointed out, this 'conditionality' of reasonable time was to make a substantial use of the goods during its season as it was difficult to tell whether the goods were suitable to use during subsequent seasons, especially as a degree of deterioration to the goods would occur in that time, and this could not be adequately compensated by damages.[401] Moreover, according to s.29(5), delivery can be considered unproductive if the goods are delivered at an unreasonable hour, even if it is within the reasonable time. 'Ineffectuality' of the delivering hour is unclear in terms of whether it is a breach of 'warranty' or a 'condition,' which can be deemed an 'intermediate term,' depending on the breach's consequences.

Some ambiguous terms regarding time may be included in the contract without specifying the exact delivery date, such as 'promptly' or 'as soon as possible/practicable.' According to *Alfred v BAI*, these phrases should not be considered 'conditions,'[402] and according to *Atwood v Emery* and *Moore v Shelley*, these phrases could be ignored, and the performance should be completed merely within a reasonable time,[403] not necessarily 'in the very next instant of time after the demand.'[404] However, although Bridge finds that these terms are subject to judicial interpretation of expediency instead of punctiliousness,[405] he sees that the seller should perform their obligations without delay.[406] These expressions were also construed, in *Hydraulic v McHaffie*, to mean that delivery should be in the shortest practicable time within a reasonable time.[407]

If the parties' intentions are unclear and it is difficult to identify whether the time can be regarded as a 'condition,'[408] such as 'around a specific date,' the court might consider it an 'intermediate term,'[409] assessing the consequences of the breach to permit termination according to commercial common sense.[410] If the result of regarding a term as a 'condition' is unreasonable, the courts may find that the parties did not intend to consider such term a 'condition.'[411] However, Diplock J in *McDougall* stated that flexible statements '[place] upon the seller a duty to deliver

400 *McDougall v Aeromarine of Emsworth* (n 399) 1132.
401 ibid.
402 *Alfred McAlpine Plc v BAI (Run-Off) Ltd* [2000] 1 All ER (Comm) 545. See also Edwin Peel, *The Law of Contract* (13th edn, Sweet & Maxwell 2011) 914 [18–091].
403 *Atwood v Emery* 140 ER 45.
404 *Moore v Shelley* (1883) 8 App Cas 285, 292.
405 Bridge, *The Sale of Goods* (n 28) [6.17].
406 ibid.
407 *Hydraulic Engineering Co Ltd v McHaffie Goslett & Co* (1878) 4 QBD 670, 672.
408 *Rice v Great Yarmouth* (n 605) [22].
409 Peel, 15th edn (n 64) 983, 984 [18–045].
410 *Thames and Mersey Marine Insurance Co Ltd v Hamilton Fraser* (1887) 12 App Cas 484, 490; *Rice v Great Yarmouth* (n 605) [24].
411 *Schuler* (n 198) 236, 237.

within a reasonable time of the specified date'[412] when the seller fails to deliver on the agreed date despite their best endeavours.[413]

Surrounding circumstances should be considered to estimate the reasonable time, and this consideration might not be confined, as stated in *Peregrine Systems v Steria*, to those circumstances contemplated by the parties or those that ought to have been anticipated at the contract conclusion.[414] Nonetheless, in *Pantland v Raymond*, it was stated that '[a] reasonable time means a time which is reasonable under ordinary circumstances, not under actual circumstances.'[415] However, Bridge finds that assessing reasonable time will depend on the nature of the goods; this period will be very short if the goods are perishable/seasonal goods but will be longer if the goods are durable.[416] Potatoes, for instance, should be available for 'immediate' delivery, within 72 hours.[417] He also states that the length of 'reasonable time' can be estimated according to the threshold of frustrating delay and the impact on the buyer's contractual purpose.[418]

The buyer can issue a prompt notice, specifying the delivery time by making time of the essence.[419] This may accelerate the buyer's potentiality to terminate the contract if the seller's performance is late[420] because the seller's delay is considered repudiation.[421] However, in *Behzadi v Shaftesbury*, it was stated that the buyer might not have given notice making time of the essence; the buyer should have waited until such a delay became unreasonable.[422] Andrews also finds that a notice may not turn the delivery time into a 'condition' unilaterally; it just serves as evidence of the reasonable date by which the seller is required to perform.[423] Delay per se does not constitute a repudiatory breach.[424] Thus, even in cases of non-performance within the time specified by subsequent notification, the innocent buyer may still show that delay goes to the root of the contract in order to terminate the contract, regarding the breach of time as an 'intermediate term.'[425]

412 *McDougall v Aeromarine of Emsworth* (n 399) 1132.

413 *Raffinerie* (n 73) 807.

414 *Peregrine v Steria* (n 462) [15].

415 *Hick v Raymond* (n 687) 23.

416 Bridge, *The Sale of Goods* (n 28) [6.14].

417 *FC Bradley & Sons v Colonial Continental Trading* [1964] 2 Lloyd's Rep 52.

418 Bridge, *The Sale of Goods* (n 28) [6.34].

419 By analogy to *Cornwall v Henson* [1900] 2 Ch. 298 (payment obligation); *United Scientific Holdings v Burnley* (n 400) 914. See Peel, 13th edn (n 691) 914 [18–091]; Bridge, *Benjamin's* (n 28) [8–026]; Davies (n 196) 3rd edn 383 [25.3.3].

420 See *Stickney v Keeble* [1915] AC 386; *Charles v Oppenheim* (n 613) 616; *Behzadi v Shaftesbury Hotels Ltd* [1992] Ch. 1, 4, 5; Andrews, *Contractual Duties* (n 78) 226; Furmston (n 30) 692.

421 Peel, 15th edn (n 64) 1029–1031 [18–127].

422 ibid *Behzadi v Shaftesbury* 13.

423 ibid, 24; *Ocular Sciences Ltd v Aspect Vision Care Ltd (No.2)* [1997] RPC 289, 302; Andrews, *Contractual Duties* (n 78) 228.

424 ibid *Ocular Sciences v Aspect Vision Care* 433.

425 *British & Commonwealth Holdings Plc v Quadrex Holdings Inc* [1995] CLC 1169, 1214; ibid; Andrews, *Contractual Duties* (n 78) 215, 216.

### *3.4.3 KLaw*

According to Article 130(1) & (3) KCOC, if no delivery date has been specified, delivery shall be implemented *as soon as the contract is concluded*,[426] unless the nature of the goods or the custom determines otherwise.[427] This means the law requires the seller to deliver the goods promptly after the contract conclusion, or the contract will be terminated pursuant to the general rule.[428] However, the seller may mistakenly assume that the contract's silence regarding the time puts them in a better situation than specifying a rigid time to deliver the goods, but the opposite is true. This situation would encourage the buyer not to provide a term of the goods' delivery time in the contract[429] to accelerate the delivery process. In one case, the buyer made a partial payment at the contract conclusion on 18 March to purchase Agfa photocopiers from Germany and paid the remainder on 19 April, as agreed. Because of non-delivery, the buyer raised a suit demanding the seller make a refund plus interest, but the seller claimed that the goods were delivered, and paying the remainder on 19 April was an assumption of the receipt; otherwise, the buyer should have withheld the remainder of the payment. The court ruled termination because the payment on 19 April was not conditional on delivery, and there was no written evidence of receipt of the goods. The court added that the contract was silent in determining the delivery time, so delivery, according to Article 130 KCOC, should have been implemented as soon as the contract was concluded; otherwise, the contract would have been terminated automatically according to the general rule of Article 131.[430] However, there was no justification for paying the price as the contract was terminated, and the buyer did not notify the seller within three days demanding the delivery. Stating in the contract that the remainder of the payment should be made a month after concluding the contract might be an implicit determination of the delivery date, especially as the nature of the goods and the custom necessitated the passage of time to bring the goods from Germany.

#### *3.4.3.1 Estimating Detrimental Consequences of Non-Delivery/Delay Is Not an Element*

KLaw does not stipulate detriment resulting from the seller's delay to terminate the contract. The Kuwaiti approach is unsuitable in the domain of contract law.[431] The seller may not perform their obligation, but, at the same time, the buyer does not suffer any detriment.[432] The law, by requiring immediate delivery or the contract will be terminated, favours keeping the goods with the seller when they do not

426 Case 17/4/1995 Appellate Court/Commercial 297/1995 p.3. Similar meaning in Art. 474 KCIC.
427 Case 14/6/1993 (n 499) 293; Case 16/12/2007 Court of Cassation/Commercial 1062/2006 in Ministry of Justice, *Civil Provisions* (n 955) 296.
428 KCOC Art. 131.
429 Al-Fadly (n 495) 91.
430 Case 9/10/1995 Appellate Court/Commercial 866/95.
431 Ayob (n 494) 318.
432 Al-Sanhory (n 279) 763.

perform immediate delivery and prefers swift settlement of the legal status of both the transaction and the parties. This is especially true when relying on reasonable time may cause situations that are difficult to manage, such as deciding whether *force majeure* occurs within or after the reasonable period. Immediate delivery may obviate such a convoluted scenario; it was held in one case that because of the seller's delay in delivering the goods, which should have been performed immediately, an unforeseen circumstance occurred, and the seller was not permitted to benefit from their negligence by relying on *force majeure*.[433]

#### *3.4.3.2 Termination Is Conditional on Non-Contractual Adherence*

When the buyer requests the execution of the contract by warning the seller to deliver the goods,[434] the buyer might no longer be able to claim that the termination right was available directly after the immediate delivery.[435] However, it is not always easy to establish whether the buyer relinquished their termination right or not as the mere postponement in taking the termination procedure might not be considered a waiver.[436] This may encourage financial speculation at the seller's expense as the buyer may wait for a few days to observe the purchased goods' value in the stock market. If it is high, they will adhere to the contract; otherwise, they will demand termination.

#### *3.4.3.3 Different Practical Standards*

The situation could be different in practice, and the court might turn a blind eye to the aforementioned provision and take one of the following case law standards:

**First**, the court could rule that the delivery time should be *when the buyer pays* the remainder of the agreed price,[437] and delivery may not take place if the buyer fails to pay the price.[438] Accordingly, when it was mentioned in a contract that a car would be handed over 'when the seller's instalment period ends towards a third party,' the court ruled that since the seller had received the full price, they were obligated to immediately pay the instalments to the third party in order to perform their duty to promptly and hand over the car to the buyer.[439] However, in another case, the seller claimed that it was inconceivable that the buyer had paid the price (by signing a cheque) without a contract regulating the sale, unless the iron scrap had already been received since Article 474 KCIC stipulated delivering/handing over the goods immediately after concluding the contract if the delivery time was not agreed upon. The court ruled that the seller had failed to prove the

433 Case 11/11/1996 Appellate Court/Commercial 574/96 p. 4.
434 Egyptian Case 27/6/1998 Supreme Court 2074/66 reproduced in Ateya (n 50) 192.
435 Similar to the autonomous termination agreement mentioned in Talaba (n 50) 88.
436 Case 24/6/1997 Egyptian Supreme Court 2372S 66Q reproduced in ibid 91, 92.
437 Case 8/1/2009 Appellate Court/Civil-4 1487–1491/2008 p. 4.
438 See Case 12/12/2001 Appellate Court/Commercial-7 1411/2001.
439 Case 28/11/2001 Commercial 1356 p. 5.

delivery, despite receiving the cheque.[440] **Secondly,** when the *buyer acknowledges* that they sufficiently see the goods, which are rented to a third party, the buyer has no right to claim not receiving the goods immediately after concluding the contract.[441] **Thirdly**, the court may *evaluate the reason* that hinders the seller from delivering the goods as soon as they are imported.[442] **Finally**, *refusal* to deliver the goods, despite deducting the outstanding instalments,[443] may result in the contract being terminated.[444]

#### *3.4.3.4 Special Case for Seasonal and Future Goods*

If the contract is silent about the delivery date, the law specifies the delivery time in relation to seasonal and future goods as follows:

**First**, according to Article 130(2) KCOC, if the goods are linked to a specific season, they must be delivered *before the end of that season.*[445] Although the legislator assumes that the season is the purpose of contracting, the phrase 'before the end of the season' is very vague; does the delivery of the goods one day before Valentine's Day suffice? Or should the goods be delivered reasonably before the end of the season? According to the literal wording of the Article, a reasonableness criterion has not been adopted, so delivering the goods one day before Ramadan could be sufficient as long as the buyer receives the goods before the end of that season, perhaps even if it is commercially inadequate, unless the judge sees otherwise. **Secondly**, according to Article 168 KCIC, the contract may be held on future goods that will inevitably exist, such as selling furniture before manufacture.[446] In this case, the delivery time, pursuant to Article 120 KCOC, is defined flexibly, depending on industrial production.[447]

### ***3.4.4 Comparative Analysis***

#### *3.4.4.1 Possible Outcomes Under the Legal Systems*

Hypothetically, a shipment of phones is purchased, and it is agreed that the goods will be delivered 'immediately.' In the month after concluding the contract, there is a national lockdown in the buyer's location, which was not envisaged under the contract. In the second month after concluding the contract, a new version of the phone is released, which was previously known by the seller. These two events negatively impact the goods' price when resold.

440 Case 17/4/1995, 297 (n 715).
441 See Case 19/3/2007 (n 502).
442 Case 3/1/2006 376/2005 Administrative Court of Cassation/Commercial-1 p. 4.
443 Case 13/4/2002 Court of Cassation/Commercial-3 418/2001.
444 See Case 2/1/2005 (n 509).
445 KCOC Art. 130(2).
446 Al-Danasory; Al-Shawarbee (n 281) 37; Abdulreda; Al-Nakas (n 257) 123, 124.
447 Al-Ahwany (n 497) 386.

**Under CISG**, the word 'immediately' does not make the deal firm, and the shipment should be delivered within a reasonable time after concluding the contract,[448] or the buyer might specify *Nachfrist* of reasonable length. The length of the reasonable period might be framed according to the contractual circumstances and shortened when considering the launching of a new phone, particularly when it was foreseeable under the contract, but without considering the lockdown because the buyer did not inform the seller of this possible occurrence. This can make the reasonable time up to two weeks after concluding the contract, and sending the goods after this time entitles the buyer to terminate the contract. However, if the buyer does not declare the contract terminated after the two-week period, the seller has the right to one of the two following procedures:

**First**, sending the goods late according to Article 48(1), even without notice, might frustrate the termination right. Nonetheless, the buyer might declare the contract terminated within a reasonable time from the receipt of the goods, according to Article 49(2)(a), due to the delay in delivery if it is a fundamental breach. **Secondly**, in the case of sending notice after the expiration of two weeks requesting the buyer to accept the delayed phones, the seller could send the delivery, and the buyer should be obliged to accept the subsequent performance if they are silent for a reasonable time after receiving notice. However, the buyer's objection to such notice and declaring termination would put an end to the contract.

**Under SGA**, there have been many interpretations of 'immediately.' According to Bridge[449] and *Hydraulic v McHaffie*,[450] the seller should deliver the goods without delay or within the shortest possible reasonable time. Nevertheless, according to *Atwood*[451] and *Moore v Shelley*,[452] the goods need not be delivered instantly after the demand, the term 'immediately' might be disregarded, and the goods should be delivered within a reasonable time. Moreover, there is controversy over specifying the length of 'reasonable time':

**First**, according to *Peregrine Systems v Steria*,[453] determining a reasonable length of time is not restricted by the circumstances contemplated by the seller; thus both the lockdown event and the launch of new phones might be considered. **Secondly**, according to *Pantland v Raymond*'s,[454] ordinary but not actual circumstances should be considered, which might exclude both events to delimit the reasonable time. **Thirdly**, according to Bridge,[455] seasonal goods could make the reasonable time shorter, so the launch of new phones might make the reasonable time less than for normal durable goods. **Lastly**, the threshold of a frustrating delay

448 Bianca; Bonell (n 155) 263; Schwenzer, *Commentary on CISG* (n 15) 574 [7].
449 Bridge, *The Sale of Goods* (n 28) [6.17].
450 *Hydraulic Engineering v McHaffie* (n 696) 672.
451 *Atwood v Emery* (n 692).
452 *Moore v Shelley* (n 696) 292.
453 *Peregrine v Steria* (n 462) [15].
454 *Hick v Raymond* (n 687) 23.
455 Bridge, *The Sale of Goods* (n 28) [6.14].

and its effect on the contractual purpose[456] delimit the reasonable time, making the launch of new phones the only event to be considered.

**Under KLaw**, in the absence of the parties' agreement on a delivery date, the goods should be delivered instantly after the contract conclusion unless the goods' nature or the custom necessitates sending the goods later. The judge might see that the shelf life of phones which will be shipped from overseas requires the delivery to be conducted at a later time, but the law does not mention any benchmark to assist the judge in determining the period within which the goods must be delivered. Thus, it is uncertain whether the judge would consider the launch of the new phones and lockdown event when determining this period. Nevertheless, if the judge considers the phones seasonal devices due to the launch of new phones, the seller should deliver the goods before the end of the season. It is unclear whether the delivery should be within a reasonable time or even few days before such a launch and whether the buyer's commercial ability to resell the phones would be deemed important. Moreover, it is up to the judge to follow one of the following two procedures:

**First**, the judge might pursue the general rule of judicial termination, which states that the seller may prevent termination by carrying out their obligation of delivery before the verdict of termination by the judiciary,[457] and, in this case, the judge should refuse termination.[458] **Secondly**, the judge might follow the rule of *autonomous termination* by agreement (similar to the rule of timely delivery), which states that the seller cannot obviate termination through performing the defaulted obligation after the proceedings and before the decision on termination.[459] The judge in this case must rule on termination[460] because they are deprived of their discretion to give the breaching seller additional time to perform their obligations.[461]

#### *3.4.4.2 Certainty in Using Termination Based on Non-Delivery/Delay*

Surprisingly, it is evident from the previous scenario that **CISG** attains a higher degree of legal clarity and predictability than SGA. This is despite the fact that the vagueness of reasonable time has a significant impact on other procedures; it is not easy for the seller to determine whether sending the goods is regarded as a

456 ibid [6.34].
457 Case 29/4/2006 (n 265) 9; Case 2/11/2010 (n 265) 8.
458 Egyptian Case 2/6/1981 Supreme Court 403S 22 S Y 48 P 1682 reproduced in Ateya (n 50) 160; Al-Shawarby (n 266) 63; Abulil (n 258) 418; AboSaad (n 257) 441; Abdulreda; Al-Nakas (n 257) 196.
459 This was mentioned in French Civil Code 1804, Art. 1134: '*conventions légalement formées tiennent lieu loi ceux qui ont faites*,' which means that legally formed agreements are the law of the parties. See Al-Sanhory (n 279) 697, 698; Al-Yaqob (n 52) 285.
460 By analogy to autonomous termination by agreement mentioned in Al-Sanhory (n 279) 808, 809; AboSaad (n 257) 443; Ateya (n 50) 218, 219; Al-Yaqob (n 52) 314.
461 By analogy to autonomous termination by agreement. EMKCIC 227, 228; Al-Jarmy (n 264) 106; Muhammad (n 255) 782.

delivery within the reasonable time or as a usage of the curability right. It is also not straightforward for the buyer to determine whether the declaration of the termination is effective, done within a reasonable time after the expiration of time for delivery or immature. Furthermore, the overlapping rules of non-delivery/delay, curability and declaration of termination could cause confusion,[462] giving rise to different interpretations,[463] even if the provisions are highly structured.[464] The competition between a termination notice, which is efficient on its dispatch according to Article 27, and a cure notice (or sending the goods without notice), which is effectual when it reaches the buyer according to Article 48(4), also minimises certainty. This will be the case if, for instance, a cure notice is sent by the seller on 1 February and reaches the buyer on 22 February, while the buyer dispatches a termination notice on 20 February. The seller will conceive that the cure notice reaches the buyer before the termination notice, and the buyer should prove that they received the cure notice after the dispatch of the termination notice. This situation perplexes both parties about knowing the position in advance.

**Under SGA**, estimating reasonable time can be vague, needing 'broad consideration, with the benefit of hindsight,'[465] and, as mentioned in the previous scenario, there are different views around which circumstances should be taken to determine a reasonable amount of time. There is also ambiguity in considering reasonable time a 'condition' or a 'warranty' and in considering 'reasonable hour' as an 'intermediate term,' and there is discrepancy around the expeditious terms, such as 'immediately.' The legal effect of the buyer's notice specifying a particular time and making it *of the essence* is also unclear. Some jurists find this method is effective[466] while others find that the buyer may not send a notice to make time of the essence unilaterally. The buyer should either wait until the reasonable time expires[467] without delivery or prove that not meeting the time specified in the notice goes to the root of the contract, according to 'intermediate term' theory,[468] to put an end to the contract. These different views might make the legal decision difficult to anticipate in advance.

**Under KLaw**, delivering the goods immediately after concluding the contract could minimise wasted money and time and hasten the fixing of the parties' legal status. This attitude could also prevent the intervention of obstacles that could hinder delivery, such as unforeseen circumstances. Nevertheless, rigid rules could be

462 A similar meaning is found in Enderlein; Maskow (n 150) 112; Albert Kritzer, *Guide to Practical Applications of the United Nations Convention on Contracts for the International Sale of Goods* (Kluwer and Taxation Publishers 2002) 200.

463 Franco Ferrari, 'CISG Case Law: A New Challenge for Interpreters?' (1999) 17 JL & Com 245, 254.

464 Spagnolo (n 54) 73.

465 *Astea (UK) Ltd v Time Group Ltd* [2003] EWHC 725 [144] (TCC).

466 By analogy with *Cornwall v Henson* (n 708) (the obligation of payment); *United Scientific Holdings v Burnley* (n 400) 914.

467 *Behzadi v Shaftesbury* (n 709) 13, 24; *Ocular Sciences v Aspect Vision Care* (n 712) 302; Andrews, *Contractual Duties* (n 78) 228.

468 *Commonwealth v Quadrex* (n 714) 1214; ibid *Ocular Sciences v Aspect Vision Care* 433; Andrews, *Contractual Duties* (n 78) 215, 216.

far from particularity and sometimes cause unjust results. Practically, however, immediate delivery is not guaranteed, and the adjudicator might resort to different standards, such as delivery being after the payment or assessing the reason for non-delivery. In other cases, the situation is subjected to the buyer's reaction, putting the seller under the heel of the buyer for a period of time not specified in law, which weakens the contractual balance between the parties. These different approaches undermine certainty and predictability.

#### *3.4.4.3 Preserving the Contract in Case of Non-Delivery/Delay*

**Under CISG**, many testimonies clarify that the Convention is keen to preserve the contract: the seller can obviate termination by sending the goods after the reasonable time/agreed date[469] as long as the termination notice has not been dispatched and open the door on assessing the breach according to the fundamental breach doctrine. But when the termination notice and curability notice are sent on the same day, the contract is terminated because its notice is effective when it is dispatched, not on its receipt, as is the case with a seller's notification. Additionally, termination is lost when it is declared late, declared within reasonable time for delivery or when it is not expressed clearly in the declaration.

**Under SGA**, not requiring acceleration in delivery and demanding reasonable time when the contract is silent about the delivery time add flexibility and reduce the possibility of termination. However, according to the majority view, not sending the goods within the reasonable time is considered a breach of 'condition,' entitling the buyer to terminate the contract. There is no room for the seller's rectification, which does not have an impact on the buyer's right to refuse the delayed goods sent after the reasonable time.

**Under KLaw**, termination based on non-delivery after concluding the contract calls for 'perfectionism,' which could be impractical and provides less protection in maintaining the contract than to CISG and SGA because:

**First**, reasonable or ordinary time has not been adopted, and there is no short time limit to recourse to termination. **Secondly**, immediate delivery after the contract conclusion, when termination would otherwise be activated, punishes the seller and ignores the fact that the buyer may not suffer any detriment. **Thirdly**, confusingly, KLaw requires the goods to be sent immediately after concluding the contract, whereas seasonal goods can be sent until the end of the season. It would make more sense if the case was the opposite: i.e. the regular goods should be sent within the usual time, which makes the contractual purpose attainable to the buyer, while seasonal goods should be sent immediately after concluding the contract. **Finally**, despite the diversity of judgements, as clarified here, a judge might see that their discretionary authority is restricted. Providing the seller with an additional period and estimating whether the use of a termination right is abusive and

469 *Auto case* (4/7/2007) 2 Ob 95/06v (Supreme Court) <https://cisgw3.law.pace.edu/cases/070704a3.html>.

the delay is insignificant would release the restricted discretionary authority and convert the termination based on breaching time, which is automatic, to judicial termination. Thus, the judge might not refuse termination even if the seller delivers most of the goods after concluding the contract.

## 3.5 Conclusion: Towards the Development of KLaw

KLaw attaches unjustified weight to a termination based on the seller's breach of delivery time, especially as termination does not require notification and could be construed as automatic. It is true that the contract has taken a prominent place in Islamic Sharia, which urges people to fulfil the covenants as it is mentioned in the Quran: 'O ye who believe! Fulfil your contracts.'[470] But this does not mean the contract can be terminated in any event of breaching this term, and it might be fairer and more compatible with the meaning of justice according to Sharia that KLaw resorts to other remedies equal to the degree of the breach.

To terminate the contract, KLaw neither assesses the *essentiality* of the breached term according to the parties' will nor estimates the *detriment* of the aggrieved buyer suffered by the non-delivery/delay or the *contractual purpose*. In practice, the situation may be different, and there might not be a strict adherence to a time provision by the judiciary. This would create incompatibility between the law in codes and the law in courts, which would severely weaken the predictability of the legal outcome, making seeking legal advice pointless. The problem is that the court could be driven behind the buyer's situation and their response to the non-delivery/delay, and this would disturb the balance between the parties. The rigidity of law and the absence of a concrete system for termination which is not commensurate with commercial contracts are the reasons for the judicial flexibility in applying this provision.

As stated in Attaiya, '[A] regrettable feature of the English provisions is that they . . . have no application to a breach of a stipulation as to time.'[471] However, according to the majority of English cases, and as Diplock LJ affirmed in *Bunge v Tradax*, there has been a sharp rebuff of the characterisation of time obligations as 'intermediate terms' in commercial contracts. There is only one possible kind of breach of time clause in a mercantile contract,[472] which is to be late, whereas 'intermediate terms' can be breached in various degrees, ranging from trivial to serious.[473] However, Bridge rightly finds that detriment caused by late performance escalates from day to day until it ultimately reaches the deprivation of substantial benefit of the bargain.[474] Furthermore, many cases do not focus on the examination of the parties' conduct and whether the buyer uses delay/non-delivery as a technical

470 The Quran, The Table 1.

471 Twigg-Flesner; Canavan (n 30) 418.

472 *Bunge v Tradax* (n 400) 717.

473 Chen-Wishart (n 77) 482 [12.2.3.3]; Peel, 15th edn (n 64) 992 [18–056].

474 Bridge, *The Sale of Goods* (n 28) [10.37].

excuse to escape an unprofitable transaction.[475] This 'black and white' approach leads the parties to understand the contractual path, lessening the unpredictability of the court decision,[476] and avoids courts being rife with prosecutions which may take years to resolve.[477] However, this approach expands the terms regarded as 'conditions' and subsequently increases the use of termination. Flexibility in relation to the delivery time is needed in commercial life, and deeming delivery time a 'condition' in all commercial contracts may render an unusual outcome. In consumer contracts, time is not considered a 'condition,' although the power of the parties is unequal, while the degree of protection in consumer sales is higher than in commercial contracts. As evidence, a very slight deviation from the contract preventing the buyer from terminating it according to s.15(A) is only applicable to commercial contracts. Moreover, the fact that the term of delivery time being a 'condition' may prevent assessing its impact by asking whether remedies other than termination is adequate. For instance, in *Bowes v Shand*, Lord Blackburn objected to the idea that the buyer can resort to compensation instead of termination when the goods are delivered at a time other than that agreed.[478]

CISG's approach could be criticised for the difficulty involved in deciding whether the non-delivery/delay is fundamental because it necessitates scrutiny of the occurrence of delay,[479] the buyer's nature, the contractual circumstances and perhaps the market, rather than depending only on the wording of the term. Deciding whether the seller has a curability right could also be controversial. Despite these criticisms, CISG has many advantages. There is no contractual fidelity to all delivery times in all contracts, but rather the issue is how to assess the impact of non-timely delivery on the buyer. The fundamentality of non-delivery/delay and the seller's curability right preserve the contract, attaining fairer outcomes, minimising waste and boosting the economy. Resorting to the criteria of 'expectations' and 'foreseeability' is an attempt to prevent the adjudicators from putting themselves in the parties' place, allowing legal predictability. Under *Nachfrist*'s system, CISG realises higher certainty to both parties when the buyer can terminate the contract directly after the expiration of such a period. These make CISG's approach a panacea to KLaw.

475 See ibid [6.28].

476 *Rice v Great Yarmouth* (n 605) [18]; Neil MacCormick, *Rhetoric and the Rule of Law* (OUP 2005) 11; RexAhdar, 'Contract Doctrine, Predictability and the Nebulous Exception' (2014) 73(1) CLJ 39, 58.

477 *Bunge v Tradax* (n 400) 720.

478 Edmund Bowes, JB Martin, and WL Kent v Charles Shand, Alexander Shand, and R A Robinson (1877) 2 App Cas 455, 480. (1876–77) L.R. 2 App. Cas. 455 (1876–77) L.R. 2 App. Cas. 455.

479 Lord Devlin, 'The Treatment of Breach of Contract' (1966) 24(2) CLJ 192, 195, 196.

# 4 Terminating a Contract Due to Misdescription

## 4.1 Introduction

Parties can delimit the required descriptions of the goods so as to secure the efficiency of the transaction and to guarantee their capabilities and needs.[1] Parties may include tangible attributes, which are 'physically present or can be seen,'[2] or intangible characteristics, including the genuine identity of the goods' creator,[3] their weight,[4] age,[5] reputation or origin.[6] Under Article 35(1) CISG, the seller is obliged to deliver the goods pursuant to the contractual description. Under SGA, s.13 states that 'there is an implied term that the goods shall correspond with the description,' but this does not necessarily spontaneously transform all descriptive words into 'conditions.'[7] The traditional distinction between mere puffery (hollow/representations), intermediate terms[8] and promissory terms might not be affected by s.13.[9] Under KLaw, Article 498 KCIC states that if the buyer finds that the goods do not meet the promised description, the buyer may request either termination with compensation or to keep the goods as well as receiving compensation.

This chapter scrutinises **first**, identification of the meaning of 'contractual descriptions' in the three legal systems, **secondly**, stipulations for termination based on non-compliance with the contractual description (misdescription) and, **lastly**, procedural requirements for termination. This chapter assumes that the breached descriptions are specified in the contract and that misdescription occurs before the risk passes to the buyer.

1 Djakhongir Saidov, *Conformity of Goods and Documents: The Vienna Sales Convention* (Hart 2015) 29.
2 Susan McDowellMudambi; Peter Doyle; Veronica Wong, 'An Exploration of Branding in Industrial Markets' (1997) 26(5) Industrial Marketing Management 433, 438.
3 Johan Erauw, 'CISG Articles 66–70: The Risk of Loss and Passing It' (2006) 25 JL & Com 203, 206.
4 *Rebar coil case* (20/11/1997) CISG/1997/32 (CIETAC arbitration proceeding) <http://cisgw3.law.pace.edu/cases/971120c1.html>.
5 Maley (n 186) 105.
6 McDowellMudambi; Doyle; Wong, (n 770) 438.
7 Poikela (n 83) 47, 48; McKendrick, *Sale of Goods* (n 202) 328; Twigg-Flesner; Canavan (n 30) 119.
8 *Alfred v Bai* (n 691) [22].
9 Roskill LJ in *Cehave* (n 126) 71.

DOI: 10.4324/9781003466130-4

## 4.2 Identifying Contractual Descriptions

Commercial transactions are generally rooted in self-interest, which gives rise to statements aimed at luring buyers into binding contracts.[10] Accordingly, a disputed statement can be categorised either as a 'contractual term,' creating a binding promise and permitting the claim of misdescription,[11] or as mere 'representations,' 'puffery' or 'opinion,' without legal effects when breached. Therefore, classification of the disputed descriptive statement is an initial critical measure, which depends on many factors: **first**, contractual formalism, the parties' intentions and the pre/post-contractual phase and **secondly**, the buyer's contractual interest and reliance on the disputed description.

### *4.2.1 Identifying Contractual Descriptions Through Contractual Formalism, Parties' Intentions and Pre/Post-Contractual Phase*

Phrasing the descriptive statement in contracts assist interpreters in identifying their legal power. Identifying the parties' intended meaning of these phrases is also crucial. In other situations, the contractual descriptions may not be comprehensive and comprehensible. Hence, negotiations and subsequent information may play a role in formulating the goods' descriptions in the contract.

#### *4.2.1.1 CISG*

##### 4.2.1.1.1 FORMALISM

Articulating descriptive statements in the contract precisely and attaching importance to them may change the legal outcome.

*4.2.1.1.1.1 Concreteness/Definitude of Descriptive Statement* General, unrealistic and elusive[12] statements might not suffice as contractual descriptions under Article 35(1).[13] For example, clearly stating a machine's power could reasonably constitute a term, more so than a comparable statement claiming that the machine is the best ever made.[14] In *Miami Valley Paper v Lebbing Engineering & Consulting*, stating that 'the machines just got out on to the market and those are a very good deal. The owner is selling them because of bankrubsy [sic]' was simply considered an opinion not constituting an obligatory term in the contract.[15] Likewise, the statement that the 'equipment was high quality and state-of-the-art' was also

10 Clayton Gillette; Steven Walt, *The UN Convention on Contracts for the International Sale of Goods: Practice and Theory* (2nd edn, CUP 2016) 215.

11 ibid 215, 216.

12 New Zealand case: *Easterbrook v Hopkins [1918] NZLR 428*, 442.

13 Saidov (n 769) 33.

14 Gillette; Walt (n 778) 218.

15 *Miami Valley Paper v Lebbing Engineering & Consulting* (26/3/2009) 1:05-CV-00702 (Federal District Court Ohio) <http://cisgw3.law.pace.edu/cases/090326u1.html>.

deemed, in *Mansonville Plastics v Kurtz GmbH*, 'too general and too difficult to measure in order to constitute a contractual [term].'[16] Additionally, the tribunal in the *Down jacket and winter coat case* did not take the attribute 'European style' for the sold jackets into consideration to assess conformity when the buyer failed to establish 'an objective, internationally recognised definition of "European style."'[17]

Conversely, statements which are meaningful, provable and concrete are considered contractual descriptions under Article 35(1).[18] When it was agreed to sell 'SUPRO Food Shaper free from genetically modified soy' in the *Soy protein products case*,[19] it was a provable description and should have been adhered to. But the seller delivered goods contaminated with genetically modified organisms (GMO) and claimed that the possible test for the absence of GMO was limited and 'impossible to be proven at the time of the conclusion of the contract, and hardly worthy of consideration due to its small amount.' The seller also claimed that when the soy was harvested, there were no concerns about GMO products. The court held the seller liable for a fundamental breach because in the first quarter of 1997, when the goods were delivered, it was illegal to import GMO products even when contamination was peripheral, but as of June 1997, GMO-soy was permitted to be imported to and sold in Switzerland.

Definite descriptions would be promissory even if they were not ordinarily stipulated. In the *Packaging machine case*, when the buyer ordered a machine, requesting a 'production line with an output of 180 units per minute' without objection from the seller, although only 'an output of not more than 127 units per minute' (which the machine met) was normally possible, the court held the seller responsible for committing a fundamental breach.[20]

Despite the foregoing, the following general statements were held to be part of the contract: '[T]he machinery would provide trouble-free, simple, reliable performance and be easy to operate'[21] and the machine is "good-as-new."[22]

*4.2.1.1.1.2 Articulating the Reason for the Description's Importance* It could be argued that there is no literal adherence to every description under CISG unless a term is emphasised by stating in the contract that a descriptive statement is important;[23] this may not only convert the statement into a binding clause[24] but also

16 *Mansonville Plastics v Kurtz GmbH* (21/8/2003) C993594 (British Columbia Supreme Court Canada) <http://www.unilex.info/cisg/case/1168>.

17 *Down jacket and winter coat case* (22/3/1995) CISG/1995/05 (CIETAC Arbitration proceeding) <http://cisgw3.law.pace.edu/cases/950322c1.html>.

18 Saidov (n 769) 33.

19 *Soy protein products case* (22/8/2003) 33/2002/SAS/so (Canton Appellate Court Basel) <http://cisgw3.law.pace.edu/cases/030822s1.html>.

20 *Packaging machine case* 26/9/2008 (n 677).

21 *Mansonville v Kurtz* (n 784) [101].

22 *CNC machine case* (21/2/2005) C1 04 162 (Appellate Court Valais/Wallis) <http://cisgw3.law.pace.edu/cases/050221s1.html>.

23 Schwenzer, *Commentary on CISG* (n 15) 428, 429 [21];[22];[23]; 431 [27].

24 Saidov (n 769) 37.

constitute a fundamental breach when not adhered to[25] because the seller could have foreseen the detriments suffered by the buyer resulting from the breach.[26] This is in contrast to the case of not attaching importance to such a description.[27] Moreover, each party might have to reveal their motivation for signing the contract at the time of conclusion.[28] Therefore, although there was a promise to provide goods of a certain origin in the *Cobalt sulphate case*, providing goods of a different origin did not constitute a fundamental breach on the basis that the essentiality of the term was not accentuated.[29] Some scholars find that the seller should be obliged to fulfil a contractual term of essence precisely, irrespective of the reason for such importance,[30] leading directly to a fundamental breach.

###### 4.2.1.1.2 PARTIES' INTENTIONS

Interpreting the contract is vital to ascertaining the descriptions the seller must adhere to,[31] relying primarily on 'what the contracting parties actually did agree upon.'[32] Thus, '[w]hen the parties' express agreement does not seem to define the contractual requirements of the goods, it is clear that such requirements should be read from the circumstances.'[33] Accordingly, unclear or implicit descriptions should be interpreted pursuant to a binary hierarchy:

**First**, finding goods' specifications which reflect the parties' *common intention*[34] and their purpose of the agreement. In the *Used automobiles case*, when the delivered vehicles suffered from scratches and a lack of components despite a stipulation in the contract that the cars should be 'in perfect mobile condition,' the court did not deem the latter phrase to reflect the parties' real intentions as the defects were the result of normal operation in the cars' previous utilisation, which was referred to in the contract.[35] Furthermore, in *Mitias v Solidea Srl*, the court construed the seller's admission of liability and their offer to replace the goods as a concession that the nonconformity could not be removed, and such a replacement was not possible without causing unreasonable inconvenience to the buyer,

25 Schlechtriem, *Commentary on CISG* (n 132) 147; Naude; Lubbe (n 146) 377, 378; Ferrari, 'Fundamental Breach' (n 161) 498; Schwenzer, *Commentary on CISG* (n 15) 419 [4]; 428 [21].

26 Flechtner, 'Transcript of a Workshop on the Sales Convention' (n 550) 254; Schwenzer, *Commentary on CISG* (n 15) 436 [36].

27 Comments by Governments and International Organizations (n 330) 113; Official Records (n 149) 12th Meeting 297; Bianca; Bonell (n 155) 217.

28 *FCF v Adriafil* (n 144).

29 *Cobalt sulphate case* 3/4/1996 (n 547).

30 Schwenzer, *Commentary on CISG* (n 15) 431, 432 [28].

31 Saidov (n 769) 30.

32 Poikela (n 83) 10.

33 Maley (n 186) 110.

34 ibid 111.

35 *Used automobiles case* (17/1/2008) 81/2001 (Supreme Court Spain) <http://cisgw3.law.pace.edu/cases/080117s4.html>.

making the breach fundamental.[36] **Secondly**, in the absence of a common intention, such as when a statement was considered sarcasm, humour or exaggeration by the seller but understood as a genuine promise by a non-native buyer according to their cultural and linguistic background,[37] the usual meaning of this statement should be according to *the understanding of a reasonable person* in the buyer's place,[38] considering '*all* relevant circumstances of the case.'[39] In *Sergueev Handelsagentur v DAT-SCHAUB*, it was held that 'Latin designation' was a part of the contract, especially according to previous practices between the parties,[40] and this revealed a reasonable person's understanding.

#### 4.2.1.1.3 IMPACT OF PRE- AND POST-CONTRACTUAL PHASE ON DESCRIPTIONS

*4.2.1.1.3.1 Impact of Negotiations on Contractual Descriptions* Some jurists find that negotiations can have a role in identifying the required descriptions, while others believe the contrary.

a. Negotiations Create Descriptions Not Mentioned in the Contract The goods' descriptions are not confined to those articulated in the contract but could include those that occur prior to concluding the contract,[41] meaning that the reading of descriptions should be consistent with the contractual circumstances, pursuant to Article 8(3).[42] Additionally, based on Article 11, description 'may be proven by any means,' which may make explicit verbal statements articulated throughout negotiations a part of description.[43] This approach was followed in *Mitchell Aircraft Spares v European Aircraft Service*, in which negotiations played a role in determining the description,[44] and in *Brown & Root v Aerotech Herman Nelson*, when brochures mentioned that the goods were new, but the seller sent used ones.[45] Similarly, in the *Milling equipment case*, when the pro forma invoice and letter of credit which were served prior to the contract conclusion mentioned that the goods would be manufactured in Germany, the seller was held liable for sending goods originating in Turkey and Russia.[46]

36 *Mitias v Solidea S.r.l.* (11/12/2008) n.2280/2007 (Tribunale di Forli District Court) <http://cisgw3.law.pace.edu/cases/081211i3.html>.
37 Gillette; Walt (n 778) 218.
38 Poikela (n 83) 10, 11.
39 CISG Art. 8(2)&(3); Gillette; Walt (n 778) 218, 219.
40 *Dr S Serguee v Handelsagentur v DAT-SCHAUB A/S* (31/1/2002) H-0126–98 (Copenhagen Maritime Commercial Court) <http://cisgw3.law.pace.edu/cases/020131d1.html>.
41 Poikela (n 83) 19.
42 Maley (n 186) 110.
43 Poikela (n 83) 19.
44 *Mitchell Aircraft Spares v European Aircraft Service* (27/10/1998) 97 C 5668 (Federal District Court Illinois) <http://cisgw3.law.pace.edu/cases/981027u1.html>.
45 CISG Art. 8(2); *Brown & Root v Aerotech Herman Nelson* (4/5/2004) MBCA 63 (Court of Appeal of Manitoba) <http://www.unilex.info/cisg/case/1009> [iv]; [vi]; [xiii]; [xiii].
46 *Milling equipment case* (2/2/2004) 7 U 4/03 (Appellate Court Zweibrücken) <http://cisgw3.law.pace.edu/cases/040202g1.html>.

b. Negotiations Cannot Create Descriptions Not Mentioned in the Contract Other jurists find that descriptive statements mentioned outside the contract and within the preliminary negotiation phase should not interfere with the descriptions within the contract, referred to by Article 35(1).[47] In the *Steel cylinders case*, it was stated that negotiations were not binding unless otherwise indicated.[48] Likewise, in the *Textile manufacturing equipment case*, the machine's description in the contract was considered, but the bid's title was not.[49]

According to a literal interpretation of Article 8(3), 'statements and conduct during the pre-contractual phase will not per se create legal obligations but will aid the interpreter to better understanding of the extent of the latter.'[50] This interpretative role of the negotiations was applied in *Gantry v Research Consulting Marketing* when the industry standards were acknowledged and written in bold letters in the seller's offer, making them a part of the goods' description when they were referred to repeatedly during the negotiations.[51]

*4.2.1.1.3.2 Impact of Subsequent Information on Contractual Descriptions* At one CISG conference, the British and Portuguese delegates suggested the referral of the seller's foreseeability of the detriment caused by their breach mentioned in Article 25 to 'the time when the contract was concluded,'[52] and some authors find this referral decisive[53] because, at that time, the situation was apparent to the seller,[54] and the parties' interests were clear.[55] However, Article 25 does not specify when the breaching seller or the reasonable person can predict the result of the breach,[56] unlike Article 74, which deals with damages and specifies the moment at which the foreseeability occurs[57] to be 'at the time of the conclusion of the contract.' Article 74's approach might be used[58] as a general principle to fill the gap of the foreseeability time in Article 25. Consequently, a judge may ignore any facts or information provided after this point, especially as it may be found that (according to the literal wording of Article 8(3)) subsequent information

47 Villyde Luca, 'The Conformity of the Goods to the Contract in International Sales' (2015) 27(1) Pace Int Law Rev 163, 186.
48 *Steel cylinders case* (19/1/2000) CISG/2000/08 (CIETAC arbitration proceeding) <http://cisgw3.law.pace.edu/cases/000119c1.html>.
49 *Textile manufacturing equipment case* (18/7/2002) CISG/2002/20 (CIETAC arbitration proceeding) <https://cisgw3.law.pace.edu/cases/020718c1.html>.
50 Luca (n 815) 186.
51 *Gantry v Research Consulting Marketing* (19/9/1995) 1707/93 (District Court Nivelles) <http://cisgw3.law.pace.edu/cases/950919b1.html>.
52 Official Records (n 149) 12th Meeting 76.
53 Ferrari, 'Fundamental Breach' (n 161) 499; Martin; Snyder (n 67) 367.
54 *Shoes case* 24/4/1997 (n 303).
55 Schwenzer, *Commentary on CISG* (n 15) 434, 435 [33].
56 Bianca; Bonell (n 155) 220; Kritzer (n 751) 205.
57 Enderlein; Maskow (n 150) 115.
58 Kröll; Mistelis; Viscasillas (n 67) 344 [20].

does not directly influence the contractual descriptions, but their role is confined to interpreting the contract though recognising the parties' intents and a reasonable person's understanding.

At the 12th meeting of the UN Conference, the Hungarian[59] and Danish[60] representatives advocated leaving the time of foreseeability to the court or tribunal in order to maintain flexibility[61] as every case has its own attributes and relevant information.[62] Therefore, other jurists may object to the recourse to Article 74 to fill the gap of a foreseeability time in Article 25 as they address different issues.[63] The absence of a foreseeability time was not 'an inadvertent omission'[64] as CISG intended to pave the way for information agreed after the contract conclusion[65] and to prevent the breaching seller from claiming their lack of knowledge of the breach's consequences on the buyer, even though they may have been given the information after the contract conclusion.[66] Thus, subsequent descriptive information, mentioned neither in the contract nor in its appendixes but rather sent in a separate document,[67] may constitute a part of the contract, clarifying the desired descriptions.[68] A reasonable person can measure whether this subsequent data should be considered and whether the buyer has provided such a statement at a time when it is likely to be implemented on a case-by-case basis.[69]

Irrespective of subsequent radical changes to the contract, such as changing the goods' type from flour to rice, which would need the seller's acceptance,[70] if the changes are minor, they are probably effective on their dispatch according to Article 27. However, the issue is not simple as it is sometimes difficult to decide whether the subsequent information is considered a radical change or not, such as altering the goods' colour, which could be a major change in some cases but not in others. When the description agreed upon in the contract was emphasised at a later time by the buyer, indicating that they wish to stick firmly to the agreed

59 Official Records (n 149) 12th Meeting 298.

60 ibid 297.

61 UN, *Commentary on the Draft Convention on Contracts for the International Sale of Goods prepared by the Secretariat* (UN DOC. A/CONF. 97/5 1978) <www.cisg-online.ch/index.cfm?pageID=644#Article23> accessed 16/7/2018.

62 Babiak (n 57) 123, 124.

63 Dessemontet (n 170) 218; *Shen* (n 131) footnote 25.

64 ibid *Shen*.

65 ibid; Bianca; Bonell (n 155) 215; Schlechtriem, *Commentary on CISG* (n 132) 176.

66 For a similar meaning see Enderlein; Maskow (n 150) 116; Bridge, 'Avoidance for Fundamental Breach' (n 158) 918; Kröll; Mistelis; Viscasillas (n 67) 344 [21]; Jason Chuah, *Law of International Trade* (6th edn, Sweet & Maxwell 2019) 210 [5–022].

67 Unavailable name (6/6/2003) 97/2002 (Arbitration proceeding Russia) <http://cisgw3.law.pace.edu/cases/030606r1.html>.

68 Saidov (n 769) 41.

69 Bianca; Bonell (n 155) 220; Grebler, 'Fundamental Breach' (n 48) 413.

70 CISG Art. 29; Art. 18(1).

description due to, for instance, their own buyers' needs, this would likely make a breach fundamental if it were communicated to the seller within a reasonable time. The foreseeability criterion would have been met even if the letter emphasising a contractual description had not reached the seller owing to its loss in the post,[71] as Article 27 places the risk of transmitting any notice on the addressee.

### *4.2.1.2 SGA*

#### 4.2.1.2.1 FORMALISM

Regarding descriptive statements as 'conditions' may depend on the following formal factors:

*4.2.1.2.1.1 Descriptive Statement's Layout and Words* The layout and typography of the statement might play a great role in deciding whether the descriptive statement falls within s.13 or not.[72] It fell within s.13 in *Tradax Export v European Grain & Shipping* when there was no 'typographical change' to render it less important.[73] As Lord Hodson stated in *Ashington*, writing the words 'NORWEGIAN HERRING MEAL' in uppercase was enough to satisfy the requirement of description,[74] and per Viscount Dilhorne in *Reardon Smith v Hansen-Tangen*, using the word 'called' or 'known' before the goods' number and name was a clear sign that they were not intended to be part of the contract but a method of identifying them.[75] This approach, however, may not necessarily be followed in all cases. In *Savage v Blakney*, when purchasing a boat with an 'estimated speed of fifteen m.p.h.,' the trial judge found that the word 'estimated' was equivalent to 'approximate' according to the dictionary, and this made the disputed clause an expression of expectancy rather than an unequivocal promise. However, the Supreme Court found that the trial judge's interpretation was an 'unwarranted substitution which stripped the words of the letter of their most significant meaning.'[76]

*4.2.1.2.1.2 Generality/Conciseness of Descriptive Statement* Excessive and preposterous commendation and vague, extravagant descriptive words extolling the goods do not normally form a basis for liability.[77] Stating that a horse was

71 Bianca; Bonell (n 155) 217.
72 McKendrick, *Sale of Goods* (n 202) 334.
73 *Tradax v European Grain* (n 422) 104, 105.
74 *Ashington Piggeries Ltd v Christopher Hill Ltd* [1972] AC 441, 470.
75 *Reardon v Hansen-Tangen* (n 417) 1000, 1001.
76 Australian case: *JJ Savage v Blakney* (1970) 119 CLR 435, 441, 442.
77 Pigott B; Martin B in Osborn v Hart (1871) 23 LT 1 851, 853; Oscar *Chess Ltd v Williams* [1957] 1 WLR 370; Bridge, *Benjamin's* (n 28) [10–001]; [10–002].

'perfectly sound in every respect'[78] and a 'shipment [would] be made in good condition'[79] were not considered promissory terms.

The buyer enjoys greater protection when descriptions are precise,[80] as Lord Hoffmann stressed in *Union Eagle*; generalisations and undefined descriptions are rejected at the expense of practical business considerations.[81] Therefore, the 'maximum 7.5% fibre (sic)' clause was formulated precisely to deem it a description,[82] and the phrase 'free from foreign and extraneous matter' means absolutely 'free from . . .'[83] As Lord Atkin emphasised in *Arcos*, '[I]f the written contract specifies conditions of weight, measurement and the like, those conditions must be complied with.'[84]

However, the following general statements were all considered part of descriptions, entitling the buyer to terminate the contract when they were breached: 'Piano . . . good tone, good order, looks as new';[85] 'there was nothing wrong' with the heifer;[86] the minicab was in 'excellent mechanical condition';[87] and 'a good little bus. I would stake my life on it. You will have no trouble with it.'[88] Moreover, the word 'normal' when selling 'normal Russian gasoil,' in *Marimpex v Louis Dreyfus* was considered a part of description on the basis that it added an attribute to 'Russian gasoil.'[89]

On the other hand, 'generality' standards could be unduly resorted to. In *Walker v Milner*, a safe bore a plate declaring it 'Picklock-Proof,' and the seller's manager stressed that it was 'thief-proof' and 'nothing can break into that safe' when the buyer insisted on asking about its suitability to leave valuable items in. When a burglar opened the safe with ease, it was held that the 'thief-proof' statement was a mere representation and could not raise the seller's liability.[90]

*4.2.1.2.1.3 Descriptions Might Not Include Quality* 'Quality' is not included in 'descriptions' under SGA.[91] Thus, the fact that goods are not commercially identical does not necessarily constitute a 'condition'[92] on which to base a termination, but the

78 Hopkins v Tanqueray (1854) 139 ER 369.
79 *Cehave* (n 126) 45.
80 *Tradax v European Grain* (n 422) 104, 105; Pistis (n 26) 4; 'United Arab Emirates: Sale by Description - Interpretation and Ambiguities' (19/2/2018) Mondaq Business Briefing, 2; Bridge, *Benjamin's* (n 28) [10–005].
81 *Union Eagle v Golden Achievement* (n 406) 519.
82 *Tradax v European Grain* (n 422) 104, 105.
83 *Hazlewood Grocery Ltd v Lion Foods Ltd* [2007] EWHC 1887 (QB) [181].
84 *Arcos v Ronaasen* (n 422) 479.
85 New Zealand case: *Turner v Anquetil* [1953] NZLR 952.
86 Harling v Eddy [1951] 2 KB 739.
87 Porter v General Guarantee Corp [1982] RTR 384, 385.
88 *Andrews v Hopkinson* [1957] 1 QB 229.
89 *Marimpex Mineralol Handels GmbH v Louis Dreyfus et Cie Mineralol GmbH* [1995] 1 Lloyd's Rep. 167.
90 Walker v Milner (1866) 176 ER 773.
91 Montedison SpA v Icroma SpA [1980] 1 WLR 48.
92 *Proton Energy Group SA v Orlen Lietuva* [2013] EWHC 2872 (Comm) [58].

goods could just be of poor quality.[93] Contractual quality should be assessed under the implied condition of s.14(2), which is a relatively low threshold in comparison to description. It was stated in *Proton Energy Group v Orlen Lietuva*: 'The parties are always free to make quality a condition of the deal but, unlike description, it is not implied by statute.'[94] When the buyer did not purchase the goods until they knew their specifications, it was an indication that these specifications were categorised as 'quality' rather than 'description.'[95]

The location of the goods' characteristics could determine their classification, as in *Grain Trade v Feed Factors International*, a stipulation of the fibre content, appearing under the 'Specifications' heading in the contract rather than 'Descriptions,' made the stipulation a matter of 'quality.'[96] Furthermore, in *Tradax Export*, a phrase was considered a description because, inter alia, it appeared before the quantity and quality clauses.[97] In *Osborn v Hart*, too, 'Superior old port' was promissory according to the wording of the clause and where it appeared, although it was not a known term in the wine trade.[98]

Sometimes functional characteristics are not a part of 'description' but a part of 'quality,' such as stating that the food purchased should be suitable for babies.[99] In *Gill v Berger*, although it was agreed that *white* Bolita beans would be supplied, it was held that the goods containing a 'commercially significant number of coloured beans, and show[ing] signs of infestation' did not affect their description as Bolita beans but only made the goods of poor quality.[100]

*4.2.1.2.1.4 Emphasis on Descriptive Detail* A descriptive representation can be directly converted to a 'condition' when the parties attribute importance to it[101] even without explaining the purpose of the purchase. In *Arcos*, the contract allowed variation in the length and breadth of staves but not in their thickness.[102] This emphasis on thickness might automatically make the term a description. In *Bannerman v White*, the buyer wanted to procure un-sulphured hops and stated verbally that they would not have enquired about the price if this particular product had not been available.[103] The seller responded that 'there was no mould this year, and therefore no occasion to use any sulphur.' When un-sulphured hops mixed with sulphured hops were delivered,[104] the court found that the assertion that sulphur was not to be used made it a 'condition.'[105] When the importance of a term is not

93 *Arcos v Ronaasen* (n 422) 470.
94 *Proton Energy v Orlen* (n 860) [60].
95 ibid [58]; [59]; [60]; [64].
96 *RG Grain Trade LLP (UK) v Feed Factors International* [2011] EWHC 1889 (Comm) [41].
97 *Tradax v European Grain* (n 422) 104, 105.
98 *Osborn v Hart* (n 845) 852.
99 Bridge, *Benjamin's* (n 28) [11–017].
100 Gill & Duffus v Berger [1984] AC 382.
101 Poikela (n 83) 27; Peel, 15th edn (n 64) 983, 984 [18–045].
102 *Arcos v Ronaasen* (n 422) 480.
103 *Bannerman v White* 142 ER 685, 686.
104 ibid.
105 ibid.

defined by the parties, a court may discover its impact by asking whether the clause is an important part of the contract, and if the answer is affirmative, the court is likely to hold it as a 'condition.'[106] However, requiring proof of the essentiality of a descriptive statement might undermine the clarifying aim of s.13 and its role in removing the need to demonstrate the importance of each contractual description.[107]

#### 4.2.1.2.2 GOODS' IDENTITY

Interpreting vague descriptions of varied meanings and assessing descriptive statements in the contract to be either 'contractual promises' or 'representations' could be pursuant to **first**, the commercial purpose of the contract;[108] **secondly**, their business sense[109] and ordinary meaning[110] 'as a matter of dictionaries and grammar,'[111] ignoring 'subjective evidence of any party's intentions';[112] or **finally**, a reasonable person's behaviour and understanding[113] if they were placed in the parties' situation,[114] 'using the language in the contract.'[115]

Some jurists find that descriptive statements are intended to be promissory and should be treated strictly as 'conditions' when they constitute a substantial ingredient of the goods' 'identity,'[116] such as its grade,[117] geographical origin or type.[118] These descriptions do not clarify 'which goods are being sold' but 'what the goods actually are,'[119] distinguishing 'them from other goods of the same general kind.'[120] In *Ashington*, it was stated that:

> [Descriptions are] confined to those words in the contract which were intended by the parties to identify the kind of goods which were to be supplied. . . . [T]heir failure to correspond with that part of what was said about

106 *Williams J in Behn v Burness* (1863) 122 ER 281, 282.

107 McKendrick, *Sale of Goods* (n 202) 324.

108 Lord Wilberforce in Reardon v Hansen-Tangen (n 417) 996; Lord Neuberger in *Arnold v Britton* [2015] UKSC 36 [15]. A similar meaning is found in *Freeman v Cooke* (1848) 154 ER 652, 653.

109 Lord Hoffmann in Investors Compensation Scheme v Bromwich (n 623) 912, 913.

110 Harlingdon and Leinster Enterprises Ltd v Christopher Hull Fine Art Ltd [1991] 1 QB 564, 584.

111 Investors Compensation Scheme v Bromwich (n 623) 912, 913.

112 Lord Neuberger in Arnold v Britton (n 876) [15]. See also *Freeman v Cooke* (n 876) 652, 653.

113 *Smith v Hughes* (1870–71) LR 6 QB 597; McKendrick, *Sale of Goods* (n 202) 320. See also Cartwright (n 114) 64.

114 Lord Wilberforce in *Reardon v Hansen-Tangen* (n 417) 996.

115 ibid; Lord Neuberger in *Arnold v Britton* (n 876) [15]. See also *Oscar Chess v Williams* [1957] 1 All ER 325, 328.

116 *Couchman v Hill* [1947] KB 554; *Ashington v Christopher* (n 842) 450; Lord Wilberforce in *Reardon v Hansen-Tangen* (n 417) 998.

117 In the contract, it was agreed that 'fine-ground meal' would be sent, thus the sending of 'coarse-ground meal' instead meant the goods were of a different grade. *Toepfer v Warinco AG* [1978] 2 Lloyd's Rep 569.

118 Bridge, *The Sale of Goods* (n 28) [7.29].

119 Twigg-Flesner; Canavan (n 30) 122.

120 Lord Diplock in *Gill v Berger* (n 880) 393.

> them in the contract makes them goods of a different kind from [those agreed upon].[121]

In *Taylor v Combined Buyers,* goods' identity was also defined as

> the class of things to which it belongs [such as selling stone as being ruby or a car as being *Ford*]. . . . Any descriptive statement so far as it goes beyond this and relates to the quality, state, [commendatory statements] or other unessential attributes of the thing sold is inoperative . . . unless on the true construction of the contract it was intended by the parties to constitute an express condition.[122]

Therefore, the clause that a soybean meal should possess 'maximum 7.5% fibre (sic)' was uncommon in the UK, making its inclusion in the contract a part of the goods' identity and evidence of the parties' intention to depart from common practice.[123] With 'butter containing a very small amount of arsenic . . . still remains butter,' misdescription might not arise,[124] but it arises when rendering scratched[125] or used cars in contrast to the agreement to sell 'new cars.'[126]

Conversely, descriptive words by which 'the goods can be identified by the buyer'[127] can be, as Lord Wilberforce stated, 'construed much more liberally than they would have to be construed if they were providing essential elements of the description,'[128] depending on whether the breach of these words goes to the root of the contract or not.[129] In *Reardon v Yngvar*, the court stated that it was clear that the name, the number and the specific company earmarked to build the goods with which the goods would be labelled had no particular importance for the parties but was only a means to identify them, which made the tendered goods those contracted for.[130]

However, confining the description to the words relating to the goods' identity may be undesirable[131] because this approach is abstract and general[132] and may give the description a very high threshold, changing the status, meaning and the straightforwardness of s.13. It might be difficult to predict whether sending

121 Lord Diplock in *Ashington v Christopher* (n 842) 503.
122 New Zealand case: *Taylor v Combined Buyers Ltd* [1924] GLR 51, 54, 55, 58, 59, 61.
123 *Tradax v European Grain* (n 422) 104, 105.
124 *Ashington v Christopher* (n 842) 450.
125 *Cehave* (n 126) 62, 63.
126 *Andrews Bros v Singer* [1934] 1 KB 17.
127 Lord Guest in *Ashington v Christopher* (n 842) 475. See also Lord Wilberforce in *Reardon v Hansen-Tangen* (n 417) 999.
128 ibid.
129 Bridge, *The Sale of Goods* (n 28) [7.29].
130 *Reardon v Hansen-Tangen* (n 417) 989, 991, 1000, 1001.
131 McKendrick, *Sale of Goods* (n 202) 341, 342.
132 ibid 330.

Swedish herring meal instead of Norwegian[133] makes it another kind. A description could be insignificant in relation to the goods' identity but still might be considered a description. In *Macpherson*, the courts held that the words 'afloat per S.S. Morton Bay due London' were part of the goods' description, entitling the buyer to reject them,[134] even though the words only identified the ship on which the goods were being transported.

#### 4.2.1.2.3 IMPACT OF PRE- AND POST-CONTRACTUAL PHRASES ON DESCRIPTIONS

*4.2.1.2.3.1 Statements Outside the Contract Do Not Delimit Descriptions* For the sake of attaining clarity, descriptive details mentioned in negotiations but not in a contract may not be a part of a description and may not play a role in contractual interpretation.[135] This is unless these details are later mentioned in writing as they are then evidence that the parties intended to include them as contractual terms.[136] Slade LJ, in *Harlingdon*, asserted that the contract could be 'sale of description' only when including the commodities' attributes in the contract.[137] Lord Gifford, in *Chartbrook*, also stated that the formal written deed determined the parties' real agreement, which made the court duty bound to confine its focus to that deed, setting aside 'all loose and preliminary negotiations,' which would normally be long and desultory discussions.[138] This is to preserve 'the integrity of written contracts by refusing to allow the admission of oral statements or previous correspondence to contradict the written agreement.'[139] Similarly, it was held in *Proton v Orlen Lietuva* that specifications attached to the offer in an email were not considered actionable representations of facts but merely a warranty to possess these specifications because the buyer relied on the contractual rather than the pre-contractual statements.[140] Thus, in *Harrison v Knowles*, when the ship's dead-weight capacity of 460 tons was stated in memorandum preliminary to the contract, it was not part of description, and when the capacity was only 360 tons, the seller was not held liable.[141] Some scholars go further, stating that descriptive words representing the preliminary negotiations mentioned in the contract[142] are not contractual terms and do not

133 ibid 341, 342.
134 *Macpherson Train v Howard Ross* [1955] 1 WLR 640.
135 *Investors Compensation Scheme v Bromwich* (n 623) 897.
136 *Oscar v Williams* (n 845) 329.
137 Harlingdon v Christopher (n 878) 584.
138 *Chartbrook Ltd v Persimmon Homes Ltd* [2009] UKHL 38 [29].
139 Larry DiMatteo, *International Contracting: Law and Practice* (4th edn, Kluwer Law International 2016) [7.06].
140 *Proton Energy v Orlen* (n 860) [60];[64]; [58];[59].
141 *T&J Harrison v Knowles* [1918] 1 KB 608.
142 Furmston (n 30) 177, 178.

allow the rejection of goods.[143] Others permit recourse to negotiations only in the absence of a formal contract.[144]

*4.2.1.2.3.2 Resorting to Statements Outside the Contract to Interpret Descriptions* The role of prior negotiations or subsequent conduct in interpreting a descriptive term and revealing the parties' intentions could be limited.[145] This is because the parties 'do not record the consensus at the moment when contractual responsibility crystallises'[146] as they might have used different and unclear statements with no agreement outside the contract, which cannot construe contractual phrases.[147] Thus, '[t]here is presently no direct recourse to post-contractual conduct as an aid for construction under English law.'[148] The main factors, therefore, on which interpretation of the contract would depend, are its 'textualism and contextualism.'[149]

However, Nicholls opposes the notion that 'pre-contract negotiations would promote uncertainty and unpredictability in dispute resolution,'[150] especially when they convey clear meaning about the disputed matter. Uncertainty could instead be created when excluding them.[151] Therefore, strict limitations to contract boundaries could be sacrificed by looking at the whole relationship[152] for 'an action for rectification,'[153] especially in extreme cases where the contract is a 'dead letter' or might convey incorrect meaning.[154] Accordingly, Lord Wilberforce, in *Prenn v Simmonds*, stated that 'we must . . . inquire beyond the language and see what the circumstances were with reference to which words were used, and the object, appearing from those circumstances, which the person using them had in view.'[155] Lord Hodge in *Wood v Capita Insurance Services* also asserted: 'The court's task is to ascertain the objective meaning of the language which the parties have chosen to express their agreement.' He continued:

> [T]his is not a literalist exercise focused solely on a parsing of the wording of the particular clause. . . . [T]he court must consider the contract as a

143 McKendrick, *Sale of Goods* (n 202) 319.

144 Lord Phillips in *MSC Mediterranean Shipping Co SA v Polish Ocean Lines* (The Tychy) [2001] EWCA Civ 1198 [29].

145 *Shore v Wilson* 8 ER 450, 532, 533.

146 Gerard Mcmeel, 'Prior Negotiations and Subsequent Conduct: The Next Step Forward for Contractual Interpretation?' (2003) 119 LQR 272, 276, 277.

147 *Prenn v Simmonds* [1971] 1 WLR 1381, 1384, 1385.

148 Vsevolod Mazurenko, *Interpretation of Contracts* (LAMBERT 2013) 18.

149 Wood v Capita Insurance Services Ltd [2017] UKSC 24.

150 Donald Nicholls, 'My Kingdom for a Horse: The Meaning of Words' (2005) 121 LQR 577, 587.

151 ibid.

152 Lord Halsbury in *Glynn v Margetson* & Co [1893] AC 351, 357.

153 Investors Compensation Scheme v Bromwich (n 623) 912.

154 Shore v Wilson (n 913) 533.

155 *Prenn v Simmonds* (n 915) 1384.

whole . . . [giving] more or less weight to elements of the wider context in reaching its view as to that objective meaning.[156]

#### *4.2.1.3 KLaw*

Misdescription can be claimed when the 'assured description' is breached. There is a gap in law, literature and even in case law about the precise meaning of 'assured description.' EMKCIC stated the following:

> The seller is obligated to hand over the commodity with the description agreed in the contract . . . The buyer may request termination with compensation . . . due to the lack of availability of the description that the seller had assured in the commodity.[157]

##### 4.2.1.3.1 FORMALISM: CLEAR PHRASING OF CONTRACTUAL DESCRIPTION PRESUMES SELLER'S ASSURANCE

Article 193(1) KCIC states: 'If the term of the contract is clear, it is not permissible to deviate from its meaning by interpreting it to identify the parties' will.'[158] This notion is ingrained even in Al-Majalla, as it states: 'It is not permissible to resort to research and analysis in the context of [clear and explicit] text [in the contract].'[159] Thus, the fact that the contract possesses a clear descriptive detail means that it must be delivered with precision,[160] reflecting an explicit, or even implicit, intention of the parties.[161] This contractual description therefore does not need the judge's intervention to determine the parties' common will to consider it either a term or a phrase holding no importance. The judge will have to take its apparent meaning without deviating from it, as there is no justification for interpretation in the existence of the text.[162] This clarity of description might consider it directly 'assured' by the seller, permitting the buyer to terminate the contract in case of misdescription.[163] The seller cannot avoid this obligation on the grounds that the missing description is not integral to the goods.[164] As Article 196 KCIC

156 Wood v Capita (n 917) [10].

157 EMKCIC 437.

158 Case 4/6/2006 Appellate Court/Commercial 2899/2005, 4, 5; Case 7/11/2006 Court of Cassation/Commercial 772/2004, 8; Case 3/10/2011 Court of Cassation/Civil 783/2010, 3.

159 Al-Majalla Art. 14.

160 Case 25/6/1990 Court of Cassation/Commercial 62/90 in Ministry of Justice, Commercial Provisions (n 259); Ayob (n 494) 64 footnote 66.

161 Case 14/6/1993 (n 499) 322; Al-Ahwany (n 497) 724, 730; Al-Defery; Al-Sayrafy (n 254) 367.

162 EMKCIC 207.

163 Stark states: '[E]st établi par cela seul que le résultat promis n'a pas été fourni.' Boris Starck, *Droit Civil Obligations* (Librairies Techniques 1972) 612, 613.

164 Al-Ahwany (n 497) 730; Al-Defery; Al-Sayrafy (n 254) 367.

states, the contract is considered the law of the parties,[165] and failure to meet the descriptions may lead to termination.[166]

This is especially true when a description is clearly expressed in writing. Although there is no obligation to record a commercial agreement in writing,[167] pursuant to Quranic verse: '[D]o not consume one another's wealth unjustly but only [in lawful] business by *mutual* consent,'[168] there is strong religious preference to solidify the agreement in writing stated in the Quran: '[R]ecord it in writing'[169] and:

> Do not show slackness in writing down the transaction. . . . That is fairest in the sight of God, more suitable as evidence, and more convenient to prevent doubts among yourselves.[170]

This importance of writing, moreover, makes every clear description mentioned in the contract an 'assured description.'

##### 4.2.1.3.2 DEDUCTION OF SELLERS' ASSURANCE FROM PARTIES' COMMON INTENTION

The parties' common intention may determine the status of the disputed description to be assured, but investigating this intention is permitted only when the description is ambiguous in its connotation: for instance, when there is heterogeneity between the parties' will and the description's meaning, or the circumstances indicate that the parties misused the descriptive expression. Judges are directed through legislation in Article 193(2) KCIC, which states:

> If the description is ambiguous, it should be interpreted according to the parties' common intention derived from the total facts and circumstances of the contract conclusion without limitation to the mere meanings of words and phrases, and this could be done through the pursuit of the transaction's

165 Case 28/11/2001 (n 728) 4; Case 31/5/2004 (n 619) 4; Case 15/10/2006, 1250 (n 261) 6; Case 3/10/2011 (n 926) 3; Case 5/3/2012 Court of Cassation/Civil 435/2010, 3, 4. This was also mentioned in French Civil Code 1804 Art. 1134: '[C]onventions légalement formées tiennent lieu loi ceux qui ont faites,' which means that legally formed agreements are the law of the parties. See also Al-Sanhory (n 279) 697, 698; Al-Yaqob (n 52) 285.

166 Case 28/11/2001 (n 728) 2.

167 Law on Evidence of Civil and Commercial Provisions No. 39 1980 Art. 39 stipulates: 'In non-commercial Articles, if the deal exceeds the value of five hundred dinars or is undetermined, the testimony of the witnesses shall not be sufficient to prove its existence or its expiry unless there is an agreement or provision of otherwise.' This Article stabilises the freedom of proof principle in commercial transactions as the concept of disparity as it says 'in non-commercial Articles.' Thus, proof of commercial transactions can be all means of proof, including testimony, acknowledgement, presumption, oath, displaying business books, correspondence and invoices or oral telephone conversations.

168 The Quran, The Women 29.

169 The Quran, The Cow 282.

170 The Quran, Al-Imran 282.

nature, the current custom and the requirement of good faith and honourable dealing.[171]

The problem is that the evaluation of the degree of clarity or vagueness is assigned to the judge's discretion, as EMKCIC stated: 'The interpretation is ultimately a matter of art, taste, wit and experience.'[172] Furthermore, in many cases, the court of cassation has asserted that trial courts hold the absolute authority in understanding the reality of cases, to interpret contracts[173] and to derive facts reflecting the parties' common intention, relying on contractual circumstances, without the censorship of higher courts, as long as its interpretation does not deviate from the apparent meaning of the contractual terms, and its ruling is based on justified reasons.[174] This affirms that if a trial court identifies a common intention with reasonable foundations, this can prevent its ruling from being challenged for misapplication of law.[175]

However, the requirement of reasonable judgement based on justified reasons does not necessarily lead to a uniform application of the law. Entrusting interpretation to the judge without concrete standards may rely heavily on their subjective convictions, which cannot be known in advance. Demonstrably, in one case, the court used an additional criterion – namely identifying the desired purposes to be achieved – in order to find the common intention.[176]

According to Article 149(1) KCIC, if the judge suspects the parties' common intention or fails to extract it with certainty,[177] then vagueness should be interpreted for the benefit of the party who would be disadvantaged when applying such a term.[178] This means the seller's assurance of a persistently vague description should be interpreted according to the buyer's interest. This approach is based on a jurisprudential rule which states that carrying out a statement by finding its real or metaphorical meaning[179] is better than neglecting it.[180] In EMKCIC, however, it is stated that there are cases in which an obscure term has been interpreted against the buyer for performing the vague obligation,[181] impeding a uniform application of law.

There is no reference to objectivity being demonstrated by a reasonable person[182] to fill a gap in KLaw, and the question regarding whether this person would

171 EMKCIC 208. See also Case 29/3/1992 Court of Cassation/Commercial 233/90; Case 27/11/2000 Court of Cassation/Commercial 145/99 in Ministry of Justice, Commercial Provisions (n 259) 23.

172 EMKCIC 209.

173 Case 20/5/1998 (n 43) 3–5; Case 16/4/2012 Court of Cassation/Civil 165/2011, 4.

174 Case 7/11/2006 (n 926) 7; Case 4/11/2000 Court of Cassation/Commercial 651/1999, 3, 4; Case 3/10/2011 (n 926) 4; Case 7/2/2012 (n 263) 8; Al-Sanhory (n 279) 675.

175 Case 7/11/2006 (n 926) 5; Case 7/2/2012 (n 263) 10; Case 16/4/2012 (n 941) 3.

176 Case 4/6/2006 (n 926) 4, 5.

177 Al-Yaqob (n 52) 289.

178 KCIC 194(2); EMKCIC 210, 211.

179 Al-Majalla Art. 62–61.

180 Al-Majalla Art. 60.

181 EMKCIC 210–211.

182 Ayob (n 494) 182 footnote 14.

consider the breached description an 'assured' term or not might not arise. However, when a judge decides there is a gap in identifying the 'assured descriptions,' they may fill it according to Article 1(2) KCIC by adopting some Islamic principles which use criteria similar to a standard person and consider them the likely behaviour of the vast majority of society.[183] Hanafi School, for instance, uses the practice of the country in which the contract was made to define or assign an element of the contract composition[184] and, 'the evaluation [in Maliki School]. . . does not differentiate according to people, but rather differentiates according to countries and times.'[185] The problem that brings us full circle is that the judge may represent a usual person through factors derived from their own view. It could be said that prevailing customs might help estimate what a reasonable person might think, and the judge would apply entrenched objective factors transcending their personal evaluation[186] to assess the descriptive detail. This is not always guaranteed as the defendant would usually prove such a custom and, when the judge is convinced of its existence, it would be applied to the case.

#### 4.2.1.3.3 PRE- AND POST-CONTRACTUAL DESCRIPTIONS

Pursuant to Article 195 KCIC, the contract shall be neither limited to what is stated implicitly or explicitly in the contract nor limited to the provisions of the law but also include what are considered necessities according to justice, good faith and honour, with the consideration of the transaction's nature.[187] Al-Yaqoub states that the necessities of the contract are those that are inherent in its nature and purpose.[188] In a car sale contract, a spare tyre may be a necessity,[189] even if it is not mentioned in the contract but is mentioned before or after. Therefore, in order to consider descriptions mentioned preceding the contract, they have to be assessed on the basis of whether they reflect the meaning of necessity, justice and honour. If not, they may have no legal effect[190] as an offer is the first component of a contract,[191]

183 Wahba AlZehely, *Islamic Jurisprudence and its Evidence* (Dar AlFeker 1985) 296 <;https://www.noor-book.com/%D9%83%D8%AA%D8%A7%D8%A8-%D8%A7%D9%84%D9%81%D9%82%D9%87-%D8%A7%D9%84%D8%A5%D8%B3%D9%84%D8%A7%D9%85%D9%8A-%D9%88%D8%A3%D8%AF%D9%84%D8%AA%D9%87-pdf-pdf>; Ayob (n 494) 224 footnote 26.

184 Ayob (n 494) 55 footnote 35.

185 Ahmed Al-Qarafy, *The Differences*: Written Between Late 13th and Early 14th Century (Part 4 Ministry of Islamic Affairs 2010) 31.

186 Atef Al-Naqeeb, *The General Theory of Liability Arising from Personal Action* (Eweedat 1983) 134, 135, 140.

187 Case 7/2/1995 Court of Cassation/Commercial 193/94 in Ministry of Justice, *The Legal Principles Decided by the Court of Cassation During Forty Years, Volume 11 in Civil Provisions* (2016).

188 Al-Yaqob (n 52) 291.

189 Abdulreda; Al-Nakas (n 257) 165.

190 Case 23/3/1983 Court of Cassation/Commercial 152/82 cited in Jamal Al-Nakas, 'Contracts and Agreements Paving the Way for Contracting and the Importance of Differentiating Between Contract and Agreement in the Pre-Contract Stage' (1996) 20(1) Kuwait Law Journal (KLJ) 133, 137, 174; Hamdy Barood, 'The Legal Value of Agreements in the Pre-Contract Negotiation Stage in the Field of International Trade Contracts' (2005) 13(2) Islamic University Journal 125, 148.

191 KCIC Art. 39.

indicating the parties' desire to establish obligations,[192] and negotiations that preceded it were nothing more than non-binding discussions and bargains[193] that pave the way for a binding contract. In one case, the financial return mentioned in the advertisement was not considered as it was not mentioned in the contract.[194] It is possible, though, to resort to pre-contract negotiations to explain the contractual terms if a dispute arises between the parties.[195]

A judge may consider the negotiations part of the final contract if they reflect the parties' intentions.[196] In one case, purchased machinery violated the agreed degree of energy related to air volume and pressure, even when this degree was mentioned in the price list.[197]

In case of post-contractual clarification of/emphasis on descriptions by the buyer, a seller's silence does not indicate a particular response[198] as Islamic jurists state, '[S]aying cannot be attributed to silence.'[199] However, 'remaining silent in the context of the *need for a speech* should be construed as a statement.'[200] It is the judge who will evaluate the seller's silence, which might make the descriptions 'assured,' as failure to object to a statement could be considered confirmation of it.[201]

#### *4.2.1.4 Comparative Analysis*

##### 4.2.1.4.1 POSSIBLE OUTCOMES UNDER THE THREE LEGAL SYSTEMS

Consider this agreement on two hypothetical shipments:

The first shipment is 'Pretty Red Dresses' to be packed in red packaging. Under the Description Section, it is mentioned that 'the size is LARGE,' and under the Quality Section, it is mentioned that they are to be 'soft dresses.' During the negotiation phase, 'silk material' has been indicated. The seller does not adhere to these descriptions and sends cotton dresses with 'size medium written on them, although the actual size is large.

The second shipment involves the delivery of 'rouge' makeup. The seller misunderstands at the contract conclusion that the buyer is seeking 'cheek blusher.' The word 'blusher' is used in the contract. Directly after concluding the contract,

192 Al-Nakas (n 958) 163.

193 For instance: Case 18/1/1993 Court of Cassation 94/92 in Ministry of Justice, Commercial Provisions (n 259) 292; Al-Nakas (n 958) 138; Hassan AlHassan, *Negotiation and Public Relations* cited in Ahmed Alshobry, 'Contract Negotiation: Its Legal Framework and Its Impact on the Obligation' (2019) 4(1) Journal of the College of Islamic and Arab Studies for Girls in Damanhour (DOAJ) 1178, 1201.

194 Case 4/11/2000 (n 942) 5, 6. See also Al-Nakas (n 958) 178.

195 Alshobry (n 961) 1188.

196 J Al-Nakas (n 958) 137, 175.

197 Case18/12/1989 Court of Cassation/Commercial reproduced in Al-Defery; Al-Sayrafy (n 254) 325.

198 KCIC Art. 196; Ibrahim Abualil, *The Contract and the Will* (Dar Alkutob 1998) 117.

199 Al-Majalla Art. 67.

200 ibid; EMKCIC 63.

201 Al-Sanhory (n 279) 238.

the buyer sends pictures of the desired goods, clarifying their intention to receive 'lipsticks,' but the seller remains silent and sends 'cheek blushers' instead.

*4.2.1.4.1.1 Under CISG* **a. Red Dresses/Red Packaging**: Sending goods in a colour other than red in miscoloured packaging might not be considered a fundamental breach[202] even if it was stated that 'it is essential to provide the goods in a red colour.' This is unless the importance was emphasised by stating that 'it is essential to provide the goods in a red colour to be resold on Valentine's Day.' This obviousness of the buyer's motivation for a specific description makes it unavoidably applicable to a reasonable person. Sometimes, this importance can be deduced from the circumstances, especially if the goods' nature and the time they were ordered make it obvious to any reasonable person that the goods were intended to be sold for Valentine's Day, and the colour should therefore be adhered to. **b. Pretty Dresses**: The word 'pretty' is general and vague and would not play a significant role in delimiting the description, even though some general phrases in a few cases, such as 'trouble-free,'[203] were considered descriptions. **c. Size:** Although using uppercase can implicitly emphasise importance, it might not be taken into account as long as the contractual expectations are met, as the actual size was large. **d. Soft Dresses**: The phrase 'silk material' mentioned in the negotiations could reflect the parties' common intention and can be used to interpret the word 'soft' mentioned in the contract. Sending cotton materials may constitute a breach of the contract, although termination might not be permitted unless this breach satisfied Article 25. **e. Lipstick**: Parties' subsequent conduct is expressly mentioned in Article 8(3), and foreseeability time has not been mentioned in the Convention to permit later information. Post-contractual clarification of 'lipsticks' could be activated, especially as it was sent immediately after concluding the contract, making its timing reasonable. Any delay or failure of this clarification to reach the seller would not deprive the buyer of their right to rely on it.[204]

*4.2.1.4.1.2 Under SGA* **a. Red Dresses/Red Packaging**: Unlike under CISG, sending goods in red could be a 'condition,' even when the buyer did not place emphasis on the colour and without having mentioned the reason for such a choice. However, stating that 'it is preferable to send the goods in red' could be interpreted as a 'representation'[205] or 'intermediate term.' Notwithstanding, demanding that the *packaging* be in red might not always be considered a 'condition,' as it may not be interpreted as a substantial part of the dresses' *identity* but could merely determine their *identification.* **b. Pretty Dresses**: The word 'pretty' might not be part of the description due to its generality, although some general phrases, like 'excellent

202 See *Down jacket* (n 785).
203 *Mansonville v Kurtz* (n 784) [101].
204 CISG Art. 27.
205 'I believe' was construed as a representation. See *Oscar v Williams* (n 845) 375.

mechanical condition,'[206] were deemed terms in previous cases. Emphasising such a phrase by using a different layout or mentioning the reason for the choice might change the outcome by providing the meaning of 'pretty,' despite the fact that, in *Walker v Milner*,[207] the term 'Picklock-Proof' was considered a 'representation,' even with the buyer's insistence on the need and reason for secure storage. **c. Size**: Emphasising 'LARGE' in uppercase might categorise it directly as a 'condition,' regardless of the fact that the actual size of the goods, labelled as medium, was large. **d. Soft Dresses**: The 'softness' of the goods would not be deemed a 'condition' as long as it appeared under the Quality Section. In *Proton Energy v Orlen Lietuva*, for instance, although the buyer claimed that 'the [disputed] specification was a matter of description' according to usual language and common sense, it was not considered so, especially as the goods' characteristics were under a 'Quality' clause rather than a 'Product' clause.[208] If the softness of the goods appeared under the Description Section, it would be interpreted under a reasonable person's understanding, without consideration of the negotiation phase. Therefore, the business sense of 'soft' might be satisfied if the cotton dresses were smooth to the touch, ignoring the parties' subjective intention. **e. Lipstick**: Considering post-contractual information can be an exception, and it might be unclear whether clarification that the goods should have been 'lipsticks' not 'blushers' could be considered one of the exceptions under which to resort to information outside the contract, especially as the contract articulates the word 'blusher.'

*4.2.1.4.1.3 Under KLaw* **a. Red Dresses/Red Packaging and Size**: In case of a wrong colour, requesting termination is allowed because colour would be considered a part of description. KLaw does not adopt the philosophy of finding out whether the contractual descriptive statement is a promise or a representation, especially when it is clearly articulated, indicating the seller's assurance of these descriptions even if the breach was related to un-emphasised descriptions and even without mentioning the purpose of this choice. This would apply to the size even if it was written in lowercase. Considering that the actual size was large, rather than the size medium the dresses were labelled, would be a matter for the judge's discretion. **b. Pretty Dresses**: It is preferable to consider a contractual descriptive statement as a term than to disregard it, even if it is vague. When the common intention to interpret the word 'pretty' is not helpful, this persistently vague term should be interpreted for the benefit of the disadvantaged party, which might be the seller. So the 'prettiness' can be interpreted according to standard criteria, such as 'public/popular taste' or 'elegance,' according to the expert appointed by the court, but not according to higher standards like 'appealing' and 'trendy,' which would be against the seller's interests. Nevertheless, this interpretation might not be guaranteed, as

206 Porter v General Guarantee Corporation Ltd v Howard Baugh & Sons Ltd (Third Party) [1999] GCCR 573, 385.

207 Walker v Milner (n 858).

208 *Proton Energy v Orlen* (n 860) [60]; [64]; [58]; [59].

the judge might find it fairer to interpret 'pretty' to the buyer's benefit, making higher standards the more appropriate measure. **d. Soft Dresses**: The position of the requirement under the Quality Section might not play a role in KLaw. If the judge considered the phrase 'silk material,' mentioned pre-contractually, as a 'new description' unrelated to the 'soft' mentioned in the contract, it is unlikely to be deemed a 'description,' as the offer is the first step of the contractual relationship, regardless of prior statements. Conversely, if the judge considered 'silk material' an interpretation of 'soft,' silk material could be considered to be part of the description. If this was not present, termination might be allowed. **c. Lipstick**: Post-contract clarification might be considered, even when the seller was silent, as silence could be a sign of consent.[209] However, another judge could find that mentioning the word 'blusher' in the contract imposes a clear obligation to provide the buyer with a specific type of goods, and later information might be construed as a change to the goods' type rather than clarification; the judge might therefore disregard this information.

#### 4.2.1.4.2 CLARITY, FLEXIBILITY AND PRESERVING THE CONTRACT

*4.2.1.4.2.1 Formalism* **Under CISG**, because foreseeability is an important factor when assessing the fundamentality of the breach, unstressed description would not constitute a breach leading to termination, and this protects the contract from being terminated for breaching immaterial clauses, which may simultaneously provide certainty. Furthermore, CISG equalises the legal effect of both quality and description once they are mentioned in the contract as they possess the same rule under Article 35(1). **Under SGA**, certainty can occur when description is breached, and termination is permitted, even if the breached description is not highlighted in the contract. However, uncertainty may occur as, **first**, although it was rightly stated in *Reardon v Yngvar* that 'the authorities as to "description" in sale of goods cases were not to be extended,'[210] not defining the descriptions that fall within s.13(1)'s sphere may create bewilderment in court[211] and leave only controversial phrases. **Secondly**, categorising a term as 'quality' or 'description' might be practically difficult.[212] 'Newly-laid eggs'[213] and the word 'hard' in 'Hard Amber Durum Wheat' could be linked to both quality and description.[214] In other cases, one word could change the phrase's status, as the phrase 'maximum 7.5% fibre (sic)' could reflect quality rather than description when the percentage was stated without the word 'maximum.'[215] **Lastly**, there is divergence in disregarding general phrases,

209 Abualil (n 966) 118, 119.
210 *Reardon v Hansen-Tangen* (n 417) 989–991.
211 Burrows, *Principles of English Commercial Law* (n 28) 69.
212 Gillette; Walt (n 778) 215.
213 *Alfred Toepferv Continental Grain* [1974] 1 Lloyd's Rep 11.
214 ibid.
215 *Tradax v European Grain* (n 422) 104, 105.

and this could cause a lack of consistency, which also applies to some cases under CISG. Although these points may weaken SGA's aim of providing certainty, they liberate the judiciary to decide according to the circumstances.[216] **Under KLaw**, breaching clear description could permit parties to request termination, irrespective of whether it was emphasised, where it was located in the contract and layout. This attains a higher degree of clarity, (unless the judiciary sees otherwise) but dramatically minimises the possibility of preserving the contract.

*4.2.1.4.2.2 Parties' Common Intention* **Under CISG and KLaw**, concentration on the parties' intentions to interpret the meaning of descriptions could be a sufficient means to recognise the contractual description in a myriad of scenarios, but similarly, it could be 'fluid and fuzzy' and lack coherence or consistency, depending on pragmatic stereotypes when establishing whether a description constitutes a contractual term or not.[217] The intention of considering a descriptive statement a contractual term could depend on external factors, such as the price,[218] but in the *Steel cylinders case*, after it was agreed that new steel cylinders would be supplied, and the seller delivered used ones, the tribunal held that the goods were nonconforming, rejecting the seller's claim that the agreed price, which revealed the parties' intention, did not correspond to brand new goods.[219] **SGA** depends on clearer standards, such as a reasonable person's understanding and business sense, instead of relying on the will and thoughts of the respective parties, which have a speculative and unidentifiable nature,[220] drifting jurists away from the factual realm and towards fiction. Nevertheless, the reference to 'identity' in order to consider a descriptive statement a term would not always achieve clarity; as Slade LJ stated in *Harlingdon*, the painter's name on the invoice can be considered equally either a term, stating the picture's origin, or a reference for the purpose of identification.[221] **Under KLaw**, in case of persistent vagueness of description, one judge may see that the seller is the debtor who delivers conforming goods, and the term could be interpreted according to the latter interest; the buyer may not claim termination for that reason. In contrast, another judge may interpret the description in the buyer's favour, since interpreting otherwise would unjustly prejudice the buyer. Predictability might not be attained, as the whole subject matter depends on the judge's perception, especially as EMKCIC stated that the judge's adopted approach might be taken 'in a manner that reassures him,'[222] maximising the recourse to prolonged and costly litigation. Conversely, in the case of the absence of common

216 Poikela (n 83) 48.

217 Saidov (n 769) 32.

218 Bruce Mann; Thomas Holdych, 'The Basis of the Bargain Requirement: A Market and Economic Based Analysis of Express Warranties – Getting What You Pay for and Paying for What You Get' (1996) 45(3) DePaul L Rev 781, 800.

219 *Steel cylinders case* (n 816).

220 Poikela (n 83) 32.

221 *Harlingdon v Christopher* (n 878) 586.

222 EMKCIC 209.

intention under CISG, a reasonable person in the buyer's place would be resorted to, which is a more certain and neutral measure than resorting to the judge's doctrine.

*4.2.1.4.2.3 Pre- and Post-Contractual Information* **Under CISG**, opinions are divided on whether to consider negotiations a source of imposing description or to interpret the contract pursuant to the literal wording of Article 8(3), which could decrease certainty. However, permitting new information after concluding the contract, when it meets the reasonability standard, achieves flexibility and practicality. **Under SGA**, exclusion of information outside the contract attains a higher degree of certainty, especially as this information might be undeveloped, discordant, outdated or non-consensual; therefore, the focus should be on the contractual text only. However, resorting to this information can be permitted in exceptional cases, and deciding these might be unclear. **Under KLaw**, determining the cases in which a statement is vague while considering the parties' common intention and assessing the possibility of the pre- and post-contract information to help interpret the vagueness are all entrusted to the judge, whose views are rooted in their beliefs, thus weakening legal clarity.

#### 4.2.1.4.3 DEVELOPING KLAW

Contractual parties want to know[223] the potential legal outcomes of their actions,[224] but this is not provided by KLaw, as it is apparent that the judge is not only a tool for law enforcement but also an instrument for creating the legal basis of the issue at hand according to their perception. Although SGA is devoted to attaining legal clarity and has succeeded in meeting this target in many ways, this aim is somewhat subtle when the legal concept of description has not been entirely defined, permitting judicial speculation. CISG attains a higher degree of both clarity and flexibility by adopting rules serving as guidelines, which could free the decision from the grip of the judge's dogma. For instance, the contractual descriptions 'should be read from the circumstances,'[225] which makes the seller particularly cautious about their statements and conduct throughout their relationship with the buyer,[226] fortifying the meaning of trust and efficiency. Additionally, resorting to the judgement of a reasonable person is considered the minimum requirement to identify the parties' intentions without the judge's ruling being influenced by the personal situation of each party.

223 Adams; Brownsword (n 218) 166–168; Ahdar (n 765) 40, 53.
224 *Bunge v Tradax* (n 400) 720.
225 Maley (n 186) 110.
226 Saidov (n 769) 33.

### *4.2.2 Buyer's Interests Under the Contract and Buyer's Reliance on Contractual Descriptions*

The distinction between *descriptive terms* and *beliefs*, deemed to be 'puffery,' can be reached by finding out the buyer's interest in continuing the contractual relationship and the buyer's reliance on the disputed statement.

#### *4.2.2.1 CISG*

##### 4.2.2.1.1 BUYER'S INTEREST

At CISG's drafting stage, the Italian representative suggested that there was a link between the concept of fundamentality and the affected party's contractual interest in performing the contract[227] to attain precision rather than abstract definitions.[228] The committee opposed this suggestion because the affected party's 'loss of interest in the contract,' as a result of the breaching party's failure to perform, could depend on a covert motive of such a party,[229] and this does not achieve objectivity.[230] The buyer could lose interest even when breaching a representation, and this would increase the likelihood of recourse to termination. Even upon applying the judgement of a reasonable person, the probability remains that this criterion could be affected by economic stimuli subject to the market situation, supply and demand and price fluctuations.

Despite this, some courts and scholars[231] rely on the buyer's loss of interest or the non-expectancy of the buyer's adherence to the contract[232] in order to understand not only the status of descriptive statement but also the misdescription's fundamentality. This is when misdescription substantially deprives the injured buyer of their contractual interest in performing the contract[233] or when the breach affects the root of the contract.[234] In the *Shoes case*, without scrutinising Article 25, the fundamentality of misdescription depended on the contractual purpose being seriously endangered, causing the aggrieved party to lose interest in implementing

227 Official Records (n 149) 12th Meeting 297.

228 ibid.

229 UN, 'International Trade Law' (n 190) 31.

230 John Honnald, *Documentary History* (n 344) 324.

231 Enderlein; Maskow (n 150) 113.

232 ibid; Kröll; Mistelis; Viscasillas (n 67) 342 [15].

233 *Computer components case* (1992) O 42/92 KfH I (District Court Heidelberg) <;http://cisgw3.law.pace.edu/cases/920703g1.html>; *Cobalt sulphate case* (14/12/1994) 5 U 224/93 (Appellate Court Oberlandesgericht) <;http://cisgw3.law.pace.edu/cases/941214g1.html>; *Packaging machine case* 18/5/2009 (n 153).

234 Van Vuuren; Elbi Janse, 'Termination of International Commercial Contracts for Breach of Contract: The Provisions of the UNIDROIT Principles of International Commercial Contracts' (1998) 15(2) ArizJIntl & CompL 583, 589; Saiegh (n 116) 452.

the contract.[235] In the *Chemical compound case*, when the seller indicated that the goods' shape would be 'microcrystals,' the tribunal found that there was no misdescription when the delivered goods were in a stone-hard condition transformable to crystals,[236] attaining the buyer's interest.

#### 4.2.2.1.2 THE BUYER'S RELIANCE ON DESCRIPTIVE STATEMENT IS NOT AN ADOPTED MEASURE TO DECIDE ITS STATUS

In the sphere of international sales, the buyer usually concludes the contract without viewing the goods because of the physical distance between the buyer and the goods' location.[237] Thus, there could be an assumption that the purchase is based on the seller's descriptive statements, and the buyer relies at all times on the seller providing goods as described in the contract. This premise should not be weakened, even if the buyer selects the products themselves.[238]

Accordingly, establishing the buyer's reliance on the seller's skill and judgement and its reasonableness to verify whether this statement is a part of the contract[239] should not emerge in relation to the goods' conformity with contractual descriptions.[240] As Gillette and Walt stress, '[C]ourts need not delve into the difficult question of whether a statement of the seller constituted a basis of the bargain.'[241] Misdescription could occur when sending nonconforming goods, even if the seller's inability to provide goods with these descriptions was apparent at the contract conclusion. Demonstratively, under Article 35(3), the seller cannot allege that the buyer knew or could not have been unaware of goods' misdescription at the contract conclusion. As stated in Secretariat Commentary, Article 35(3) 'does not go to those characteristics of the goods explicitly required by the contract.'[242] The buyer may conceive that the nonconformity at the contract conclusion will be remedied at delivery time.[243]

However, it may be found that despite excluding the application of Article 35(3) to Article 35(1), the buyer's prior knowledge of nonconformity would be considered to reveal the parties' intentions and to categorise the seller's descriptive

235 *Shoes case* 17/9/1991 (n 564). See also Official Records, Czechoslovakian representative (n 149) 12th Meeting 297, 298.

236 *Chemical compound case* (1996) 8247 (ICC arbitration) <http://cisgw3.law.pace.edu/cases/968247i1.html>.

237 René Franz Henschel, 'Conformity of Goods in International Sales Governed by CISG Article 35: Caveat Venditor, Caveat Emptor and Contract Law as Background Law and as a Competing Set of Rules' (2014) 1 Nord J Commer Law 1, 3.

238 Gillette; Walt (n 778) 215.

239 ibid 215, 216.

240 The reliance defence was expressly mentioned only in relation to the goods' fitness for particular purpose according to Art. 35(2)(b).

241 Gillette; Walt (n 778) 215.

242 Secretariat Commentary, 'Guide to CISG Article 35' <https://cisgw3.law.pace.edu/cisg/text/secomm/secomm-35.html>.

243 Gillette; Walt (n 778) 250.

statements as either 'terms' or 'puffery,' making the buyer's reliability crucial. Otherwise, it would be contrary to the good faith principle.[244] Saidov stresses that when the buyer's expertise is greater than that of the seller, the latter's representation may be considered a mere opinion[245] because the buyer's reliance cannot be inferred.[246] This conclusion is unfortunately based on an English case, and this may impede a uniform application, but it has been followed by some courts. In *Kunsthaus v Wilhelmina*, the First Instance Court found that the seller was not liable for a painting not being attributed to the agreed artist, Henry Velde, on the basis that the buyer was an expert, knew more than the seller and could not rely on the latter.[247] Furthermore, in *Roland Schmidt v Textil-Werke*, it was stated that when the buyer, who was an expert and had professional knowledge of mechanics, purchased a machine built 14 years before, the goods would not suffer from misdescription even if the machine was unable to meet the contractual capacity.[248] Notwithstanding, regarding reliance as a factor to determine the descriptive statement's nature, whether it is obligatory or not, will indirectly activate Article 35(3).

### *4.2.2.2 SGA*

#### 4.2.2.2.1 THE INFLUENTIAL ROLE OF DESCRIPTIVE STATEMENT TO INDUCE THE BUYER TO SIGN THE CONTRACT

When the disputed descriptive statement has influenced the buyer's decision to purchase, this statement is promissory.[249] In other words, when the seller intentionally, culpably or perhaps even unknowingly makes the buyer believe in the existence of a description, the seller cannot afterwards dispute that the description has not been agreed upon.[250] When a seller induced a buyer to purchase, rendering information about the commercial significance of a boat's speed in the industry,[251] the phrase 'estimated speed of fifteen m.p.h.' was considered promissory. It was tested in *Budd v Fairmaner* that a horse being a four-year-old colt was not a promissory description,[252] and when the horse's actual age was three years old, there was no misdescription as long as this specific age did not play an influential part in

244 Saidov (n 769) 39.

245 ibid 34.

246 ibid 37.

247 Maley (n 186) 106. Maley refers to *Kunsthaus Mathias Lempertz v Wilhelmina van der Geld* (9/2/1999) rolnr. 97/805 <http://www.unilex.info/cisg/case/452>. (The full text in English is unavailable.)

248 *Roland Schmidt GmbH v Textil-Werke Blumenegg AG* (22/12/2000) 4C.296/2000/rnd (Federal Supreme Court Switzerland) <http://cisgw3.law.pace.edu/cases/001222s1.html>.

249 Lord Mackenzie in Edgar v Hector (1912) SC 348, 352; *Easterbrook v Hopkins (n 780)* 442; Lord Denning MR in *Dick Bentley Productions Ltd v Harold Smith* (Motors) Ltd [1965] 1 WLR 623, 627; Nourse LJ in *Harlingdon v Christopher* (n 878) 574.

250 Freeman v Cooke (n 876) 652, 653.

251 *Savage v Blakney (n 844)* 441, 442.

252 *Budd v Fairmaner* (1831) 131 ER 318.

inducing the buyer to sign the contract. Some jurists were more objective, referring to a reasonable person's understanding rather than the actual buyer for the application of this measure.[253]

On the other hand, this measure was opposed in *Savage v Blakney*, as it was emphasised that it was insufficient to establish a descriptive phrase as a 'condition' by discovering that, without such a phrase, the buyer would not have signed the contract since innocent 'representation' can also induce a purchase.[254] Similarly, in *Smith v Hughes*, the parties' minds were not *ad idem*; the buyer intended to purchase old oats, but the seller intended to sell new ones. Blackburn J found that as long as the seller was not guilty of fraud, the buyer should accept the purchased goods, even if they did not have the intended characteristic and even if the seller was aware that the buyer would not have entered into the contract unless the goods had such characteristics. The sole fact that the seller abstained from correcting the buyer did not break a legal rule.[255]

#### 4.2.2.2.2 THE IMPACT OF BUYER'S RELIANCE ON DESCRIPTIVE STATEMENTS

In *Cremdean Properties v Nash*, Bridge LJ stated: 'The word "representation" is an extremely wide term; I cannot see why one should not be making a representation when giving information or when stating one's opinion or belief.'[256] There is division under SGA in considering 'reliance' a decisive element in deciding whether a specific descriptive detail is a 'term' or mere 'puffery.'

*4.2.2.2.2.1 Reliance Is Decisive Factor* Some jurists find that the buyer's reliance on the seller's skill and judgement, mentioned in s.14(3), for the goods' fitness of particular purpose should be applied to s.13 as well[257] so that a description is regarded as a 'condition.'[258] When purchasing the goods exactly 'as they are,' the decisive factor of the buyer's reliance is missing; this situation means the sale goes ahead but not by description.[259] In *Joseph v Longel*, calling anti-gas boots 'waders' simply used the name to distinguish the goods; the buyer did not rely on such a word, even though normal waders are waterproof.[260]

253 Salmon LJ in *Bentley v Harold* (n 1017) 629.
254 *Savage v Blakney (n 844)* 442.
255 *Smith v Hughes* (n 881) 597.
256 *Cremdean Properties Ltd and another v Nash and others* [1977] 2 EGLR 80.
257 See *Henry Kendall & Sons v William Lillico & Sons Ltd* [1969] 2 AC 31, 32; Bridge, *Benjamin's* (n 28) [11–009].
258 *Beale v Taylor* (n 30) 1194; *Harlingdon v Christopher* (n 878) 572; Thomas Holdych, 'Warranties and Conditions in the Sale of Goods: A Market-based Assessment of English and European Community Warranty Law' (1998) 29 Cambr Law Rev 73, 74; Bridge, *Benjamin's* (n 28) [11–009].
259 Nourse LJ in *Harlingdon v Christopher* (n 878) 566, 567.
260 *Travers (Joseph) v Longel* (1948) 64 TLR 150.

a. The Impact of Parties' Experience on Descriptions' Status Reliance can be apparent when the seller expounds on facts that are unknown to the buyer,[261] even when the descriptive detail is a matter of indifference to the buyer,[262] as opposed to merely providing an opinion about which the seller has no knowledge.[263] Reliance could be diminished in cases in which the seller is not a professional[264] and states false information which is likely to be an innocent misrepresentation, especially when goods are sold sequentially by one seller and then another.[265] In *Oscar v Williams*, the registration book of a second-hand Morris motor car showed that it was a 1948 model, but it later became evident to the buyer, a motor dealer, that the car was a 1939 model. The court held that the false description of the model was merely an innocent misrepresentation, as it was obvious that the seller did not intend to bind themselves with this statement, and the buyer knew the seller had no knowledge of the actual date of the car's manufacture.[266] Therefore, it was not an integral part of the contract unless this assertion had been known to be untrue by the seller, and they had acted deceitfully.[267]

This notion was followed in *Harlingdon*, when a painting which sold for £6,000 had been described as being by the German expressionist Münter in both the contract and the auction catalogue[268] but turned out to be a forgery, which could only be resold for £50. The seller was a specialist in British contemporary art and made it plain to the buyer that they were not an expert and had never heard of Münter,[269] and the buyer was a dealer, running a fine art gallery specialising in German art.[270] Nourse LJ indicated that the buyer purchased the painting believing it was by Münter based on their own examination and experience and not on the description,[271] which did not have a 'substantial influence' on the buyer.[272] This means the sale was not based on the description,[273] which prevented the buyer from repudiating the contract.[274] This approach was also pursued in *Jendwine v Slade*, when it was stated that the mere inclusion of the artist's name in the catalogue was not a promise that the paintings were by this artist; it was rather an expression of

261 Oscar v Williams (n 845) 329. See Bridge, *Benjamin's* (n 28) [10–005].
262 *Reardon v Hansen-Tangen* (n 417) 1002, 1003.
263 *De Lassalle v Guildford* [1901] 2 KB 215, 221; *Bisset v Wilkinson* [1927] AC 177.
264 Lord Wilberforce in *Ashington v Christopher* (n 842) 452.
265 *Routledge v McKay v Nugent, Ashgrove, Mawson* [1954] 1 WLR 615, 623.
266 *Oscar v Williams* (n 845) 325.
267 Williams J in *Behn v Burness* (n 874) 281.
268 *Harlingdon v Christopher* (n 878) 568.
269 ibid 569.
270 ibid 568.
271 ibid 566.
272 ibid 568.
273 ibid 574.
274 ibid 564.

opinion, and the seller was not liable if they were mistaken.[275] Lord Kenyon stated that, as

> the pictures were the work of artists some centuries back, and there being no way of tracing the picture itself, it could only be matter of opinion whether the picture in question was the work of the artist whose name it bore, or not.[276]

Furthermore, in *Power v Barham*, Littledale J stated that 'I think that all the auctioneers in London would be alarmed if they thought that such words as ["Views in Venice, Canaletto"] were to be understood as [promissory].'[277]

Conversely, in *Leaf v International Galleries*, the name of the painter was considered a 'condition,' as Denning LJ stated that '[t]here was a term in the contract . . . as to the person by whom the picture was painted.'[278] Moreover, in *Nicholson v Smith-Marriott*, although it was stated in the contract that the authenticity of the tablecloths and napkins belonging to 'Charles I' was not guaranteed, the court considered the goods' genuineness a contractual description.[279]

b. Dependency on Goods' Type The goods' type might indicate that there is no reliance on a descriptive detail, excluding it from being a promissory term,[280] especially when the buyer purchased **specific goods**, possessing apparently unique characteristics, entirely on their own judgement and assessment or where the goods are second-hand.[281] In these cases, the sale would unlikely be a 'sale by description,' but rathera 'sale of a specific thing,' and misdescription would be irrelevant.[282] Bailhache J asserted, in *Harrison,* that in cases concerning specific existing chattels, the absence of their descriptive attributes could not be a breach of a 'condition' unless this absence made the chattel a different kind from that described in the contract.[283] However, in *Grant v Australian Knitting Mills*, it was asserted that a sale by description had occurred even though the goods were of a specific kind, as long as the parties agreed on their descriptions.[284]

On the other hand, there is a technical view that 'all sales of **unascertained goods** are necessarily sales by description'[285] (emphasis added), and every descriptive word is a promise, even if it is related to unessential characteristics.[286]

275 *Jendwine v Slade* (1797) 170 ER 459.
276 ibid 459, 460.
277 *Power v Barham* (1836) 111 ER 865, 866.
278 *Leaf v International Galleries* [1950] 2 KB 86, 89.
279 *Nicholson and Venn v Smith-Marriott* [1947] 1 WLUK 428.
280 Lord Wilberforce in Reardon v Hansen-Tangen (n 417) 996–998.
281 Poikela (n 83) 48, 49. 61.
282 *Beale v Taylor* (n 30) 1196.
283 *Harrison v Knowles* (n 909) 610.
284 *Grant v Australian Knitting Mills Ltd* [1936] AC 85, 100.
285 *Taylor v Combined Buyers* (n 890) 54, 55, 58, 59, 61. See also *Reardon v Hansen-Tangen* (n 417) 989–991.
286 ibid *Taylor v Combined Buyers* 51, 54, 55, 58, 59, 61.

However, in *Ashington*, it was stated that even in cases in which unascertained goods were sold, descriptions were merely those which identified the goods' kind.[287]

c. Relevance of Seeing and Examining the Goods When a contract between present parties is concluded and the buyer sees the goods, a sale may not be made by description.[288] Conversely, when the buyer proceeds with the transaction depending solely on the description of the goods,[289] such as in the case of future goods[290] or goods manufactured to a particular design,[291] almost all descriptive statements are considered descriptions.[292] In *Varley*, when a machine was sold as 'it had been new the previous year,'[293] and the buyer, who had never seen it,[294] discovered that it was much older upon arrival, the goods suffered from misdescription.[295] Even cases of sales of specific goods can be classified as sales by description when the goods were not seen at the time of purchase.[296] Despite the foregoing, in *Grant v Australian Knitting Mills*, it was pointed out that a sale by description had taken place even if the buyer bought items in front of them[297] as s.13 is broad enough to include these cases,[298] especially as divergence from the description may be invisible.[299]

Other jurists find that when buyers actually examine the goods before purchase[300] and the nonconformity is apparent from ordinary examination,[301] there is no implied condition to correspond with the contractual description, as buyers have relied on their own skill and judgement and may ignore any criticism on their mal-assessment.[302] The buyer thereby should not be allowed to use their own error in assessment as grounds for alleging that the goods rendered suffered from misdescription.[303] In *Beale v Taylor*, when the description of 'Herald convertible, white, 1961' turned out, after purchase, to be incorrect, this made the car different from the one agreed, as this could not have been established by initial examination.[304] However, in *Beale v Taylor*, it was held that even if the buyer had inspected

287 Lord Diplock in *Ashington v Christopher* (n 842) 503.
288 Burrows, *Principles of English Commercial Law* (n 28) 70.
289 *Varley v Whipp* [1900] 1 QB 513; Sellers LJ in *Beale v Taylor* (n 30) 1194; Channell J and Bucknill J in *Harlingdon v Christopher* (n 878) 572; 'Sale By Description' (n 848) 3.
290 *Reardon v Hansen-Tangen* (n 417) 998.
291 Twigg-Flesner; Canavan (n 30) 125.
292 *Varley v Whipp* (n 1057) 516.
293 ibid.
294 ibid 514.
295 ibid.
296 Bridge, *Benjamin's* (n 28) [11–008].
297 *Grant v Australian Knitting Mills* (n 1052) 100; *Beale v Taylor* (n 30) 1194.
298 Poikela (n 83) 48, 49, 61.
299 *Beale v Taylor* (n 30) 1197.
300 *Thornett & Fehr v Beers & Son* [1919] 1 KB 486, 486–489.
301 *Beale v Taylor* (n 30) 1197.
302 Nourse LJ in *Harlingdon v Christopher* (n 878) 570.
303 *Harlingdon v Christopher* (n 878) 576.
304 *Beale v Taylor* (n 30) 1196, 1197. See also *Steels v Bleecker Bik* [1956] 1 Lloyd's Rep 228.

the goods, the sale occurred by description, as the descriptions mentioned in the advertisement (on which the buyer relied) had changed the contract's nature from merely being a sale of specific things to sale by description.[305]

*4.2.2.2.2.2 Reluctance to Consider Reliance a Decisive Factor* Other jurists may be reluctant to accept 'reliance' as a stimulator to consider a descriptive detail a contractual term as 'reliance' is never mentioned in s.13 and is not considered a common principle of contract law but was mentioned purely in relation to the goods' fitness for the particular purpose.[306] More problematically, 'reliance' can be considered parallel to the 'going to the root of the contract' standard, which distinguishes between 'warranty' and 'condition,' making the codification of s.13(1) redundant.

In *Harlingdon*, Slade LJ emphasised: 'While some judicial dicta seem to support the view that there can be no sale by description unless there is actual reliance on the description by the purchaser, I am not sure that this is strictly correct in principle.'[307] Resorting to 'reliance' might give the seller the opportunity to escape their breach by proving there was no actual reliance on the breached description.[308] However, His Lordship indicated that the buyer's non-reliance could serve as evidence of the parties' intentions, at the contract conclusion, that this description did not constitute a term, but the seller was 'selling the goods as they were.'[309] Oddie J stated that it was erroneous to establish that 'reliance' was the yardstick by which to determine whether or not a sale was by description.[310] Nourse LJ also asserted that 'reliance' could not delimit the nature of the disputed clause as the painter's name amounted to a 'substantial ingredient' in the goods' identity.[311] However, His Lordship concluded that a description not relied upon could, theoretically, be an essential term of a contract, but practically, a description should possess 'sufficient influence' to be considered an essential term, and the sign of this influence could be 'reliance.'[312] Stuart-Smith LJ affirmed that a buyer did not have to demonstrate their reliance on every contractual statement,[313] and neither a seller's sole claim that they were not experts on a sold painting nor the mere fact that the buyer was more knowledgeable than the seller necessarily meant the description was withdrawn. The buyer's experience may not necessarily assist them in determining the authenticity or falsification of the sold paintings.[314]

305 ibid *Beale v Taylor* 1194.
306 SGA s.14(3).
307 *Harlingdon v Christopher* (n 878) 584.
308 ibid 584.
309 ibid 584, 585.
310 ibid 566.
311 ibid 566, 574.
312 ibid 574.
313 ibid 579.
314 ibid.

#### *4.2.2.3 KLaw*

##### 4.2.2.3.1 IDENTIFYING THE SELLER'S ASSURANCE OF DESCRIPTION BY THE BUYER'S DESIRE TO ENTER THE CONTRACTUAL RELATIONSHIP

According to Articles 470(2), 469, 485(1) and 479 KCIC, unrelated to misdescription, KLaw adopts a specific criterion to permit the buyer to ask for termination: namely that if the nonconformity existed at the time of sale, the buyer would not have entered into the contract.[315] This standard could be applied to fill the loophole in the definition of 'assured description.' The question is how we can know the buyer's attitude at the time of sale or if misdescription occurred then. This attitude might be recognised by perceiving the deal's purpose as being derived from the contractual terms,[316] adopted in Article 663(1) KCIC, which states that 'the materials must be sufficient for the *aimed purpose*.'

The dilemma is that the law does not establish an obligation to reveal the buyer's purchase purpose to the seller, making the subject matter excessively dependent on the buyer's circumstances. In one case, when some Italian marble differed from the agreed engraving and colour, the expert assigned by the court reported that this difference changed and disturbed the beauty of the buyer's floors due to contrasting patterns and different shades of colour, even though the price matched both the market price and the contractual price. The court held that the seller breached the intended purpose.[317] In another case, a buyer requested termination due to a violation of the purchase purpose, but the termination claim was rejected[318] because the disputed description was not indicated in the contract.[319] By *argumentum a contrario*, if the description had been specified in the contract and the misdescription had hindered the purchase purpose, the description could be deemed 'assured.' The predicament is that as long as the description's purpose is not tied to the contract to make the description 'assured,' any pretence can be presented to activate the termination, especially if the buyer finds a more cost-effective alternative transaction.

##### 4.2.2.3.2 THE IMPACT OF THE BUYER'S RELIANCE ON DESCRIPTION TO BE CONSIDERED 'ASSURED'

Reliance could play a role in determining the assured status of the description as follows:

*4.2.2.3.2.1 Solely Attracting the Buyer* A descriptive statement which merely attracts the buyer could make it difficult to determine if the buyer relied on it, and

315 KCIC Art. 469; 470(2); 485(1).

316 Corenblit in Mustafa Al-Karjy, *Termination of the Contract* (Dar Alnahda 1988) 103; Al-Ahwany (n 497) 356, 357; Al-Danasory; Al-Shawarbee (n 281) 60.

317 Case 18/11/1996 Appellate Court/Commercial 1024/1995.

318 Case 20/11/2006 Appellate Court/Commercial 1106/2006, 3.

319 Case 10/11/2006 Appellate Court/Civil 1106/2206, 7.

this may categorise it as a 'non-assured' description. In one case,[320] the court did not consider potential post-sale financial gains mentioned in an advertisement as a term and stated that the purposr of these statements was only to attract buyers.[321]

*4.2.2.3.2.2 Parties' Proficiency* When cases involve professional sellers who specialise in a particular type of goods,[322] courts will assume that all descriptive details are 'assured,' even if those descriptions are considered implicitly, more than when sellers deal in a variety of goods.[323] However, when a buyer agrees to purchase goods in their current condition, a termination claim may be rejected.[324]

According to case law, a buyer's proficiency or the discoverability of misdescription can determine their reliance and then delineate the descriptive detail as 'assured.' This is true even when examination is not mentioned in relation to misdescription and could make the court apply rules for hidden defect (explained in the next chapter) to misdescription. When a buyer worked in the field of trading cars, the court of first instance and the appellate court decided that the difference in both the chassis numbers and the odometer from those agreed did not make the seller liable as the buyer was able to discover it,[325] making the description 'non-assured' due to the lack of reliance. Additionally, when a car was found not to be new as agreed, but it would have been easy for an ordinary person to discover the car's drift when its speed reached 130 kmph or when the brakes were suddenly used, and it was easy to hear an external sound in the car while driving,[326] these signs might indicate the buyer's non-reliance on the description, making it 'non-assured.' Likewise, when a Mercedes 506 SEL turned out to be a 420 SEL, which could only be ascertained by specialists in the car's type, the buyer was entitled to terminate the contract[327] since it would have been difficult for an ordinary person to discover through regular inspection.[328] Similarly, when it was agreed to sell a new car, but it turned out to be second-hand by the presence of ventilation from the side of the car's rear doors and the effect of a recent paint job,[329] the description was activated. However, misdescription arose when a Lexus that was sold was discovered to be a 1992 model, instead of a 1998 as agreed (without examining the discoverability of the breach), applying the rules of misdescription instead of hidden defect.[330]

320 Case 4/11/2000 (n 942) 5, 6.
321 ibid.
322 A similar meaning is found in Ayob (n 494) 218; Ibrahim Dawood, *Cognitive Imbalance in Contracts* (Dar Aljama Aljadeda 2014) 49.
323 A similar meaning in Ayob (n 494) 217 footnote 13.
324 Case 10/11/2006 (n 1087) 7.
325 Case 29/5/2007 Court of Cassation/Commercial-1 384/2006 p. 4, 5.
326 Case 20/4/2002 Court of Cassation/Commercial 2 529/2001 p. 1–4. See also Case 4/11/2000 (n 942) 5, 6; Case 10/11/2006 (n 1087) 7.
327 Case 9/12/1996 Appellate Court/Commercial 4 1368/1995 p. 4.
328 ibid.
329 Case 17/12/2005 Court of Cassation/Commercial 3 2004/1011 p. 2.
330 Case 11/2/2006 Court of Cassation/Commercial 2 391, 399/2005 p. 2–4.

*4.2.2.3.2.3 Goods Different From the Original Condition at the Time of Sale* Al-Majalla[331] affirms that when goods are seen by the buyer, descriptions are 'chitchat,' but when goods are not seen, these descriptions are highly significant. Thus, if a seller says that a sold horse is white and points to a black horse, this 'white' description is not considered, but when the horse is not seen, there is misdescription[332] leading to termination. Article 467 KCIC includes a similar rule when the parties are present in the same place, but this provision mentions nothing about seeing the goods. It states that the seller shall deliver the goods to the buyer in the same state as at the time of concluding the contract.[333] This makes the goods' state an assured description on which the buyer relies. If the seller still holds the goods after concluding the contract, they shall be obliged to maintain them, without making any physical amendment,[334] in order to remain in the same state as at the time of sale until delivery.[335] In one case, the court stated that the seller was obliged to deliver the goods in the same state as at the time of sale, and the seller was held liable when a change in the goods' state was proven harmful to the buyer.[336]

#### *4.2.2.4 Comparative Analysis*

##### 4.2.2.4.1 POSSIBLE OUTCOMES UNDER THE THREE LEGAL SYSTEMS

Consider this hypothetical example: A contract mentions that a machine is capable of working for ten hours without stopping, despite the fact that the buyer, who inspects the goods, does not need this full capacity at the time of purchase, and the buyer knows the seller's firm does not sell machines of such high capacity. Following the purchase, the production process at the buyer's premises noticeably increases, which results in a machine of full capacity becoming a persistent need,[337] but the machine does not conform to the contractual capacity.

**Under CISG**, although the *buyer's loss of interest* is not adopted, the contractual purpose could be undermined on the basis that the mal-capacity substantially deprived the buyer of the contractual benefit,[338] making the machine's capacity a promissory term despite the fact that the buyer did not rely on this feature when the machine was purchased. This is true unless the seller proves that the result of the breach was unforeseeable. **Under SGA**, the machine's capacity did not form an influential factor inducing the buyer to contract, especially as it was clear, from the buyer's experience, that the seller's capability did not match this requirement. Moreover, the buyer's inspection could indicate that they relied on their own

331 Art. 65.
332 Al-Majalla Art. 65. It overtly states that in this case, the contract is not concluded.
333 KCIC Art. 467.
334 Al-Ahwany (n 497) 340; Al-Shawarby (n 266) 371; Tnago (n 291) 220.
335 Case 4/4/2007 Appellate Court/Commercial 2006/3348, 8; Al-Jarmy (n 264) 71.
336 Case 7/11/1995 Appellate Court/Commercial 400/1995, 2–7.
337 Gillette; Walt (n 778) 215, 216.
338 *Hong Kong* (n 219) 27, 28.

assessment, irrespective of the contractual clauses, making the contract a sale of a specific thing rather than by description. However, a minority of scholars see that SGA favours imposing promises, regardless of whether there is real reliance on the contractual promise, which can be fictional and may not be easy to prove.[339] **Under KLaw**, the court could use the purpose of the purchase to decide on the description's nature, and the buyer could allege that the mal-capacity obstructed their personal purpose on their premises, regardless of the lack of predictability based on the contract, making the criterion very subjective. A judge might not consider the seller's capability and the buyer's proficiency in determining the description's status as assured, activating the capacity clause as a promissory term, upon which requesting termination would be allowed. The fact that the buyer did not need full capacity at the time of purchase, alongside their knowledge of the seller's limitation, would not change the legal outcome, as long as the capacity had been articulated in the contract. However, the buyer's inspection and the discoverability of misdescription may upend the situation. If the mal-capacity was discoverable by normal means, hidden defect rules might be applied instead of misdescription, as examination was not mentioned therein. Furthermore, if the seller sends a machine with a higher capacity that is better than the one shown to the buyer at the time of sale, termination might be permitted, as the seller did not deliver the commodity in the same state as when it was viewed. The buyer can cite any reason to request termination, such as that this high capacity consumes more electricity or demands more voltage than is available on their premises. They can even cite no specific reason as the difference in itself may constitute a breach, permitting the request for termination.

#### 4.2.2.4.2 CLARITY, FLEXIBILITY AND PRESERVING THE CONTRACT

**Under CISG**, the 'buyer's contractual interest' was considered in some cases in order to determine both the status of the breached descriptive statement and the fundamentality of the breach. This was true despite the fact that this criterion, which was refused by the CISG committee, could cause uncertainty when defining this interest. On the other hand, the 'buyer's reliance' on a descriptive statement may not represent a factor to verify the description's legal power as Article 35(3) clearly excludes description from its scope: i.e. the buyer's knowledge of misdescription at the contract conclusion (reflecting the buyer's non-reliance on descriptions) does not affect a misdescription claim. This obviates engaging in controversies over whether 'reliance' was presented or not, especially as this contention could be unclear and difficult to prove. Despite this exclusion, in some cases, for the sake of applying the good faith principle or revealing parties' intentions, the buyer's expertise, which was more than that of the seller, was examined (representing reliance) to categorise the descriptive statement, diminishing certainty and unintentionally activating Article 35(3). However, this would reduce the recourse to termination.

339 Cohen (n 249) 578–580.

**Under SGA**, in order to estimate the obligatory nature of the disputed description, opinion is divided with regards to considering the influential role of the phrase to induce the buyer to contract, the buyer's reliance, the goods' kind being specific goods or unascertained and the visibility and examination of the goods. This divergence in views reduces the chances of providing clarity. For instance, a car's model was a representation in *Oscar v Williams*[340] due to the seller's lack of knowledge but considered a promissory term in *Beale v Taylor*[341], depending on the buyer's examination. On the other hand, comparing the parties' experience to assess the buyer's reliance could reduce the risk of termination because it minimises the technical requirement of applying the contract, providing increased flexibility by assessing the situation according to the contractual circumstances, but, at the same time, it would reduce predictability and consistency. When the goods' maker is mentioned in the contract, determining the legal power of this clause requires a) assessment of the parties' dialogue throughout the contractual relationship to reveal their knowledge; b) finding out the parties' expertise, which might not be known to the other party at the time of sale; and 3) observing whether the buyer depended on their own judgement or on the seller's. In contrast, other courts found that the creator's name per se was a 'condition.'[342]

**Under KLaw**, focusing on the buyer's situation to determine their purchase motive and then to establish whether a description is 'assured' impedes predictability and objectivity. Furthermore, in some cases, the factors of examination and discoverability are applied to assess the description's status, and this made some courts apply the hidden defect rules, especially when the misdescription was hidden. This may reduce the recourse to termination as hidden defect rules are stricter than those of misdescription, but this conflation causes uncertainty and misapplication of law.

Nonetheless, if a judge acknowledges that there is a legal gap in defining the 'seller's assurance of description,' they may rule pursuant to Article 1(2) KCIC, in accordance with 'Islamic jurisprudence compatible with the reality of the country and its interests.' By using consensus, analogical reasoning, juristic preference, public interest and customs, Islamic rules can be reached.[343] The ruling, thus, will vary depending on the adopted Islamic school and the judge's Islamic perspective.

The situation of KLaw would leave the parties confused and cause judgements to vary from one case to another, even if the facts of the cases are the same, due to the diversity of the adopted criteria and the dependency on the judge's legal characterisation of the case. In principle, CISG permits claims of misdescription, even if the buyer did not rely on the breached description and regardless of whether the buyer was interested in completing the contractual relationship or not. This attains more certainty than SGA but could increase the number of misdescription claims.

340 *Oscar v Williams* (n 845).

341 *Beale v Taylor* (n 30) 1196.

342 *Leaf v Galleries* (n 1046) 89; *Nicholson v Smith-Marriott* (n 1047).

343 Kourides (n 36) 490.

However, such claims should always be assessed under Article 25, retaining the aim of contract preservation. This makes CISG an inspirational source for KLaw's reform.

## 4.3 Stipulations for Termination Based on Misdescription

Each legal system has its own approach to permitting termination of a contract based on misdescription.

### *4.3.1 CISG*

One hypothesis is that any descriptive statement in the contract can incite a nonconformity claim when it is breached by the seller.[344] As stated by the Secretariat Commentary, '[T]he overriding source for the standard of conformity is the contract between the parties.'[345] However, this does not mean that when the goods suffer from misdescription, the buyer is automatically permitted to terminate the contract; misdescription should be fundamental, according to Article 25.

#### *4.3.1.1 Substantial Deprivation of Contractual Expectations and Its Foreseeability*

Misdescription will not be fundamental unless the defaulting seller or a reasonable person can foresee[346] that a particular description will create particular expectation,[347] and misdescription will substantially deprive the buyer of this legitimate expectation.[348]

Some jurists may find that deprivation should be measured by establishing how the buyer's normal financial activities are affected.[349] In *FCF v Adriafil*, the court refused the buyer's right to declare the contract terminated when the nonconformity did not acutely jeopardize profits and the business-orientated contractual aim.[350] Additionally, in *Delchi Carrier v Rotorex*, the court considered the effect of the nonconformity (pertinent to 'the cooling power and energy consumption of an air conditioner compressor') on the goods' value an important determinant in deciding

344 Henschel, 'Conformity of Goods' (n 1005) 6; Gillette; Walt (n 778) 215, 219, 250. See also Saidov (n 769) 29.

345 Secretariat Commentary, 'Guide to Article 35' (n 1010).

346 CISG Art. 25.

347 A similar meaning is found in Schwenzer, *Commentary on CISG* (n 15) 431 [27].

348 See ibid 177, 178 [66]. For example, if the good which have been promised are seasonal, a reasonable supplier (in the same branch of trade) would perceive that delivery of such goods at the end of its season would undoubtedly impair their value.

349 Babiak (n 57) 120.

350 *Industrial furnace case* (26/7/2007) I.37/04 (Appellate Court Canton) <http://cisgw3.law.pace.edu/cases/070726s1.html>.

the breach was fundamental.[351] In the *Shoes case*, too, the court found that the seller's breach was fundamental when the shoes subsequently had no value to the buyer.[352]

However, the detriment might not directly affect the contractual financial aim, but it could affect the buyer's integrity or could implicate the buyer in a legal plight, such as infringing intellectual property law or consumer protection. Suppose that carcinogenic flavours/colours contained in some edible goods made the taste far more appealing than the healthier version, as stipulated in the contract, which accordingly enhanced the goods' marketability; no economic detriment was suffered by the buyer, but the breach could damage the ethics of the profession.

#### *4.3.1.2 Curability of Misdescription*

The relationship between the curability right and termination mentioned in Chapter 3 is applicable to misdescription. Some distinct aspects, with case law associated with misdescription, will be mentioned here. Pursuant to Article 48(1), immediate termination might not be permitted when misdescription could still be superceded by the seller's reasonable curability, without putting the buyer's main interest at definitive risk.[353] A buyer could accept a seller's offer to cure,[354] particularly as the buyer could collect damages for any inconvenience.[355] It may be found, moreover, that misdescription might not be fundamental when curability of this breach is feasible within a reasonable time,[356] especially when it is easy[357] and inexpensive.[358] The seller's offer to cure could be evidence that the buyer will not lose a substantial part of the bargain.[359] However, Article 48(2), (3) and (4) give an implicit right to the buyer to refuse the seller's attempt to cure when this refusal is conducted within a reasonable time, starting from when the seller requests to cure.

351 *Delchi Carrier v Rotorex* (6/12/1995) 185, 717, Dockets 95–7182, 95–7186 (Federal Appellate Court) <https://cisgw3.law.pace.edu/cases/951206u1.html>.

352 See also *Shoes case* 17/9/1991 (n 564).

353 *Inflatable triumphal arch case* (n 345); Honnold, *Uniform Law* (n 320) 426, 427; Piia Kalamees, 'Hierarchy of Buyer's Remedies in Case of Lack of Conformity of the Goods' (2011) 18 Juridica International 63, 68.

354 *Furniture case* (27/4/1992) 6252 (District Court Locarno Campagna) <http://cisgw3.law.pace.edu/cases/920427s1.html>. A similar conclusion was reached in *Acrylic blankets case* (n 350). It was stated that if there had been a serious proposal to cure the non-conformity, there would have been no fundamental breach.

355 Martin; Snyder (n 67) 364.

356 *Inflatable triumphal arch case* (n 345); *Arens Sondermaschinen v Smit Draad/Draad* (n 312).

357 *Saltwater isolation tank case* (26/4/1995) HG 920670 (Commercial Court Zürich) <http://cisgw3.law.pace.edu/cases/950426s1.html>.

358 *Industrial furnace case* (n 1118).

359 Martin; Snyder (n 67) 364.

If misdescription is obviously incurable or of 'irremovable character'[360] or it is curable but causes unreasonable inconvenience or expense to the buyer,[361] the buyer is entitled to terminate the contract.[362] This is the case especially when the concerned goods are those associated with either price fluctuation or rapid technological development.[363] In the *Organic barley case*, when the goods lacked documents confirming their classification as 'organic,' the issuing of a certificate after the goods were shipped did not have any retroactive effect,[364] making the breach fundamental.

Despite the foregoing, it could be argued that it does not matter that misdescription is remediable when Article 25's stipulations are met. According to the approach of *Cobalt sulphate*, the reparability of the breach is not the decisive factor in differentiating between a fundamental breach and a simple breach.[365] Nevertheless, pursuant to Article 37, when the seller delivers the goods before the agreed date and the buyer accepts early delivery,[366] the seller has the right to remedy the fundamental nonconformity until the agreed delivery date, with the stipulation of not causing the buyer unreasonable inconvenience or expense.[367]

#### *4.3.1.3 Suggested Criteria to Assess the Fundamentality of Misdescription*

Perhaps the vagueness of the 'substantial deprivation' and its foreseeability mentioned in Article 25 has driven some jurists to create alternative criteria, outlined next:

##### 4.3.1.3.1 GOODS' USABILITY/SALABILITY

Re-salability/usability of goods may prevent misdescription from being considered fundamental[368] as long as they can be found on the international market and have a purchasing value, irrespective of the fact that the resale could incur expense or

360 *Varnish and paint machine case* (18/10/2005) 21/2005 (Arbitration proceeding Russia) <;http://cisgw3.law.pace.edu/cases/051018r1.html>; *Sr Carlos Manuel del Corazón de Jesús Bravo Barros v Salvador Martínez Gares* (31/5/2007) 87484, Registro de Cámera No. 102.876/2002 (National Commercial Court of Appeals) <http://cisgw3.law.pace.edu/cases/070531a1.html>.

361 Honnold, *Uniform Law* (n 320) 352.

362 *Dust ventilator case* (21/6/2006) 1 C 1025/05 (Lower Court Landsberg) <http://cisgw3.law.pace.edu/cases/060621g1.html>. A similar conclusion was reached in the *Automobile case* (2006) CISG/2006/03 (CIETAC arbitration proceeding) <http://cisgw3.law.pace.edu/cases/061200c1.html>.

363 Schlechtriem, 'Subsequent Performance' (n 349) 90.

364 *Organic barley case* (13/11/2002) 27 U 346/02 (Appellate Court München) <http://cisgw3.law.pace.edu/cases/021113g1.html>.

365 *Cobalt sulphate case* 3/4/1996 (n 547). A similar statement was mentioned in *FCF v Adriafil* (n 144).

366 CISG Art. 51(1).

367 Honnold, *Uniform Law* (n 320) 350, 351.

368 Enderlein; Maskow (n 150) 114; Dessemontet (n 170) 209; Lookofsky; Bernstein (n 541) 124; Martin; Snyder (n 67) 368;

require a discounted price.[369] In the *GMS modules case*, the court stated that 'there will be no objective and grave non-conformity if the goods can be put to a different use in the course of normal business without causing any unreasonable commercial detriment upon the buyer.'[370] The court continued, '[T]he fact [that] the buyer is in a position to make limited use of the defective goods in combination with a price reduction or damages claim [might make the breach non-fundamental].'[371] Thus, when the buyer in the *Shoes case* complained that the material used to manufacture the shoes was different from that agreed, which made them rough, distorted and wrinkled, the court indicated that a fundamental breach had not occurred if the buyer could have made use of the goods.[372] Similarly, in the *Souvenir coins case*, when the buyer's customers complained that the coins were not authentic as described in their certificates, the tribunal found there was no fundamental breach, owing to the ability to sell 'three-quarters of the goods,' which meant the buyer was not substantially deprived of what they were contractually entitled to expect.[373] In the *Cobalt sulphate case*, too, the court refused to consider the violation fundamental when lower-quality goods of South African origin were sent rather than British ones, as had expressly been stipulated in the contract, as the buyer failed to demonstrate that the goods sent were unsalable or unusable, either in their country or abroad.[374] Furthermore, in the *Meat case*, the court asserted that the feasibility of disposing the goods in the normal course of commerce without inconvenient effort should be taken into account in order to objectively assess the fundamentality of misdescription.[375]

However, as Schlechtriem asserts, 'The conformity of the goods with the contract is not determined objectively but depends first and foremost on the "subjective" description of the goods in the contract,'[376] and as Luca emphasised, 'Goods are deemed to be conforming not when they meet abstract and objective standards, but rather when they correspond to the concrete description contained in the contractual agreement.'[377] Relying on the 'salability' test may not render each case its particularity; the breach will be assessed in a generic way instead. Thus, in the *Weaving machines case*, the court found that it was reasonable for the buyer to request the return of the goods as long as the goods were not manufactured

369 Anna Veneziano, 'Non Conformity of Goods in International Sales- A Survey of Current Caselaw on CISG' (1997) 1 IBLJ 39, 57; Martin; Snyder (n 67) 368.

370 *GMS modules* (n 135).

371 ibid.

372 *Shoes case* (18/1/1994) 5U15/93 (Appellate Court Frankfurt) <https://cisgw3.law.pace.edu/cases/940118g1.html>.

373 *Souvenir coins case* (2000) CISG/2000/17 (CIETAC arbitration proceeding) <http://cisgw3.law.pace.edu/cases/000000c1.html>.

374 *Cobalt sulphate case* 3/4/1996 (n 547).

375 *Meat case* (n 171).

376 Peter Schlechtriem; Petra Butler, *UN Law on International Sales: the UN Convention on the International Sale of Goods* (Springer 2009) 113, 114.

377 Luca (n 815) 184.

in Switzerland as agreed upon,[378] without assessing their salability or usability. Furthermore, in the *Packaging machine case*, it was stated that 'the usability or retailability of sub-standard goods will have to be denied for producers or ultimate buyers who do not deal in such goods.'[379]

###### 4.3.1.3.2 INSUFFICIENCY OF OTHER REMEDIES

If the buyer is unsatisfied with less drastic compensatory remedies,[380] such as damages or a price reduction, or when these remedies are reasonably inappropriate to fix the detriment,[381] some jurists rule this a sign of fundamental misdescription. In the *Globes case*, the judge found that the buyer was not substantially deprived of their main expectations on the basis that, inter alia, the breach could be remedied by price reduction.[382] In the *GMS modules case*, it was stated that 'the term "fundamental". . . includes an assessment of the fact whether the expectations of the buyer can be fully satisfied by means of a damages claim or a reduction in price.'[383] However, one might argue that when the compensation for the detriment resulting from a breach is considered an adequate remedial solution, it might not be a sign that Article 25's stipulations are unmet.[384]

### *4.3.2 SGA*

#### *4.3.2.1 Conditionality of Descriptions*

Descriptions as such are elevated to 'conditions' by operation of law,[385] and this status gives the buyer an immediate right to treat the whole contract as terminated when it is broken,[386] regardless of the gravity of its consequences,[387] even though many degrees of breaches might occur.[388] Sending goods resembling those ordered,[389] supplying partially coarse-ground goods instead of fine-ground ones for the whole delivery as agreed[390] and sending soybean meal with a percentage

378 *Weaving machines, tools and accessories case* (5/9/1994) CIETAC Arbitration proceeding <http://cisgw3.law.pace.edu/cases/940905c2.html>.

379 *Packaging machine case* 18/5/2009 (n 153).

380 Ferrari, 'Fundamental Breach' (n 161) 489; Kröll; Mistelis; Viscasillas (n 67) 341 [12].

381 *Computer components case* (n 1001); Zeller, 'Fundamental Breach' (n 184) 82; Ferrari, 'Fundamental Breach' (n 161) 496, 497; Bridge, 'Avoidance for Fundamental Breach' (n 158) 921.

382 *Globes case* (n 185).

383 *GMS modules* (n 135).

384 Enderlein; Maskow (n 150) 113.

385 McKendrick, *Sale of Goods* (n 202) 324. See also *Bentley v Harold* (n 1017) 629.

386 Smith, *Atiyah's* (n 198) 198; Burrows, *Principles of English Commercial Law* (n 28) 77; McKendrick, *Contract law* (n 206) 737.

387 *FW Moore & Co Ltd v Landauer & Co* [1921] 2 KB 519.

388 Smith, *Atiyah's* (n 198) 200.

389 *Arcos v Ronaasen* (n 422) 470; Ebrahim *Dawood Ltd v Heath* [1961] 2 Lloyd's Rep 512.

390 *Toepfer v Warinco* (n 885) 569.

of fibre exceeding that agreed[391] entitled buyers to reject the whole cargo.[392] When it was agreed in *Moore* to sell Australian canned fruit packed in cases, each case containing thirty cans, and the seller sent the correct total quantity, but some cases contained twenty-four cans instead of thirty, the court held that the sale was by description, and the buyer was entitled to reject the whole consignment.[393] In *Arcos*, when it was contractually stipulated that the staves' thickness must be half an inch and it was discovered on the goods' arrival that they were fractionally different (over half an inch but not more than an inch), the court affirmed the buyer's right to reject the goods, even though the staves were commercially merchantable and fit for the buyer's purpose in making cement barrels.[394] As Lord Atkin emphasised, '½ inch' did not mean 'about ½ inch.'[395] In *Rapalli v Take*, when some onions were about 6% undersized and around 5% were sprouting, the buyer was entitled to reject the consignment, despite the court's holding that the onions were not sub-standard.[396] Stating in the contract that the 'goods [are] to be taken with all faults and defects; damaged or inferior'[397] or stating that the seller did not guarantee any description[398] did not change the result that the shipments should have complied with the descriptions, even if the goods were displayed before the buyer.[399]

#### *4.3.2.2 S.15A*

According to s.15A, when misdescription is 'so slight,' making rejecting the goods unreasonable, termination is not an option, avoiding strained application of the agreed description[400] and imposing a new norm of flexibility and fairness.[401] Some decisions before the enactment of s.15A followed quantitative *modus operandi*, which could have had a notion similar to s.15A. In *Cehave*, when a small part of the goods was a little below the agreed standard, 'shipped in good condition'[402] was not a repudiatory breach.[403] As Lord Denning mentioned, it could be unfair that a small difference permits rejection of the whole consignment.[404] In *Glass' Fruit Markets v Southwell*, when a shipment of 'sound' potatoes was agreed upon but the buyer received blighted potatoes, it was held that the word 'sound' would not be applicable if the blight was insignificant, not entitling the buyer to reject the whole

391 *Tradax v European Grain* (n 422) 100.
392 *Levy v Green* (1859) 120 E.R. 1174.
393 *Moore v Landauer* (n 1155).
394 *Arcos v Ronaasen* (n 422) 470.
395 ibid 479.
396 *Rapalli v Take* (n 422) 469.
397 *Robert A Munro & Co v Meyer* [1930] 2 KB 312.
398 *Wallis Son & Wells v Pratt & Haynes* [1911] AC 394.
399 *Grant v Australian Knitting Mills* (n 1052) 100.
400 Bridge, *The Sale of Goods* (n 28) [10.26].
401 McKendrick, *Sale of Goods* (n 202) 491, 492.
402 The clause 'shipped in good condition' was not considered to be a promissory statement.
403 *Cehave* (n 126) 61.
404 ibid 63.

delivery.[405] Furthermore, in *Tradax Internacional v Goldschmidt*, when the buyer discovered that the shipment of barley contained 4.10% foreign matter, whereas the agreed percentage was 4%, it was held that the excess amount was not commercially significant.[406]

Nevertheless, s.15A adds some complexity[407] and causes 'regrettable uncertainty'[408] 'without attaining justice,'[409] making it difficult to predict not only its application but also the legal outcome, and this makes seeking legal advice worthless.[410] A slight breach of description might be apparent in cases in which damages are a reasonable remedy for the breach,[411] as stated in *Ruxley Electronics v Forsyth*: 'It is unreasonable of a plaintiff to claim an expensive remedy if there is some cheaper alternative which would make good his loss.'[412] However, in *Arcos*, it was stated:

> No doubt there may be microscopic deviations which business men and therefore lawyers will ignore. . . . But apart from this consideration the right view is that the conditions of the contract must be strictly performed.[413]

Although some scholars[414] find that a slight misdescription should not be converted to an 'intermediate term,' it is stated in s.15A that a term that is slightly breached 'may be treated as a breach of warranty.' Using the phrase 'may be' seems to imply that it is possible instead to treat the slightly breached description as an 'intermediate term.' This may position a slightly breached description outside the realm of 'conditions' under s.13(1) by virtue of s.15A, but at the same time, this excluded breach could be placed under an 'intermediate term' classification to examine its consequences, and, if they are substantial, termination would be activated again. In *Ashington*, Lord Guest stated that misdescription occurred when there was a substantial addition to the ordered commodity,[415] and the admixture of only 0.0008 did not make the goods different.[416] If this case recurred, the impact of this slight addition, which resulted in the death of farmed mink, could be considered, and termination might be permitted.

405 Glass' Fruit Markets v Southwell (A) & Son (Fruit) [1969] 2 Lloyd's Rep 398.
406 *Tradax v Goldschmidt* (n 421) 604, 605, 614.
407 Peacock (n 140) 111.
408 Peel, 15th edn (n 64) 996 [18–060].
409 Peel, 13th edn (n 691) 889 [18–054]. See also Burrows, *Principles of English Commercial Law* (n 28) 77, 78; Chen-Wishart (n 77) 479 [12.2.3.1].
410 Yan M, 'Remedies under the Convention on Contracts for the International Sale of Goods and the United Kingdom's Sale of Goods Act: A Comparative Examination' (2011) 3 CityUHK LR 120, 121; Peel, 15th edn (n 64) 997 [18–061].
411 ibid Peel 1031 [18–129].
412 Staughton LJ in *Ruxley Electronics v Forsyth* [1996] AC 344, 364.
413 *Arcos v Ronaasen* (n 422) 479, 480.
414 Burrows, *Principles of English Commercial Law* (n 28) 77, 78 Footnote 263; Peel, 15th edn (n 64) 996, 997 [18–060].
415 *Ashington v Christopher* (n 842) 472.
416 ibid 459.

#### *4.3.2.3 Reasonable Application of Description*

The parties' reasonable expectations[417] and the reasonable recipient's understanding could be factors in clarifying the extent to which the description will be applied.[418] Lord Reid, in *Schuler v Wickman*, stated that:

> The fact that a particular construction leads to a very unreasonable result must be a relevant consideration. The more unreasonable the result the more unlikely it is that the parties can have intended it.[419]

In *Grenfell*, it was held that a pair of flying goggles did not breach the contractual description 'safety-glass lenses,' even when the buyer's eye was injured by a splinter from the goggles in a flying accident. They were manufactured from laminated glass, complying with the general understanding of people making or using them to be 'safety-glass,' and the general sense of this phrase did not equate to absolute safety.[420] Additionally, in *Peter Darlington v Gosho*, it was agreed in the contract that Moroccan canary seed would be of 'pure basis.' When some of the goods possessed a purity of 98%, this was ruled as adequate as 'pure basis' was not necessarily equivalent to 100% purity.[421]

Problematically, common understanding could be recognised according to the court's perspective. Lord Wilberforce, in *Reardon Smith*, stated that 'what the court must do must be to place itself in thought in the same factual matrix as that in which the parties were.'[422] This is even though it was stated in *Skanska v Somerfield* that:

> Judges are not always the most commercially-minded, let alone the most commercially experienced, of people, and should . . . avoid arrogating to themselves overconfidently the role of arbiter of commercial reasonableness or likelihood.[423]

Moreover, over-recourse to common sense might be inconsistent with the parties' intention[424] and may attribute to the parties an intention which is clearly not theirs, and this is not suggested by the law.[425] In *Chadwick v Oxford Forecasting Services*, it was stated that deviating from the literal construction of contractual proviso on the pretext that it was incompatible with 'any sensible commercial objective or

417 *Equitable Life Assurance Society v Hyman* [2002] 1 AC 408.

418 *Mannai Investment Co Ltd v Eagle Star Life Assurance Co Ltd* [1997] AC 749, 767; Bridge, *Benjamin's* (n 28) [11–021].

419 *Schuler* (n 198) 236, 237.

420 *Grenfell v E B Meyrowitz Ltd* [1936] 2 All ER 1313.

421 *Peter Darlington Partners v Gosho* [1964] 1 Lloyd's Rep 149.

422 *Reardon v Hansen-Tangen* (n 417) 995.

423 *Skanska Rasleigh Weatherfoil Ltd v Somerfield Stores Ltd* [2006] EWCA Civ 1732 [22].

424 Chadwick LJ in *City Alliance Ltd v Oxford Forecasting Services Ltd* [2001] 1 All ER [12];[13].

425 Lord Hoffmann in *Investors Compensation Scheme v Bromwich* (n 623) 913; ibid.

purpose' might likely be unacceptable.[426] Lord Pearson in *Trollope v Regional Hospital Board* stated, '[I]t is not enough for the court to find that such a term would have been adopted by the parties as reasonable men.'[427] This is especially true as certainty could be favoured even at the expense of justice,[428] as Lord Hope stated: '[T]o avoid any commitment to over-arching principles in favour of piecemeal solutions in response to demonstrated problems of unfairness.'[429] The courts, therefore, may endeavour to enhance predictability[430] without any deviation to create new unfamiliar doctrines.[431]

#### *4.3.2.4 Substantiality of the Result*

When it is difficult to categorise descriptive statements as either 'terms' or 'puffery,' they could be considered 'intermediate terms.' To decide whether termination is an option or not,[432] it would depend on the seriousness[433] of the breach's consequences, which must have deprived the buyer 'of substantially the whole benefit . . . intended [to be obtained] from the contract.'[434] This could be contingent on the practical considerations of the judicial perspective.[435] Although this consequential method is only a complementary approach,[436] there is a fear that if this goes further,[437] displacing the 'condition' rule rather than supplementing it,[438] it undesirably reduces the strictness of s.13.

### ***4.3.3 KLaw***

Article 197 KCIC asserted that 'the contract must be executed in accordance with the provisions it contains';[439] in some cases, the court stated that according to Article 498 KCIC, if the agreed description does not exist in the goods, the buyer has

426 *City Alliance v Oxford Forecasting* (n 1192) [12]; [13].
427 Lord Pearson in *Trollope & Colls Ltd v North West Metropolitan Regional Hospital Board* [1973] 1 WLR 601, 609.
428 Peel, 15th edn (n 64) 974 [18–032].
429 *R. (on the application of European Roma Rights Centre) v Immigration Officer, Prague Airport* [2005] 2 AC 1 [95].
430 Ahdar (n 765) 56.
431 Andrew Stewart, 'What's Wrong With the Australian of Contract?' (2012) 29(1) JCL 74, 80.
432 Twigg-Flesner; Canavan (n 30) 120, 122, 123.
433 *Cehave* (n 126) 61.
434 ibid 71.
435 Peel, 15th edn (n 64) 974 [18–032].
436 Adams; Brownsword (n 218) 169, 170.
437 *Schuler* (n 198) 236, 237.
438 Adams; Brownsword (n 218) 168, 169. See also *Dick Bentley Productions Ltd v Harold Smith (Motors) Ltd* [1965] 1 W.L.R. 623, 627.
439 Case 12/12/2001 (n 727) 5. See also Case 18/1/1993 (n 961) in Ministry of Justice, *Commercial Provisions* (n 259) 65.

a choice between terminating the contract or keeping it.[440] EMKCIC also includes statements such as '[T]he contract is the primary source of commitment,' and '[T]he contract generates the obligation.'[441] It also explains the importance of complying with the agreed descriptions, stating:

> One of the most important foundations of KLaw is determined by Art.196, which is that the contract is the law of the parties. It says in the Quran: 'Believers, fulfil your obligations.' The Messenger Muhammed (PBUH) also stated: 'Muslims should fulfil their promises.'[442]

However, neither the law,[443] case law nor literature provides concrete stipulations to request termination for misdescription. It is merely repeatedly stated that termination is subject to the estimation of the trial court in terms of assessing the adequacy of its causes and justifications,[444] as long as the judgement is based on justified reasons.[445]

#### *4.3.3.1 Absence of the Requirement of Detriment for Termination Based on Misdescription*

Under contractual liability, the seller is responsible for accomplishing the result promised in the contract[446] in order to avoid the buyer's recourse to termination. Assessing the breach, the detriment and the causal relationship between them is confined to claim compensation[447] and tort liability.[448]

440 Case 29/12/2009 (n 260) 7, 8. See also Case 11/2/2006 (n 1098) in Ministry of Justice, *Civil Provisions* (n 955) 295.

441 EMKCIC 42.

442 ibid 213.

443 KCIC Art. 498.

444 Case 13/5/2001 (n 617) 5.

445 Case 20/5/1998 (n 43) 5; Case 17/2/1999 Appellate Court/Commercial 1453/1998, 5; Case 6/2/2001 (n 263) 4; Case 31/5/2004 (n 619) 4; Case 12/11/2005 Court of Cassation/Commercial 3 1080/2004, 5; Case 29/4/2006 (n 265) 9; Case 15/10/2006, 1250 (n 261) 6; Case 7/11/2006 (n 926) 5–8; Case 25/9/2008 Court of Cassation/Commercial 1314–1330/2005, 8; Case 30/12/2008 Court of Cassation/Commercial 92/2008, 6; Case 29/12/2009 (n 260) 4–6, 10; Case 27/4/2010 Court of Cassation/Commercial 2008/865, 6; Case 2/11/2010 (n 265) 6; Case 3/10/2011 (n 926) 3; Case 20/12/2011 Court of Cassation/Commercial 2009/1498, 8; Case 7/2/2012 (n 263) 8, 11; Case 14/2/2012 Court of Cassation/Commercial 2011/499, 2, 3; Case 5/3/2012 (n 933) 3, 4.

446 Al-Sanhory (n 279) 739.

447 This liability is designed especially for compensation, which can be deduced from KCIC Art. 227, 230, 231 and 234.

448 Case 20/5/1998 (n 43) 3; Case 11/10/1999 Appellate Court/Commercial 1988–2072/1998, 5; Case 6/2/2001 (n 263) 5; Case 29/3/2006 (n 503) 5; Case 7/11/2006 (n 926) 2; Case 27/4/2010 (n 1213) 6; Case 7/2/2012 (n 263) 11.

#### 4.3.3.1.1 MISDESCRIPTION RAISES TERMINATION RIGHT

There are no stipulations to request termination other than that the disputed description should be assured by the seller, as discussed earlier. This puts termination on a par with other remedies, despite its nature as a dangerous mechanism. Thus, the descriptions laid down in the contract shall be applied, or the contract shall be terminated when these terms are not presented.[449] Requesting termination could be permitted even if the misdescription is not considered a breach according to the usage of the same goods.[450]

This conduct has been deduced from Article 310 Al-Majalla,[451] which states that if goods are sold according to a specific description and, after the purchase, it turns out that the goods lack this description, the buyer has the option of either terminating the contract or accepting the goods for the agreed price. Al-Majalla gives examples, stating that if a cow is sold as 'milch' but it emerges afterwards that it is 'non-milch,' or if a stone is sold as red sapphire but later appears to be yellow, a buyer would have this choice.[452] These examples emphasise the importance of compliance with descriptions, whether they are functional or physical, but these examples could also indicate that the breach should not be trivial.

However, some courts stated that the mere lack of an agreed description assured by the seller, raised the liability of the latter.[453] Hence, partial failure to implement the agreed descriptions[454] is considered a breach per se, entitling the buyer to request termination.[455] It has been emphasised in many cases that the legislator authorised under Article 209 that both parties can demand termination if the other party has failed to fulfil their contractual obligation,[456] and the judge is *obliged* to answer if they request termination.[457]

#### 4.3.3.1.2 NO DETRIMENT REQUIREMENT IN REQUESTING TERMINATION

KLaw does not stipulate a buyer's detriment resultant from misdescription in order to terminate the contract, nor does it stipulate a certain degree of deviation from the contractual description. In one case, a seller's defence that misdescription was not substantial, did not cause detriment to the buyer and did not influence the buyer to

449 Case 14/12/1983 Court of Cassation/Commercial 70/83 in Ministry of Justice, *Commercial Provisions* (n 259); Ayob (n 494) 49.

450 Case 14/6/1993 (n 499).

451 Al-Majalla Art. 310.

452 ibid Art. 311.

453 Case 16/3/2008 Court of Cassation/Commercial 467, 476/2008, 8, 9; Case 29/12/2009 (n 260) 7, 8.

454 Case 14/6/1999 Appellate Court/Commercial 1207/1998, 4.

455 Case 9/10/1995 (n 719) 2; Case 20/5/1998 (n 43) 2; Case 19/6/2000 Court of Cassation/Civil 249/1999, 3; Case 13/5/2001 (n 617) 5; Case 13/4/2002 (n 732) 4; Case 31/5/2004 (n 619) 2, 4; Case 12/12/2007 (n 618) 2; Case 29/12/2009 (n 260) 4; Case 27/4/2010 (n 1213) 6; Case 3/10/2011 (n 926) 3–5; Case 14/2/2012 (n 1213) 4.

456 Case 27/11/1996 (n 276) 2, 3; Case 20/5/1998 (n 43) 5; Case 12/12/2001 (n 727) 7; Case 16/4/2012 (n 941) 4.

457 Case 14/6/1999 (n 1222) 4.

refrain from signing the contract was refused by the court.[458] Furthermore, when a machine violated the agreed degree of energy related to air volume and pressure,[459] termination was activated even though this equipment would have been very good and perhaps better than average, and no detriment was suffered by the buyer. Additionally, when a shipment of paper arrived and was discovered to have been made in Korea and not Japan, England or Switzerland as agreed, the buyer (a bank) refused to take the goods and began proceedings to terminate the contract. The court of first instance decided that the shipment was in conformity with the agreed specifications as long as the paper had been made in a Japanese factory in Korea, and this decision was upheld on appeal. However, the court of cassation applied Article 498 KCIC and decided that the contractual terms were clear regarding the place of manufacture, which reflected the parties' will without the need for interpretation, pursuant to Article 193(1) KCIC.[460] This ruling investigated neither the significance of misdescription nor the substantiality of the detriment suffered by the buyer.

#### 4.3.3.1.3 DETRIMENT COULD BE A REQUIREMENT, DEPENDING ON JUDGES' PERSPECTIVE

Despite the foregoing, judges might require 'detriment' to have been suffered by the buyer in order to decide on termination.[461] In some cases, the court of cassation highlighted that extracting the availability of the detriment was left to the trial court's discretion.[462] This may make the court hold the seller liable for misdescription according to the personal detriment[463] suffered by the buyer.[464] In some cases, the court of cassation stressed that the judge should adhere to regulations set by law and should consider the personal circumstances of the injured party,[465] such as prejudice against their reputation, dignity, honour or image[466] or deprivation of investment.[467] In one case, misdescription led to termination based, inter alia, on the personal, moral and material detriment suffered by the buyer.[468]

This policy of taking into account personal detriment may follow that adopted in tort law as Article 247 stipulates that the judge should determine compensation by

458 Case 18/6/1996 Appellate Court/Commercial-4 427/1995, 4, 5; Case 29/12/2009 (n 260) 7, 8. See also Case 1/11/1998 Court of Cassation/Commercial 636/1997, 2, 3.
459 Case 18/12/1989 Court of Cassation/Commercial reproduced in Al-Defery; Al-Sayrafy (n 254) 325.
460 Case 18/1/1993 (n 961) in Ministry of Justice, *Commercial Provisions* (n 259) 65.
461 Case 7/11/1995 (n 1104) 2–7.
462 Case 6/2/2001 (n 263) 15; Case 16/3/2008 (n 1221) 8, 9; Case 2/11/2010 (n 265) 2 and 4; Case 14/2/2012 (n 1213) 4.
463 Case 7/11/1995 (n 1104) 2–7; Case 18/11/1996 (n 1085).
464 Abdulreda (n 40) 465.
465 Case 6/2/2001 (n 263) 16.
466 Case 20/3/2005 (n 263) 4.
467 ibid 6.
468 Case 9/12/1996 (n 1095).

considering the personal circumstances of the injured party. Article 230(1) KCIC, related to compensation, might also be followed; it states that the detriment suffered by the buyer should be the natural result of the seller's breach in order to compensate the buyer. However, the phrase 'natural result' (which indicates the causal relationship between the breach and detriment)[469] might encompass personal detriments, unlike expected damage,[470] which would be foreseeable by any sensible person.[471]

Some jurists state that when the buyer is a specialised dealer, they are able to resell the goods, even if they differ from the goods agreed upon.[472] With counter-interpretation of this opinion, detriment could be construed through the buyer's inability to resell the goods of different descriptions. In one case, it was stated that nonconformity did not establish that the delivered machines were *reduced in their value* by such a breach, and this made the nonconformity insubstantial.[473] However, others may find that the salability of goods suffering from misdescription could hinder the buyer from achieving their intended purpose, causing harm to their reputation, especially when they are known for selling a specific standard of goods.[474] This contradiction indicates that this criterion might be unviable as it might encourage the seller to breach the contractual clauses, alleging that the contract cannot be terminated as long as the goods are merchantable. Generally, this does not align with KLaw's perspective, unless customs indicate the contrary.

#### *4.3.3.2 Abuse of Rights*

After scrutinising other general provisions not exclusively related to contract law, there is a possibility that judges may not permit termination based on misdescription when buyers exploit the right to termination, according to Article 30 KCIC.

469 Atef Al-Naqeeb, *The General Theory of Responsibility Arising From Things* (Eweedat 1981) 137, 138; Abdulrasheed Mammon, *Causal Relationship in Civil Liability* (Dar Alnahda) 2, 25.

470 Demogue states: '*[U]ne atteinte au droit et la fait d'avoir aperçu ou pu apercevoir que l'on portait atteinte au droit d'autrui.*' René Demogue, *Des Obligations en Général* (Librairie Arthur Rousseau 1923) 367. This approach is followed by Mammon (ibid 35). See also René Savatier, *Traite de la Responsabilité Civile en Droit Français, Tome II* (Librairie Générale de Droit et du Jurisprudence 1951) 26. Savatier mentioned the phrase '*la cause directe.*' François Chabas, *L'influence de la Pluralité de Causes sur le Droit a Réparation* (Librairie Générale de Droit et du Jurisprudence 1967) 87, 88.

471 Al-Naqeeb, *Liability Arising From Personal Action* (n 954) 114. See also Chabas ibid 87. Chabas mentioned that there should be 'Nomological Knowledge' of the result: i.e. knowing the result of an action through an objective possibility of the result by deducing such an effect of such a cause of a normal man.

472 Sarko (n 258) 51; Abdulfadeel Ahmed, *Commercial Contracts and Banking Operations in Kuwaiti Law* (Dar AlKotob 2015) 24.

473 Case 17/4/1995, 293 (n 517).

474 Ahmed (n 1213) 24.

However, not a single case that applies Article 30 to misdescription could be found. Article 30 states that:

> The use of a right is unlawful if its holder *deviates from the purpose of the right or its social function*, and in particular:
>
> (a) [n/a]
> (b) [n/a]
> (c) if the *benefit* resulting from it is *in no sense commensurate with the damage* caused to others.
> (d) if it would cause *extraordinary colossal damage* to others.

#### 4.3.3.2.1 DEVIATION FROM TERMINATION'S PURPOSE AND ITS SOCIAL FUNCTION

Termination may not be allowed if it deviates from its purpose, although it is unclear what constitutes the purpose and social function of termination. It could be submitted that the parties enter into the contractual relationship consciously and selectively, and this free will creates the contract, which becomes the parties' law,[475] making the purpose of termination to encourage the application of the contract and respect all its terms as a moral duty,[476] mirroring the principle of enforcing promises.[477]

Accordingly, when termination is used to guarantee the existence of contractual descriptions, this refutes the assumption of deviation from its purpose, making this sub-rule rarely applicable to contract law.

#### 4.3.3.2.2 TERMINATION'S NON-COMMENSURABILITY WITH THE OTHER'S (SELLER'S) DAMAGE OR CAUSING THEM UNUSUALLY EXTRAORDINARY DAMAGE

Article 30(c) and (d) open the door for sellers to claim that termination would be incommensurate with the damage suffered, leading to competition between the parties to win the battle of persuading and propitiating the judge, which creates an unsettled status for both parties. Moreover, these sub-rules are excessively subjective, lack precision and depend on the seller's situation. The law scrutinises the detriment suffered by sellers as a result of using the termination right, rather than assessing 1) the magnitude of the breach, 2) the detriment suffered by the buyer because of the breach or 3) 'what [the buyer] would have gained if the promise had been kept.'[478]

It is stated in EMKCIC that 'a lack of proportionality between the interest of the holder of the rights, and the harm caused to others, could be a presumption of the

475 KCIC Art. 32; Kourides (n 36) 420; Abdulreda; Al-Nakas (n 257) 157.
476 Cartwright (n 114) 273, 274.
477 Smith, *Contract Theory* (n 85) 52.
478 Cohen (n 249) 553, 578–580.

*intention to harm others.*'[479] Similarly, in many cases (not related to misdescription), it was established that:

> Whoever uses their rights legitimately is not responsible for the harm that arises from such a use. . . . The use of these rights outside this lawful circle is an exception stated in Article 30 KCIC. . . . [T]he intention to harm [could be] active, by deliberately seeking to harm others without obtaining benefits to the holder of the rights, or passive, by underestimating the serious harm to others resulting from exercising their rights, which is apparently regarding their usage as a luxury. . . . Estimating the existence of this deviation is left to the trial court.[480]

Hence, it could be argued that this provision should not be applied in cases of misdescription for the following reasons: **First**, in contract law, the parties rarely use their rights maliciously[481] to harm the other party but rather, in most cases to maintain their own interests.[482] **Secondly**, the doctrine of *lex specialis* makes specific laws override the general rule, and this, accordingly, makes contractual adherence[483] prevail over the general rule of not causing harm to others, making this sub-rule more appropriate to tort law. **Lastly**, one can simply claim that the phrase 'damage caused to *others*' used in the Article 30(d) most likely does not refer to contractual parties, but third parties.

Nonetheless, it could be argued that Article 197 KCIC states that the contract must be executed pursuant to the requirements of good faith and honour, which may exclude trivial misdescription from consideration because of the incommensurability with damage to the seller. However, because there is no express adoption of objective criterion in law, the buyer can always demonstrate that the trivial breach in the court's perspective could be considerable in their particular situation.

#### *4.3.3.3 Special Case: Goods Are Different From Agreed Category under KCOC*

Article 132(1) KCOC states that if the delivered goods differ from the goods agreed upon in terms of their class/category, the buyer may not request termination unless this difference is substantial. Article 132(1) asserts that the substantiality in this case depends on the invalidity of the delivered goods for their prepared purpose.

479 EMKCIC 33.

480 Case 4/12/2000 Appellate Court/Civil 1303/2000, 5–7. A similar meaning was found in Case 31/12/1995 Appellate Court/Civil 407/1995, 4; Case 13/2/1996 Appellate Court/Commercial 1429/95, 2, 3; Case 20/3/2005 (n 263) 5, 6, 8, 10, 13.

481 Case 20/3/2005 (n 263) 5, 6.

482 Ayob (n 494) 230 footnote 39.

483 KCIC Art. 196, 197.

#### 4.3.3.3.1 NONCONFORMING CATEGORY AND MISDESCRIPTION

Not one single case could be found in which Article 132 had been applied to the 'category' of goods, but there were cases which applied Article 132 to 'quantity,'[484] which also falls within its scope. Problematically, Article 132(1) does not clearly differentiate between sending goods of a different category and sending goods suffering from misdescription, which has its own rule, mentioned earlier. The scope of whether or not Article 132(1) applies to 'misdescription' and/or 'quality' is also unclear. Moreover, 'different category' is not defined; does it mean goods of a different origin from that agreed? A different manufacturer or brand?

Seemingly, 'category' specifies the goods' class, but 'description' indicates a certain kind of goods[485] within the agreed category. Examples of nonconforming category could be sending timber instead of English coal[486] and delivering American wheat instead of Australian wheat, entitling the buyer to request termination[487] because these differences are considered substantial. However, receiving Basmati rice from Bihar (an area in India) instead of Basmati rice from Punjab (another area in India) can be deemed relatively insubstantial, especially as the rice is still Basmati and from India, possessing the same features. The dilemma lies in the fact that these goods' categories could be classified as descriptions, as long as they were mentioned in the contract.

#### 4.3.3.3.2 DEFINING SUBSTANTIALITY BY IDENTIFYING THE PREPARED PURPOSE

Referring 'substantiality' of the nonconforming category to the goods' 'prepared purpose' might not offer much help in the absence of defining such a purpose. Is the 'prepared purpose' dependent on the buyer, a sensible person, the contractual circumstances or the judge's perspective? A reasonable purpose is not considered following Marty, who was opposed to the reasonable person standard because it required the buyer to behave in a manner unknown to all buyers.[488]

Thus, the purpose might be confined that related neither to the contract nor to the concerned goods, permitting the inclusion of the buyer's personal purposes. These purposes might not be revealed to the seller at the contract conclusion but might be proved at the time of litigation by showing, for instance, the buyer's commitment to their customers. This conduct is the antithesis of the objective criteria, which are logical, reliable, easier to apply and more accurate.[489]

484 Case 12/1/1987 Court of Cassation/Civil 18/86; Case 1/6/1987 Court of Cassation/Civil 11/87 Ministry of Justice, *Commercial Provisions* (n 259); Case 17/4/1995, 293 (n 517); Case 25/5/2005 Court of Cassation/Commercial 857/2003 in Ministry of Justice, *Civil Provisions* (n 955) 459.

485 Al-Ahwany (n 497) 728, 729.

486 Egyptian Court of Cassation (20/3/1958) S 9 P 223 cited in AboSaad (n 257) 120.

487 Al-Ahwany (n 497) 355.

488 Marty and Raynaud state, *'[L]'observateur type dispose après coup d'éléments d'information et d'appréciation très supérieurs a ceux que l'on peut exiger.'* Gabriel Marty; Pierre Raynaud, *Les Droit Personnels Theorie Générale des Obligations Volume I Tome II* (Sirey 1962) 521.

489 Al-Naqeeb, *Liability Arising from Personal Action* (n 954) 136.

Linking the purchase's purpose to the contract would not be panacea. If, for instance, the seller uses a kind of wood in furniture diverging from the type agreed upon, such mal-implementation might not permit termination as long as it does not affect the 'elegance' mentioned as a purpose in the contract.[490] If the buyer did not state their purpose, the difference in the type of wood used could be considered 'misdescription,' entitling the buyer to request termination without stipulating 'substantiality.' This encourages the buyer not to disclose the purpose of their purchase. Other jurists might find the opposite; the mere indication of this purpose in the contract may convert any requirement to 'assured description,' which does not necessitate proof of 'substantiality.' Through this bewilderment, judges may resort to various benchmarks under their discretionary authority[491] whenever they are satisfied with the evidence.[492]

#### 4.3.3.3.3 IS SUBSTANTIALITY (APPLIED TO NONCONFORMING CATEGORY) A STIPULATION FOR MISDESCRIPTION?

'Substantiality,' stipulated in Article 132 KCOC to terminate the contract for sending goods of nonconforming category, may not be extended to include the misdescription mentioned in Article 498 KCIC for two reasons:

**First**, regarding Article 498 KCIC, EMKCIC states that

> the legislator has . . . introduced a new provision regarding the conditional description in a commodity, as it is noted that *the current commercial law* [in which Article 132 KCOC is mentioned regarding goods of a different category] *is devoid of ruling therein.*[493]

**Secondly**, according to the jurisprudential rules, 'the exception [of Article 132 KCOC] can neither be a basis for reasoning by analogy nor be elaborated in its interpretation,' and the general statement in Article 498 KCIC will be implemented on its generality unless there is an apparent linked provision that restricts it.[494] Demonstratively, in most of the misdescription cases mentioned earlier, 'substantiality' was not raised, with one exception, in which the court resorted to the 'substantiality' of the misdescription to rule for termination.[495]

490 Al-Jarmy (n 264) 100.
491 ibid 87; Al-Ahwany (n 497) 459.
492 Case 30/12/2008 (n 1213) 6.
493 EMKCIC 437. See also Case 18/1/1993 (n 961) in Ministry of Justice, *Commercial Provisions* (n 259) 65.
494 Al-Majalla Art. 64.
495 Case 7/11/1995 (n 1104) 2–7.

### *4.3.4 Comparative Analysis*

#### *4.3.4.1 Possible Outcomes Under the Three Legal Systems*

Suppose that in a hypothetical contract, it is *emphasised* that used machines will be of a specific brand. On their arrival, the goods' compatibility is confirmed, except for their cables, which are of a different brand name and more powerful. The cables are not compatible with the facilities at the buyer's premises, located in a rural area, which was unknown to the seller at the time of sale. The seller offers to cure their performance.

**Under CISG**, misdescription per se does not constitute a reason for termination; it must be evaluated under Article 25, as follows:

**First**, misdescription should substantially deprive the buyer of their contractual expectations. If the contractual consequences resulting from misdescription are focused on more than the brand, there is no substantial deprivation, as long as the contractual purpose of the goods is achieved. On the other hand, if the brand is the main focus, there might be an objective deprivation of the expectation in performing such a term, especially as this term is emphasised in the contract, but this deprivation might not be substantial. **Secondly**, the buyer might not suffer detrimental consequences under the contract as long as the goods are intact, especially if the court/tribunal finds that the goods can be resold and used in premises other than the buyer's, and other, less harsh remedies can redress the non-compliance. **Thirdly**, even if the judge/arbitrator finds that the buyer is substantially deprived of their contractual expectations, misdescription is non-fundamental because the goods' unsuitability to the buyer's personal needs is not envisaged under the contract and therefore might not have been foreseeable to either the seller or a reasonable person. **Finally**, if we assume that this misdescription objectively constitutes a fundamental breach because it is emphasised in the contract, immediate termination might not be permitted as long as the seller offers to cure their performance within a reasonable time by providing the buyer with complying cables without causing them any inconvenience.

**Under SGA**, the dependency on an automatic grouping of descriptions as 'conditions' makes the brand a promissory term. The cables being of another brand does not constitute a slight breach, and this automatically grants the buyer the right to termination once the brand description is breached, irrespective of the seller's offer to cure. The prudence of SGA is protecting the expectations linked to the promises rather than merely redressing injuries.[496] Lord Wilberforce, in *Ashington*, did not 'believe that [SGA] was designed to provoke metaphysical discussions as to the nature of what is delivered, in comparison with what is sold.'[497] This entitlement to termination occurs even if the buyer's circumstances are not revealed under the contract. In *Bostock v Nicholson*, while the purpose for purchasing 'sulphuric acid commercially free from arsenic' (in order to manufacture brewing sugar to

496 Cohen (n 249) 578–580.
497 *Ashington v Christopher* (n 842) 489.

be sold to brewers for manufacturing beer) was not mentioned in the contractual relationship, it was held that the seller was liable for breaching the description as it ultimately made the beer poisonous.[498]

**Under KLaw**, theoretically, the buyer is entitled to request termination based on non-compliance with the required brand, especially if the formulation of this term is clear in the contract, making it 'assured.' However, judicially, the courts might pursue different approaches:

**First**, some judges would follow the literal application of law, which does not demand 'detriment' be suffered by the buyer to permit termination. **Secondly**, other judges might require such 'detriment,' encompassing the personal detriment that the cables are unsuitable for the buyer's premises, as long as it is the 'natural result' of misdescription. **Thirdly**, other courts might not permit termination if the buyer is a trader, except in cases of inability to dispose of the goods or if the goods' value is reduced because of this misdescription. **Fourthly**, other dicta might find that the buyer abuses the right to termination, especially when the damage suffered by the buyer is in no sense commensurate with the significant harm that would occur to the seller in case of termination (which could also be personal). This could be true particularly if the seller demonstrates their willingness to cure their performance. However, if the buyer proves that the wait for repair would cause them loss or they have already bought other machines from another supplier, a repair might not be an option. Nevertheless, the threshold to prevent buyers from resorting to termination according to the rule of abuse of rights could be too high as using phrases like 'deviate,' 'in no sense commensurate' and 'extraordinary colossal damage' might only exclude termination for trivial misdescription, inapplicable in this example case. **Fifthly**, other judges might find that the seller may avoid termination by providing the buyer with compliant cables before the judicial issuance of termination according to the general rules. **Finally**, judges might find that the machines' brand could be deemed a 'category' rather than a 'description,' and, in order to permit termination, the breach should be substantial. 'Substantiality' is defined by referring to the goods invalidity for the 'prepared purpose,' which itself needs a definition. This makes the situation dependent on the buyer's ability to prove the substantial invalidity of the goods for the prepared purpose, even if this is subjective.

### *4.3.4.2 Contract Preservation and Certainty of Using Termination*

#### 4.3.4.2.1 UNDER CISG

*a) Certainty* The references to general abstract[499] concepts, such as 'substantiality,' 'deprivation' and 'foreseeability,' might reduce predictability since this approach

498 *Bostock v Nicholson* [1904] 1 KB 725.

499 Alison Williams, 'Forecasting the Potential Impact of the Vienna Sales Convention on International Sales Law in the United Kingdom' [2001] <https://cisgw3.law.pace.edu/cisg/biblio/williams.html> 9, 21; Nathalie Hofmann, 'Interpretation Rules and Good Faith as Obstacles to the

depends on the judiciary to assess the breach's consequences.[500] Thus, the buyer's assessment of a fundamental breach might be refuted by the judge, who may find the consequences do not meet Article 25,[501] despite the fact that termination is a remedy that does not necessitate litigation. 'Substantial deprivation,' for instance, can be interpreted in two ways: *qualitatively*, according to which the aggrieved buyer suffers a deprivation of their core contractual expectations, and the detriment resulting from the breach of the most important descriptions makes the breach fundamental. Substantial deprivation can be interpreted *quantitatively* instead, meaning that the adjudicator will rely on the number of breached descriptions in the contract,[502] and when cumulative contraventions reach a high threshold of substantiality,[503] the misdescription is fundamental. Additionally, when applying 'foreseeability' in a court of the buyer's country, the judge is unlikely to know about a standard merchant's thoughts in the seller's country (where the 'reasonable person' is from), causing confusion in interpreting the 'reasonability' standard.

*b) Contract Preservation* Resorting to termination as a remedy of last resort and attaining objectivity could be demonstrated as follows: **Firstl**, Article 35 does not allow technical termination; a further step of fundamental breach should be met, according to which substantial deprivation of contractual expectations should be suffered in order to qualify. Moreover, according to Article 7.3.1(3) UPICC, when it is apparent that the seller 'will suffer disproportionate loss . . . [more than the substantial deprivation suffered by the buyer] if the contract is terminated,' the buyer may refrain from resorting to this remedy. **Secondly**, CISG links the detriment suffered by the buyer with the seller's foreseeability, attaining a fair balance between the parties without considering personal detriment not revealed in the contract. **Finally**, because both parties act subjectively according to their culture, education and morality, this may prevent them from considering the other party's position in cases of breaching a contract. Adding the stipulation of a reasonable person's foreseeability reduces termination to the lowest level, as a reasonable person always acts objectively and in a sensible manner.[504]

#### 4.3.4.2.2 UNDER SGA

*a) Certainty* Due to the categorisation of 'conditions,' termination based on misdescription is simple and straightforward; less than perfect compliance with

---

UK's Ratification of the CISG and to the Harmonization of Contract Law in Europe' (2010) 22(1) Pace Int Law Rev 145, 153.

500 A similar meaning is found in Peel, 15th edn (n 64) 974 [13–032].

501 A similar meaning can be seen in Fisher (n 429) 101, 102.

502 See the *Old boxboard corrugated cartons case* (8/3/1996) CISG/1996/12 (CIETAC arbitration proceeding) <http://cisgw3.law.pace.edu/cases/960308c1.html>.

503 Kröll; Mistelis; Viscasillas (n 67) 341 [11].

504 John Honnald, *Documentary History* (n 344) 89.

descriptions will allow the immediate right to deem the whole contract terminated,[505] even if no detriment is suffered by the buyer in any respect. This avoids the delay of recourse to litigation because it assists the buyer in being more decisive and confident in knowing the possibility of termination beforehand,[506] and it makes judicial interpretation literal and gives it less discretion. In *Maredelanto*, Megaw LJ stated that:

> [I]n commercial law, there are . . . substantial advantages in having . . . a firm and definite rule. . . . It is surely much better, [for both parties and their advisors]. . . to be able to say categorically: 'If a breach is proved, then the [innocent party] can put an end to the contract,' rather than that they should be left to ponder whether or not the courts would be likely . . . to decide . . . the breach was or was not such as 'to go to the root of the contract.'[507]

Despite the foregoing, it is true that there is not much recognition of 'reasonableness' in case of misdescription, but the court might see that description should be applied according to reasonable understanding, although many jurists oppose this approach, which aims to attain a fairer outcome not adopted by SGA. Determination of 'reasonability' could be assigned to the court and could be inconsistent with the parties' intention, jeopardising the assurance of certainty. Additionally, applying the 'intermediate term' rule when it is difficult to categorise the descriptive term either as a promissory term or puffery may also lessen this aim as 'intermediate term' does not provide the parties with the availability of termination on the contract date but, rather, relies on future events[508] without formulating a 'satisfactory fixed rule.'[509] Furthermore, the matter of slight breaches is relative. It is unclear, for instance, whether or not s.15A is excluded when there is emphasis on specific contractual description,[510] leaving its interpretation to the courts.

*b) Contract Preservation* '[A]ny deviation from the contractual description of the goods amounts to a breach of contract,'[511] entitling termination, so long as the breach is more than slight. The insignificancy of consequences resulting from misdescription, the goods' fitness for purpose[512] or their merchantability do not change the outcome, increasing the number of terminations. Moreover, SGA does not prohibit termination if the buyer's main motive is to escape from a

505 Smith, *Atiyah's* (n 198) 198; Furmston (n 30) 661; Bridge, *Benjamin's* (n 28) [10–029].
506 Fisher (n 429) 104; ibid Furmston 212.
507 *Maredelanto* (n 78) 205.
508 Furmston (n 30) 208. See also Davies (n 196) 3rd edn 377, 378 [25.2].
509 Arden LJ in *Valilas v Januzaj* [2014] EWCA Civ 436 [59].
510 Bridge, *Benjamin's* (n 28) [12–026].
511 Peter Huber; Alastair Mullis, *The CISG: A New Textbook for Students and Practitioners* (Sellier 2007) 132.
512 Beale (n 213) 1324 [43–076].

contract not generating profits.[513] Additionally, accepting a repudiatory breach to terminate a contract does not require giving the breaching seller any opportunity to rectify their breach,[514] even in cases in which this rectification does not cause any inconvenience and does not demand money from the buyer, contrary to CISG. However, SGA adopts an approach which protects sellers from buyers' overzealous or meticulous requests for accurate performance and avoids termination for slight breaches, constituting an antidote to the draconian system of 'conditions' through the provision of s.15A.[515]

#### 4.3.4.2.3 UNDER KLAW

*a) Certainty* KLaw does not require many stipulations for termination based on misdescription, and this means certainty is theoretically attained as breaching almost any 'assured descriptive detail' mentioned in the contract would generate the right to request termination. However, in practice, the situation is uncertain, as a lack of a felicitous conception of 'assured descriptions' encourages the adoption of many criteria having different meanings and may be affected by judges' political, socialist or capitalist leanings, making the legal outcome indecisive. Judges can also pick and choose from many rules not specified particularly for misdescription, as long as the judgement is based on justifiable criteria. As emphasised bAU: y the court of cassation, the seller's failure to fulfil their obligation is a sufficient justification for terminating the contract, and the trial court may use its discretion to estimate the justification for termination.[516] Furthermore, the adoption of an array of rules in relation to 'misdescription' and a nonconforming 'category' without definitions leads to a mixture of the two being used. Hence, the required approach lacks clarity and therefore depends upon the judge's perspective and conviction. This situation increases both the recourse to termination and the discretionary authority. As Lord Lowry stated in *Bunge v Tradax*, '[L]itigation would be rife and years might elapse before the results were known.'[517]

*b) Contract Preservation* KLaw's orientation goes to extremes: either literal implementation of the contractual description or contractual termination, neither of which provides a compromise. The legislation does not measure whether other sanctions would suffice to cure the breach,[518] unless, as mentioned in Chapter 2,

513 See *Bowes v Shand* (n 404) 455.

514 Cartwright (n 114) 283.

515 Andrews, *Contractual Duties* (n 78) 239; Stone; Devenney (n 64) 645.

516 Case 2/11/2010 (n 265) 7, 8.

517 *Bunge v Tradax* (n 400) 720.

518 This conduct opposes French Civil Code 2016, as Art. 1226 states that '[u]nless there is urgency, [the buyer] must previously have put the [seller] in default on notice to perform his undertaking within a reasonable time.' Moroccan Obligations Law (1913) modified in 2016. Art. 259 states that there is no option for the buyer to terminate the contract as long as specific performance is possible. <http://adala.justice.gov.ma/production/legislation/ar/Nouveautes/%D9%82%D8%A7%

there is extreme necessity. The estimation of this necessity, however, would be according to the judge's discretion. 'Detriment' is not a statutory stipulation for termination based on misdescription as a rule; the mere deviation from contractual descriptions, without specifying a degree, permits termination, even when the misdescription is reparable. Even if some courts do occasionally resort to the detriment standard to terminate contracts, an objective assessment of the detriment is not definite, unless an unbiased criterion is judicially adopted. Depending subjectively on the buyer's situation opposes social logic[519] and makes the scale of assessment fraught with risk due to its variability and instability, even in cases in which the facts are convergent. This standard facilitates the use of scenarios and evidence to rule for termination judicially.

It is unwise to stipulate 'substantiality' when sending goods of a different 'category,' which could be a considerable breach per se. On the other hand, there is no stipulation of 'substantiality' when the goods suffer from 'misdescription,' such as sending miscoloured goods, in which the nonconformity ranges from a trivial breach to a considerable one.

#### *4.3.4.4 Developing KLaw*

Misdescription should be measured substantively, rather than discretionarily; otherwise, the claimant buyer could be encouraged to seek a judge with a philosophy and perspective that matches their own, enabling the buyer to terminate the contract without demanding 'detriment.' This was especially true in one case, when it was affirmed that nothing in the law requires the judge to follow certain criteria to solve the dispute.[520] KLaw is neither flexible (as presented in CISG), due to its tendency to adhere strictly to the contract, nor clear (as characterised in SGA), due to overreliance on the judge's discretionary authority.

It is true that SGA is generally straightforward and leads to predictable outcomes.[521] As Lord Hoffmann in *Attorney General of Belize* stated, 'The court has no power to improve . . . a contract, [or] a statute . . . [to] introduce terms to make it fairer or more reasonable. It is concerned only to discover what [this] instrument means.'[522] However, applying strict rules could permit the buyer to assert control over the contract by misusing termination for any breach, serving as a loophole to escape from the contract for purposes of self-interest.

To declare termination, CISG rightly focuses on the breach's consequences, which can be envisaged by the seller when agreeing the contract. This is to permit the seller to determine the possible occurrence of detriment in the event of

D9%86%D9%88%D9%86%20%D8%A7%D9%84%D8%A7%D9%84%D8%AA%D8%B2%D8%A7%D9%85%D8%A7%D8%AA%20%D9%88%D8%A7%D9%84%D8%B9%D9%82%D9%88%D8%AF%20.pdf>.

519 Al-Naqeeb, *Liability Arising From Personal Action* (n 954) 135, 136.

520 Case 6/2/2001 (n 263) 11.

521 Mullis, 'Termination for Breach of Contract' in Guest (n 226) 142.

522 *Attorney General of Belize v Belize Telecom Ltd* [2009] UKPC 10 [16].

misdescription. CISG's approach is fair, prevents disordering the contractual equation and minimises waste. This could be used for the reform of KLaw.

## 4.4 Procedural Requirements for Termination Based on Misdescription

In order to terminate a contract for misdescription, the buyer should not only meet the substantive requirements but also comply with procedural prerequisites.

### *4.4.1 CISG*

The buyer has a duty to examine the goods in a timely fashion and notify the seller of nonconformity when it arises. Otherwise, the buyer will lose their termination right, even if the nonconformity is fundamental.

#### *4.4.1.1 Examination of Goods*

Extraordinary examination, requiring great effort, is not required, nor does a brief visual examination suffice, but an inspection in the way a reasonable person in the same circumstances would be expected to carry it out is necessary.[523] Inspection necessitating the damaging of the goods, would make testing random samples sufficient.[524] The question now concerns the time frame in which the goods should be inspected.

##### 4.4.1.1.1 CONDUCTED WITHIN AS SHORT A PERIOD AS PRACTICAL

Under Article 38(1), buyers should examine the goods in 'as short a period as is practicable in the circumstances.' In the *Shoes case*, the court was satisfied with the buyer's conduct in examining the goods on their arrival and notifying the seller the next day.[525] In the *Aluminium hydroxide case*, the court stated that the buyer was expected to conduct the examination immediately, especially as the miscolour was detectable by sight.[526] Thus, in *Delphic Wholesalers*, when the buyer kept silent for a long time after they received complaints from their customers about the source of

523 *Paperboard containers case* (12/1/2007) 19 U 11/07 (Appellate Court Köln) <;http://cisgw3.law.pace.edu/cases/070112g1.html>; Franco Ferrari, *Contracts for the International Sale of Goods: Applicability and Applications of The 1980 United Nations Sales Convention* (BRILL 2011) 216, 217.

524 ibid *Paperboard containers case*.

525 *Shoes case* (3/4/1990) 41 O 198/89 (District Court Aachen) <http://cisgw3.law.pace.edu/cases/900403g1.html>.

526 *Aluminium hydroxide case* (21/8/1997) (Appellate Court Oberlandesgericht) <http://cisgw3.law.pace.edu/cases/970821g1.html>.

the cheese and continued accepting new shipments from the seller,[527] the buyer lost their right to claim misdescription.

Pursuant to the *Audio CDs case*, examination time depends on the 'objective circumstances of the individual case,' such as 'the type of goods,' 'the nature of the lack of conformity' and 'the time which is necessary to carry out the examination.'[528] Personal obstacles hindering the buyer from examining the goods are irrelevant, as opposed to general impediments, such as a general strike.[529] Nonetheless, in the *Machines case*, it was stated that the buyer's position and cultural differences and the infrastructure of the place where the examination was expected to be conducted should also be considered in order to determine the examination time.[530]

#### 4.4.1.1.2 DEFERRING EXAMINATION FOR REDIRECTED/RE-DISPATCHED GOODS

Under Article 38(3), when the goods are 'redirected in transit or re-dispatched by the buyer,' the examination can be deferred until the goods arrive at their new destination. It was held in the *Check valves case* that examining the goods prior to reselling them was not obligatory.[531] This is subject to two conditions: **First**, the buyer should not have any reasonable opportunity to examine the goods before redirection/re-dispatch. In the *Doors case*, when the goods were stored in the buyer's storehouse until they were resold, examination should have been conducted promptly after delivery.[532] In the *Tinned cucumbers case*, the buyer notified the seller seven days from the goods' loading, which resulted in an untimely notice because there was a prior reasonable opportunity to examine the goods as the buyer's representative supervised the loading.[533] **Secondly**, the seller should have known at the contract conclusion of the possibility of redirecting/re-dispatching the goods. In the *Watermelon case*, the buyer's failure to examine the goods before they were shipped made the notification untimely because the contract did not involve transporting the goods.[534] In the *Doors case*, the deferral of examination

527 *Delphic Wholesalers (Aust) Pty Ltd v Agrilex Co Ltd* [2010] VSC 328 <http://cisgw3.law.pace.edu/cases/100806a2.html>.

528 *Audio CDs case* (11/2/2003) HG.2001.11-HGK (Commercial Court St. Gallen) <http://cisgw3.law.pace.edu/cases/030211s1.html>. See also *Paperboard containers case* (n1314).

529 Ferrari, *Contracts for the International Sale of Goods* (n 1291) 212, 213.

530 *Machines, devices and replacement parts case* (2002) 12/1997/322 (District Court Schaffhausen) <http://cisgw3.law.pace.edu/cases/020225s1.html>.

531 *Check valves case* (21/12/2004) (Western Appellate Court) <http://cisgw3.law.pace.edu/cases/041221d1.html>.

532 *Doors case* (13/1/1993) 1 U 69/92 (Appellate Court Saarbrücken) <http://cisgw3.law.pace.edu/cases/930113g1.html>.

533 *Tinned cucumbers case* (8/1/1993) 17U82/92 (Appellate Court Düsseldorf) <http://cisgw3.law.pace.edu/cases/930108g1.html>.

534 *Watermelon case* (16/1/2009) 197586/KGZA08–659 *(Rechtbank* District Court Breda) <http://cisgw3.law.pace.edu/cases/090116n1.html>.

was confined to the situation in which the buyer was a 'pure intermediary,' or the goods were 'directly delivered to the ultimate consumer.'[535]

### *4.4.1.2 Timely Notification*

Under Article 39(1), the buyer should notify the seller about the nonconformity within a reasonable time, commencing from the buyer's *actual* discovery of nonconformity or from the time the buyer ought to have discovered such a lack (*assumed* discovery); otherwise, the buyer loses their right to rely on nonconformity,[536] preventing them from resorting to termination.[537] Notably, pursuant to Article 27, if the notice of nonconformity is sent by means appropriate to the circumstances in time, any delay, error or failure of its transmission to reach the seller within the notification's reasonable time does not deprive the buyer of the opportunity to rely on it.[538]

#### 4.4.1.2.1 CASE LAW'S CRITERIA DETERMINING NOTIFICATION TIME

There is no general measure to determine the reasonability of the notice time;[539] it is flexible, avoiding *faux amis*, but could lack clarity,[540] leading to case law adopting different criteria. The **goods' nature** – whether they are perishable, durable or seasonal – may determine the length of the reasonable period for notice.[541] Goods comprising cheese and watermelon required notice to be sent either immediately on the delivery day or, at most, a few days after delivery.[542] In the *Trekking shoes case*, notification about nonconforming hiking shoes sent three weeks after the last shipment exceeded the time limit, which was within 14 days from delivery, considering subjective and objective circumstances, such as the size of the buyer's firm and the shoes' seasonal nature.[543] In the *Doors case*, opening the wrapped doors in piles on pallets to examine them was deemed reasonable, but sending the notice more than two months after the delivery exceeded the reasonable time.[544]

535 *Doors case* (n 1300).

536 *Second-hand bulldozer case* (n 649).

537 Ferrari, *Contracts for the International Sale of Goods* (n 1291) 184.

538 *Wire and cable case* (11/2/2004) 304/II/2003/wuda/scch (Appellate Court Bern) <;http://cisgw3.law.pace.edu/cases/040211s1.html>; *Dust ventilator case* (17/11/2006) 24 U 501/06 (Appellate Court Oberlandesgericht) <;http://cisgw3.law.pace.edu/cases/061117g1.html>; *Shoe case* (6/7/2007) 4C4003/06 (Lower Court Freiburg) <;http://cisgw3.law.pace.edu/cases/070706g1.html>; ibid 218, 219.

539 Luca (n 815) 244.

540 Camilla Andersen, 'Reasonable Time in Article 39(1) of the CISG – Is Article 39(1) Truly a Uniform Provision?' [1999] <https://www.cisg.law.pace.edu/cisg/biblio/andersen.html>.

541 *Oven case* (27/4/2007) Canton Appellate Court Valais <;https://cisgw3.law.pace.edu/cases/070427s1.html>; Honnold, *Uniform Law* (n 320) 369.

542 *Fallini Stefano v Foodik* (19/12/1991) 900336 (District Court Roermond) <;http://cisgw3.law.pace.edu/cases/911219n1.html>; *Watermelon case* (n 1302).

543 *Trekking shoes case* (27/8/1999) 1 Ob 223/99x (Supreme Court Austria) <http://cisgw3.law.pace.edu/cases/990827a3.html>.

544 *Doors case* (n 1300).

**Obvious nonconformity** should be discovered instantly, shortening the notification period,[545] but other, less apparent nonconformities, such as a machine's operating power, are likely to be discovered later,[546] affecting the notification time. In the *Organic barley case*, the missing certificates that would have stated that the delivered barley was organic, as stipulated in the contract, were apparent nonconformity, which normally allows between two weeks and a month to send a notice, but the buyer exceeded these limits and, accordingly, lost their right to rely on this misdescription.[547]

#### 4.4.1.2.2 NOTIFICATION INFORMATION

The buyer should notify the seller of nonconformity 'with sufficient specificity' by putting 'the seller in the position of having been adequately informed.'[548] Using general phrases, such as 'the goods are not all right,' 'the goods possess inadequate characteristics,' or 'we received the wrong delivery'[549] is deemed improper notice.[550] However, there are two different opinions on what information should be contained in the notice:

*a. Precise Information About Nonconformity Is Requisite* Following this opinion, buyers should specify the nonconformity 'as precisely as possible,'[551] describing, for instance, the discrepancy of the size and appearance;[552] otherwise, the notice will be inadequate.[553] Some aspects that should have been mentioned in notices were discussed in the following examples of case law:

**First**, the buyer should clearly specify the *nonconforming part* of the goods. In the *Printing system case*, the court found that:

> Since the printer unit . . . consisted of a thermal transfer printer, a color monitor, a computer and a software package, the term 'printer'. . . was, without further specification,. . . ambiguous because it could relate to the unit as well as to the individual element. Therefore, in order to meet the requirements of CISG Art.39(1), the [buyer] would have been obligated to describe the defect in such a detailed manner that any misunderstandings were impossible and to

545 Ferrari, *Contracts for the International Sale of Goods* (n 1291).
546 Honnold, *Uniform Law* (n 320) 369.
547 *Organic barley case* (n 1132).
548 *Catalogue case* (21/9/1998) HG 960527/O (Commercial Court Zürich) <http://cisgw3.law.pace.edu/cases/980921s1.html>.
549 *GMS modules* (n 135).
550 *Catalogue case* (n 1316).
551 *Commercial vehicles case* (10/3/2004) 7U147/03 (Appellate Court Celle) <http://cisgw3.law.pace.edu/cases/040310g1.html>. See also *Doors case* (n 1300).
552 *Flowers case* (3/6/1998) 1 U 703/97–143 (Appellate Court Saarbrücken) <http://cisgw3.law.pace.edu/cases/980603g1.html>.
553 *Shoes case* 18/1/1994 (n 1140).

enable the seller to determine unmistakably what was meant. . . . Therefore, the ambiguity of the term "printer" goes against the [buyer].[554]

Additionally, it was emphasised in the *Agricultural machine case* that 'the notice must precisely identify the defective components by serial number . . . in order to spare the seller the inconvenience of researching the sales documentation with respect to all of the components.'[555] **Secondly**, the buyer should specify the *nature of nonconformity* in detail,[556] specifying deviation from what was agreed in the contract.[557] Since the buyer's notices in the *Shoe soles case* failed to expand on the nature of the soles' nonconformity, the buyer could not rely on it.[558] **Thirdly**, the buyer should specify the *degree of nonconformity*. In the *Shoes case*, the court found that the buyer did not specify the exact level of nonconformity the shoes suffered upon which the remedy could have been envisaged.[559] **Fourthly**, the buyer should specify sufficiently in the notice *all nonconformities* in the goods to allow the seller to visualise the goods' condition.[560] In the *New Zealand mussels case*, when the goods suffered from misdescription in many aspects, the buyer should have described all these aspects individually.[561] Only nonconformities mentioned in the notice will be considered in assessing whether they equate to a fundamental breach or not.[562] **Finally**, the buyer's expertise may have an impact on the notice information. In the *Catalogue case*, it was stated that '[a] more precise description can be expected from a specialist than from a lay person.'[563]

*b. Reasonable Information (Not Necessarily Detailed) Suffices* Specifying the nonconformity adequately in the notice (written or verbal) is not supposed to burden the buyer with too high a threshold.[564] There must not be a tendency to resort to 'overly-demanding standards of specificity,'[565] and it must be understood that the notification's content may not be used to entrap a naive buyer as the seller can always inquire, in the era of e-communication, to discover more about the

554 *Printing system and software case* (4/12/1996) VIIIZR306/95 (Supreme Court) <http://cisgw3.law.pace.edu/cases/961204g1.html>.
555 *Agricultural machine case* (12/12/1995) 2O246/95 (District Court Marburg) <http://cisgw3.law.pace.edu/cases/951212g1.html>.
556 *Recycling machine case* (8.11.2005) 4Ob179/05k (Supreme Court) <http://cisgw3.law.pace.edu/cases/051108a3.html>.
557 *Shoe soles case* (29/7/1998) 3HKO43/98 (District Court Erfurt) <http://cisgw3.law.pace.edu/cases/980729g1.html>.
558 ibid.
559 *Shoes case* 18/1/1994 (n 1140).
560 Ferrari, *Contracts for the International Sale of Goods* (n 1291) 232.
561 *New Zealand mussels case* (8/3/1995) VIIIZR159/94 (Supreme Court) <http://cisgw3.law.pace.edu/cases/950308g3.html>.
562 *Trekking shoes case* (n 1311).
563 *Catalogue case* (n 1316).
564 *Lumber case* (28/5/2002) 4C.395/2001/rnd (Federal Supreme Court) <http://cisgw3.law.pace.edu/cases/020528s1.html>.
565 *Shoe soles case* (n 1325).

buyer's notification.[566] This is true especially as the repercussion of the deficiency of the notification's content is severe, costing the buyer all rights, and the buyer is obliged to accept the goods and pay the agreed purchase price. Therefore, this harsh sanction should not be applied too hastily by tribunals, particularly in the absence of denotations that the seller suffers considerable prejudice by improper notice.[567] In the *Check valves case*, it was held that mentioning only some of the goods in the nonconformity notice was sufficient.[568] In the *Plants case*, also, it was stated that the buyer should not specify the nonconformity in relation to every delivered item; this conduct would be an undesirable exaggeration.[569]

#### 4.4.1.2.3 TWO-YEAR ABSOLUTE CUT-OFF PERIOD

The buyer's failure to notify the seller within two years, starting in all cases from the date of the physical handing over of the goods, will result in their losing the right to rely on nonconformity.[570] It is stated in the official records of the UN conference that:

> [I]t is . . . important to protect the seller against claims which arise long after the goods have been delivered. [This is because they] are often of doubtful validity and when the seller receives his first notice of such contention at a late date, it would be difficult for him to obtain evidence as to the condition of the goods at the time of delivery.[571]

Notably, as mentioned in the *Laminated glass case*, the period of up to two years can be resorted to only when the buyer had no practicable prior point in time to examine the goods, to discover the nonconformity or to notify the seller.[572]

#### 4.4.1.2.4 NONCONFORMITY NOTICE VERSUS TERMINATION NOTICE

The termination notice mentioned in Chapter 3 is applicable in cases of misdescription. Yet a pertinent question arises regarding as to whether there is any conflict between a nonconformity notice and a termination declaration. The court in the *Saltwater isolation tank case* held that both notices should be provided within a

566 Honnold, *Uniform Law* (n 320) 367, 368.

567 ibid 368, 372, 373.

568 *Check valves case* (n 1299).

569 *Plants case* (23/10/2006) 2O51/02 (District Court Bamberg) <http://cisgw3.law.pace.edu/cases/061023g1.html>.

570 CISG Art. 39(2); *Coke case* (1994) 7565 (ICC arbitration) <http://cisgw3.law.pace.edu/cases/947565i1.html>.

571 UN, *United Nations Conference on Contracts for The International Sale of Goods* (1991) <https://uncitral.un.org/sites/uncitral.un.org/files/media-documents/uncitral/en/a-conf-97-19-ocred-eng.pdf> 35.

572 *Laminated glass case* (19/12/2007) 9 Ob 75/07f (Supreme Court) <http://cisgw3.law.pace.edu/cases/071219a3.html>.

reasonable period of time, commencing from the same starting point. The court did not differentiate between the statement 'after [the buyer] knew or ought to have known of the breach' (mentioned as a starting point of reasonable period for declaring termination in Article 49(2)(b)(i)) and 'after [the buyer] has discovered or ought to have discovered it' (mentioned as a starting point of reasonable period for nonconformity notice in Article 39(1)). Thus, the court concluded that 'the buyer generally has to declare the contract avoided when notifying lack of conformity if it wants to avoid the contract in case of a fundamental breach.'[573] This, however, may contradict the seller's curability right. In the *Dust Ventilator case*, sending a nonconformity notice on 18 March 2005 and sending a termination notice on 6 May 2005 were both considered to have been within a reasonable period.[574]

#### *4.4.1.3 The Linkage Between Timely Examination and Timely Notification*

Case law has adopted different views to clarify the relationship between examination and notification:

##### 4.4.1.3.1 EXAMINATION DETERMINES THE STARTING POINT OF A REASONABLE PERIOD FOR NOTIFICATION

According to this view, the task of specifying that the examination time must be 'as short a period as is practicable' is to recognise the starting point from which the required 'reasonable time' for notification should run.[575] Examination necessitating specialist testing lengthens the notice's reasonable period.[576] In the *Model locomotives case*, notifying the seller of nonconformity within three weeks of delivery was timely, especially as the goods were appurtenances for model railways and model cars, requiring lengthy time for examination, ranging from 75 to 150 hours.[577] However, in the *Engines for hydraulic presses case*, a period of four months to examine the sold engine was not considered as short a period as practicable, causing untimely notification.[578] When the goods in the *Cisterns and accessories case* were inspected by an independent agency on 31 March 2000 and the nonconformity was discoverable on that date, a notice sent on 7 May 2001 was considered too late.[579] Moreover, in the *Fabrics case*, when the buyer ordered the goods urgently, this necessitated the buyer's urgent examination and notification of nonconformity

573 *Saltwater isolation tank case* (n 1125).

574 *Dust ventilator case* 17/11/2006 (n 1306).

575 *Tinned cucumbers case* (n 1301); Ferrari, *Contracts for the International Sale of Goods* (n 1291) 204–207. See also Honnold, *Uniform Law* (n 320) 369.

576 Honnold, *Uniform Law* (n 320) 369.

577 *Model locomotives case* (27/1/2004) 11/1999/99 (District Court Schaffhausen) <http://cisgw3.law.pace.edu/cases/040127s1.html>.

578 *Engines for hydraulic presses and welding machines case* (23/6/1994) 31O231/94 (District Court Düsseldorf) <http://cisgw3.law.pace.edu/cases/940623g1.html>.

579 *Cisterns and accessories case* (16/2/2009) (Tribunale di Forli District Court) <http://cisgw3.law.pace.edu/cases/090216i3.html>.

within a month at the latest. Giving notice seven weeks from the goods' receipt was considered untimely, and this was due to the buyer's delay in examining the goods.[580]

#### 4.4.1.3.2 EXAMINATION IS ONLY A RECOMMENDATION AND THE KEY IS TIMELY NOTIFICATION

Some jurists find that the mere default of examination at its required time would not constitute a reason for the buyer's loss of their ability to rely on nonconformity.[581] In *Al Palazzo v Bernardaud di Limoges*, it was stated that there was no sanction on the buyer's lack of examination as long as the notification was conducted before the reasonable period elapsed.[582] Furthermore, in the *Frozen vegetable case*, the court disregarded the fact that the examination was conducted by the buyer's customer, not by the buyer themselves, as 'prior examination [was] not to be seen as [a] requirement for an effective notice. If the buyer gives timely notice . . . it is irrelevant whether the examination has taken place within reasonable time and in a reasonable form.'[583] Some courts determined that the reasonable time for notification included the time of examination.[584] As stated in the *Timber case*, 'a time limit of fourteen days for [both] examination and notice of defect [was] ample.'[585]

#### 4.4.1.3.3 EXAMINATION IS A SEPARATE OBLIGATION

This view sees that untimely examination would lead to the buyer's loss of their ability to rely on nonconformity, even when notification was sent in time. In the *Bullet-proof vest case*, it was indicated that deferring the examination until after the expiration of the short period (commencing at the soonest practicable opportunity) would lead to the loss of the right to notify the seller of nonconformity.[586] The court also stated in *Bronneberg v Belvédère* that the buyer erred in postponing the inspection of the tiles until the buyer's customer complained, even though, according to the buyer's argument, the wearing off of the tiles' glazing took time to be discovered.[587] Moreover, in the *Used shoes case*, while a clause indicating

580 *Fabrics case* (21/3/2003) (District Court Berlin) <http://cisgw3.law.pace.edu/cases/030321g1.html>.

581 Honnold, *Uniform Law* (n 320) 353; Ferrari, *Contracts for the International Sale of Goods* (n 1291) 204–207.

582 *Palazzo* (n 67).

583 *Frozen vegetable case* (29/11/2005) 5HKO10734/02 (District Court München) <http://cisgw3.law.pace.edu/cases/051129g1.html>.

584 *Audio CDs case* (n 1296).

585 *Timber case* (15/10/1998) 2Ob191/98x (Supreme Court) <http://cisgw3.law.pace.edu/cases/981015a3.html>.

586 *Proof vest case* (2009) 4505/2009 (Multi-Member Court of First Instance of Athens) <http://cisgw3.law.pace.edu/cases/094505gr.html>.

587 *Bronneberg v Belvédère* (20/2/1998) 16.442 (Supreme Court) <http://cisgw3.law.pace.edu/cases/980220n1.html>.

C&F FOB Mombasa/Kenya was included in the contract, after the goods arrived, they were re-dispatched to Kampala/Uganda, where the buyer examined them and sent a nonconformity notice. The court found that the buyer should have examined the goods in Mombasa and sent the notice earlier, despite the buyer's assertion that the seller knew about the dispatch, and there was no reasonable opportunity to examine the goods in Mombasa because it would have been necessary to damage the seal and pay additional customs. The court denied the buyer's claims as it was the buyer's responsibility to deal with these expenses[588] and stated that Mombasa was chosen as the goods' destination by the buyer; they could have agreed on Kampala instead.[589] However, even if the examination could have been conducted in Mombasa, the notice was given within reasonable time as the goods arrived on 24 May and the notice was given on 17 June.[590]

#### *4.4.1.4 The Seller's Knowledge of Nonconformity Is an Exception to the Notification Rule*

According to Article 40, if a seller knew or could not have been unaware of facts relating to nonconformity and did not disclose them to the buyer, this seller's fraudulent conduct would permit the buyer's reliance on nonconformity, even if the buyer was negligent and failed to examine[591] and notify the seller of nonconformity in a timely manner,[592] and the cut-off two-year period has elapsed without notification.[593] This is to prevent the seller from profiting from their wrongdoing.[594] The time at which the seller knew of the nonconformity is not specified, but it can be initiated 'by the end of the period for timely notice,' whether it is the 'reasonable time period' or a 'two-year period,' depending on the case.[595]

The seller's **real knowledge** can be apparent if nonconformity reflects obvious facts,[596] such as rendering metal covers for sewerage systems with resistance of only 25 to 35 tons rather than 'resistance of up to 40 tons' as agreed, although the seller undertook a resistance test before delivery.[597] In the *Used car case*, when the

588 *Used shoes case* (11/4/2005) *(Landgericht* District Court Frankfurt) <http://cisgw3.law.pace.edu/cases/050411g1.html>.

589 ibid.

590 Honnold, *Uniform Law* (n 320) 359, 360.

591 *Wine case* (12/10/1995) 7 HO 78/95 (District Court Trier) <http://cisgw3.law.pace.edu/cases/951012g1.html>.

592 *Used car case* (21/5/1996) 22 U 4/96 (Appellate Court Köln Oberlandesgericht) <http://cisgw3.law.pace.edu/cases/960521g1.html>.

593 Ferrari, *Contracts for the International Sale of Goods* (n 1291) 242.

594 *Srl RC v BV BA R.T* (27/6/2001) 1997/AR/1554 (Appellate Court Antwerp) <;http://cisgw3.law.pace.edu/cases/010627b1.html>; Luca (n 815) 254.

595 Honnold, *Uniform Law* (n 320) 376.

596 *Clay case* (26/9/2012) VIII ZR 100/11 (Supreme Court) <http://cisgw3.law.pace.edu/cases/120926g1.html> [19].

597 *Metallic covers case* (28/4/2004) 862/2003-B (Appellate Court Barcelona) <http://cisgw3.law.pace.edu/cases/040428s4.html>.

buyer's customer discovered that the car was licensed in 1990 rather than 1992, as written in the car's documents, and the mileage was much higher than that shown on the odometer, the court found that the seller had breached Article 35(1), and the buyer's possibility of discovering the nonconformity earlier was irrelevant.[598]

The buyer can establish that the nonconformity was apparent to any reasonable person in the seller's place in order to prove the seller's **assumed knowledge.**[599] This could be based on the seller's gross negligence even if they did not act in bad faith.[600] In *Shanghai Anlili v Golden Wings*, the seller could not have been unaware of sending a shipment of only one type of liquor, although a shipment of six types was ordered.[601] In the *Spanish paprika case*, too, when it was agreed that the goods should be suitable for human consumption in Germany, the buyer did not have to discover that the goods 'contained approximately 150% of the maximum concentration of ethyl oxide admissible under German food and drug law' any earlier because the seller's previous consignments were not contaminated with ethylene oxide,[602] presuming the seller's knowledge of nonconformity. However, in the *Frozen fish case*, a fish shipment which was intended to be sold to a different customer was not a product of the 1997 catch quota but of the 1996 quota, and this fact was not disclosed to the buyer. The trial court found that, as the fish were intended to be sold to a previous buyer, the seller knew about the goods' age, and therefore, they could not rely on the buyer's improper examination and notification to avoid termination. Nonetheless, the appellate court found that the assumption of the seller's knowledge was not convincing.[603]

#### *4.4.1.5 Nonconformity and Non-Delivery*

One may wonder whether delivering totally different goods from the agreed description (*Aliud*), such as sending peas instead of beans[604] or sending cargoes of coke breeze blended with 'substantial amounts of coal, [which] cannot be considered as coke breeze,'[605] is equivalent to sending goods that don't conform to the required description (*Peius*) or committing non-delivery. There is a split in dicta:

598 *Used car case* (n 1360).

599 Luca (n 815) 254.

600 *Stainless steel plate case* (23/1/2004) 17U110/02 (Appellate Court Düsseldorf) <;http://cisgw3.law.pace.edu/cases/040123g1.html>; *Commercial vehicles case* (n 1296); *Miami Valley Paper, LLC v Lebbing Engineering & Consulting GmbH* (10/10/2006) 1:05-CV-00702 (Federal District Court Ohio) <;http://cisgw3.law.pace.edu/cases/061010u1.html>; Ferrari, *Contracts for the International Sale of Goods* (n 1291) 242, 243.

601 *Shanghai* (n 72).

602 *Spanish paprika case* (21/8/1995) 1 KfH O 32/95 (District Court Ellwangen) <http://cisgw3.law.pace.edu/cases/950821g2.html>.

603 *Frozen fish case* (27/2/2003) 2 Ob 48/02a (Supreme Court Austria) <http://cisgw3.law.pace.edu/cases/030227a3.html>.

604 Huber; Mullis (n 1279) 132, 133.

605 *Coke case* (n 1338).

#### 4.4.1.5.1 *ALIUD* IS A CASE OF *PEIUS*

This view sees that *Aliud* can be classified under *Peius*, rather than being considered a case of non-delivery.[606] Thus, sending the wrong type of goods invokes timely examination and notification required under Article 39,[607] and there is no obligation imposed on the buyer to extend the time by setting *Nachfrist*, a procedure appertaining to non-delivery under Article 47 and Article 49(1)(b).[608] In the *Audio CDs case*, the court indicated that nonconformity should be interpreted broadly; including both 'defective deliveries of the correct type of goods as well as deliveries of a wrong type of goods,'[609] which was also held in the *Dividing wall panels case*.[610]

#### 4.4.1.5.2 *ALIUD* IS A CASE OF NON-DELIVERY

There is implicit indication in case law that, in some extreme cases, *Aliud* delivery can be considered non-delivery, which does not require notice but requires the fixing of *Nachfrist* under Article 49(1)(b).[611] In *Pallets case*, *Aliud* delivery was treated as *Peius* under Article 35, but the court noted that *Aliud* delivery could be considered non-delivery in exceptional cases in which there was obvious divergence between the agreed goods and the delivered ones.[612] In the *Thread case*, it was also stated that 'differences in . . . contractual requirements can only be regarded as nonconforming goods . . . if the defects reach a certain level of seriousness, and the buyer must raise timely objections as required by Article 39 CISG.'[613] This means that if the discrepancy exceeds that 'certain level of seriousness,' the goods could be considered undelivered rather than nonconforming. Furthermore, in the *Cobalt sulphate case*, it was stated that *Aliud* delivery amounted to *Peius* as CISG does not distinguish between these categories of delivery.[614] However, it was later stated that '[t]he Court does not need to resolve whether, in the event of a blatant divergence from the contractual condition, a non-delivery in the meaning

606 *Used agricultural machine* (14/4/1993) (Lower Court Cloppenburg) <;http://cisgw3.law.pace.edu/cases/930414g1.html>; *Cobalt sulphate case* 3/4/1996 (n 547); *Dividing wall panels case* (29/6/1999) 1Ob74/99k (Supreme Court Austria) <;http://cisgw3.law.pace.edu/cases/990629a3.html>; *Commercial vehicles case* (n 1296); Secretariat Commentary, 'Guide to CISG Article 31' <https://www.cisg.law.pace.edu/cisg/text/secomm/secomm-31.html>.

607 *Audio CDs case* (n 1296); Schlechtriem, *Commentary on CISG* (n 4) 278 [10]; Honnold, *Uniform Law* (n 320) 368, 369; Ferrari, *Contracts for the International Sale of Goods* (n 1291) 190, 191.

608 Schlechtriem, 'Subsequent Performance' (n 349) 85. This is even though Art. 47 gives the buyer a non-obligatory option to grant the seller *Nachfrist*.

609 *Audio CDs case* (n 1296).

610 *Dividing wall panels case* (n 1374).

611 Huber; Mullis (n 1279) 132, 133; Gillette; Walt (n 778) 220.

612 *Pallets case* (11/12/2002) 1 C 419/01 (Lower Court Viechtach) <http://cisgw3.law.pace.edu/cases/021211g1.html>.

613 *Thread case* (21/4/2004) 15 U 222/02 (Appellate Court Düsseldorf) <http://cisgw3.law.pace.edu/cases/040421g2.html>.

614 *Cobalt sulphate case* 3/4/1996 (n 547).

of Article 49(1)(b) CISG can arise' as '[s]uch a violation of contract did not occur in the present case.'[615] It can be understood that, in cases of blatant divergence, it is possible to consider the goods undelivered.[616]

More explicitly, it was mentioned in Secretariat Commentary that 'if the contract calls for the delivery of corn, the seller has not delivered if he provides potatoes,'[617] a view which Bianca advocated.[618] Moreover, the appellate court in the *Fabrics case* held that when a partial quantity of delivered textiles were miscoloured, 'such a delivery constituted partial non-performance' according to Article 51(1), and because 'the [buyer] failed to fix an additional period of time . . . for performance by the [seller],' 'the [buyer] could not exercise [termination according to] 49(1)(b) CISG.'[619]

#### *4.4.1.6 Restitution of the Goods in Their Original Condition*

According to Article 82(1), if it is impossible for the buyer to return the goods in a state substantially similar to that in which they received them, they will lose the termination right. This is unless the impossibility of restitution is due to either nonconformity itself,[620] reasonable examination[621] or the normal course of use (by selling, consuming or transforming the goods) before the buyer's actual or assumed discovery of nonconformity.[622] Thus, in order to terminate the contract, the buyer 'should have returned the [nonconforming] machinery to the seller instead of still operating it and making profit out of it.'[623]

### *4.4.2 SGA*[624]

The sole recognition that the breached clause is considered a 'description' and then a 'condition' under s.13(1) is insufficient grounds for termination. It depends on the buyer's conduct whether to proceed with the contract's performance[625] and sue

615 ibid.
616 Gillette; Walt (n 778) 221.
617 Secretariat Commentary, 'Guide to Article 31' (n 1374).
618 ibid [3].
619 *Fabrics case* (10/2/1994) 6 U 119/93 (Appellate Court Düsseldorf) <http://cisgw3.law.pace.edu/cases/940210g2.html>.
620 CISG Art. 82(2)(a).
621 CISG Art. 82(2)(b).
622 CISG Art. 82(2)(c); *Marble slabs case* (27/9/1991) 2U1899/89 (Appellate Court Koblenz) <;http://cisgw3.law.pace.edu/cases/910927g1.html>; *Spanish paprika case* (n 1370). See also *Fabrics case* 10/2/1994 (n 1387).
623 *Machinery case* (30/7/2007) (Chamber of National and International Arbitration Milan) <cisgw3.law.pace.edu/cases/070730i3.html>.
624 This applies to delay as well.
625 Peel, 15th edn (n 64) 970, 971 [18–026].

only for damages or to accept repudiation and terminate the contract with damages.[626] This decision is irrevocable.[627]

#### 4.4.2.1 *Terminating the Contract by Accepting Repudiatory Breach*

Repudiatory breach by the seller represents an offer for termination,[628] insofar as it will take legal effect once it is accepted by the buyer:[629] for instance, by refusing to take the delivery[630] and treating the whole contract as terminated.[631] Nonetheless, the buyer will be liable for wrongful termination[632] if they treat the seller's action as repudiatory, and the court does not consider it so. This puts the buyer at risk of committing a repudiatory breach themselves,[633] which is what happened in *Hong Kong* and *Cehave*, when the seller was permitted to terminate the contract and claim damages.[634]

#### 4.4.2.2 *Notifying the Defaulting Seller of Termination*

As stipulated in s.35(4) and s.36(1), there should be notice to the seller within reasonable time that the goods have been rejected. Opinions are divided on when considering notification of termination to the seller essential, reflecting the meaning of 'notice':

##### A. INFORMING THE SELLER IS A REQUISITE

It is true that the buyer, in order to resort to the termination right, should merely demonstrate their intention to 'throw the goods back on the seller,'[635] and 'notice' is not an explicit stipulation needed to terminate the contract. However, case law requires, when bringing the contract to an end, that the seller be notified of termination.[636] It was stated in *Couston v Chapman* that the purchaser should have examined

626 Andrews, *Contract Law* (n 223) 442, 468. See *Harbutt's Plasticine Ltd v Wayne Tank & Pump Co Ltd* [1970] 1 QB 447, 646; Chen-Wishart (n 77) 483 [12.2.4].

627 *Peyman v Lanjani* [1985] Ch 457, 585; Andrews, *Contractual Duties* (n 78) 249; Burrows, *Principles of English Commercial Law* (n 28) 78; Andrews, *Contract Law* (n 223) 468; Cartwright (n 114) 283; McKendrick, *Contract law* (n 206) 737; Davies (n 196) 3rd edn 386 [25.5].

628 *Fercometal Sarl v MSC Mediterranean Shipping Co SA (The Simona)* [1989] AC 788, 792.

629 J Thomson, 'The Effect of a Repudiatory Breach' (1978) 41(2) ModLRev 137, 141; Smith, *Atiyah's* (n 198) 203.

630 McKendrick, *Sale of Goods* (n 202) 308.

631 *Fercometal v Mediterranean Shipping* (n 1396) 792; Thomson (n 1397) 141; Smith, *Atiyah's* (n 198) 203.

632 Macdonald; Atkins (n 64) 448; McKendrick, *Contract Law* (n 206) 738.

633 Stone; Devenney (n 64) 679.

634 *Gill v Berger* (n 880) 382.

635 Bridge, *The Sale of Goods* (n 28) [10.49].

636 *Vitol SA v Norelf Ltd* (The Santa Clara) [1996] AC 800, 810, 811. See also Cartwright (n 114) 283.

the goods 'without delay,' and if they had been found to be nonconforming, the buyer could have terminated the contract by sending 'immediate notice.'[637] In *Hardy v Hillerns*, the buyer's conduct in giving a notice of rejection was praised, especially as it was prior to the expiration of a reasonable time for examining the goods.[638]

B. SILENCE COULD ACTIVATE TERMINATION

As a rule, a buyer's silence may be construed as affirmation of the contract and might not be deemed acceptance of repudiatory breach, permitting termination.[639] Exceptionally, silence can be considered acceptance of repudiatory breach, if it can be understood as such by a reasonable person.[640] Therefore, there is no need to express the intent to terminate the contract once repudiatory breach has been committed, and the goods have been rejected.[641] Littledale J, in *Poulton v Lattimore*, pointed out that if the goods had no value, the buyer was entitled to reject them, even if the buyer did not send notice to the seller of the defective characteristics.[642] It was also stated, in *Bernstein v Pamson Motors*, that apparent defects rendering the goods useless would make delivery incomplete;[643] thus, informing the seller of the rejection might not be needed.

### *4.4.2.3 Losing the Termination Right by Accepting the Goods*

According to s.34 and s.35(2), even if the buyer accepts the goods, this acceptance is not an effective way of preventing rejection unless they had had a reasonable opportunity to examine the goods before acceptance.[644] The buyer loses the right to reject the goods and then to terminate the contract in the three following situations:

#### 4.4.2.3.1 THE BUYER'S ACCEPTING GOODS WITH THEIR DEFECTS

'Acceptance of goods' does not mean a buyer merely acknowledges the receipt of delivery before having had a chance to examine the goods.[645] It means that the buyer unequivocally affirms the contract despite the breach.[646] The buyer can irreversibly downgrade the broken 'condition' and treat it as a 'warranty' by a)

637 *Couston Thomson & Co v Chapman* (1870–75) LR 2 Sc 250.
638 *E Hardy & Co (London) Ltd v Hillerns & Fowler* [1923] 2 KB 490, 492.
639 *Vitol SA v Beta Renowable Group SA* [2017] EWHC 1734 (Comm) [46].
640 *Vitol v Norelf* (n 1404) 812.
641 Thomson (n 1405) 141.
642 *Poulton v Lattimore* (1829) 109 ER 96, 97.
643 *Bernstein v Pamson Motors (Golders Green)* [1987] RTR 384 391.
644 *Truk (UK) Ltd v Tokmakidis GmbH* [2000] 2 All ER (Comm) 594.
645 SGA s.11(1); Beale; Bishop; Furmston (n 614) 618; McKendrick, *Sale of Goods* (n 202) 309; Twigg-Flesner; Canavan (n 30) 427.
646 *China National Foreign Trade Transportation Corp v Evlogia Shipping Co SA of Panama (The Mihalios Xilas)* [1979] 1 WLR 1018, 1037; Beatson; Burrows; Cartwright (n 247) 506.

electing to keep the goods and **claiming damages**,[647] b) demanding a **second performance**[648] (despite the fact that some scholars find that affirmation of the contract cannot be embodied by simply calling on the seller to perform their obligation)[649] or c) giving the seller **additional time** for performance. (The contract may only be terminated if the seller fails to comply with the description within that additional time.[650])

A question arises concerning the legal effect of the buyer's accepting the goods before the discovery of the default. Some jurists find that the buyer's acceptance can be effectual,[651] and, accordingly, the right of rejection can be lost.[652] In *Hardy v Hillerns*, Atkin LJ stated that the buyer would be considered to have accepted the goods by indicating so to the seller, even without having a reasonable opportunity of examination.[653] Other jurists find that the buyer's acceptance of the goods should occur after their knowledge of their right to reject.[654] In *Broadcrest v DOC*, it was clarified that when the buyer accepted the machines but later discovered they were not the ones ordered, their acceptance was ineffective,[655] enabling them to terminate the contract.

#### 4.4.2.3.2 ACTING INCOMPATIBLY WITH THE SELLER'S OWNERSHIP

Buyers may be deemed to have accepted goods if they act inconsistently with the seller's ownership (and this prevents the buyer from returning the goods and claiming a refund),[656] such as in cases of reselling, renting or transforming the goods,[657] even when only part of the goods are used/resold.[658] Even though some of the buyer's actions can be deemed inconsistent with the seller's ownership, SGA and case law have not considered them barriers to termination. In *Clegg v Andersson*, the buyer's act of insuring the goods was not considered inconsistent with the seller's ownership.[659] Under s.35(6)(a) and s.35(6)(b), the mere inquiry or agreement on the goods' repair and the sub-sale of the goods (even if the seller is not informed of the resale intent) are not considered inconsistent actions.

647 SGA s.53(1); *Rowland v Divall* [1923] 2 KB 500, 503; *Couchman v Hill* (n 884).
648 A similar meaning is found in *Charles v Oppenheim* (n 613) 619, 620.
649 Chen-Wishart (n 77) 484, 485 [12.3]; McKendrick, *Contract law* (n 206) 777, 778.
650 A similar meaning is found in *Charles v Oppenheim* (n 613) 616.
651 Bridge, *The Sale of Goods* (n 28) [10.02]; Twigg-Flesner; Canavan (n 30) 424, 425.
652 SGA s.11(4).
653 *Hardy v Hillerns* (n 1406) 498.
654 *Evans v Bartlam* [1937] AC 473, 479; *Peyman v Lanjani* (n 1395); Chitty (n 64) [24–003].
655 *Broadcrest CD Ltd v DOC Data (UK) Ltd* [2000] 5 WLUK 124 [30].
656 *Harnor v Groves* (1855) 139 ER 587, 673.
657 *Charles Henshaw v Antlerport* [1995] 6 WLUK 27.
658 *Harnor v Groves* (n 1424) 673.
659 *Clegg v Andersson (t/a Nordic Marine)* [2003] EWCA Civ 320 [59]. This is true even though the case is regarding the sale of goods and labour.

#### 4.4.2.3.3 ACCEPTING GOODS WHEN REASONABLE TIME LAPSES

According to s.35(4), retaining the goods and failing to reject them within a reasonable time strips the buyer of their termination right.[660] In *Kwei v British Traders*, it was stated that merely retaining the goods and using them would not have prevented the buyer from rejecting them,[661] but using the goods for a long time would eliminated their right to reject the goods if there had been a fall in market price.[662]

The Law Commission affirmed that 'there is no limit on the number of factors which the court is entitled to take into account when deciding what period of retention is reasonable.'[663] The goods' nature may be a crucial factor in lengthening the required time[664] as the reasonable time for a bicycle would be much less than that of nuclear submarines.[665] Three weeks did not transcend the reasonable time for terminating a yacht purchase in *Clegg v Andersson*,[666] but rejecting new cars 26 days after receipt could exceed the reasonable period according to *Bernstein v Pamson Motors*.[667] In the case of goods to be resold, reasonable time can be extended until the goods reach the ultimate buyer and are tested by them.[668] However, if a buyer has had a reasonable opportunity to examine the goods before reselling them,[669] the resale is considered acceptance of the goods, and the buyer loses their right to reject them.[670] In *Molling v Dean*, in which the court held that since the buyer had made it known to the seller that the 40,000 books were going to be sold overseas, the buyer had not had a reasonable opportunity to examine the goods, and they were entitled to reject them at a later date when their customers complained.[671] Problematically, in *Bernstein v Pamson*, the court concluded that a buyer's situation should contribute to determining the length of the reasonable period and extended the reasonable period for the same amount of time that the buyer was ill.[672]

### 4.4.3 KLaw

KLaw does not mention any special procedures for requesting termination based on misdescription. Specific procedures are mentioned in terms of hidden defects, but legislators do not refer to them in terms of both the misdescription and nonconforming category. Demonstrably, EMKCIC states that 'Art.489 to 497 are related

660 *Kwei* (n 75) 498.
661 *Rowland v Divall* (n 1415) 500, 501.
662 *Kwei* (n 75) 498.
663 The Law Commission (n 230) [2.48].
664 *Charles Henshaw & Sons Ltd v Antlerport Ltd* [1995] 6 WLUK 27.
665 *Bernstein v Pamson* (n 1411) 397.
666 *Clegg v Andersson* (n 1427) [64].
667 *Bernstein v Pamson* (n 1411).
668 *Truk v Tokmakidis* (n 1412) 594.
669 SGA s.34.
670 *Perkins v Bell* [1893] 1 QB 193; *Saunt v Belcher and Gibbons* [1920] All ER Rep 142.
671 *Hardy v Hillerns* (n 1406) 492; *E&S Ruben Ltd v Faire Bros & Co Ltd* [1949] 1 KB 254, 256.
672 *Bernstein v Pamson* (n 1411) 397.

to hidden defects only, and this contrasts with Egyptian law, which merges hidden defects and misdescriptions.'[673] EMKCIC also states that legislators differentiated between these two legal subjects by providing a distinguishing provision to each.[674] Thus, the buyer's knowledge of misdescription at the time of sale, their ability to discern the misdescription,[675] the nature of the misdescription (being hidden or apparent)[676] and the seller's actions being of good faith do not negatively affect the buyer's termination right.[677]

#### *4.4.3.1 General Procedural Stipulations of Judicial Termination*[678]

Procedurally, the courts mainly built their judiciary on the following statement:

> [I]f one of the parties fails to fulfil their obligation in due time and after being notified, the other party may . . . request the judge to terminate the contract, with compensation if needed, unless the applicant of termination is also a violator to their obligations.[679]

##### 4.4.3.1.1 THE BUYER PERFORMS THEIR CONTRACTUAL OBLIGATIONS

According to Article 209(1) KCIC, a buyer's choice of termination is conditional on their payment or at least their willingness to make payment.[680] Otherwise, the buyer would be defaulting and therefore could not ask for a penalty which could be applied to them.[681] In many cases, the buyer's request for termination was refused due to their own failure to perform their obligations without legitimate reason.[682] Nevertheless, the buyer is entitled to resort to *exceptio non adimpleti contractus*:

673 EMKCIC 433.

674 ibid 437.

675 Case 29/12/2009 (n 260) 7, 8.

676 Case 13/11/1989 Court of Cassation 116/89 in Ministry of Justice, *Civil Provisions* (n 955) 295; Case 11/2/2006 (n 1098).

677 ibid.

678 This type of termination applies to contracts, regardless of the nature of the sale contract, either civil or commercial. Al-Defery; Al-Sayrafy (n 254) 367.

679 Case 27/11/1996 (n 276) 2, 3; Case 28/11/2001 (n 728) 4; Case 31/5/2004 (n 619) 4; Case 15/10/2006, 1250 (n 261) 6; Case 3/10/2011 (n 926) 3; Case 5/3/2012 (n 933) 3, 4. See also Case 11/12/2004 Court of Cassation/Commercial 728/2003, 5.

680 Case 6/11/1985 Court of Cassation/Commercial 18/85 Ministry of Justice, *Commercial Provisions* (n 259) 412. See also Egyptian Supreme Court (21/3/1946) 62 Y 15 Qreproduced in Saeed Shoala, *The Civil Cassation Court in the Sale Contract* (Manshaat AlMaared) 359; Egyptian Supreme Court (2/6/1981) 402/48 Q 22 P 1683 reproduced in Ateya (n 50) 159; Al-Sanhory (n 279) 787; Al-Ahwany (n 497) 807; Al-Shawarby (n 266) 62; Al-Yaqob (n 52) 313; Abdulreda; Al-Nakas (n 257) 195.

681 Al-Jarmy (n 264) 88.

682 Case 25/3/1996 Appellate Court/Commercial 357/1995; Case 29/12/2009 (n 260) 5, 6. A similar meaning is found in Egyptian Supreme Court (28/4/1975) 6 Y 41 S 26 P 840reproduced in Ateya (n

i.e. to withhold their own performance up to the time that the seller has duly performed their exact obligations, especially when the counter-obligations are due at the same time.[683]

#### 4.4.3.1.2 NOTIFICATION OF NONCONFORMITY

The buyer should notify the seller of nonconformity,[684] and if the seller has failed to correctly perform their obligation despite the buyer's notice, the buyer can request a ruling for termination in court.[685] It was stated in one case that a termination was a licence and could be used when the other party failed to perform a due obligation after sufficient time had passed since the innocent party notified them of the need to perform.[686]

*a. Official Notification* According to Article 108 KCOC, the buyer should notify the seller of their mal-performance through an official paper, written by public officials (all those appointed in government agencies)[687] or through a registered letter with acknowledgement of the receipt, and, in cases of urgency, the notification can be in writing via fax or email.[688] Notification is not mandatory when a seller explicitly refuses to fulfil their obligation[689] or if the execution of the obligation is rendered impossible or ineffective to a buyer.[690]

This stipulation could be impractical due to the rapid nature of sales contracts and their abundance in commercial life.[691] It also opposes the fact that there is no requirement of formalism in sale contracts.[692] Despite this stipulation, in one case, it was oddly stated that the law does not specify a special form for notification, so it was valid even when it was conducted orally.[693]

*b. Notification and Specific Performance* It is unclear whether the legal effect of notification is only to position the seller as a defaulting party or to give the seller another chance to perform their obligation as agreed. In fact, there is no provision in KLaw that encourages the buyer to give an opportunity to the seller to correct their performance. Specific performance, by repairing the goods or sending a replacement, is dependent on the request of the injured buyer, who has the choice

---

50) 187. See also Egyptian Supreme Court (28/4/1975) 6/41 Q S 26 P 840 reproduced in Muhammad (n 255)793 .

683 KCIC Art. 219; Case 16/4/2012 (n 941) 3.

684 KCIC Art. 209(1); Case 27/4/2010 (n 1213) 7.

685 Egyptian Supreme Court (8/3/1951) 85/19Q reproduced in Shoala (n 1448) 361.

686 Case 27/11/1996 (n 276) 5.

687 Civil and Commercial Procedure Law (Part 2) Art. 8.

688 Sarko (n 258) 30; Al-Hayan (n 40) 20. Journal article.

689 Abulil (n 258) 416.

690 Al-Sanhory (n 279) 795; AboSaad (n 257) 452; Abdulreda; Al-Nakas (n 257) 195.

691 Sarko (n 258) 13.

692 Case 12/11/2005 (n 1213) 5; Case 29/12/2009 (n 260) 10.

693 Case 15/10/2006, 1250 (n 261) 4, 5.

between specific performance or requesting termination[694] according to the wording of Article 284 and many cases.[695] Pragmatically, termination provides buyers with an excellent option[696] in the possible case of a seller's bankruptcy, contrary to the request for specific performance. This is because, after termination, the buyer will take possession of the payment, but in the case of specific performance, the buyer will be in an equal position to the seller's other creditors, and the money will be divided between them according to the share apportionment.[697]

*c. Notification Time* The challenge is that KLaw does not specify the time when buyers should notify sellers of the nonconformity. In one case, it was stated that the period in which the notification should be carried out was one of the substantive issues estimated by the trial judge in light of the circumstances of each case.[698] A judge might find Article 499(1) KCIC (relating to the seller's guarantee for the goods' validity for a specific time), in which the buyer should notify the seller of any defect within a *month* of its appearance, suitable to be applied for nonconformity. Another judge might apply Article 456(4) KCIC (relating to the nullification of the contract based on the buyer's lack of knowledge of the goods but not to termination) which states: 'If the buyer receives the goods and does not object to them within a *reasonable period*, this action shall be deemed as an acceptance of the goods.'

*d. Notification's Contents* KLaw does not specify the notification's contents, making any notification sufficient, even without determining the misdescription's aspects or without an express warning to resort to termination. However, not specifying the aspects of nonconformity at all would be impractical and could be used against the buyer. In one case, the buyer notified the seller and only stated that the supplied air conditioning equipment was nonconforming with the agreed characteristics. In the trial, the expert assigned by the court clarified that it was difficult to conduct an inspection to specify the nonconformity due to the passage of five years from the delivery time, especially as the buyer failed to specifically disclose the elements of nonconformity in the notice.[699]

*e. Filing a Lawsuit Equates to Notification* Some jurists regard the mere filing of the lawsuit in court to terminate the contract as a notification to the seller[700] of misdescription. In one case, the court denied the seller's defence that the buyer did not notify them before requesting termination, based on the fact that filing a

694 Case 27/11/1996 (n 276) 3.

695 Case 20/4/2002 (n 1094) 2; Case 30/12/2008 (n 1213) 2 and 5.

696 Abdulmenaam Al-Badrawe, *General Theory of Obligations* (Part 1 Dar Alnahda 1968) 451; Al-Jarmy (n 264) 133.

697 ibid Al-Jarmy 87.

698 Case 15/10/2006, 1250 (n 261) 4, 5.

699 Case 17/4/1995, 293 (n 517).

700 Case 20/5/1998 (n 43) 5; Case 17/2/1999 (n 1213) 5; Case 14/6/1999 (n 1222) 4; Al-Sanhory (n 279) 794; Abulil (n 258) 415; AboSaad (n 257) 452; Abdulreda; Al-Nakas (n 257) 195.

termination lawsuit and writ of summons was considered in itself notification to the defendant.[701]

This leniency could encourage buyers to initiate judicial proceedings to terminate contracts and lessen the importance of notification as a means of avoiding termination and to prove the seller's failure to perform their obligation.[702]

#### 4.4.3.1.3 FILING A LAWSUIT FOR TERMINATION

Fulfilling these conditions is insufficient to terminate the contract based on nonconformity, and filing a lawsuit before the judiciary and the issuance of termination ruling are prerequisites.[703] The seller may avoid termination if they offer goods that meet the assured description[704] before termination is issued. The judge is required to abide by the limits of the requests submitted to them[705] and cannot terminate the contract based on reasons not mentioned by the plaintiff, even if the facts of the case reveal stronger reasons for termination.

The right to request termination for nonconforming category/class elapses one year after the actual delivery date.[706] This special period is inapplicable to termination claims based on misdescription,[707] which, according to Article 498 KCIC, is subject to a long prescription:[708] ten years[709] from the due date on which the obligation should have been fulfilled, or the date that the breaching seller was notified of nonconformity.[710]

701 Case 18/6/1996 (n 1226) 6; Case 25/9/2008 (n 1213) 9.
702 Egyptian Supreme Court (18/1/1989) 537/56 Q 40/201 M reproduced in Ateya (n 50) 154; AboSaad (n 257) 452; Abdulreda; Al-Nakas (n 257) 195.
703 KCIC Art. 209(1); Al-Sanhory (n 279) 795; AboSaad (n 257) 440.
704 EMKCIC 437.
705 Case 5/5/2001 Court of Cassation/Commercial 390/2000, 4; Case 25/9/2008 (n 1213) 4.
706 KCOC Art. 132(2); Case 18/6/1996 (n 1226).6.
707 Case 5/6/1988 Court of Cassation/Commercial 55/88 Ministry of Justice, *Commercial Provisions* (n 259) 513; Al-Defery; Al-Sayrafy (n 254) 335.
708 KCOC Art. 118; Case 25/3/1996 (n 1427); Case 11/2/2006 (n 1098) 2–4; Case 25/9/2008 (n 1213) 5; Case 29/6/2010 Court of Cassation/Commercial 3 656/2007 p. 4–7; Al-Ahwany (n 497) 734; Al-Defery; Al-Sayrafy (n 254) 335.
709 Case 26/6/1990 Court of Cassation/Commercial 15/89; Case 17/11/1991 Court of Cassation/Commercial 123/1990; Case 30/12/1991 Court of Cassation/Commercial 214/90; Case 21/2/1993 Court of Cassation/Commercial 147/92 in Ministry of Justice, *Commercial Provisions* (n 259) 509; Case 29/1/2001 Court of Cassation/Commercial 517/2000; Case 20/3/2007 Court of Cassation/Commercial 291/2003 in Ministry of Justice, *Civil Provisions* (n 955) 431; Case 10/6/2007 Court of Cassation/Commercial 1430/2005; Case 6/12/2007 Court of Cassation/Commercial 825–819–825/2006.
710 KCOC Art. 118; Abulil (n 258) 417, 418; Sarko (n 258) 31; Shaaban (n 258) 164, 165.

#### *4.4.3.2 Losing Termination*

##### 4.4.3.2.1 THE BUYER'S WAIVER OF TERMINATION

There is a lack of legal clarity in cases in which the possibility of claiming termination is lost. Therefore, judges may derive some principles from other provisions or scholarly opinions, as follows:

**First**, some scholars find that the right to request termination can be waived if the buyer relinquishes it implicitly or explicitly,[711] deduced from the buyer's actions.[712] **Secondly**, Article 312 Al-Majalla clarifies that the buyer loses their termination right when they dispose of the goods as owners. Using or reselling the goods[713] may be construed as acknowledgement that the goods are identical to those agreed.[714] **Thirdly**, if the goods are apparently nonconforming but the buyer takes them without reservation, this may be interpreted as a disclaimer of their adherence to the contractual descriptions. **Fourthly**, Article 106 KCOC (relating to the case of retaining the termination right exclusively in exchange for paying a certain amount)[715] denies the buyer their termination right when they perform their contractual obligations or accept the seller's performance. **Finally**, Article 456(4) KCIC (relating to nullification of the contract)[716] deems the buyer's receipt of the goods without conducting an objection within a reasonable period as an acceptance of the goods.[717] However, pursuant to the rule imposed by jurisprudence, exceptions can neither be a basis for reasoning by analogy nor be elaborated in its interpretation; the last two provisions mentioned might not be resorted to, other than for their scope, unless the judge sees a legal reason to do so.

##### 4.4.3.2.2 THE BUYER'S INABILITY TO MAKE RESTITUTION

Some scholars believe that the buyer must be able to return the goods in the state they were in at the time of sale.[718] The buyer may not resort to termination,[719] for example, if clothes are cut, sewed or dyed by the buyer before their misdescription is discovered.[720] Furthermore, if the buyer sells the nonconforming goods, they cannot retrieve them from the sub-buyer because there is a presumption that the latter is the title holder as long as they possess the goods physically. This may deprive

711 Egyptian Supreme Court (25/5/1975) 286/40 Q 26 P 1683 reproduced in Ateya (n 50) 179.

712 Al-Karjy (n 1084) 54.

713 Al-Ahwany (n 497) 35; Al-Defery; Al-Sayrafy (n 254) 211.

714 A similar meaning is found in Al-Ahwany (n 497) 426, 446, 448; Ayob (n 494) 157.

715 EMKCIC 412.

716 ibid 415.

717 KCIC Art. 456(4); Al-Ahwany (n 497) 355; Al-Defery; Al-Sayrafy (n 254) 211.

718 Al-Sanhory (n 279) 787; Al-Ahwany (n 497) 807; Al-Shawarby (n 266) 62; Al-Yaqob (n 52) 313; Abdulreda; Al-Nakas (n 257) 195.

719 KCIC Art. 494; Abdulreda (n 40) 492, 493.

720 Al-Ahwany (n 497) 808; Abdulreda (n 40) 394, 395.

the first buyer of claiming termination because they cannot repossess the goods to return them to the seller.[721] Nonetheless, it is true that termination has the retroactive effect of returning parties to the pre-contractual status,[722] but the impossibility of reinstating the situation to its original state does not prevent termination.[723] According to Article 211(2) KCIC, if it is impossible to return the goods to the seller in a similar state as before the contract was concluded, a fair cash equivalent can be ruled.[724]

### 4.4.4 Comparative Analysis

#### *4.4.4.1 Possible Outcomes Under the Three Legal Systems*

**a)** In the *Audio CDs case*, the CDs did not contain a performance recorded in the year 2000 as agreed but an old version with an identical title. The buyer did not notify the seller of this breach until three months after receiving the goods.[725]

**Under CISG**, as long as the CDs' discrepancy could have been discovered easily by a reasonable person and did not need unusual efforts, notification time should have been a few days, commencing from the time the buyer ought to have discovered the nonconformity. Therefore, the buyer's late notification resulted in the loss of the right to rely on misdescription,[726] unless it was proven that the seller had known of the nonconformity, or the seller ought to have known of it, by either proving that any reasonable person with the seller's expertise would have known about the nonconformity or by proving that the seller exercised gross negligence. In the event of sufficient evidence, the buyer could still have relied on nonconformity despite their late notification. **Under SGA**, three months could have exceeded the reasonable time within which the buyer should have indicated to the seller that the goods had been rejected, and this would have prevented termination. However, if the buyer proved that they had had no reasonable opportunity to examine the goods according to s.35(2), termination might still have been available. Proving the seller's knowledge of the nonconformity would not have changed the situation. **KLaw** requires notification, but its time is not specified, leaving its appropriateness to the trial judge to determine according to the contractual circumstances.[727] Because the law generally stipulates official notification, the buyer could have proven to the judge that the delay of notification was due to the process of sending

721 Al-Sanhory (n 279) 793; Ateya (n 50) 177.
722 KCIC Art. 211(1); Talaba (n 50) 138.
723 Al-Jarmy (n 264) 123.
724 Case 29/12/2004 Appellate Court/Civil 1586/2004, 4; Case 22/10/2005 Court of Cassation/Commercial 839/2004; Case 7/11/2006 (n 926) 2, 3; Case 29/4/2007 (n 500) 12, 13; Case 31/1/2008 Appellate Court/Commercial 2486–2529/2007, 3, 9. See also Ballantyne (n 36) 95; Al-Shawarby (n 266) 65; Al-Fadly (n 495) 91.
725 *Audio CDs case* (n 1296).
726 ibid.
727 Case 15/10/2006, 1250 (n 261) 4, 5.

the notification officially. Proving the seller's knowledge of nonconformity may be considered by some judges who might deem the notification time to be open ended, as Article 197 KCIC imposes a requirement on the parties to fulfil the contract along with the requirements of good faith and honour.[728] However, assumed knowledge, similar to that adopted by CISG, might not be considered. Other judges might see that the seller's bad faith does not affect the outcome.[729] In any case, notification would not have an effect unless the buyer filed a lawsuit to terminate the contract.

**b)** Suppose a buyer in this same scenario redirected the CDs (for resale) to a new destination, a fact the seller did not know of at the time of sale. Because there was no reasonable opportunity to examine the goods at the first destination, the buyer deferred the examination until its final destination.

**Under CISG**, as the seller did not know about the redirection of the goods at the contract conclusion, the examination should not have been deferred until the goods' final destination, and the notification period would therefore not have been extended. However, if the notification had been objectively conducted within a reasonable time, regardless of the fact that the goods were redirected, and the court/arbitral had found that examination was not a separate obligation but a mere recommendation, the buyer might still have relied on the misdescription. Conversely, if it had been found that examination was a separate obligation, irrespective of notification, or it was deemed that the short time for examination was important for determining the starting point of notification, notification should have been conducted in a shorter timeframe than the one set by the buyer, and, therefore, the buyer might not have relied on misdescription. **Under SGA**, resale would not have been inconsistent with the seller's ownership if there had been no prior opportunity to examine the goods, which would have made the rejection of the goods and termination of the contract still available. Unlike CISG, SGA does not impose on the buyer an obligation to inform the seller at the time of sale about the intention of reselling the goods, (despite considering it in *Molling v Dean*), which means the seller may not have known that the inspection would be carried out by someone other than the first buyer, and the intimation for rejection may have been extended. **Under KLaw**, this situation would have been referred to the judge, who may have deemed the notification effective, especially if they had found that the traders' normal occupation was mainly centred on reselling goods.

**c)** Suppose that the buyer in this scenario sent immediate notification, stating only: 'CDs are rejected due to their nonconformity.'

**Under CISG**, this notification might not have been considered adequately specific as it did not spell out the exact nature of the nonconformity, the examination's result or the diversion extent, which would have lost the buyer their right to rely on misdescription. **Under SGA**, no special content would have been required for

728 KCIC Art. 197.

729 Case 13/11/1989 (n 1444) in Ministry of Justice, *Civil Provisions* (n 955) 295; Case 11/2/2006 (n 1098).

intimation, as long as the buyer had clarified to the seller that the goods had been rejected. Moreover, the indication of rejection might not exclusively mean notification as silence could activate rejection and termination if a reasonable person were to understand the buyer's attitude, especially if the goods were valueless/useless. **Under KLaw**, there is no requirement to specify the exact aspects of nonconformity, making the notification in the earlier scenario sufficient. This, however, might have confused the seller regarding the buyer's goal of notification. It could have meant either giving the seller a second tender to comply with the description or informing them that the buyer intended recourse to termination. Nevertheless, the deficiency of information explaining the nonconformity might have been held against the buyer as it would have been difficult to prove the misdescription, especially if a long time had passed. More problematically, filing a termination lawsuit could have been regarded as tantamount to notification.

#### *4.4.4.2 Certainty of Using Termination Based on Misdescription*

There are some procedural aspects **under CISG** that might reduce decipherability, two of which are mentioned next:

**First**, some jurists may find that the intention to declare termination should be mentioned in a notification, although it might contradict the seller's curability right, which may make others see that notification of nonconformity and declaration of termination should be conducted separately. **Secondly**, some decisions found that extreme *Aliud* is a case of non-delivery, although the majority of the dicta have found that *Aliud* is a case of *Peius*, and this difference of opinion might make the parties unsure of which procedures to apply. The decision in the *Fabrics case* went too far by regarding the miscoloured goods as non-delivery rather than nonconforming goods,[730] necessitating the application of non-delivery procedures.

Conversely, there are procedural features in CISG that achieve certainty:

**First**, despite the foregoing, the prevailing opinion considers *Aliud* as *Peius*, applying the procedural requirement for nonconformity, which avoids engagement in the discussion of whether nonconformity goes to the goods' very essence to be considered non-delivery or not.[731] **Secondly**, specifying flexible and logical time for examination and notification could be apparent to any reasonable merchant. **Finally**, the two-year absolute cut-off period for notification starts, in all cases, from the buyer's physical handling.

**Under SGA**, permission to use termination is virtually automatic once the seller breaches descriptions,[732] making the judicial outcome highly predictable and the use of termination by parties without a court order understandable. Procedurally, the aim of legal clarity is enforced, as when the buyer uses the goods, which is

730 *Fabrics case* 10/2/1994 (n 1387).
731 Saidov (n 769) 44, 45.
732 Yan (n 1178) 120, 121.

regarded as inconsistent act with the seller's ownership, by for instance, incorporating the goods into buildings, it constitutes acceptance of the goods according to s.35(1)(b), perhaps even before the knowledge of misdescription. This situation obviates the dispute over whether the buyer knew about the breach or not. Additionally, there is clear non-differentiation between *Aliud* and *Peius* under s.13(1),[733] although some cases concluded that useless goods in fact nullified delivery.[734] Certainty is still attained in the latter case as the procedures of non-delivery and nonconforming goods are similar.

However, certainty is weakened by some procedural features of SGA, such as:

**First**, indication of the goods rejection may *not* signify that the buyer would like to terminate the contract; rejecting the goods could rather be interpreted by the seller as a demand to repair/replace the goods. **Secondly**, adopting a 'reasonable time' for rejection or notification may cause indecision, making it 'difficult to give advice on the subject.'[735] It is a question of fact[736] and may cause practical difficulty[737] in achieving consistent application, as many factors, perhaps even subjective ones,[738] will be considered. **Finally**, the buyer's acceleration in accepting the goods (not just the receipt) before discovering the misdescription could be found either effective, making the misdescription a 'warranty,' or ineffective, making termination still available.

**Under KLaw**, there is a heavy dependency on the judiciary, not only substantively, to determine whether or not misdescription justifies termination, but also procedurally, by not specifying concrete guidelines, making the predictability of the outcome minimal in comparison to SGA or CISG. Some demonstrations of uncertainty in the required procedures are:

**First**, the law does not specify the notification time, which could lead to diversity of rules, especially as some courts may consider personal circumstances, but others may not. It is possible that notification can be acknowledged either **1)** as soon as the nonconformity is discovered, **2)** within one month pursuant to Article 499(1) KCIC or **3)** within a reasonable period according to Article 456(4) KCIC. Despite these suggestions, a judge may not focus on the notification time and could be keen to apply the contract as the law of the parties. **Secondly**, although the law stipulates official written notification for commercial contracts, some cases found that it could be done orally. **Thirdly**, the statute of limitation for sending goods suffering from a nonconforming category is one year, beginning from actual delivery of the goods, but for misdescription, it is ten years, commencing either from notification or from the fulfilment date.

733 Bridge, *Benjamin's* (n 28) [11–004].
734 *Bernstein v Pamson* (n 1411) 391.
735 Bridge, *The Sale of Goods* (n 28) [10.76].
736 SGA s.59.
737 Bridge, *The Sale of Goods* (n 28) [10.76].
738 See *Bernstein v Pamson* (n 1411) 397.

This could lead to confusion between the two, as long as there is no clear differentiation between 'misdescription' and the 'nonconforming category.' **Finally**, it is unclear if the buyer waives their termination right either **1)** when they act as owners, **2)** when they accept the goods without objection, or **3)** when they do not object within a reasonable time.

#### *4.4.4.3 Contract Preservation*

**CISG** strives to maintain the contractual relationship and to procedurally reduce termination by:

**First**, requiring prompt inspection, with the notice of nonconformity being given within a short period: either within a reasonable time beginning from the moment of actual/presumed discovery of the nonconformity or within a two-year period;[739] otherwise, termination is inapplicable. **Secondly**, in order to determine the examination and notification period, not only objective factors would be considered, but also the buyer's subjective circumstances, especially when these factors shorten such periods more than the objective ones, resulting in a reduction of the available time for termination. **Thirdly**, proper notice requires precise information, especially when the buyer is an expert. A notice with general information would not suffice. **Finally**, restitution of the goods in a condition similar to that received by the buyer is a requirement. There are exceptions to this, including if consumption/transformation of the goods occurs before the discovery of nonconformity. This exception, however, applies in cases of not only *actual* but also *presumed* discovery, lessening the applicability of this exception. Additionally, any difficulty in restitution would hinder termination even if it was caused by examination unless it is reasonable.

**Under SGA**, the contract could be preserved in these situations:

**First**, the buyer's wrongful recourse to rejection constitutes a repudiatory breach, which should make buyers more mindful and cognizant before resorting to termination. **Secondly**, termination is unavailable, and the reasonable time for intimation of rejecting the goods elapses when the buyer confirms their acceptance of the goods or uses the goods inconsistently with the seller's ownership. The availability of a reasonable opportunity to examine the goods may be irrelevant as the buyer implicitly, through their conduct, relinquishes their opportunity to examine the goods. Using a lorry, for example, for a 'business trip' could be considered acceptance barring the termination right, even if misdescription became apparent during such a trip;[740] otherwise, it would always be open to the buyer to allege that this utility could be considered an opportunity to examine the goods. **Finally**, there is no prescriptive period resembling the two-year period in CISG for claiming termination, and this absence makes a reasonable period the only period for rejecting the goods, reducing the possibility of termination.

739 CISG Art. 39.
740 *Long v Lloyd* [1958] 1 WLR 753.

Conversely, there are features in SGA that would increase the recourse to termination:

**First**, knowing the outcome of litigation beforehand minimises the recourse to actual prosecution.[741] This easily measurable self-remedy with legal clarity could increase termination. **Secondly**, if the intimated acceptance or the buyer's action inconsistent with the seller's ownership is not taken into account when it occurs before the buyer has had an opportunity to examine the goods or, as found by some scholars, when it happens before their knowledge of their right to reject, this makes the only pragmatic case of losing termination the lapse of a reasonable period. **Thirdly**, s.34 does not explain the examination process, so the reasonable time could be prolonged by using the goods under the pretext of the examination right,[742] and the buyer could reject the goods even after some extent of beneficial use.[743] **Finally**, there is no obligation on the buyer to return the goods in a state that substantially resembles the state they received them in or to return them to the seller at all, which permits the buyer to leave them in the port, making the termination easier to conduct.

**Under KLaw**, the recourse to termination could be frequent because:

**First**, it is true that demanding judicial termination could minimise termination, but opening the legal door for claiming termination based on misdescription for up to ten years without adopting a clear requirement for notification would upend the situation. This period would unsettle the legal status of the seller, threatening them with termination for a long period of time, contrary to CISG and SGA. **Secondly**, the buyer could request termination even if restitution is impossible, as long as making an equivalent payment is permissible. This would permit termination even when the goods were changed, resold or used after the discovery of nonconformity. **Thirdly**, the buyer could be encouraged to initiate judicial proceedings for termination because a termination lawsuit is considered a notification. **Fourthly**, a buyer's refusal to accept the goods could constitute proof that the right to termination is not waived, putting the buyer in a situation in which they feel the contract will inevitably be terminated, even though termination necessitates judicial intervention. This unilateral refusal of the goods is perilous, especially with the vague and diverse rules in law. **Finally**, there is no explicit obligation to return the nonconforming goods to the seller.

#### *4.4.4.4 Developing KLaw*

The absence of concrete procedural rules and entrusting the judge with the task of creating appropriate rules, not only according to the case being assessed but also

741 Cohen (n 249) 586.

742 Bridge, *The Sale of Goods* (n 28) [10.55].

743 ibid [10.67].

according to the judge's subjective views and culture, greatly weaken the legal predictability of the judicial outcome. It is unfair to punish a party for their procedural default when the law does not specifically and precisely determine the cases that give rise to such defaults, unlike CISG and SGA. CISG's flexible rules, shaped according to the circumstances to a large extent, attain predictability and comprehensibility due to their reflection of logical reasoning. This stabilises the parties' legal centres and reduces the waste of time, money and effort, making it crucially important to be adopted by KLaw.

## 4.5 Conclusion

KLaw 'should not be regarded as permanent reforms upon which an attorney or business executive can rely'[744] because:

1. It is true that the law stipulates 'substantiality' for termination, but this is confined to cases on which the goods are of a 'nonconforming category.' Even in stipulating 'substantiality' for the latter case, it suffers from ambiguity.
2. Termination based on misdescription depends on the seller's malperformance, not on the detriment suffered by the buyer,[745] and this may lead to arbitrary behaviour from the buyer, who may wish to terminate the contract for their own benefit.
3. If the detriment of the breach is considered by the judge, it largely depends on the buyer's personal situation, without necessitating the revelation of this situation to the seller, which opposes the aim of achieving both neutrality and balance between the parties.
4. Applying different rules to each breach is confusing, and resorting to either KCOC or KCIC is misleading.
5. To some extent, KLaw follows the approach of Article 25 CISG, but unfortunately, it is confined to tort law. It would be an appropriate method with which to assess contractual termination if it was adopted.
6. Ambiguity, legal lacunae and inconsistency arise in many areas of misdescription, leaving the direction of the court in the hands of the judge 'according to [their] experience and inclination.'[746] However, each judge may support different ideologies, such as 'corrective justice, liberal autonomy, social constructivism, or economic efficiency.'[747] There is the possibility that judges will apply the principles of other provisions unrelated to 'misdescriptions' or the 'nonconforming category' because, for instance, they reflect the requisites of good faith

744 '[T]he application and interpretation of [commercial law] rules remain a matter for debate.' Sayed Amin, *Commercial Law of Iran* (Bell and Bain 1986) 37. This is particularly applicable to KLaw. David Karl, 'Islamic Law in Saudi Arabia: What Foreign Attorneys Should Know' (1991) 25(1) George Wash J Int Law Econ 131, 167; Shaaban (n 258) 162.

745 Al-Jarmy (n 264) 88.

746 Shaaban (n 258) 161.

747 McCormack (n 36) 3.

and honour required by Article 197 KCIC or for the sake of alleviating leniency in terminating the contract in the name of justice. Other judges may adhere to the letter of the law without using any supplementary tools to confront the law's tolerance of termination. This obviously leads to a diverse range of interpretations, rulings, and outcomes.

S.13(1) SGA is straightforward, but such simplicity has led either to strict application for all descriptive details mentioned in the contract or to diverse outcomes in case law when considering a 'descriptive detail' a 'term.' On one hand, sale by description could be, as mentioned in *Reardon Smith v Hansen-Tangen*, 'excessively technical,'[748] leading to a noticeable dependency on termination for the sake of the pursuit of certainty.[749] However, certainty may contradict the principle of respecting the parties' will when regarding all descriptive statements in the contract as descriptions,[750] rather than seeking the parties' intention as conveyed in the contract.[751] This has led many jurists, such as Lord Kilbrandon, to criticise this strictness, which counters the flexibility of modern inclination to a 'business-like content.'[752] On the other hand, a multitude of factors could be relevant if considering a term a description, such as in *Bisset v Wilkinson*, where it was stated 'the material facts of the transaction, the knowledge of the parties, the words used, and the actual condition of the subject-matter' must be taken into account.[753] This makes s.13(1) one of the most burdensome conceptual provisions in SGA,[754] especially as there is a fine line between 'puffy statements' and 'contractual terms,' making it easy to confuse the two.[755]

In contrast, it could be argued that CISG does not precisely delimit the definition of descriptions to outline nonconformity, and the fundamentality of misdescription may not be easily applied, encouraging the adoption of different criteria, especially as case law does not elaborate on these gaps but focuses on procedural rules, as Veneziano asserts:

> Case law interpreting article 35 CISG is scarcer than one would think. Many decisions leave in fact open the question of the existence of a defect and are solved on the basis of lack of examination and/or notice by the buyer, or lack of evidence regarding those requirements. The limited number of cases is also explained by the fact that quite a few decisions concern requirements for avoidance of the contract and therefore focus on the different question

748 *Reardon v Hansen-Tangen* (n 417) 989–991.
749 Burrows, *Principles of English Commercial Law* (n 28) 76, 77.
750 Poikela (n 83) 27.
751 *Elliot v Von Glehn* (1849) 116 ER 1404, 1407; *Taylor v Combined Buyers* (n 890) 51.
752 *Reardon v Hansen-Tangen* (n 417) 1001.
753 *Bisset v Wilkinson* (n 1031) 177.
754 Bridge, *Benjamin's* (n 28) [11–002].
755 ibid [10–005].

> of what kind of lack of conformity causes a fundamental breach and permits avoidance.[756]

However, CISG has a conspicuous tendency to protect the contract and complicate the route towards termination substantively and procedurally.[757] This solidifies the overall stability of legal centres and strengthens credit, reliance, trust and effectiveness in business transactions,[758] which should therefore encourage Kuwait to join CISG or at least to consider it as a model law when reforming its own.

756 Veneziano (n 1137) 41, 43, 44. See also Poikela (n 83) 18.
757 Williams (n 1267) 21; Plate (n 372) 79.
758 Al-Masry, *Commercial Law of Kuwait* (n 38) 83.

# 5 Terminating the Contract Due to the Inferior Quality of Goods

## 5.1 Introduction

Outlining that goods should possess a certain degree of quality by law is necessary[1] as goods are normally ordered according to their general descriptions without any further details.[2] This legal requirement affords the buyer a high level of protection and prevents sellers from sending substandard products when contractual agreements on the goods' quality or particular purpose for using the goods are absent.[3]

One of the major provisions in CISG is Article 35(2)(a),[4] which demands that the seller delivers goods fit for 'the purposes for which goods of the same description would ordinarily be used.' Under SGA, s.14(2), which is only operative when the sale is conducted 'in the course of business,'[5] contains an implied condition requiring the goods to be of 'satisfactory quality.' This level of quality can be identified by two main elements. First, the 'satisfactoriness' of the goods should be tested according to a reasonable person's perspective, considering the goods' descriptions, the price and any other factors.[6] Secondly, there is a non-comprehensive list of aspects that should be applied where appropriate: namely, 'fitness for all common purposes,' 'appearance and finish,' 'freedom from minor defects,' 'safety' and 'durability.'[7]

1 Poikela (n 83) 5; Peter Schlechtriem, 'Uniform Sales Law in the Decisions of the Bundesgerichtshof' <https://cisgw3.law.pace.edu/cisg/biblio/schlechtriem3.html>.

2 Kröll; Mistelis; Viscasillas (n 67) 504 [70].

3 The curability right discussed in the chapters on delay and description is applicable here. Luca (n 815) 197.

4 Fritz Enderlein, 'Rights and Obligations of the Seller under the UN Convention on Contracts for the International Sale of Goods' in Petar Sarcevic; Paul Volken, *International Sale of Goods* (Dubrovnik Lectures 1996) 160 <;https://cisgw3.law.pace.edu/cisg/biblio/enderlein1.html>; Harry Flechtner, 'Conformity of Goods, Third Party Claims, and Buyer's Notice of Breach under the United Nations Sales Convention ("CISG"), with Comments on the "Mussels Case," the "Stolen Automobile Case," and the "Ugandan Used Shoes Case"' <https://law.bepress.com/cgi/viewcontent.cgi?article=1065&context=pittlwps> 1, 5.

5 SGA s.14(2).

6 SGA s.14 (2A).

7 Dora Neo, 'The Sale of Goods (Amendment) Act 1996: Satisfactory Quality, an Undivided Share in a Bulk and Other Amendments' (1997) 9(2) SAcLJ 362, 364.

DOI: 10.4324/9781003466130-5

KLaw includes provisions on hidden defects, addressing issues when the delivered goods apparently conform with the contract but possess a flaw which does not exist in similar goods,[8] such as mites in wood or rust in iron,[9] preventing their intended utility.[10] KCOC does not tackle hidden defects,[11] so the goods' quality in commercial contracts is determined in accordance with the KCIC,[12] which is mainly applicable to consumer contracts. Article 489 states that:

> The seller must guarantee the commodity in accordance with the rules of Art.485 if the commodity at the time of sale had defect(s) that diminished its value or its usefulness according to the intended purpose, utilising from what is stated in the contract, the goods' nature, or the purpose for which the goods were prepared.

According to Al-Majalla,[13] hidden defects in goods give the purchaser the right to terminate upon discovery, and this is followed by KCIC,[14] as Article 489 refers to Article 485, which permits returning the goods and recovering the price from the seller with compensation.[15]

## 5.2 Substantive Requirements to Terminate the Contract Due to Inferior Quality

Many aspects require scrutiny to determine the threshold at which goods can be of lower quality than that legally required, as outlined next.

### *5.2.1 Degree of Inferior Quality*

In order to activate termination for inferior quality, the breach should reach a required degree.

#### *5.2.1.1 CISG*

Termination of a contract based on inferior quality should be confined to cases in which the breach, as aforementioned, is fundamental. 'Substantial deprivation'

8 Egyptian Court of Cassation (8/4/1948) Group Rules Part 1 P 36 reproduced in Al-Fadly (n 495)123.
9 Some faulty components that affected the function of a theme park ride (Case 23/6/2004 Court of Cassation/Commercial 2 732/737) and a short-circuit in cars, which caused a fire (Case 12/11/2006 Court of Cassation/Commercial-2 1149/2005 p. 2–4) were regarded as hidden defects; Al-Ahwany (n 497) 631.
10 Al-Ahwany (n 497) 412; Al-Danasory; Al-Shawarbee (n 281) 69.
11 EMKCIC p. 434.
12 Sarko (n 258) 48.
13 Al-Majalla Art. 335, 336; Kourides (n 36) 407; Ayob (n 494) 61, 65; John Donboli; Farnaz Kashefi, 'Doing Business in the Middle East: A Primer for US Companies' (2005) 38(2) CornellIntlLJ 413, 415, 421; Al-Masry, *Commercial Law of Kuwait* (n 38) 43.
14 Al-Masry, *Commercial Contracts in Kuwaiti Law* (n 538) 81.
15 EMKCIC 434.

suffered by the buyer may, in many cases, reflect the meaning of 'substantial detriment,'[16] excluding two types of inferior quality:

**First**, sending goods with *minor damage*[17] does not constitute a fundamental breach per se, especially when this inferiority is not 'objectively of considerable importance.'[18] There was a breach of Article 35(2)(a) in the following cases: carts needed significant assembly to be functional and race-ready;[19] soles of shoes were separated, hooks came off and the upper leather was defective;[20] the rancid taste of powdered milk was caused by a lipase infestation;[21] and clothes suffered shrinkage of 6.5% after washing.[22] In the *Check valves case,* when the buyer complained about cracks and a leak in the valves due to an additive, MTBE, in petrol, the seller was held liable.[23] In the *Clay* case, the appellate court found that clay on potatoes contained a dioxin far above the permissible limit. However, because 'the clay could have easily been fully and completely washed off,' it did not breach Article 35(2)(a).[24] Nevertheless, the Federal Supreme Court of Germany rejected the latter finding as neither undesirable impurities, prohibited by food/animal feed law and causing abnormal risk, nor the indispensable extra measure of cleaning 'the separated potatoes after passing through the clay-water bath' to dispose of its dioxin contamination was normally expected by the ordinary user.[25]

**Secondly**, defects in appearance as such may not violate Article 35(2)(a), as in *La San Giuseppe v Forti Moulding*, the presence of cross grain and curly grain in

16 Martin; Snyder (n 67) 368.

17 *Drukkerij Moderna v IVA Groep* (28/6/2006) A.R. 06/1347 (Commercial Court Hasselt) <http://cisgw3.law.pace.edu/cases/060628b1.html>.

18 *Coke case* (n 1338).

19 *Racing carts case* (25/3/2003) 3 O 196/01 (District Court Köln) <http://cisgw3.law.pace.edu/cases/030325g1.html>.

20 *Trekking shoes case* (n 1311).

21 *Powdered milk case* (9/1/2002) VIII ZR 304/00 (Supreme Court Germany) <http://cisgw3.law.pace.edu/cases/020109g1.html>.

22 *Flippe Christian v Douet Sport Collections* (19/1/1998) 97 009265 (District Court Besançon) <http://cisgw3.law.pace.edu/cases/980119f1.html>. Substantial deprivation can be measured by non-usability when deciding whether Art. 35(2)(a) is fundamentally breached or not. Trousers were unusable since they were too tight in the thigh area to be pulled up to the crotch area; *Designer clothes case* (n 352). A machine's function was frequently interrupted due to its defective design; *Textile product machines case* (2002) 10377/2002 (ICC arbitration) <http://cisgw3.law.pace.edu/cases/020377i1.html> [23]. Dust ventilators could not be used for their normal purposes because they diffused the dust instead of sucking it in, and the dust containers in the machines were cramped, causing them to turn off too soon; *Dust Ventilator case* 17/11/2006 (n 1306). Broken and sticky pepper slices violated Art. 35(2)(a), and the buyer was entitled to terminate the contract; *Frozen vegetable case* (n 1351). Vine waxes breached Art. 35(2)(a) if they damaged the vines instead of protecting them from drying and infection; *Vine wax case* (24/3/1999) VIII ZR 121/98 (Supreme Court Germany) <http://cisgw3.law.pace.edu/cases/990324g1.html>. The fabrics were fit for their ordinary purpose to produce skirts and dresses according to Art. 35(2)(a); therefore, the buyer's statement that the fabrics were unable to be cut economically was dismissed; *Cloth case* (n 347).

23 *Check valves case* (n 1299).

24 *Clay case* (n 1364) [19].

25 ibid [21]; [26].

the purchased picture frame mouldings and dents in the finish ranging from 5% to 8% were held to be within the tolerance zone and might be expected.[26] Likewise, scratches, scrapes and deterioration of some of the vehicles' components in the *Used automobiles case* were considered normal as the vehicles had been described as second-hand in the contract.[27] Furthermore, in *Deforche v Prins Gebroeders*, the court held that the formation of mould and spots, due to sold greenhouses' plates being placed non-vertically, did not cause the plates' disintegration or rotting, and it was merely a cosmetic issue.[28] However, Article 35(2)(a) may be breached due to considerable defects in the goods' appearance, such as when towels were stained and of uneven length in the *Cotton bath towel case*.[29]

#### *5.2.1.2 SGA*

Apart from s.15A, any breach of quality entitles the buyer to terminate the contract[30] without the need to assess the seriousness or triviality of the breach and its consequences,[31] even when a breach causes little or even no prejudice to the buyer.[32] This is because a breach of implied condition *might* cause severe consequences, regardless of whether they *actually* occurred in the case at hand.[33]

S.14(2B)(c) demands sending goods without minor defects to eliminate the likelihood of supplying goods that are 'far from perfect.'[34] In *Bernstein v Pamson*, when a car broke down within three weeks of delivery due to a very minor breach – a defective piece of sealant in the lubricating system, causing a blockage of the oil supply – there was a breach of quality, even though the seller repaired the car without any cost to the buyer and, moreover, offered the buyer a new car.[35] Likewise, in *Parsons v Uttley*, the fault was very small, breaching satisfactory quality, when pignut hoppers were installed by the seller, but the seller failed to open the ventilator, resulting in mouldy pignuts, causing the death of many pigs.[36] In *Millars of Falkirk v Turpie*, the oil leak in a new car was regarded minor since it could easily be cured by tightening a screw or replacing the power steering for a maximum of £25. However, if the car had been used for a long time without fixing the leak, the hydraulic oil reservoir could have dried out, causing danger. It was

26 *La San Giuseppe v Forti Moulding* (31/8/1999) 98-CV-142493CM (Ontario Superior Court of Justice) <http://cisgw3.law.pace.edu/cases/990831c4.html> [33];[37].
27 *Used automobiles case* (n 803).
28 *Deforche v Prins Gebroeders Bouwstoffenhandel* (4/10/2004) 2003/AR/2763 (Appellate Court Ghent) <http://cisgw3.law.pace.edu/cases/041004b1.html>.
29 *Cotton bath towel case* (26/10/1996) CISG/1996/49 (CIETAC arbitration proceeding) <http://cisgw3.law.pace.edu/cases/961026c1.html>.
30 SGA s.11(3).
31 *Maredelanto* (n 78) 205; Roskill LJ in *Bunge v Tradax* (n 400) 724.
32 Stone; Devenney (n 64) 646; Peel, 15th edn (n 64) 987 [18–050].
33 ibid Peel 987, 988 [18–050].
34 Twigg-Flesner; Canavan (n 30) 150.
35 *Bernstein v Pamson* (n 1411) 385.
36 *Parsons (Livestock) Ltd v Uttley Ingham & Co Ltd* [1978] QB 791, 792.

stated that it was not exceptional to find new cars with some defects, and the sheriff held that the car was, according to the previous SGA, of the required quality due to the defect being negligible.[37] However, The Law Commission asserts that if a court was presented with these same facts under the current SGA, a different conclusion would be reached.[38]

S.14(2B)(b) requires sending goods without a lack in their aesthetic appearance. A car which operates perfectly but has some dents on its bonnet[39] breaches the requirements associated with appearance.[40] Therefore, there should be an 'appropriate degree . . . of pride in the vehicle's outward and interior appearance.'[41] S.14(2B)(b) may give the buyer the right to reject the whole consignment, even when only some of the goods are dented, scratched and discoloured[42] and despite the fact that the damaged parts can be made marketable at a small cost.[43]

It should be observed that the goods' descriptions, the price, and other contractual circumstances are considered when applying the obligation of freedom from 'minor defects.'[44] Therefore, s.14(2B)(b) may be more relevant to new goods than second-hand goods.[45] In cases in which cars are sold for scrap, the appearance or absence of minor defects is totally irrelevant.[46]

However, s.14 (2B)(a) and (b) can unnecessarily render the goods unsatisfactory,[47] entitling the buyer to terminate the contract even if the goods are perfectly suitable for their purpose while possessing minor defects, such as discolouration, scratches, dusty parts, missing small parts or ancillary parts that do not work properly,[48] even if a reasonable person might accept the goods[49] with these defects. The dilemma is that the requirement of being free from minor defects could contradict s.15A, which considers termination unreasonable when the breach is 'so slight.' Minor defects can be equivalent to slight breaches, which do not permit termination. The Law Commission states:

> [D]ents, scratches, minor blemishes and discolourations, and small malfunctions will in appropriate cases be breaches of the implied term as to quality,

37 Millars v Turpie (n 243) 67.
38 The Law Commission (n 230) [3.43].
39 Neo (n 1533) 364, 365.
40 The Law Commission (n 230) [3.52].
41 Neo (n 1533) 368.
42 *Jackson v Rotax Motor and Cycle Co* [1910] 2 KB 937, 938.
43 ibid 939.
44 Neo (n 1533) 364, 365.
45 The Law Commission (n 230) [3.40].
46 ibid [3.24]; [3.41]; Mustill LJ in *Rogers v Parish (Scarborough) Ltd* [1987] QB 933, 944; W.C.H. Ervine, 'Satisfactory Quality: What Does It Mean?' [2004] J. Bus. Law 684, 699.
47 Bridge, *Benjamin's* (n 28) [11–033].
48 Twigg-Flesner; Canavan (n 30) 151.
49 ibid 154.

> provided they are not so trifling as to fall within the principle that matters which are quite negligible are not breaches of contract at all.[50]

Establishing the difference in terminology between 'minor' and 'so slight' to facilitate considering the former and ignoring the latter could be impractical.

#### *5.2.1.3 KLaw*

The seller is liable if the commodity has a defect at the time of sale that diminishes its value and/or usefulness.[51] KLaw does not clearly state whether this reduction needs to be detrimental to the buyer or whether such a reduction should be substantial enough to be considered for termination.

##### 5.2.1.3.1 THE DETRIMENT OF REDUCTION IN GOODS' VALUE/BENEFIT

To claim 'hidden defect,' KLaw solely requires deficiency in the goods' value and/or utility due to the defect.[52] However, this does not always represent the detriment to the buyer. A defect may impact the goods' *usefulness*, but there may simultaneously be a scarcity of such goods on the market, generating huge demand and minimising the significance of such a defect, especially if reselling the goods was the purpose of the purchase. In other instances, a defect may cause a decrease in the goods' *value* under normal circumstances, but in a market recession, even if there is no defect, the goods' value will decrease anyway. In both cases, the reduction in goods' value/utility may not cause actual detriment to the buyer but may still be considered a hidden defect judicially.

However, Al-Sanhory finds that the seller's liability does not arise from the mere poor state of defective goods but from the impact the defect has on the buyer.[53] The material detriment was considered in some cases, despite the fact that this consideration could be vitiated by subjectivity a) when reselling the goods at a price much lower than the prevailing price in the local market due to the defect, causing severe damage to the buyer,[54] b) when the court justified the termination's refusal by stating, inter alia, that the buyer did not prove any detriment suffered as a result of the defect[55] and c) when an expert was appointed to decide whether the buyer suffered any material damage as a result of the defect.[56] More clearly, in one case, the court was convinced by the expert's report, which stated that there was a hidden industrial defect in a Jaguar car's airbag. The court considered the medical report, which established that, by not opening, the defective airbags caused chest and head injuries to the buyer's daughter, which caused pain and emotional

50 The Law Commission (n 230) [3.40].
51 Al-Defery; Al-Sayrafy (n 254) 284.
52 A similar meaning is found in Al-Ahwany (n 497) 666; Abdulreda (n 40) 126, 131.
53 Al-Sanhory (n 279) 742. Some Islamic jurists stipulate detriment. See Abdulreda (n 40) 123.
54 Case 7/11/1995 (n 1104) 2–7.
55 Case 17/6/2007 Court of Cassation/Commercial 2 660/2006 p. 5, 6.
56 Case 9/12/1996 (n 1095) 4.

suffering to the buyer and their family.[57] The seller objected, presenting a written technical report concluding that Jaguar experts confirmed, after inspecting the car, that the airbags were not supposed to have deployed (as was the case) in the scenario that took place, and their inflation may have caused the passenger more damage than was suffered.[58] The seller's defence was refused.[59] In another case, the courts ruled termination when a car's malfunction led to its stopping in the motorway, and this forced the buyer to rent another car.[60] These cases firmly indicate that judges may consider either the personal detriment suffered by the buyer from defective goods or the mere reduction of goods' value/benefits as detrimental.

##### 5.2.1.3.2 SUBSTANTIALITY OF THE DECREASE OF THE GOODS' VALUE/BENEFIT

KLaw does not address whether the mere decrease in the goods' value/benefit raises the seller's liability or if the decrease should reach a certain extent.[61] Nevertheless, there is a reference in Article 489 to Article 485, (about a third party's rights over parts of goods), in which the latter permits termination only when the buyer's loss (resultant from a third party's rights over such parts) is so great that, if they had known about it, they would not have concluded the contract. Accordingly, the question arises as to whether the 'substantiality' mentioned in Article 485 is a requirement under Article 489.

*5.2.1.3.2.1 Substantiality Is Required* Some scholars find that buyers can request contractual termination when the degree of the decrease of the goods' value/usefulness is 'substantial.'[62] Al-Ahwani states that a seller is liable for hidden defects when a buyer expects to obtain certain benefits from the commodity and would not have concluded the contract if they were aware that the commodity had defects; these defects are 'substantial.'[63] In some cases, the court required 'substantiality' of the defects and stated that its estimation would be entrusted to the trial judge.[64]

*5.2.1.3.2.2 Substantiality Is Not Required* Simply a decrease in the goods' value/benefit may permit the buyer to request contractual termination without their specifying the degree of the deficiency.[65] It can be found that the reference to

57 Case 8/3/2006 Appellate Court/Commercial 6 3303, 3450/2005 p. 14.

58 ibid 9, 10.

59 ibid. Even though the hidden defect claim was refused due to the expiration of the statute of limitations.

60 Case 12/11/2005 (n 1213) 4, 5.

61 Al-Ahwany (n 497) 668.

62 Al-Defery; Al-Sayrafy (n 254) 310.

63 Al-Ahwany (n 497) 626.

64 Case 12/11/2005 (n 1213) 4, 5; Case 30/12/2008 (n 1213) 6.

65 Other laws follow CISG, which requires 'substantiality' of the defect, such as Lebanese Contract Law Art. 442 and Moroccan Law Art. 549. These laws stipulate the substantiality of the defect that diminishes the value or usefulness of the goods; Al-Fadly (n 495) 123. Although the 'substantiality' criterion is vague, each of these laws specifies the degree of the decrease required.

Article 485 is supposed to include the breach's effect – namely, termination with compensation – but not to embrace the requirement of 'substantiality' as a main stipulation of hidden defect. This is because Article 489 merely mentions 'deficiency' in value/utility, whereas 'substantiality,' if it is a stipulation, is something intrinsic that should be mentioned in Article 489's text. The Kuwaiti approach might follow Article 420 Al-Murshed, which requires the defect to diminish the price, even slightly, or cause a common purpose with the majority of similar goods to be missed in order to permit the return of the commodity.[66] Evidently, in interpreting Article 489, EMKCIC does not mention the 'substantiality' requirement and is confined to stating:

> The defect is required to be effective in such a way that it diminishes the goods' value or its usefulness . . . and the defect is not effective if it is customarily tolerable.[67]

This means that termination is permissible, whether the defect is 'substantial' or not, unless there is a custom requiring otherwise.[68] In many cases, it was mentioned that the defect must be 'effective' in order to permit a hidden defect claim, and this 'effectiveness' was defined as a mere reduction in the commodity's value/benefit at the time of receipt.[69] It was also emphasised that the reduction should be assessed in a purely objective manner.[70] However, the criterion adopted in Article 485 is subjective, according to the actions of the buyer had they known about the defect at the time of sale. More clearly, in one case, on appeal, the seller claimed that the judgement had considered the defect 'substantial' without the loss reaching a degree to which if the buyer had known, they would not have completed the contract. The court responded that Article 485 deals only with the case of a third party's rights in relation to the sold commodity, and this was not within the scope of the dispute at hand,[71] which related to a hidden defect.

##### 5.2.1.3.3 DISCRETION OF TRIAL COURT

It was emphasised in many cases that all substantive matters of hidden defect claims are entrusted to the trial court, which has full discretionary authority[72] in

66 Muhammad Basha, *"Murshid Al-Hiran" on the Knowledge of Human Conditions in the Legal Dealings According to the Doctrine of Imam Abu Hanifa al-Nu'man* (Egyptian Library 1889).

67 EMKCIC 343.

68 Al-Masry, *Commercial Contracts in Kuwaiti Law* (n 538) 81.

69 Case 20/4/2002 (n 1094) 1–4; Case 24/4/2004 Court of Cassation/Commercial-3 457/2003 p. 2–4; Case 12/11/2005 (n 1213) 4, 5; Case 15/10/2006, 1250 (n 261) 5; Case 29/5/2007 (n 1093) 4, 5; Case 17/6/2007 (n 1581) 5, 6; Case 30/12/2008 (n 1213) 6; Case 17/4/2012 Court of Cassation/Commercial-1 1720/2010 p. 4, 5.

70 Case 20/4/2002 (n 1094) 1–4; ibid Case 24/4/2004, 2–4; ibid Case 17/4/2012, 4, 5.

71 Case 18/6/1996 (n 1226).

72 Case 30/12/2008 (n 1213) 5, 6.

assessing the justifications for termination and the adequacy of the causes,[73] determining the defaulting party and extracting what it deems consistent with the reality of the case according to its contentment.[74] This authority is independent, meaning that the judgement is not reviewed by the higher courts[75] as long as it establishes its reasons are justifiable.[76] This is despite the fact that it is necessary for the rules on these issues to be identified in advance.

To clearly demonstrate that the matter is assigned to the trial judge, in one case, the court of first instance ruled termination because the appointed expert affirmed that a car's vibration when exceeding 100 km/h was a hidden defect which prevented the buyer from using it properly, but the appellate court quashed this ruling, deciding that this defect was an advantage, preventing the driver from exceeding this speed and therefore helping save lives and money, thus negating the availability of detriment.[77]

#### *5.2.1.4 Comparative Analysis*

##### 5.2.1.4.1 SCENARIOS' OUTCOMES UNDER THE THREE LEGAL SYSTEMS

**First Scenario**: In the *Mussels case*, the mussels delivered contained a cadmium concentration exceeding the recommended limit.[78]

**Under CISG**, it was asserted that, as long as the mussels remained edible despite the contamination of cadmium concentration, the seller was not liable for nonconformity.[79] This was apparently because there was no substantial deprivation of contractual expectations, especially when the permissible percentage of contamination was simply 'guidelines indicating an unwanted concentration of harmful substances in food for purposes of preventative consumer health protection' recommended by the federal public health agency and not legally binding.[80] **Under SGA**, this contamination would probably constitute a breach of satisfactory quality as an implied condition, entitling the buyer to terminate the contract without requiring any additional stipulations, except that the contamination should be more than 'slight,' as referred to in s.15A. **Under KLaw**, the mere fact that contamination had reduced the goods' value/benefit might entitle the buyer to terminate the contract. However, if the court had considered the 'detrimentality' and/or 'substantiality' of

73 Case 12/11/2005 (n 1213) 4, 5.

74 Case 29/1/1996 Appellate Court/Commercial 1 1302/95 p. 4; Case 9/12/2001 Court of Cassation/ Commercial 2 747/2000 p. 2; Case 12/11/2005 (n 1213) 4, 5; Case 17/6/2007 (n 1581) 5, 6; Case 30/12/2008 (n 1213) 5, 6; Case 29/6/2010 (n 1475) 4–7.

75 Case 30/9/1998 Appellate Court/Commercial 5 1416/1998 p. 6, 7; Case 15/10/2006, 1250 (n 261) 6.

76 Case 29/1/1996 (n 1600) 4; Case 9/12/2001 (n 1600) 2; Case 20/4/2002 (n 1094) 1–4; Case 12/11/2005 (n 1213) 4, 5; Case 15/10/2006, 1250 (n 261) 6; Case 17/6/2007 (n 1581) 5, 6; Case 30/12/2008 (n 1213) 5, 6; Case 29/6/2010 (n 1475) 4–7; Case 7/2/2012 (n 263) 11.

77 Case 24/4/2004 (n 1572) 2–4.

78 *New Zealand mussels case* (n 1329).

79 ibid.

80 ibid.

the reduction elements to permit termination, the buyer should have proved that the loss suffered from such contamination would have made them unwilling to sign the contract if they had known of it at the time of sale.

**Second Scenario:** In *Jackson v Rotax*, the motor horns were badly polished, but they were completely fit for their function, and rectifying the imperfection in appearance would have a trivial cost.[81]

**Under CISG**, the requirement of 'fitness for purpose,' which can be defined as usability,[82] might obscure the possibility of applying non-functional aspects such as cosmetic imperfections. Substandard appearance does not on its own necessarily constitute a fundamental breach, especially if the imperfection can easily be rectified. However, poorly finished goods are easily rendered unsatisfactory **under SGA**, as it expressly articulates the aspects constituting quality, allowing a minor defect in appearance to raise termination, despite the goods' complete fitness for their function, even if the rectification of this imperfection would be at a nominal cost.[83] **Under KLaw**, if the defect reduces the goods' value/benefit, the buyer may raise a termination claim. However, the 'detrimentality' and 'substantiality' of such a reduction and the assessment of whether to take objective or subjective criterion are entrusted to the trial judge.[84]

##### 5.2.1.4.2 CERTAINTY AND FLEXIBILITY

**Under CISG**, rather than providing a general rule and automatic answers, Article 35(2) is 'highly fact-sensitive' and established on a case-by-case basis[85] to extract parties' expectations of 'ordinary purposes,' making Article 35(2) 'extremely pliable.'[86] Nevertheless, the 'centrism' on fundamental breaches, combining flexibility and practicality, attains fairer outcomes. However, **under SGA**, not demanding any additional requirement for termination other than breaching the satisfaction quality (which does not fall within the 'so slight' criterion mentioned in s.15A), can lead to an almost automatic termination right. However, the lack of a 'one solution fits all' approach for aspects of quality, such as in the case of substandard appearance and freedom from minor defects, and requiring 'appropriateness' to apply these aspects reduces the degree of certainty. For instance, second-hand goods are assessed less stringently if they have few scratches, but if the wipers are defective or there is a small leak in the gas tank, the situation is not apparent and cannot be fully predictable.[87] On the other hand, **under KLaw**, the reference in Article 489 to Article 485 associated with hidden defects and a third party's rights can

81 *Jackson v Rotax* (n 1568).
82 The Law Commission (n 230) [3.31].
83 *Jackson v Rotax* (n 1568).
84 Case 30/12/2008 (n 1213) 5, 6.
85 CISG Advisory Council, 'Opinion No. 19 Standards and Conformity of the Goods Under Article 35 CISG' (2019) 2019 (2) NJCL 34, 45.
86 Honnold, *Uniform Law* (n 320) 333, 335 [225]; [252].
87 Neo (n 1533) 367.

be confusing and puts the adjudicator in a difficult situation when deciding which rules to follow. More importantly, overdependence on the discretionary authority to interpret the vagueness of the hidden defects' requirements makes the litigants expect the unexpected.

###### 5.2.1.4.3 PRESERVING THE CONTRACT

**CISG** permits termination only on the occurrence of Article 25's conditions, achieving the highest level of contract preservation, as opposed to to **SGA**, under which any breach (except *de minimis*) of the required quality permits termination. This is true even when the goods suffer from a minor defect, the goods are perfectly suitable for their purpose,[88] or the buyer's main motive is to escape from a contract.[89] In *Clegg*, although the buyer manoeuvred to find a better deal, the judge found that the motivation to reject the goods was irrelevant if the buyer had the right to do so.[90] Therefore, the buyer 'does not have to act reasonably in choosing rejection rather than damages or cure. He can reject for whatever reason he chooses.'[91] Under **KLaw**, the contract can be preserved when 'detrimentality' and 'substantiality' are clearly adopted by law, but in the current situation, the principles of 'contract preservation' and 'balance between counter-interests' depend on the trial judge's doctrine.

### *5.2.2 The Goods' Fitness for All Purposes, Any Purpose, or Intended Purpose to Comply With the Quality Requirement*

The functional aspect of quality is crystallised in the goods' 'fitness for purpose.' The meaning of this aspect varies under the three legal systems.

#### *5.2.2.1 Fitness for Purpose Depends on the Contractual Circumstances and the Adopted Criteria Under CISG*

Article 35(2)(a) states that the goods should 'fit for the purposes for which goods of the same description would ordinarily be used.' It does not, however, provide any benchmark by which 'ordinary purposes' can be ascertained.[92] Recourse to the historical aspects of the provision for interpretative purposes is advised.[93] At one CISG conference, the Canadian delegate recommended determining ordinary

88 Ervine (n 1572) 693; Twigg-Flesner; Canavan (n 30) 151.

89 See *Bowes v Shand* (n 404) 455.

90 *Clegg v Andersson* (n 1427) [65].

91 Hale LJ in *Clegg v Olle Andersson* [2003] EWCA Civ 320 [74].

92 Luca (n 815) 236.

93 Vienna Convention on the Law of Treaties 1969 Art. 32, which states that '[r]ecourse may be had to supplementary means of interpretation, including the preparatory work of the treaty and the circumstances of its conclusion' in order to clarify ambiguous provisions. *Condensate crude oil mix case* (15/10/2002) 2319 (Netherlands Arbitration Institute) <https://cisgw3.law.pace.edu/cases/021015n1.html>[111].

uses by considering, inter alia, the goods' fitness for 'fair average quality.'[94] This suggestion, however, was withdrawn.[95] This withdrawal can be interpreted in two ways: either implicit acceptance of 'merchantable quality'[96] (the opposite of the Canadian's suggestion) or mere reflection of non-consensus,[97] without imposing or excluding 'average quality.'[98] Therefore, some adjudicators have determined ordinary purposes by resorting to the meaning of either 'merchantable' or 'average quality.'[99]

###### 5.2.2.1.1 COMPLIANCE WITH ANY PURPOSE UNDER MERCHANTABLE QUALITY

According to case law, the goods' merchantability in the normal course of business has been heavily relied on to define their fitness for their ordinary purposes:[100] 'i.e. it must be possible to resell them in the view of a person in the trade sector concerned'[101] and is considered by some scholars 'the best standard to apply.'[102] When the goods lack normal characteristics or have defects that considerably lessen their value and affect their tradability, they might be unfit for their purposes, although they could be fit for their normal use.[103] Emphasis is added in the Secretariat Commentary on the drafting of CISG that the goods 'must be honestly resalable in the ordinary course of business.'[104] In *Fryer Holdings v Liaoning MEC Group*, McDougall J of the Supreme Court of New South Wales stated:

> The test which has been applied in this country is that fitness for purpose equates to being of merchantable quality. . . . It seems to me that I should

94 Official Records (n 149) 308.
95 ibid 103, 104.
96 *Condensate crude oil mix case* (n 1619) [113].
97 ibid [114].
98 ibid [116].
99 Clayton Gillette; Franco Ferrari, 'Warranties and "Lemons" under CISG Article 35(2)(a)' (2010) 1 Internationales Handesrecht <https://cisgw3.law.pace.edu/cisg/biblio/gillette-ferrari.html> 2–4.
100 For instance: *Sacovini/M Marrazza v Les fils de Henri Ramel* (23/1/1996) (Supreme Court) <;http://cisgw3.law.pace.edu/cases/960123f1.html>; *Ginza v Vista Corporation* (17/1/2003) WASC 11 CIV 1647 of 1998 (Supreme Court of Western Australia) <http://cisgw3.law.pace.edu/cases/030117a2.html> [190]; *Frozen pork case* (2/3/2005) (Federal Supreme Court) VIII ZR 67/04 <http://cisgw3.law.pace.edu/cases/050302g1.html>. It was also expressly stated in *International Housewares v SEB* (31/3/2003) (High Court, Auckland) <http://cisgw3.law.pace.edu/cases/030331n6.html> [59] that merchantable quality was recognised internationally as forming the basis for quality in CISG.
101 *Crudex Chemicals Oy v Landmark Chemicals S.A.* (31/5/2004) S 01/269 (Hovioikeus/hovrätt Appellate Court Helsinki) <http://cisgw3.law.pace.edu/cases/040531f5.html>.
102 Gillette; Walt (n 778) 229, 241.
103 Bianca; Bonell (n 155) 274, 275 [2.5.1]; Poikela (n 83) 5.
104 Secretariat Commentary, *Commentary on the Draft Convention* (n 647); Official Records (n 149) 33.

follow that test, particularly since it has been applied in other common law jurisdictions.[105]

In *Mitias v Solidea*, it was asserted that because contracts governed by CISG were generally contracts between traders, ordinary purposes should be construed according to the reasonable trader's expectations in the same circumstances, and the minimum expectation was that the goods should be merchantable.[106] For example, in *Crudex Chemicals v Landmark Chemicals*, sending coloured phenol (instead of colourless) restricted the goods' ordinary use and negatively impacted the resale process, especially as the coloured phenol had no recognised market.[107] In the *Shoes case*, the court of first instance held that the purchased shoes were faulty due to dissolved glue, cracked leather and looseness of the seams and soles, but the court ordered a price reduction and refused termination on the grounds that only 36 out of the 319 pairs of shoes were defective. However, on appeal, the court ruled contract termination on the grounds of 'fear that there would be a decline in sales, as a lack in quality [could] lead to a general loss of trust on behalf of one's customers.'[108] Similarly, in the *Clothes case*, when the buyer's customers returned the garments due to the goods' poor quality, the goods were 'not fit for commercial sale.'[109] Hence, in *Delphic Wholesalers v Agrilex*, when there was no evidence that the quality of the cheese was the cause of a sales reduction, the goods were not unfit for ordinary purposes.[110]

Honnold states that '[t]he basic standard in paragraph (2)(a) is similar to the warranty of "merchantable quality" developed in early English case law incorporated in the Sale of Goods Act (1893).'[111] Under 'merchantable quality' in the old SGA, it was sufficient to reasonably satisfy any common purpose for which such goods were normally purchased.[112] In *Canada Atlantic Grain v Eilers*, Wright J stated that the goods were of merchantable quality when it was understood that they could be used for one or more of the common purposes of the goods, even if they were unfit for the purpose for which the buyer purchased them.[113] In *Cammell Laird v Manganese Bronze*, Lord Wright stated that the goods might have been in breach

105 *Fryer Holdings Pty Ltd v Liaoning MEC Group Co Ltd* [2012] NSWSC 18 <http://www.cisg-online.ch/content/api/cisg/urteile/2325.pdf> [19].

106 *Mitias v Solidea* (n 804). According to *Van Wyk v Norden Laboratories* 345 NW2d (Iowa 1984) 81–84, a purchaser can reasonably expect the merchantability of goods. See also Schwenzer, *Commentary on CISG* (n 15) 603; 601 [17]; [15].

107 *Crudex v Landmark* (n 1627).

108 *Shoes case* (21/11/2007) (Appellate Court Koblenz) <http://cisgw3.law.pace.edu/cases/071121g1.html>.

109 *Clothes case* (3/6/2003) CISG/2003/01 (CIETAC arbitration proceeding) <http://cisgw3.law.pace.edu/cases/030603c1.html>.

110 *Delphic Wholesalers v Agrilex* (n 1295).

111 Honnold, *Uniform Law* (n 320) 332 [225]. See also Gillette; Walt (n 778) 222.

112 *Harlingdon v Christopher* (n 878) 567, 568. See Sale of Goods Act 1979 <https://www.legislation.gov.uk/ukpga/1979/54/1991-02-01>.

113 *Canada Atlantic Grain Export Co (Inc) v Eilers* (1929) 35 LlL Rep 206, 213.

of merchantable quality when they were, in their tendered form, of 'no use for any purpose' for which the same goods would commonly be used and were unsalable under the contractual description.[114] Therefore, the compounded meal sold containing a toxic substance, which caused the death of many young pheasants after eating it,[115] was held to be of merchantable quality,[116] despite the fact that the goods 'were not reasonably fit for use in compound food for poultry and its use in a compound food for pheasants was an ordinary and reasonable use.'[117] This was on the grounds that the compounded meal was not commercially unsalable[118] as it was suitable for older poultry without inflicting harm.[119] Furthermore, the paintings in *Harlingdon* were reasonably resalable for the purpose of aesthetic appreciation even though they were unfit to be sold as works of Münter.[120] This approach encourages the buyer to specifically determine the purchase purpose from the beginning of the contractual relationship to give the seller a chance to refuse a contract if the buyer is looking for something beyond the seller's capabilities.

##### 5.2.2.1.2 COMPLIANCE WITH PURPOSES – BELOW-AVERAGE QUALITY

Alternatively, some jurists may think that the 'goods must be of average quality, and it does not suffice that they can only just be traded.'[121] In the *Mussels* case, it was stated that the impact of the cadmium concentration on the tradability of the mussels, exposing them to 'official seizure,' could not be applied to determine the goods' conformity.[122] This approach obliges the seller to deliver average goods, especially as goods which are fit for purpose range from the 'perfect fit' to an 'OK fit.'[123] This is particularly true as goods' merchantability, as outlined in *Taylor v Combined Buyers*, 'does not mean of good, or fair, or average quality. Goods may be of inferior or even bad quality yet fulfil the legal requirement of merchantable quality.'[124] Nevertheless, determining the required purposes for goods of below-average quality could be troublesome, for many reasons:

**First**, in international contracts, 'average quality' can differ from one country to another, necessitating a limitation to the relevant market.[125] **Secondly**, this approach requires an assessment of the quality according to the market,

114 *Cammell Laird & Co Ltd v Manganese Bronze & Brass Co Ltd* [1934] AC 402, 430.
115 Lord Pearcein *Henry v William* (n 1025) 117. However, the seller was held liable for breaching the particular purpose.
116 ibid 32.
117 ibid 33.
118 Havers J at the trial in ibid 32, 117.
119 ibid 54, 79.
120 *Harlingdon v Christopher* (n 878) 567, 568.
121 *Shoes case* (15/9/1994) 52 S 247/94 (District Court Berlin) <http://cisgw3.law.pace.edu/cases/940915g1.html>.
122 *New Zealand mussels case* (n 1329).
123 Poikela (n 83) 5. See also Bianca; Bonell (n 155) 274, 275 [2.5.1.].
124 Taylor v Combined Buyers (n 890) 51.
125 *Condensate crude oil mix case* (n 1619) [92].

encompassing the 'full range' of the relevant product.[126] In the *Mussels* case, the buyer did not prove that the average quality of the New Zealand mussels had much less cadmium contamination than those that were delivered. Submitting a report stating, '[T]here are also other imported New Zealand mussels on the market . . . that do not show a comparable cadmium contamination' did not constitute a proof of the goods' average quality.[127] **Thirdly**, it is difficult to designate an average quality level for all goods. In the *Condensate crude oil case*, it was stated that the fact that the goods contained a higher level of mercury did not directly place them in the category of below-average quality,[128] and it was unclear 'whether there [was] a common understanding in the refining industry what average quality for blended condensates . . . should have been and what levels of mercury [were] tolerable.'[129] The seller attempted to evidence that there was 'general awareness of mercury levels in condensates' at the purchase time, but this evidence did not help much as the court still could not determine an acceptable level of mercury according to which average quality could be established.[130] **Fourthly**, an 'average quality' of goods could reflect a number of levels, comprising a broad spectrum ranging from high to low, complying with Article 32(2)(a), although their grades are significantly different.[131] **Finally**, average quality creates a 'moving target'[132] by dropping goods of below-average quality out of the market. This shift alters the position of goods of average quality by elevating them, and this could make both parties uncertain about the required quality.[133]

#### 5.2.2.1.3 COMPLIANCE WITH ALL PURPOSES

Other adjudicators advocate that goods do not meet Article 35(2)(a) if they are fit for only one or some of their purposes; the goods should instead be fit for *all* usual purposes for which the goods may be utilised.[134] The Secretariat Commentary, on drafting CISG, stated that when goods are bought according to their general description, they should be 'fit for all the purposes for which goods of the same description are ordinarily used,'[135] compatible with consumers' expectations, which are constantly increasing.[136] In *Mitias v Solidea*, the court stated that goods should be fit for 'all (and not only some) of the [ordinary] purposes.'[137] However,

126 ibid [93].
127 *New Zealand mussels case* (n 1329).
128 *Condensate crude oil mix case* (n 1619) [98].
129 ibid [100].
130 ibid [101].
131 Saidov (n 769) 117.
132 Gillette; Walt (n 778) 230.
133 Gillette; Ferrari (n 1625) 12; Saidov (n 769) 116, 117.
134 Luca (n 815) 198. See also Gillette; Walt (n 778) 228.
135 Secretariat Commentary, *Commentary on the Draft Convention* (n 647); Official Records (n 149) 33.
136 Gillette; Ferrari (n 1625) 6; Saidov (n 769) 122.
137 *Mitias v Solidea* (n 804).

the goods' unsuitability for all their purposes would not permit termination unless an assessment was being made according to Article 25. In the aforementioned case, it was stated that, as long as the non-defective shoes' value was less than one tenth of the overall goods' value, the buyer was substantially deprived of what they were entitled to expect, and subsequently, it was found to be a fundamental breach.[138]

#### *5.2.2.2 Fitness for All Purposes Under SGA as a Rule*

In 1994, SGA switched 'merchantable quality,' in which meeting *any* purpose would suffice, to 'satisfactory quality,'[139] under which the seller is obliged, where relevant, to supply goods that are fit for *all* common purposes for which the same goods are normally supplied.[140] The Law Commission accentuates that 'goods of a particular description and price should be fit for all their common purposes unless there is an indication to the contrary.'[141] This indication could be deduced from contractual circumstances, such as in cases in which the seller expressly clarifies that the goods are unsuitable for a specific common usage, or the price implicitly indicates this unsuitability.[142]

Some judicial conclusions which occurred under 'merchantable quality' requirement would be rendered the opposite way under 'satisfactory quality.' In *Ashington*, the buyer would have been entitled, under satisfactory quality, to reject the whole consignment and terminate the contract when the animal foodstuff delivered contained toxic chemical preservatives and caused the death of mink, so long as feeding mink was one of the goods' common purposes. This would have been true even though the goods' purpose of feeding mink was not made known to the seller,[143] and the chemical ingredient was not verified unsuitable for animals other than mink. In *Aswan v Lupdine*, plastic pails containing a water-proofing compound, described as 'shipping container,' 'heavy duty container' and 'Stackability – 6 high,' were shipped to Kuwait, where they were left stacked six pails high for several days on the quayside, and the inner temperature of the goods reached 70° centigrade. This caused the pails to collapse and resulted in a total loss of the compound. Although export trade was the purpose for which the same kind of pails were commonly bought, they were held to be of 'merchantable quality,' even when the pails were truly unsuitable for use when stacked six high in all regions of the world, but they were suitable, if so stacked, for use in many regions of the world.[144] However, as Lloyd LJ stated, Parliament referring to *all* purposes

138 ibid.

139 See Sale of Goods Act 1979 <https://www.legislation.gov.uk/ukpga/1979/54/section/14/1991-02-01>.

140 SGA s.14(2B)(a); The Law Commission (n 230) [3.35]; Poikela (n 83) 27.

141 ibid The Law Commission [3.36].

142 Ervine (n 1572) 698.

143 *Henry v William* (n 1025) 117; Ashington v *Christopher* (n 842) 461. If the facts of the *Henry Kendall* case reoccur, the goods would probably be deemed unsatisfactory.

144 *Aswan Engineering Establishment v Lupdine Ltd* [1987] 1 WLR 1, 13.

would change the result.[145] This makes the pails of unsatisfactory quality under the current SGA, unless the seller proves that the pails' being stacked in a high temperature is not a purpose for which they are commonly used.[146]

#### *5.2.2.3 Fitness for the Intended Purpose Under KLaw*

KLaw considers the goods' freedom of defects rather than their suitability for their purposes. Al-Ahwani states that his may make a defect's existence in goods one stipulation and its reduction of the goods' value/benefit another.[147] However, other scholars find that a defect can be 'physical,' such as a broken chassis on a car,[148] or 'functional,' in which case there is no need for the buyer to prove the defect's existence as it is sufficient to prove that the commodity's utility has been affected, even if the commodity itself is intact. Evidently, in one case, the court rejected the request for termination because the defect was not hidden from the buyer as the voltage of the machines (which was Volt C (110) while the voltage required in Kuwait was Volt C (220)) was displayed on the goods.[149] As indicated by Al-Defery and Al-Sayrafy, if this defect had not been apparent, the termination could have been permitted despite the absence of a physical defect, and the goods' invalidity for the purpose could be considered a defect.[150]

The right to claim a hidden defect, pursuant to Article 489, is based on 'defect(s) that diminish its value or its usefulness according to the *intended purpose*.'[151] Therefore, if the commodity has a hidden defect that makes it invalid for some uses and denies the buyer of a benefit that is one of those intended, they have the right to claim termination even though the commodity retains its monetary value.[152] Article 489 continues that the intended purpose can be determined through two factors:

**First**, it depends upon the goods' nature and their prepared purpose. When the commodity is second-hand, the intended purpose can be deduced according to its age and price,[153] while if the commodity is new, it is easy to consider any defect as hidden, even if the buyer is a specialist.[154] **Secondly**, it depends on the contract and whether the intended purpose is mentioned implicitly or explicitly, meaning that the assessment of the defect must be based on objective grounds that relate not to the parties' personal considerations but to their common intention.[155] However, this intended purpose mentioned in the contract reflects the meaning of a 'particular

145 ibid.
146 Neo (n 1533) 370.
147 Al-Ahwany (n 497) 666.
148 Al-Defery; Al-Sayrafy (n 254) 285.
149 Case 15/2/1988 Court of Cassation 234/87 reproduced in ibid 290.
150 Al-Defery; Al-Sayrafy (n 254) 290, 291.
151 See Case 18/12/1989 Court of Cassation/Commercial 170–172/89 in Ministry of Justice, *Civil Provisions* (n 955) 292.
152 Al-Fadly (n 495) 128; Al-Defery; Al-Sayrafy (n 254) 292.
153 Al-Ahwany (n 497) 655, 656.
154 ibid 656.
155 ibid 673.

purpose,' such as using a car for racing, though this is outside the scope of this study. Nevertheless, the contractual contents, such as the goods' descriptions, could assist in the identification of the reduction of the goods' value/benefits due to the hidden defect.

Despite this reference in law to 'the contract, the goods' nature or the purpose for which the goods were prepared,' it is unclear whether these factors should be followed exclusively or if other elements could be resorted to. Article 489 uses the word 'utilising' before enumerating these factors, which gives the impression that these elements are merely for guidance, and other elements can be resorted to, such as the parties' position, purchase price or even the buyer's personal loss. Presumably, if following these elements is compulsory, legislation should have used the word 'according' rather than 'utilising.'[156] As stated by EMKCIC, estimation of the reduction can be (i.e. not obligatorily) through recourse to these elements.[157] Additionally, using the conjunction 'or' and not 'and' could permit the selection of any standard. Despite this fact, some jurists find that determining the significance of the defect depends mainly on these elements,[158] making them obligatory. Notwithstanding, the judge may estimate the situation according to the buyer's circumstances as the court indicated, in one case, that the intended purpose was that for which the *buyer* bought the goods.[159] In another case, the court stated that the buyer would not have been able to use the rods for the desired purpose in construction work,[160] and it was unclear whether this purpose was mentioned in the contract, this purpose was for goods which are alike, or it reflected the buyer's personal situation.

#### 5.2.2.4 *Comparative Analysis*

##### 5.2.2.4.1 POSSIBLE OUTCOMES UNDER THE THREE LEGAL SYSTEMS

Bunker coal was only suitable for one type of ship,[161] which was not the one the purchaser had. The buyer did not disclose the type of ship for which the coal was bought.

**Under CISG**, when applying *merchantable quality*, the coal could have been merchantable despite the fact that it was unsuitable for all types of ships. As Lord Morris affirmed, one could expect goods corresponding with the agreed descriptions to satisfy one of the normal purposes for which these goods were usually bought if there were various qualities and multiple purposes associated with these goods.[162] When applying *average quality*, the coal might also have corresponded

156 As seen in Lebanese Law (The Code of Obligations and Contracts of 1932) Art. 442.
157 EMKCIC 434.
158 Al-Danasory; Al-Shawarbee (n 281) 91.
159 For instance, Case 17/6/2007 (n 1581) 5, 6.
160 Case 7/11/1995 (n 1104) 7.
161 *Henry v William* (n 1025) 42, 43.
162 ibid 54, 79; George Akerlof, 'The Market for "Lemons": Quality Uncertainty and the Market Mechanism' (1970) 84(3) QJE 488, 490, 495.

with the average quality of similar coal in the market and so might not breach Article 35(2)(a). Fitness for all types of ships may not have reflected a reasonable expectation, as long as there was no indication of this requirement throughout the contractual relationship. So, under CISG, the contract would not have been terminated if the goods were suitable for one, some or most common purposes, unless the parties had agreed otherwise. **Under SGA**, if there was no indication otherwise, the coal should have been suitable for *all* common types of ships, and, if not, the buyer would have been entitled to terminate the contract. **Under KLaw**, if 'physical defect theory' had been pursued and the coal was intact and did not possess defects, then the claim of hidden defect could not have been raised. If 'functional defect theory' or 'non-usability' had been followed instead, the goods would have been regarded as defective. The effectiveness of considering goods defective depends on their reduction in value/benefit. If the coal's unsuitability for all types of ships caused this decrease, this reduction could have entitled the buyer to claim termination. Another judiciary opinion could perceive that this reduction should have been estimated according to the 'contract' and the 'nature of the goods,' and if the contract had been silent and the goods' nature had not indicated that the coal was suitable for all ships, then termination would not have been permitted. Another judge may find that resorting to these elements (i.e. the contract and the goods' nature) was not meant to be comprehensive and could evaluate the situation according to the buyer's evidence that they suffered detriment due to the unsuitability of the coal for specific types of ships, even if the contract had been silent, permitting the buyer to terminate the contract.

#### 5.2.2.4.2 CERTAINTY AND FLEXIBILITY

*Gillette* and *Ferrari* state that the obligation for goods to be fit for ordinary purposes is 'inherently ambiguous' **under CISG**; however, it might be impossible to identify the frequency of common uses in practice, and this prevents the adoption of a general rule applicable to a diverse range of goods and uses.[163] Therefore, many courts have resorted to the use of 'merchantable' or 'average' quality.[164] Nevertheless, '[I]t may well happen that the goods are below average quality but are still merchantable or fit for their ordinary purpose and vice versa,'[165] and this hinders the uniform application of Article 35(2)(a). **SGA** avoids these uncertainties by demanding that the goods meet all common purposes, although there could be an issue regarding the establishment of all common purposes in advance as '[s]ometimes [a purpose] is uncommon in certain contexts and is perfectly common in a different context.'[166] **Under KLaw**, is there ambiguity not only around interpreting the rule for the goods' validity for certain purposes and the legal outcomes of such a rule but also around which ideology should be adopted, giving the law a high degree of uncertainty when

163 Kröll; Mistelis; Viscasillas (n 67) 505 [74].
164 *Condensate crude oil mix case* (n 1619) [117].
165 Kröll; Mistelis; Viscasillas (n 67) 506 [80].
166 Twigg-Flesner; Canavan (n 30) 144.

pursuing either 'physical defect theory' or 'functional defect theory' and whether the intended purpose should be construed objectively, according to the contract and the goods' nature, or subjectively, according to the buyer's circumstances.

##### 5.2.2.4.3 PRESERVING THE CONTRACT

**Under CISG**, interpretations of quality (merchantability or average quality) are not required to meet all purposes, unless agreed otherwise, as the buyer is better positioned and has superior information about the intended use and should disclose this to the seller; otherwise, the contract should be preserved and not terminated. **Under SGA**, however, stipulating the suitability of all purposes is a very broad requirement involving many legitimate purposes, and this may cover even uncommon purposes. Therefore, 'it would be unreasonable to require that a manufacturer should be cognisant of all the purposes to which the article he manufactures might be applied.'[167] Rougier J remained sceptical about the fact that an 'all-embracing definition of . . . [satisfactory] quality [of a type of goods] could ever be made.'[168] SGA effectively elevates the level of both quality and legal certainty, but this permits the buyer to reject the goods because they are unsuitable for even one of the common purposes – one for which the buyer does not intend to use them,[169] especially in the event of a price decline, allowing the buyer to be released from an unprofitable deal rather than unfit goods.[170] **Under KLaw**, when termination is strictly confined to cases of 'physical defects' and the reduction in value/benefit caused by these defects is estimated objectively and exclusively according to the contract and the goods' nature, preserving the contract is an apparent feature. On the contrary, when cases are assessed subjectively, according to the buyer's situation or the reduction in value/benefit caused by the goods' unsuitability for the unrevealed purpose, the usage of termination increases.

### *5.2.3 The Role of Reasonableness in Determining Quality*

In order to identify the required quality, the 'reasonability standard' is adopted expressly by SGA and implicitly by CISG, reflecting the meaning of objectivity. Under KLaw, objective criteria might not be the only benchmark; the judge may consider the buyer's subjective circumstances.

#### *5.2.3.1 Reasonability Is the General Principle Under CISG*

Although Article 35(2)(a) does not mention that the quality should be 'reasonable,' some adjudicators have resolved the vague nature of 'goods' fitness for ordinary

167 *Drummond & Sons v Van Ingen & Co* (1887) 12 App Cas. 284, 293.
168 *Bernstein v Pamson* (n 1411) 387.
169 Bridge, *The Sale of Goods* (n 28) [7.68].
170 A similar meaning is found in Gillette; Ferrari (n 1625) 6.

purposes' by resorting to a 'reasonable quality' standard.[171] Because 'reasonable quality' cannot be identified without context[172] but depends on the circumstances of the case, the more detailed the contract is, the more easily contractual expectations of quality and their ordinary purposes can be envisaged.

CISG perceives the contract as a continuum of a relationship, including descriptive aspects not consolidated in the contract but mentioned in the negotiations,[173] in lieu of confining the contract to its boundaries,[174] unless the parties' intentions exclude any statements made prior to the contract.[175] In the *Textile manufacturing equipment* case, the tribunal stated that the machine was described in the contract as '350 grams chemical heavy fabric' but not as 'heated-air shaping method,' and the latter was the best machine to reach 28m/minute in the shaping of anti-pilling polar fleeces. This speed was not considered an ordinary purpose of the sold machine despite the buyer's argument that the title of the bid was 'Production Line of Anti-Pilling Polar Fleece.' The court did not consider the bid's title because it was only an inviting formal act and should not affect the parties' expression of real intention in the contract.[176]

Reasonable quality is founded on the 'information-based rationale' of the asymmetric information theory[177] as there is a presumption that the seller knows more about the goods' characteristics than the buyer,[178] and the seller is in a better position to avoid nonconformity.[179] Therefore, only when sellers possess information-based advantages[180] relating to the concerned purpose is this purpose relevant. In *BV v AS*, when a diesel tram's speed was 25 km/h, the seller was not held liable on the basis that the buyer did not prove that 40 km/h was the minimum speed of similar trams, particularly as the tram was a small tourist train, and its speed was well matched to its ordinary purposes.[181] In the *Condensate crude oil* case, the arbitral tribunal held that when early instalments of crude oil did not contain high levels of mercury, there was a breach of Article 35(2)(a) when goods sent later did[182] as this violated the buyer's expectations of obtaining goods of a consistent quality.[183] The tribunal explained that the 'reasonable quality' approach was the best standard to define the ordinary purposes on three grounds: **First**, it was the least divergent

171 *Condensate crude oil mix case* (n 1619) [117].
172 Huber; Mullis (n 1279) 135.
173 *Mitchell v European Aircraft Service* (n 812). See also *Gantry v Research Consulting Marketing* (n 819).
174 Saidov (n 769) 32.
175 ibid 31.
176 *Textile manufacturing equipment case* (n 817).
177 Gillette; Ferrari (n 1625) 6.
178 Henschel, 'Conformity of Goods' (n 1005) 3.
179 *Condensate crude oil mix case* (n 1619) [123].
180 Gillette; Ferrari (n 1625) 7, 8.
181 *BV BA G-2 v AS C.B.* (25/4/2001) A/00/00665 (District Court Veurne) <https://cisgw3.law.pace.edu/cases/010425b1.html>.
182 *Condensate crude oil mix case* (n 1619) [124].
183 ibid [121].

standard by national parallels and respected the international character of CISG, consistent with Article 7. **Secondly**, it was compatible with the buyer's reasonable expectations under Article 25. **Finally**, reasonableness was considered one of the main general principles implied in many of CISG's provisions, which can play a gap-filling role.[184]

On the other hand, when applying the reasonable person criterion to decide the required quality, the expression 'of the same kind,' mentioned in Article 25 and Article 8(2), could be used, placing the focus on an imaginary merchant who is engaging in the same type of trade as the buyer and belongs to the same class of merchants.[185] Some scholars further believe that this hypothetical trader should also possess the same 'socio-economic background, including religion, language [and] average professional standard' of the parties.[186] It is obviously true that the more specific the characteristics applied to the reasonable person are, the closer we approach the subjectivity standard and individualisation.[187] This might make the objectivity of the reasonable person approach redundant.

#### *5.2.3.2 Reasonable Person Is the Test of Satisfactory Quality Under SGA*

Goods are rendered unsatisfactory when a reasonable person regards them so, taking into account descriptions, price and other circumstances.[188] However, the descriptive statement in the contract should first be considered a contractual term in order to constitute an element of a reasonable person's perspective of quality. Goods described as 'used' are not comparable to new ones.[189] Also, according to *Alfred Toepferv Continental Grain*, 'amber durum' was not the same as 'hard amber durum wheat.'[190] In *Harlingdon v Christopher*, Stuart-Smith LJ established that paintings of the required quality should have been made according to the description,[191] and as long as the artist's identity was not considered a 'contractual term,' there was no room for a 'quality' claim regarding this identity. Otherwise, as Slade LJ asserted, the buyer could always have used the 'back door' approach of breaching *quality* to make a descriptive statement a term when they had failed to establish it using the 'front door' of breaching *description*.[192]

Therefore, as stated by Farwell LJ in *Bristol Tramways v Fiat Motors*, the matter depended on a reasonable person and whether they would have accepted an

184 ibid [103].
185 Official Records (n 149) 261; Gyula Eörsi, 'A Propos the 1980 Vienna Convention on Contracts for the International Sale of Goods' (1983) 31(2) AmJCompL 333, 341; Bianca; Bonell (n 155) 209, 219; Babiak (n 57) 122; Graffi (n 155) 341.
186 ibid Bianca; Bonell 219; ibid Babiak 113, footnote 57.
187 ibid Bianca; Bonell.
188 *Jewson v Boyhan* [2003] EWCA Civ 1030 [78]; Ervine (n 1572) 695; Twigg-Flesner; Canavan (n 30) 153, 154.
189 Ervine (n 1572) 688.
190 *Alfred v Grain* (n 981) 14.
191 *Harlingdon v Christopher* (n 878) 565, 583.
192 ibid 586.

omnibus for either using or reselling after their full inspection.[193] In *Marimpex v Louis Dreyfus*, if a reasonable buyer had been made aware of the contamination level present in the gasoil, they would not have bought the goods as 'normal Russian gasoil,' as described in the contract, but as abnormal gasoil;[194] even if they were using the gasoil for the purpose of heating, as Clarke J stated, the user would not have cared about the contamination.[195]

Despite the foregoing, the 'reasonable' standard is ambiguous. For instance, Auld LJ in *Bramhill v Edwards* stated that 'focus [should be] on the attitude of a "reasonable person" to the quality of the goods in question rather than on that of a person who would be willing to accept or buy them.'[196] Rather ambiguously, the Law Commission defines the reasonable person standard as follows:

> The question which the definition asks is not whether the reasonable person would find the goods acceptable; it is an objective comparison of the state of the goods with the standard which a reasonable person would find acceptable.[197]

To exemplify how resorting to a reasonable person is not always predictable, take the facts from *Bramhill v Edwards*. The vehicle was 102 inches wide, which exceeded the maximum of 100 inches permitted by road regulations,[198] and this illegality might have been considered a prosecution risk,[199] affecting the goods' satisfactory quality. The problem arose when the authorities 'turned a blind eye' to the breach,[200] making the reasonable person's attitude unclear, as the reasonable person 'could hold either opinion':[201] i.e. one reasonable person might consider regulation infraction a major factor that rendered the goods unsatisfactory while another might regard goods satisfactory when widespread breaches of the regulations had not resulted in any prosecution.

Additionally, it is difficult to determine what to apply: the reasonableness according to the parties' situation or the reasonableness according to an external observer. In *Mannai v Eagle*, the assessment of whether satisfactory quality was breached was subjected to 'what reasonable persons, circumstanced as the actual parties were, would have had in mind'[202] and not to the observation of a reasonable third party who has nothing to do with the transaction.[203] However,

193 Bristol Tramways, & C, Carriage Company, Limited v Fiat Motors, Limited [1910] 2 KB 831, 841.
194 *Marimpex v Louis Dreyfus* (n 857) 168.
195 ibid 168.
196 *Bramhill v Edwards* [2004] EWCA Civ 403 [39].
197 The Law Commission (n 230) [3.25].
198 *Bramhill v Edwards* (n 1722) [3].
199 ibid [28].
200 ibid [24].
201 Auld LJ in ibid [40].
202 *Mannai v Eagle* (n 1186) 768. See also *Rogers v Parish* (n 1572) 936, 946; *Bernstein v Pamson* (n 1411) 385; *Shine v General Guarantee Corp* [1988] 1 All E.R. 911.
203 *Bramhill v Edwards* (n 1722) [39]; Bridge, *Benjamin's* (n 28) [11–031].

in *Jewson v Boyhan*, Sedley LJ stated that the reasonable person should not be 'equipped with the buyer's personal agenda.'[204] Nevertheless, the approach pursued in *Investors Compensation Scheme* was establishing the contractual meanings from the perspective of a reasonable person who possesses all parties' reasonable background knowledge according to the words' meaning in dictionaries but excluding consideration of the previous negotiations and the parties' declarations of subjective intent.[205] Equally, in *Chartbrook v Persimmon*, it was submitted that the pre-contractual negotiation should be excluded as it reflected uncertainty and subjectivity.[206]

#### *5.2.3.3 Subjectivity or Objectivity of Reduction in Goods' Value/Benefit Caused by a Defect Under KLaw*

Contractual descriptions could play a significant role in estimating the reduction caused by the defect, pursuant to the jurisprudential rule that 'the contract is the law of the contractors' on which both KCIC and KCOC are based. In one case, it was considered that the buyer had bought a vehicle according to high-security specifications, making the failure of the airbags to deploy at the time of an accident a defect, even if the airbags were not supposed to deploy.[207] Pre-contractual descriptions could also play a role especially in interpreting the contract to know the parties' common intention from the total contractual facts,[208] unless otherwise indicated.

Nonetheless, when the contract is silent about the goods' descriptions, on what basis can one say there is a defect in goods causing a reduction in their value/benefit? If, for instance, tissues are discovered not to be soft, what is the benchmark to decide whether this defect is effective, reducing the goods' value/benefits? This question does not have a simple answer, especially as resorting to the goods' nature, their prepared purpose or an average commodity[209] does not help if there are a number of grades for the concerned goods. There are no criteria to estimate hidden defects in KLaw, but it has been stressed in many cases that all substantive matters of hidden defect claims were assigned to the discretionary authority of the trial judge,[210] which potentially replaces the 'reasonable person' in CISG and SGA.

If the defect only decreases the goods' benefits without affecting their value, the loss is 'utilitarian' rather than 'monetary,' which can easily be fabricated, especially as the law resorts subjectively to the buyer to define the 'substantiality' according to Article 485. The buyer only needs to prove that the loss reaches 'a certain extent,

204 *Jewson v Boyhan* (n 1714) [78].
205 *Investors Compensation Scheme v Bromwich* (n 623) 912, 913; *Arnold v Britton* (n 876) [15].
206 *Chartbrook v Persimmon* (n 906) [38].
207 Case 8/3/2006 (n 1583) 14.
208 Case 4/6/2006 (n 926) 4, 5.
209 Case 18/12/1989 Court of Cassation/Commercial 170–172/89 in Ministry of Justice, *Civil Provisions* (n 955) 292.
210 Case 30/12/2008 (n 1213) 5, 6.

being that if the buyer had known about it at the time of sale, they would have been dissuaded from concluding the contract.' Despite this linkage between the defect's substantiality and the purchaser instead of the contract, Islamic jurisprudents, such as Shafi'i school, do not take the parties' intent into consideration. This is because it reflects internal psychological thoughts contrary to the parties' declared will,[211] revealed by material standards of acts and behaviours, adhering to the appearance of the contract[212] for the sake of securing 'social security.'[213] The unrevealed intentions are known only by God, as it says in the Quran: 'He (God) certainly has (full) knowledge, of the secrets of (all) hearts.'[214] Correspondingly, Article 3 Al-Majalla states that 'the core in contracts is its purposes and meanings,' which means that the purposes deduced from the contract form the nucleus of the agreement.

KLaw, however, is more attuned to the buyer because KCIC applies to the consumers, and therefore the law seeks to protect them. In many cases, however, when KCOC has gaps, like concerning hidden defects, KCIC is applicable[215] to merchants, positioning the law on the merchant buyer's side more than on the selling merchant's. Interestingly, in one case, 'substantiality' was defined objectively as having a hugely negative impact on the goods' usual use, and it was only after this recognition that the buyer had the right to request termination,[216] despite the fact that the literal meaning of 'substantiality' reflects subjectivity. Dr Al-Fadly suggests a new objective standard to define 'substantiality': namely, the inability of the goods to be repaired.[217] This approach was taken in one case in which the buyer repeatedly visited the seller's garage, and the seller could not fix the defect, which led to the judgement of termination.[218] Al-Ahwany adopts a different objective approach, believing that if the purpose of the purchase was reselling the goods, the defect is not substantial if the goods can be sold at a higher price than the purchase price, despite the defect.[219] These attempts, which strive to avoid subjectivity, are not found in Article 485, causing unpredictability.

### *5.2.3.4 Comparative Analysis*

#### 5.2.3.4.1 POSSIBLE OUTCOMES UNDER THE THREE LEGAL SYSTEMS

Consider this hypothetical situation: In the pre-contractual stage, a buyer is unsatisfied with the option of purchasing a photocopier with the capacity to print only 20

211 Ayob (n 494) 51, 53; Al-Qarafy (n 953) 227.

212 ibid Ayob 53.

213 ibid 318.

214 The Quran. 'Translation of Surah Al-Mulk: Verse 13' <http://search-the-quran.com/search/Surah+Al-Mulk/8>.

215 KCOC Art. 2; Art. 96.

216 Case 9/12/2001 (n 1600) 2, 3; Case 17/6/2007 (n 1581) 5, 6.

217 Al-Fadly (n 495) 130.

218 Case 30/12/2008 (n 1213) 6.

219 Al-Ahwany (n 497) 668.

pages a minute. It is then agreed in the contract that the seller will supply a 'fast photocopier.' As the brand is not mentioned in the contract, it will be more difficult for courts to determine the printing capacity of similar photocopiers. The reasonable capacity of most photocopiers in the market ranges from 15 to 100 pages a minute. The seller, who is less experienced than the buyer, then supplies photocopiers with a speed of 30 pages a minute, which subsequently causes personal loss to the buyer.

**Under CISG**, according to 'asymmetric information theory,'[220] the buyer is better positioned to estimate the goods' fitness than the seller[221] because of their experience. But the buyer's refusal at the negotiation stage to accept photocopiers with a capacity to print 20 pages a minute is likely to have an impact on the assessment of reasonable quality. The seller can refuse to do business due to the buyer's high expectations,[222] which may not be met because of the seller's limited capabilities. This strongly indicates that the parties intend to regard 'fast' as a contractual description, and this should require a minimum speed of 40 pages a minute, therefore breaching Article 35(2)(a). In order to describe this breach as fundamental,[223] it needs to have a hugely negative impact on the buyer's contractual expectations, and this result can be foreseeable from the seller's side. Printing 10 pages less than the required minimum per minute can entitle termination, unless other criteria, such as the seller's curability right or the suitability of other, less harsh remedies, are applicable.

**Under SGA**, negotiations are not a factor in assessing the quality according to the perspective of a reasonable person, which makes the buyer's refusal at the negotiation stage irrelevant. This will lead to the consideration of 'fast' not as a description but simply as a representation, especially as the buyer is more experienced than the seller, analogous to the *Harlingdon* case. Because SGA expressly adopts a reasonable person benchmark, the buyer's subjective loss will not be considered, and, therefore, the seller may not breach s.14(2) as long as the goods' capacity is within the reasonable range.

**Under KLaw**, Articles 196 and 197 KCIC emphasise that any contract is the law of the parties and should be fulfilled in accordance with its terms. So the term 'fast' is highly likely to be considered when estimating the goods' defectiveness. The pre-contractual stage will not play a role in this scenario as the contract is clear and does not need to be interpreted to identify the common intention. The reasonable capacity of 15 to 100 pages a minute might not be considered because reasonability is not a criterion, unless the court sees otherwise. Accordingly, there is a legal gap regarding the measure of whether the capacity of printing 30 pages a minute is considered a defect and whether the supplied capacity causes a reduction in the goods' value/benefit, especially as referring to the contract and the goods'

220 Gillette; Ferrari (n 1625) 6.

221 A similar meaning is found in the previous text, ibid.

222 CISG Art. 8.

223 This is in tandem with other Art. 25 stipulations.

nature will not help. Assigning this task to the judge without adopting a clear criterion could give either party the opportunity to win the case by persuading of the judge. The buyer's subjective loss based on capacity can reinforce their right to termination, especially as, if they were aware of this loss at the time of sale, they might have been dissuaded from concluding the contract. Defining 'substantiality' according to the buyer's whims and personal needs disturbs the contractual equilibrium between the parties and places the fate of the contract in the buyer's hands, enabling them to portray the breach as substantial.

#### 5.2.3.4.2 CERTAINTY, FLEXIBILITY AND PRESERVING THE CONTRACT

The reasonability criterion is neutral,[224] objective and flexible[225] in order to strike a balance between the parties[226] and prevent the buyer from using irrelevant departures as a pretext for termination at the expense of the seller.[227] However, this fictitious measure might make the seller anxious about the possibility of violating reasonable expectations at all contractual stages, simply because they may not know what the reasonable person expects. The constituents of 'reasonable quality' are similar to those of Article 25, which could be complicated, especially when the contract does not elucidate the goods' details. This gives little guidance about the required quality,[228] reducing legal certainty[229] for the following reasons:

**First**, there is no definition that specifies who a 'reasonable person' might be, as neither CISG nor SGA specifies the degree of awareness and prevision that that person should possess.[230] However, there have been some attempts to define them. They could represent 'merchants with a reasonable degree of knowledge and experience in their trade, including knowledge of the relevant market conditions.'[231] Nonetheless, specifying the required degree of experience can itself be problematic and diverse. **Secondly**, 'reasonability' is variable and is rooted in culture.[232] It might be difficult to decide whether to pursue a particular nation's sense of reasonableness.[233] Even within the same region, the attitude of a reasonable person may be inconsistent. **Thirdly**, at one CISG conference, some delegates recommended entrusting the task of interpreting the 'reasonable person' standard to the courts,[234] which means the reasonable person might always be conceived according to the

224 Saidov (n 769) 116, 117.

225 Kröll; Mistelis; Viscasillas (n 67) 507 [85].

226 Burrows, *Principles of English Commercial Law* (n 28) 77, 78.

227 Charles Fried, *Contract as Promise: A Theory of Contractual Obligation* (OUP 2015) 119.

228 The Law Commission (n 230) [3.21]; Neo (n 1533) 367; Roger Brownsword, *Contract Law: Themes for the Twenty-First Century* (OUP 2006) 104; Burrows, *Principles of English Commercial Law* (n 28) 71; Twigg-Flesner; Canavan (n 30) 141.

229 ibid Burrows 77, 78.

230 John Honnald, *Documentary History* (n 344) 52.

231 Babiak (n 57) 122; Kröll; Mistelis; Viscasillas (n 67) 344 [22]. See also Graffi (n 155) 341.

232 Official Records (n 149) 261.

233 *Schuler* (n 198) 263.

234 John Honnald, *Documentary History* (n 344) 65.

country of the jurisdiction,[235] reflecting the court's sense of justice.[236] In *Davis v Fareham*, Lord Radcliffe stated that '[a] reasonable man who represents after all no more than the anthropomorphic conception of justice, is and must be the court itself.'[237] This gives the judge 'plenty of scope . . . to manoeuvre, so that the outcome of particular cases will no doubt continue to be influenced by the view the judge forms of the reasonableness of the . . . behaviour.'[238] This could lead to a variety of applications and make the contract's fate unknown beforehand. **Lastly**, reasonableness is an unstable factor and susceptible to external market-related circumstances, which may change over time.[239]

Despite the foregoing, a reasonable person is not the sole decisive factor in determining quality **under SGA**. Other aspects should be considered, such as the goods' fitness for all common purposes, appearance and finish and freedom from minor defects,[240] a breach of which entitles the rejection of the goods even when the seller is able to establish that a reasonable person would consider the goods satisfactory with such a breach,[241] boosting legal certainty and lifting the required quality but reducing the chance to preserve the contract. **Under CISG**, when the goods are described broadly in the contract, encompassing numerous diverse classes, 'reasonable quality' suffers from imprecision, requiring a complementary standard such as 'merchantable' or 'average' quality, which could hinder the parties' prior knowledge of the required quality.[242] CISG achieves flexibility by requiring analysis[243] of all the contractual circumstances, such as the consumers' reasonable expectations, the parties' previous dealings,[244] the goods' nature and the interpretation of the contract[245] to extract the required quality, but this could be conducted differently by the parties than by the adjudicators. This, however, achieves a high level of contract preservation.

**Under KLaw**, Article 489 seemingly adopts an objective criterion to identify the reduction of the goods' value/benefit caused by a defect according to the contract and the goods' nature, but Article 485 adopts a subjective criterion to define the 'substantiality' of such a reduction, leading to confusion. Personal criteria are fraught with risks of variability and instability, leading to different solutions from

235 ibid.

236 Twigg-Flesner; Canavan (n 30) 131, 141.

237 *Davis Contractors v Fareham Urban DC* [1956] AC 696, 728, 729.

238 Adams; MacQueen (n 126) 158.

239 Public perception can change over time. This aspect can be added to the non-exhaustive matters mentioned in SGA s.14(2B).

240 SGA s.14(2B)(a),(b),(c),(d),(e).

241 Ervine (n 1572) 697, 698.

242 Richard Hyland, 'Conformity of Goods to the Contract under the United Nations Sales Convention and the Uniform Commercial Code' in Peter Schlechtriem, *Einheitliches Kaufrecht und nationals Obligationenrecht* (Nomos 1987) <https://www.cisg.law.pace.edu/cisg/biblio/hyland1.html> 313; Gillette; Walt (n 778) 229.

243 *Shoe leather case* (n 282).

244 CISG Advisory Council (n 1611) 48.

245 Schwenzer, *Commentary on CISG* (n 15) 601; 603 [15][17]; ibid 51, 52.

case to case, despite the similarity of the non-performed obligation. More problematically, when resorting to the contract and the goods' nature is not much help in deciding whether the goods are defective or not, the evaluation is assigned to the judge's discretion, sacrificing certainty and making cases variable from one judge to another. Despite the aforementioned concerns about the uncertainty of the 'reasonable' standard, the 'expectations of an average user'[246] and of a reasonable person in the buyer's place[247] aim to represent objectivity. Certainty can be attained far more efficiently than with the KLaw approach by deducing sensible neutral behaviour, removed from the individual and expelling from international commerce those who are intellectually, ethically and professionally inferior to a reasonable merchant.[248] This plays a role in preserving the contract more than following the buyer's subjective circumstances, which permits the buyer to terminate the contract as long as their purpose is not tied to the contract.

### *5.2.4 The Role of Price in Determining Quality*

The concept of inferior quality might be limited in the context of inexpensive goods as it may be argued that the buyer cannot expect them to be in the same condition as goods of the same type with much higher prices.[249] However, the price has a different role in each legal system.

#### *5.2.4.1 Price Is Core in 'Merchantability' and Is a Single Element in 'Reasonability' Under CISG*

Non-merchantability of the goods breaches Article 35(2)(a)[250] if a reasonable buyer in the same market is unwilling 'at times comparable to [the purchase time]. . . to pay the [agreed] price'[251] when they are fully acquainted with the goods' actual state,[252] such as in the *Frozen fish case*, when fish from the previous year were difficult to sell until the price was substantially discounted.[253] Alternatively, Article

246 *Plants case* (12/12/2006) 22 O 38/06 (District Court Coburg) <http://cisgw3.law.pace.edu/cases/061212g1.html>.

247 Akerlof (n 1688) 499, 500; Huber; Mullis (n 1279) 135; Luca (n 815) 242.

248 Bianca; Bonell (n 155) 219.

249 Al-Ahwany (n 497) 655; Al-Fadly (n 495) 126; Al-Defery; Al-Sayrafy (n 254) 300.

250 For instance, *Sacovini/M Marrazza v Les fils de Henri Ramel* (n 1626); *Ginza v Vista Corporation* (n 1626) [190]; *International Housewares v SEB* (n 1626) [59]; *Frozen pork case* (n 1626); Gillette; Walt (n 778) 229, 241.

251 *Condensate crude oil mix case* (n 1619) [90] Despite this conclusion, the court did not take the approach of merchantability.

252 ibid [90]; *Fryer Holdings v Liaoning MEC* (n 1631) [20]. See also Dixon Jin *Australian Knitting Mills v Grant* [1933] HCA 35, 50 CLR 387, 418 <https://jade.io/article/63653>. This case is mentioned here because it was referred to by *Aswan v Lupdine* (n 1670); Gillette; Ferrari (n 1625) 13, 14.

253 *Frozen fish case* (n 1371).

35(2)(a) can be breached when the value of the delivered goods is lower than that of the conforming goods if they are supplied at the agreed delivery time.[254]

Reliance on the price can make the 'merchantable quality' 'less susceptible [than 'average' and 'reasonable' quality] to interpretation that is inconsistent with optimal risk bearing.'[255] The price mirrors the informational advantage of receiving goods of equivalent quality, so the lower the price, the lower the expectation of quality and vice versa.[256] In the *Down jacket* case, although the jackets suffered from being disproportionate and a report was issued from a quality control body that declared that the goods were 'below-grade,' the court held that the purchase price was significantly below the market price, which made the buyer's expectation of obtaining goods of a higher standard unreasonable.[257] In *Rynpoort Trading v Meneba Meel*, it was stated that the price of flour did not indicate that the buyer should not have expected the goods' quality to meet international standards.[258] However, the drawbacks of this approach are:

**First**, this test interferes with the parties' agreement by linking it to quality, preventing the parties from bargaining for a better price. **Secondly**, the price could be affected by factors other than quality,[259] such as transportation and production costs; an oligopolistic market; the goods being seasonal,[260] luxurious or fashionable; or sellers being new entrants to the market.[261] **Thirdly**, the real reason for a reasonable buyer's unwillingness to buy the goods without price abatement may be due not to the goods' inferior quality but to external factors in the market, such as the emergence of more sophisticated, cheaper goods between the time of concluding the contract and the delivery date. In one case, the buyer claimed that the inferior quality of the first consignment helped foster a bad reputation, leading to a considerable decrease in prices and a slowdown in sales of the second consignment, but the court found that the buyer failed to prove that linkage.[262] In *argumentum e contrario*, if the buyer succeeded in proving this linkage, a bad reputation negatively affecting the buyer's 'later sales and the expected profit'[263] could lead to a breach of Article 35(2)(a).[264] **Lastly**, this standard depends on the market price, and finding out which market should be resorted to might be problematic, especially

254 *Catalogue case* (n 1316).

255 Gillette; Ferrari (n 1625) 14.

256 Akerlof (n 1688) 488, 490, 495; ibid 13.

257 *Down jacket case* (n 785).

258 *Rynpoort Trading v Meneba Meel* (23/4/2003) 99/474 (Appellate Court Gravenhage) <http://cisgw3.law.pace.edu/cases/030423n1.html>.

259 Gillette; Ferrari (n 1625) 15, 16; Saidov (n 769) 114, 115.

260 Saidov (n 769) 116, 117.

261 Gillette; Ferrari (n 1625) 15, 16.

262 Unavailable Name (24/1/2000) (Arbitration proceeding Russia) 54/1999 <http://cisgw3.law.pace.edu/cases/000124r1.html>.

263 *Electric heaters case* (n 633). See also Maley (n 186) 114.

264 This occurred in *Pocket ash-trays case* (10/10/2005) 4P.146/2005/biz (Supreme Court) <http://cisgw3.law.pace.edu/cases/051010s1.html>. The case is not translated online; Maley's translation was relied on. Maley (n 186) 113, 114.

as some goods do not have a market at all,[265] making this benchmark suitable for goods bought to be sold but not applicable to specialist machinery, for example.[266] The Arbitral Tribunal in the *Condensate crude oil* case stated that 'there was no market for Rijn Blend (the goods) with increased mercury levels at prices comparable to the sales contracts.'[267]

Conversely, when applying 'reasonable quality,' the surrounding facts of the contractual circumstances, such as the parties' prior dealings, practices and usages,[268] formulate the ordinary purposes more than 'merchantable quality,' the price can only be considered one contractual element. Therefore, when described as 'new' or 'first-class' or when of an expensive and sophisticated nature, goods should be suitable for use for an average of three years,[269] irrespective of the price. Still, when the price is comparatively high, the goods may be unfit for their ordinary purpose if they suffer damage, especially if there is a *big* difference between the value of delivered goods and that of equivalent goods in pristine condition.[270] Yet termination might not be an option unless the breach meets Article 25's stipulations, and the seller fails to cure the defect. This is besides assessing the insufficiency of less harsh remedies in redressing the contractual detriment in order to determine the substantiality of the deprivation of contractual expectation. This is contrary to the merchantability criterion, in which Article 25's stipulations could automatically be met when the goods are unmerchantable.

#### *5.2.4.2 Price (If Relevant) Could Be a Strong Indicator of Quality Under SGA*

The Law Commission states that 'the price will often be a guide to the quality of the goods';[271] thus, the 'buyer [should be] entitled to value for his money.'[272] Price could reflect the goods' age and characteristics,[273] and the goods' purposes can be estimated accordingly. If cars are sold at a very low price, it is likely that they are to be used as scrap, not as roadworthy vehicles,[274] and the expectation of their quality should be far lower than for drivable cars.[275] According to case law, contaminated Russian gasoil breached quality when its market value was considerably less than

265 Saidov (n 769) 116, 117.
266 ibid 117–119.
267 *Condensate crude oil mix case* (n 1619) [90].
268 CISG Art. 8(3).
269 *Globes case* (n 185).
270 Saidov (n 769) 133, 134.
271 The Law Commission (n 230) [3.27].
272 Mustill LJ in Rogers v Parish (n 1572) 944. See also *Henry v William* (n 1025) 42, 79; Hale LJ in *Clegg v Olle* (n 1617) [72].
273 *Goldup v John Manson Ltd* [1982] QB 161, 163; *Thain v Anniesland Trade Centre* (1997) SLT (Sh Ct) 102, 104.
274 Twigg-Flesner; Canavan (n 30) 157.
275 *Business Applications Specialists Ltd v Nationwide Credit Corp Ltd* [1988] RTR 332, 335; *Thain v Anniesland* (n 1799) 106.

that of uncontaminated gasoil.[276] The unsuitability of material for manufacturing dresses did not render it below the required quality because its price was very low.[277] Similarly, generators that shut down automatically when the temperature reached 55° centigrade,[278] causing a reduction in production, were of satisfactory quality on the grounds that the goods were obtained from stock and were not high priced.[279]

This emphasis on price under the current SGA may render opposing decisions in old cases. In *Harlingdon v Christopher*, it was held that paintings which were discovered to be forged did not breach quality due to, inter alia, their fitness for their common purpose – namely, 'resale and/or aesthetic appreciation' – despite the fact that the paintings were sold at £6,000.[280] Currently, it would likely be concluded that a reasonable person would not consider fake paintings satisfactory at this price. In *Cehave v Bremer*, after the contract was concluded, the market price of citrus pulp pellets sold at £100,000 fell, and on their arrival, the buyer rejected the whole cargo on the grounds that some of the goods were damaged due to overheating. The seller resorted to court, which ordered the sale of the whole cargo for £30,000 to an importer, who then sold it at the latter price to the original buyer to use for the original purpose of feeding cattle. Since all the pellets were suitable and ultimately used for cattle feed, the goods were held to be of 'merchantable quality,' and the buyer was not entitled to terminate the contract.[281] However, according to the 'satisfactory quality' requirement, if the heat damage had an impact on reducing the goods' price (irrespective of the decline in the goods' price in the market), a reasonable person might not consider the goods satisfactory, regardless of their suitability for purpose; the goods could be unsatisfactory at £100,000 as some of them were damaged but could be satisfactory, even with the defect, at £30,000.

#### *5.2.4.3 Reduction in Price Due to a Defect Permits Termination Under KLaw*

Price has a different role under KLaw. When a commodity's value decreases due to a defect, even without detracting from its usefulness, the defect is effective, and the buyer has the right to claim termination. Some scholars find that the judge should not need to resort to the contract or the commodity's nature in order to know whether the defect has a negative impact on the goods' value, but rather, this decrease can be determined from the value of the commodity with the defect in the market according to the rules of supply and demand.[282] In one case, the court found that rust on the edge of rods shipped from Japan was an effective defect when the

276 *Marimpex v Louis Dreyfus* (n 857) 168.
277 *BS Brown v Craiks* [1970] 1 WLR 752.
278 *Wärtsilä France SAS v Genergy plc* [2003] EWHC 1966 (TCC) [43].
279 ibid [44]. Additionally, in *Goldup v John* (n 1799) 162, the percentage of fat in minced beef was linked to the price.
280 *Harlingdon v Christopher* (n 878).
281 *Cehave* (n 126) 71.
282 Al-Ahwany (n 497) 666; Al-Defery; Al-Sayrafy (n 254) 294, 295.

commodity was sold in the local market for less than the price of its purchase and lower than the price in the local market.[283]

However, comparing the goods' value at purchase with their value at delivery or perhaps at litigation (to decide the effectiveness of the defect, entitling the buyer to claim termination) permits the intervention of market factors. This necessitates studies of the market to identify whether the defect was the real reason for the reduction in the commodity's value, which could be time consuming and require the opinion of economic experts. For instance, in a 'buyer's market,' the supply of goods exceeds their demand,[284] decreasing the goods' value, even if they are totally intact, and any defect is put under the microscope, further reducing the price. Conversely, in a 'seller's market,' where there is a low supply of goods with high demand,[285] the same defect will not be considered, and the price could increase, even with a defect. In contrast, Al-Majalla,[286] Al-Murshed[287] and some Muslim jurists[288] resort to the perspective of merchants and experts as a clear objective criterion to estimate the defect's impact on the goods' value, and this may exclude both external factors of the market situation and the parties' subjective circumstances. Thus, any decrease in the goods' price would not necessarily activate a hidden defect claim, especially when the decrease in price is minor in an expert's opinion.[289]

More problematically, Article 489 strangely holds the seller liable for hidden defects when they exist in the goods at the time of sale.[290] This means that if the defect emerges after the contract is concluded and just before delivery, it might not be included in Article 489. The seller has another obligation: namely, delivering the goods in their state at the time of sale, which is regarded as a promised description,[291] without the requirement of proving the hidden defect's stipulations,

283 Case 7/11/1995 (n 1104) 7.

284 Akhilesh Ganti, 'Buyer's Market' (9/9/2019) <https://www.investopedia.com/terms/b/buyers market.asp> accessed 9/10/2020.

285 Will Kenton, 'Seller's Market' (12/5/2018) <https://www.investopedia.com/terms/s/sellersmarket.asp> accessed 9/10/2020.

286 Al-Majella Art. 338; Iraqi Civil Code 1951 Art. 558(2) expressly adopted this objective obligatory standard, stating that the effectiveness of a reduction in price caused by a hidden defect should be assessed by *traders and experts*.

287 Basha (n 1592) Art. 432.

288 Ayob (n 494) 157.

289 Al-Fadly (n 495) 132.

290 This is contrary to what was mentioned in Al-Majalla Art. 339 and Art. 340, stating that a defect is old if it existed in the goods when they were in the seller's possession. This provision regards any defects as hidden if they exist from the time of sale until the time of delivery. The problem with this provision is that the seller is liable as long as the goods are in their possession, even if the seller notifies a negligent buyer that the goods are ready for collection. Al-Majalla was clearer than KLaw in determining the point in time when defects take effect. Art. 558(2) of the Iraqi Civil Code regards a defect as old if it occurs in the goods at the time of concluding the contract or afterwards, in the hands of the seller and before delivery. Seemingly, this provision adds the phrase 'before delivery' in order to avoid the remark of Al-Majalla mentioned earlier.

291 KCIC Art. 467; Al-Ahwany (n 497) 663, 664.

such as its negative impact on the goods' value. Despite this, Al-Majalla[292] and Al-Murshed,[293] as well as other scholars[294] and cases,[295] apply the hidden defect rules even when the defect exists after concluding the contract and before the buyer's receipt. Designing different rules for different points in time may be neither practical nor predictable.

#### *5.2.4.4 Comparative Analysis*

##### 5.2.4.4.1 POSSIBLE OUTCOMES UNDER THE THREE LEGAL SYSTEMS

Suppose a specific brand of cheese is normally considered top quality. In this example, the price is reduced because the cheese has been stored in the wrong conditions, which makes it third class. However, the buyer is not informed of the poor storage or the reason for the lower price.

**Under CISG**, when applying 'merchantable quality,' if the goods are merchantable when revealing the condition of the cheese without reducing the purchase price, there is no breach to Article 35(2)(a). As stated in *Condensate crude oil case*, the agreed price would not have been paid by alternate buyers for Rijn Blend when the increased level of mercury was disclosed.[296] Conversely, when pursuing 'reasonable quality,' the price may not be the only factor, and the goods' description including a specific brand might cause the buyer to reasonably expect the equivalent quality. However, this breach would not permit termination per se unless it is substantial and foreseeable according to Article 25.

**Under SGA**, a reasonable person may recognise that the price is not the expected one, and this indicates the relinquishment of the cheese's normal class, making the cheese of satisfactory quality. The outcome may be different if the purchase is made at the normal price, and the cheese is second class, as the mere difference in classification, even if it is not significant, permits termination.

**Under KLaw**, the price can be an inherent indicator when considering a defect effective. If the low quality reduces the cheese's value to below the purchase price according to the rules of supply and demand in the market, the buyer will have the right to terminate. Alternatively, if the defect does not reduce the price but reduces its benefits, hindering the buyer's intended purpose, the buyer can also request termination.

##### 5.2.4.4.2 CERTAINTY AND FLEXIBILITY

**Under CISG**, 'merchantability' can represent Article 25's stipulations, constituting a clear and assessable yardstick due to its dependence on the market price.[297]

292 Al-Majalla Art. 430, 339.
293 Basha (n 1592) Art. 422.
294 Al-Fadly (n 495) 132, 133; Abdulreda (n 40) 198; Al-Danasory; Al-Shawarbee (n 281) 90.
295 Case 20/4/2002 (n 1094) 1–4; Case 24/4/2004 (n 1572) 2–4; Case 17/4/2012 (n 1572) 4, 5.
296 *Condensate crude oil mix case* (n 1619) [120].
297 Saidov (n 769) 117–119.

When 'the resale possibility is fundamentally impaired' or 'when the defects, though not affecting the material use of the goods, *considerably lessen their trade value*,'[298] the goods breach Article 35(2)(a),[299] substantially depriving the buyer of their contractual expectations and making this result foreseeable for any reasonable person in the seller's place.[300] In the *Catalogue* case, when one line on one page in an art catalogue was misplaced without affecting its readability and accordingly did not devalue the product, the court asserted that 'although a seller can be held liable even for a non-essential lack of conformity, this is only if the defect lowers the value of the goods.'[301] Poikela additionally states:

> In the case of goods intended for resale, even slight defects in quality in respect of which a repair is not possible or is unreasonable or is not performed by the seller, are likely to amount to a fundamental breach of contract. However, if the buyer can reasonably sell the imperfect goods elsewhere, there has been no fundamental breach.[302]

Nevertheless, pursuing 'reasonable quality' may lessen certainty by considering and assessing many contractual circumstances other than price, but this approach is fairer and more flexible.

**Under SGA**, even in cases in which the price is reduced only to quicken the sale without signifying a decrease in quality,[303] the price remains an important element in assessing quality.[304] If there is a substantial disparity between the price and the quality, the goods can be classed as unsatisfactory[305] from a reasonable person's perspective. Therefore, the *purchase* price is the core of estimating the required quality in all relevant cases. This makes the situation clearer and more predictable without intervention of the state of the market because the *resale* price may not play a role, contrary to merchantable quality.

**Under KLaw**, depending on the market's situation when deciding whether a defect is effective invites the intervention of the market's external factors. Moreover, requiring the reduction of the goods' value due to those defects existing at the time of sale without those existing thereafter hinders predictability and requires proof of the time of the defect's occurrence, which wastes time and effort.

### *5.2.5 Goods' Safety*

The seller may infringe on the required quality when not implementing the relevant safety standards. Each legal system's attitude towards this violation is different.

298 Enderlein; Maskow (n 150) 144. See also Maley (n 186) 113.
299 *Designer clothes case* (n 352).
300 See *Spanish paprika case* (n 1370).
301 *Catalogue case* (n 1316).
302 Poikela (n 83) 5.
303 Ervine (n 1572) 697.
304 ibid 688.
305 Twigg-Flesner; Canavan (n 30) 159.

#### 5.2.5.1 CISG

Any governmental sanctions imposed on goods due to the breach of international safety requirements might breach Article 35(2)(a) as it could be foreseeable to any trader in the concerned field that these sanctions can cause severe detriment, substantially depriving the purchaser of what they are entitled to expect.[306] Therefore, machines lacking safety measures which injured workers[307] and a 'bread improver' infringing international standards and containing a carcinogenic additive, which had harmful effects on human health,[308] were held unfit for their ordinary purposes. However, mussels that contained cadmium concentration did not constitute a breach of Article 35(2)(a) because, inter alia, the goods were not toxicologically harmful as they were not consumed in vast quantities in a short period of time, and even during excessive consumption, there was no danger to the consumer's health.[309] If there is a lack of necessary data or warning of the goods' characteristics, particularly when they're bought from a specialised seller, this may also breach Article 35(2)(a).[310] However, it was stated in *Deforche v Prins* that 'the duty of information towards a specialist is much less stringent than the duty of information towards a layman.'[311]

Safety requirements are implemented strictly, even in cases of suspicion about goods' risks, as this suspicion might badly affect the goods tradability,[312] especially when 'merchantable quality' is adopted. In the *Frozen pork case*, a consignment of Belgian pork was seized by the German government (the buyer's country) because of the enactment of a new regulation in the month of delivery, June 1999, prohibiting the trade of such goods due to dioxin contamination. A similar measure was adopted in Belgium (the seller's country), declaring that the meat was unmarketable when the animals were slaughtered in/before July 1999. The seller demanded payment the buyer took the goods before the regulation was implemented. The Appellate Court and the Federal Court of Justice dismissed the seller's claim and emphasised that, in international trade, the suspicion of the goods' harm to health constituted a breach of conformity, especially if the suspicion led to measures disqualifying the goods' re-salability and particularly as the dioxin contaminate, which was the cause of the goods' loss of tradability, was inherent before the passage of risk.[313] Nevertheless, this may contradict what is stressed in the opinion of the Advisory Council: that only standards at the time of concluding the contract

306 *Rynpoort v Meneba* (n 1784); *Red Pepper Powder Case* (25/5/2012) 267/2012 (Appellate Court Murcia) <http://cisgw3.law.pace.edu/cases/120525s4.html>.

307 *Textile product machines case* (n 1548) [22].

308 *Rynpoort v Meneba* (n 1784).

309 *New Zealand mussels case* (n 1329).

310 *Printing system and software case* (n 1322); *Beijing Light Automobile v Connell* (5/6/1998) (Stockholm Chamber of Commerce Arbitration) <http://cisgw3.law.pace.edu/cases/980605s5.html>. See also Al-Ahwany (n 497) 464–466.

311 *Deforche v Prins* (n 1554).

312 *Frozen pork case* (n 1626).

313 ibid.

should be taken into account, and any new scientific study or change in regulations that emerges after such a point in time may not be considered. Otherwise, the seller would be placed in an inequitable and worrying position since there would not be any time identified to test the conformity.[314]

The question now is which safety regulations[315] should be considered in order to assess the breach of Article 35(2)(a): Those of the seller's country or the buyer's?

### VIEWPOINT ONE: STANDARDS OF THE EXPORTING/SELLER'S COUNTRY

From this perspective, when the seller is from a highly developed country and the purchaser is from a less developed one, it is right to expect to receive reliable products corresponding with higher standards.[316] For instance, in *Rynpoort v Meneba*, the shipment of wheat flour which was confiscated in Mozambique (importing country) because it contained potassium bromate was held to be nonconforming due to the seller's non-compliance with the norms recommended in the 'Codex Alimentarius' to protect consumers' health, operational in the Netherlands (exporting country), even if such norms were not operative in Mozambique at the passage of risk.[317]

Nevertheless, the seller's knowledge that the goods would be resold/used in a specific country could not be considered an agreement to ensure the goods' re-salability in that country by complying with all its interior operative standards.[318] Therefore, mussels containing a cadmium concentration exceeding the limit recommended by the health authority of the importing country, did not breach Article 35(2)(a).[319] However, the seller is obliged to comply with the importing country's standards[320] operative at the contract conclusion in the following cases:

**First**, the buyer informs the seller of the necessity of complying with the regulations of that country.[321] **Secondly**, the standards of the utilising/importing country

314 CISG Advisory Council (n 1611) 41, 42.

315 This is applicable to any relevant public law or even voluntary standards relating, for example, to environmental considerations operative in the state where the market is located. CISG Advisory Council (n 1611) 38, 39, 41; Kröll; Mistelis; Viscasillas (n 67) 508 [90].

316 *Rynpoort v Meneba* (n 1784).

317 ibid.

318 *Machines case* (13/4/2000) 2Ob100/00w (Supreme Court Austria) <;http://cisgw3.law.pace.edu/cases/000413a3.html>; *Frozen fish case* (n 1371); *Frozen pork case* (n 1626). This was also followed in the *Frozen pork liver case* (25/1/2006) 7 Ob 302/05w (Oberster Gerichtshof Supreme Court) <http://cisgw3.law.pace.edu/cases/060125a3.html]>; *Eyroflam S.A. v P.C.C. Rotterdam B.V* (15/10/2008) 295401/HA ZA 07–2802 (Rechtbank District Court Rotterdam) <;http://cisgw3.law.pace.edu/cases/081015n2.html>; Bianca; Bonell (n 155) 274, 275, 283 [3.2.]; [2.5.1.].

319 *New Zealand mussels case* (n 1329).

320 ibid.

321 ibid; *RJ & AM Smallmon v Transport Sales Limited and Grant Alan Miller* (30/7/2010) CIV-2009-409-000363 (High Court of New Zealand) <;http://cisgw3.law.pace.edu/cases/100730n6.html>; *Cortem SpA v Controlmatic Pty Ltd* (13/8/2010) VID 414 of 2008 (Federal Court of Australia) <;http://cisgw3.law.pace.edu/cases/100813a2.html>; Bianca; Bonell (n 155) 283 [3.2.]; Gillette; Walt (n 778) 225; Schlechtriem, 'Uniform Sales Law' (n 1527). See also

are applicable in the seller's country as well.[322] Thus, toys containing pearls that could be ingested by infants were nonconforming due to their infringement of the European Directive's standards operational in both parties' countries.[323] **Thirdly**, there are circumstances signifying that the seller has been made aware or should have been aware of these standards: for instance, when the seller has complied with these standards in recent transactions with other buyers from the same country;[324] the seller has a branch in the importing country; they have had a longstanding business relationship with the buyer;[325] the seller delivers the goods directly to the buyer's ultimate consumers;[326] or the seller has made a public commitment to apply any relevant standards to the concerned goods.[327]

#### VIEWPOINT TWO: STANDARDS OF UTILISATION/BUYER'S COUNTRY

Few jurists support the idea that the seller's knowledge of the country where the goods will be used may impose on them an obligation to respect its interior standards. The Federal Supreme Court of Germany (Bundesgerichtshof) asserts: 'If the seller knows where the goods are intended to be used, then he will usually be expected to have taken the factors that influence the possibility of their use in that country into consideration.'[328] The court in *ISEA v Lu* followed this approach, indicating that as long as France was the place of delivery, '[t]he disputed obligation of conformity thus had to be performed in that place.'[329]

---

*Spanish paprika case* (n 1370); *Machines case* 13/4/2000 (n 1844); *Frozen fish case* (n 1371); *Frozen pork liver case* (n 1844); *Eyroflam v Rotterdam* (n 1844).

322 *New Zealand mussels case* (n 1329); *Frozen fish case* (n 1371); *Frozen pork case* (n 1626); *Eyroflam v Rotterdam* (n 1844); Bianca; Bonell (n 155) 283 [3.2.]; Schlechtriem, 'Uniform Sales Law' (n 1527).

323 *Caterpillar toys case* (13/10/2005) 04/04128 (Appellate Court Versailles) <http://cisgw3.law.pace.edu/cases/051013f1.html>. See also *Wine case* (n 1359).

324 CISG Advisory Council (n 1611) 38, 39; *Frozen pork case* (n 1626); *Eyroflam v Rotterdam* (n 1844); *Smallmon v Transport Sales Limited* (n 1847); Bianca; Bonell (n 155) 283 [3.2.]; René Franz Henschel, 'Creation of Rules in National and International Business Law: A Non-National, Analytical-Synthetic Comparative Method' in Camilla Andersen; Ulrich Schroeter; Albert Kritzer, *Sharing International Commercial Law Across National Boundaries: Festschrift For Albert H. Kritzer on the Occasion of his Eightieth Birthday* (Wildy, Simmonds & Hill, 2008) 184, 185 <;https://www.cisg.law.pace.edu/cisg/biblio/henschel1.html>; Gillette; Walt (n 778) 226.

325 CISG Advisory Council (n 1611) 38, 39, 48, 51, 52; *New Zealand mussels case* (n 1329); Huber; Mullis (n 1279) 137; Saidov (n 769) 143.

326 Kröll; Mistelis; Viscasillas (n 67) 509, 510 [93–96].

327 CISG Advisory Council (n 1611) 47.

328 Schlechtriem, 'Uniform Sales Law' (n 1527).

329 *ISEA Industrie v Lu* (13/12/1995) 95–018179 (Appellate Court Paris) <http://cisgw3.law.pace.edu/cases/951213f1.html>. See also *Caito Roger v. Société française de factoring* (13/9/1995) 93/4126 (Appellate Court Grenoble) <;http://cisgw3.law.pace.edu/cases/950913f1.html>; Mitias v Solidea (n 804).

### *5.2.5.2 SGA*

Because 'safety' as an aspect of satisfactory quality is mentioned separately, it could be classed as a requirement, irrespective of a reasonable person's attitude. Accordingly, unsafe goods would easily render the goods unsatisfactory,[330] such as an explosion of coalite;[331] arsenic in beer;[332] the snapping of a toy plastic catapult;[333] the bursting of one of many bottles, even though they were hired, and only the drinks inside them were sold;[334] and contamination of additives, colours or preservatives in foodstuff injurious to health, especially when public bodies adopted a zero-tolerance policy of such substances.[335] In *Pinnock v Lewis*, when 'copra cake' was contaminated with a large amount of castor beans, making it poisonous to the cattle, the seller was liable,[336] despite the fact that toxicity is relative, causing death to some creatures but not effecting others.[337] Proposing rectification of the defects which cause unsafe results may not be germane, as in *Clegg v Olle*, the heavy keel of a yacht adversely affected, inter alia, rig safety, and although several proposals were offered to rectify the overweight keel, it was concluded that the yacht, which needed 'more than minimal remedial work,' was unsatisfactory.[338]

Goods can be dangerous, but providing a clear warning may make them of satisfactory quality.[339] Under the previous SGA, Lord Pearce, in *Kendall v Lillico*, stated that the absence of a warning that groundnut extraction was specifically unsuitable to feed pheasants, was a substantial defect per se, even if the extraction was suitable for other animals.[340] This is applicable to the current SGA, as groundnut extraction should be safe for all purposes, including feeding pheasants, unless a warning is provided. In *Aswan*, the court refused to accept the manufacturers' liability for damage because of the lack of warning that the pails should not have been stacked six high, especially in intense heat.[341] However, this oversight would violate safety requirements under the current SGA.

The question arises as to whether the goods' non-compliance to health regulations of the buyer's country could render the goods unsatisfactory. In *Sumner v Webb*, although the quality of tonic water was unfit for human consumption according to Argentinean law (importing country) because it contained salicylic acid, the court found that merchantability did not mean legal salability of the

330 *Bernstein v Pamson* (n 1411) 395.
331 *Wilson v Rickett Cockerell* [1954] 1 QB 598, 606.
332 *Wren v Holt* [1903] 1 KB 610.
333 Godley v Perry [1960] 1 WLR 9.
334 *Geddling v Marsh* [1920] 1 KB 668, 669.
335 See *Hazlewood Grocery v Lion* (n 851) [191].
336 *Pinnock Bros v Lewis & Peat Ltd* [1923] 1 KB 690.
337 Bridge, *Benjamin's* (n 28) [11–020].
338 Hale LJ in *Clegg v Olle* (n 1617) [49].
339 *Wormell v RHM Agricultural (East)* Ltd [1987] 1 WLR 1091, 1091, 1092.
340 *Henry v William* (n 1025) 119.
341 *Aswan v Lupdine* (n 1670).

goods,[342] but merchantability should be assessed 'irrespective of the place where they are intended to be resold.'[343] This was because it was impossible to suggest that the seller should have warranted the goods' salability in their destination, even if the seller had known about such place,[344] unless the seller had targeted a specific market for a long time and was expected to know the operational health law of that market.[345] This case relates to the old SGA, in which 'safety' was not an explicit legal requisite. Currently, a different decision would probably be rendered, particularly if the purchaser proves that the contaminated goods constitute a risk to health regardless of the law under which the matter is considered, even though the risk is based on a recommended health study only and includes cases in which the risk is very low. In *SW Tubes*, it was held that a saw was of unsatisfactory quality due to the failure to provide guards for it, although the saw was second-hand and was to be used without guards.[346] Furthermore, in *Hazlewood v Lion*, when chilli powder was only marginally contaminated with the outlawed industrial dye Para Red and did not cause any health risk,[347] it was held that the buyer was entitled to reject the goods[348] as they were unfit for commercial purpose,[349] especially as the Food Standards Agency had advised merchants to destroy such goods and had posted this advice on its website.[350]

#### *5.2.5.3 KLaw*

Safety infringements generally assume the seller's liability, entitling the buyer to terminate the contract. When a manufacturing defect in the brake system was proved, violating safe driving, termination was permissible.[351] When bubbles and foam appeared once food was placed in oil, causing a fire in a school kitchen, the court ruled that this hidden defect made the oil unfit for food use and refused the seller's defence that the Ministry of Education (the buyer) chemically examined the goods and confirmed their validity,[352] even though the defect may have been caused by the buyer's inadequate storage. Additionally, a buyer's medical report[353] based on an airbag's failure to activate during a serious accident[354] was considered by the court, which held the seller liable without accepting their

342 *Sumner Permain v Webb* [1922] 1 KB 55.
343 Atkin LJ in ibid 64.
344 ibid.
345 Twigg-Flesner; Canavan (n 30) 144.
346 *SW Tubes v Owen Stuart* [2002] EWCA Civ 854 [39].
347 *Hazlewood Grocery v Lion* (n 851) [2].
348 ibid [180].
349 ibid [161].
350 ibid [86]; [72]; [191].
351 Case 12/11/2005 (n 1213) 4, 5; Case 30/12/2008 (n 1213) 5, 6.
352 Case 14/12/1967 Court of Cassation/Commercial 127/67 reproduced in Abdulreda (n 40) 83.
353 Case 8/3/2006 (n 1583) 14.
354 ibid.

expert report that the airbags were not supposed to have deployed in this specific accident.[355]

Overseas goods which do not correspond with Kuwaiti safety standards might permit a hidden defect to be claimed. In one case, the buyer requested termination on the grounds that the goods did not correspond with Kuwaiti standards (the buyer's country), but the court rejected the request because the defect was not hidden; the specifications were displayed on the goods.[356] Presumably, this means if these specifications were not clearly displayed on the goods, the buyer might have claimed termination, imposing on the seller an obligation to ensure the goods' safe workability and consumption in Kuwait.

There is an independent obligation under Article 468 KCIC, arising from sales contracts,[357] to provide buyers with all necessary information about the commodity, such as precautions necessary for safe use,[358] unless this information is already known to the buyer, or it is obvious to the consumer if the buyer wants to resell it.[359] The breach of this obligation is assessed according to the general rules, without requiring the stipulations of a hidden defect, which are mainly 1) reducing the goods' benefit/value and/or 2) causing detriment.

### *5.2.5.4 Comparative Analysis*

#### 5.2.5.4.1 POSSIBLE OUTCOMES UNDER THE THREE LEGAL SYSTEMS

**First Scenario**: In *Britvic v Messer*, it was discovered that carbon dioxide used for manufacturing drinks was contaminated with benzene, which is carcinogenic in high quantities, but the actual quantity was small and medically negligible, posing no risk to health.[360] The following discussion assumes that this contamination made the drinks unsalable in the importing country.

**Under CISG**, as long as the additive was not harmful, detriment would not have been suffered, and the buyer would not have been substantially deprived of their contractual expectation. Even in cases in which similar situations caused substantial deprivation, this result might not have been foreseeable by the seller or any reasonable person in their place because the standards were not stipulated in the contract, preventing the breach from being fundamental. The un-salability of the goods due to their infringement of the safe standards in the importing country might mean the goods were nonconforming if compliance with these standards was also operative in the seller's country or in circumstances that indicated the seller's

355 ibid 9, 10.

356 Case 15/2/1988 Court of Cassation 234/87 reproduced in Al-Defery; Al-Sayrafy (n 254) 290.

357 Al-Ahwany (n 497) 468, 469; Al-Danasory; Al-Shawarbee (n 281) 69; Salem Al-Azawy, *Producer's Liabilityin Civil Laws and International Conventions* (Dar Althaqafa 2008) 215.

358 ibid Al-Ahwany 466, 467; Assayed Omran, *The Obligation of Information* (Academic Publications 1994) 33; ibid Al-Azawy 213.

359 Al-Defery; Al-Sayrafy (n 254) 239–242.

360 Britvic Soft Drinks Ltd v Messer UK Ltd [2002] EWCA Civ 548 [3];[11]; [35].

knowledge of these standards, making the goods' infringement foreseeable to the seller. Otherwise, as stated in one English case under the previous SGA,

> it would place an intolerable burden on suppliers . . . and therefore would represent a serious interference with normal commerce . . . [as] it could be shown that the article concerned could have been safer . . . than it actually was.[361]

**Under SGA**, the goods in this scenario were deemed unsatisfactory,[362] focusing on the impact of the concern about public health on the goods' salability.[363] SGA expressly articulates safety requirements which are assessed as such, irrespective of the degree of violation, its rectifiability or which country the applicable standard is operative in.

**Under KLaw**, the judge may, or may not, consider the substantial reduction in the goods' benefit/value a stipulation. Similarly, they may, or may not, consider the substantial detriment suffered by the buyer is a stipulation. The substantial detriment may be identified, if recognised a stipulation, by measuring the loss reaching a degree to which if the buyer had known, they would not have completed the contract. Generally, if this contamination reduced the goods' benefit/value, it would be deemed that there was a hidden defect. Because the safety standard was infringed, the goods' un-salability in Kuwait would be an evident element of their reduction in benefit.

**Second Scenario**: Consider *Vacwell Engineering v BDH Chemicals*, in which chemical goods which were relatively new at the time of the case contained a 'harmful vapour' warning. An explosion occurred when the chemicals, in glass ampoules, made contact with water.[364]

**Under CISG**, the seller might not have been held liable, on the basis that the explosion might not have been foreseeable, especially as the field was new, making a general warning sufficient. **Under SGA**, the goods were held unmerchantable[365] and would likely have been of unsatisfactory quality under the current SGA on the basis that a general warning might not suffice.[366] Under **KLaw**, any lack of necessary information would permit the buyer to claim termination, even if the buyer did not suffer any detriment. But the necessity of the missing information would be determined by the judiciary.

#### 5.2.5.4.2 CERTAINTY, FLEXIBILITY AND PRESERVING THE CONTRACT

**Under CISG**, safety requirements should be met to reach the required quality of Article 35(2)(a), but this does not generally permit termination unless the

361 Neuberger J in *Medivance Instruments v Gaslane Pipework Services* [2002] EWCA Civ 500 [22].
362 *Britvic v Messer* (n 1886) [3]; [11].
363 ibid [3];[11]; [35].
364 *Vacwell Engineering v BDH Chemicals* [1971] 1 QB 88, 89.
365 ibid.
366 *Wormell v RHM* (n 1856) 1091, 1092.

conditions of Article 25 occur. Additionally, the goods might not have to be safe for all the normal purposes of similar goods, unless the contractual circumstances indicate otherwise. This approach would likely decrease certainty due to CISG's ruling on a case-by-case basis. On the other hand, this approach accomplishes a high degree of contract preservation and flexibility. **Under SGA**, however, the goods should be safe when used for any of their common purposes,[367] and this might require the consideration of extrinsic factors, such as public concern.[368] This gives a high degree of predictability to the legal outcome but a low degree of both contract preservation and flexibility according to each case's facts. **Under KLaw**, the presumption that breaching safety requirements is mostly attributed to the seller can attain certainty, but the availability of termination remains unclear due to its vague substantive stipulations, and it is hard to predict the judge's mentality towards this vagueness. On the other hand, in cases where the goods lack the necessary warning, this breach permits the buyer to claim termination without any additional conditions, unless the judge finds it necessary to consider the missing information.

### *5.2.6 Buyers' Knowledge of Inferior Quality*

The act of a buyer signing a contract despite their knowledge of the goods' inferior quality at the time of sale signifies their acceptance of the goods in their condition. Nevertheless, this knowledge is interpreted differently under the three legal systems.

#### *5.2.6.1 CISG*

According to Article 35(3), the seller is exempt from liability for inferior quality when the buyer 'knew or could not have been unaware' of the goods' unfitness for their ordinary purposes at the time of concluding the contract.[369]

##### A) ACTUAL KNOWLEDGE

When the buyer inspects the goods at the contract conclusion and the defects are discoverable via normal inspection, or when the seller informs them of a specific aspect of the goods' nonconformity, the buyer possesses real knowledge of the nonconformity,[370] preventing them from alleging afterwards that the goods are unfit for their normal purposes.[371] In the *Frozen chicken legs case*, when the buyer's representative inspected the frozen chicken at the contract conclusion without expressing any objections to its nonconformity to the hygienic requirements in the

367 The Law Commission (n 230) [3.44].
368 *Aswan v Lupdine* (n 1670); *Jewson v Boyhan* (n 1714).
369 Schwenzer, *Commentary on CISG* (n 15) 613 [37]. See also Bianca; Bonell (n 155) 278 [2.8.1].
370 *Second-hand bulldozer case* (n 649); Luca (n 815) 180.
371 Bianca; Bonell (n 155) 278 [2.8.1.]; Schwenzer, *Commentary on CISG* (n 15) 614 [38].

importing country,[372] or in the *Hydraulic press case*, when purchasing the same model of hydraulic press, which suffered from the same inferior quality, from the same seller, the buyer's actions indicated their acceptance of the goods' quality.[373]

#### B) PRESUMED KNOWLEDGE

When the buyer does not possess actual knowledge but they 'could not have been unaware' of nonconformity at the time of sale, the buyer cannot claim breach of Article 35(1)(a). This presumed knowledge has not been defined in CISG but can be equivalent to many concepts: it could be simple negligence, gross negligence or the cunning actions of the buyer.[374] In *Deforche v Prins Gebroeders Bouwstoffenhandel*, the buyer was expected to have known of a nonconformity as they were greenhouse specialists.[375] Similarly, in the *Skin-care products case*, the buyer was expected to have known that Vitamin A in skin-care products decomposes over time.[376] However, some scholars find that negligence does not suffice when determining the buyer's presumed knowledge as the buyer is not obliged to examine the goods before concluding the contract,[377] and presumed knowledge can be related to a nonconformity that is 'before eyes.'[378] In *Smallmon v Transport Sales*, the seller was not held liable as the absence of a vehicle's plates was clearly apparent to the buyer.[379]

#### C) SELLER'S BAD FAITH

When the seller knows that the goods are of an inferior quality to that required by Article 35(2)(a) and they do not disclose this to the buyer,[380] the seller will not rely on the buyer's presumed knowledge. A grossly negligent buyer who should know about nonconformity deserves protection more than a fraudulent seller who deceptively sends nonconforming goods.[381] However, the buyer's real knowledge of nonconformity excludes the seller's liability, even when the seller acts in bad faith.[382]

372 *Frozen chicken legs case* (2/3/2000) 546/1999 (Appellate Court Granada) <http://cisgw3.law.pace.edu/cases/000302s4.html>.
373 *Hydraulic press case* (20/1/1994) CISG/1994/02 (CIETAC arbitration proceeding) <http://cisgw3.law.pace.edu/cases/940120c1.html>.
374 Luca (n 815) 178; Vivian Curran, 'Cross-References and Editorial Analysis, Article 40' <https://cisgw3.law.pace.edu/cisg/text/cross/cross-40.html>.
375 *Deforche v Prins* (n 1554).
376 *Skin-care products case* (30/7/1998) S96/1215 (Helsinki Court of Appeal) <http://cisgw3.law.pace.edu/cases/980630f5.html>.
377 Hyland, 'Conformity of Goods' in Schlechtriem, 'Einheitliches Kaufrecht' (n 1768) 324, 325; Enderlein, 'Rights and Obligations' in Sarcevic; Volken (n 1530) 160.
378 Honnold, Uniform Law (n 320) [229].
379 *Smallmon v Transport Sales Limited* (n 1847).
380 Kröll; Mistelis; Viscasillas (n 67) 527 [168].
381 According to the good faith principle adopted in Art. 40 and Art. 7(1); *Used car case* (n 1360); Poikela (n 83) 5; Schwenzer, *Commentary on CISG* (n 15) 614 [40].
382 Kröll; Mistelis; Viscasillas (n 67) 527 [168].

### *5.2.6.2 SGA*

The requirement of satisfactory quality is not extended in two situations:

#### A) WHEN DRAWN TO THE BUYER'S ATTENTION

According to s.14(2C)(a), when the default in quality is clearly and specifically drawn to the buyer's attention at the contract conclusion, the seller is not liable for satisfactory quality. In *Wormell v RHM*, when weedkiller used to control wild oats was ineffective in wet weather, it was unfit for a reasonable purpose since the instructions should have clearly mentioned the unsuitability of the goods in wet weather.[383] Small print or a general statement in the contract stating that the goods may be defective does not satisfy this exception.[384] In *Turnock v Fortune*, although it was communicated to the buyer that a car had been involved in an accident, it was rejected by a company due to its extensive damage; the sales manager strongly advised the buyer not to buy the car. It was held that these facts did not equate to informing the buyer that the car was unroadworthy.[385]

#### B) THE BUYER'S EXAMINATION OF GOODS

The second case that exempts the seller from liability for satisfactory quality is when the buyer examines the goods before the contract is made, and such examination would have revealed the inferior quality.[386] It does not suffice that there is the mere opportunity to examine the goods by the buyer; there should be an actual inspection.[387] Thus, when it is undiscoverable through the buyer's examination that beer contains arsenic,[388] the beer is very likely to be unsatisfactory. Some courts consider the reasonable result of the buyer's actual examination; in *Thornett v Beers*, it was held that as long as the goods were examined by the buyer, there was no implied condition of quality as a minimal inspection should have revealed the defects,[389] quite apart from the fact that the buyer did not properly inspect the goods because there was 'no time.'[390] Other courts took the actual result of the examination; in *Crowther v Shannon*, after driving a second-hand Jaguar for 2,354 miles, within three weeks of the purchase, huge oil consumption and the need to replace the engine were discovered. The car was held unfit for its purposes despite the fact that the buyer (who was a young man lacking mechanical experience) had inspected the car before purchase; the mileage on the milometer was 82,165; the

383 *Wormell v RHM* (n 1856) 1098.

384 Donald Harris; Denis Tallon, *Contract Law Today: Anglo-French Comparisons* (Clarendon 1989) 34.

385 Turnock v Fortune (1989) SLT (Sh Ct) 32, 33, 34.

386 SGA s.14(2C)(b)

387 Bray J in Thornett v Beers (n 1068) 489.

388 *Wren v Holt* (n 1858) 611.

389 Bray J in *Thornett v Beers* (n 1068) 489, 490.

390 ibid 489.

car was bought for £390; the car passed the MOT; and the buyer then made significant use of the car.[391]

#### *5.2.6.3 KLaw*

Under Article 491, the seller is not responsible for a defect known to the buyer at the time of sale,[392] such as when the seller informs the buyer that the goods are defective[393] or when the buyer could have discovered this by themselves if they had examined the goods with due care. In one case, although an expert concluded that an oil leak from the steering wheel that damaged the steering system in a Chevrolet Caprice was an apparent defect, the appellate court decided on termination. The seller challenged the decision, and the court of cassation revoked the decision for termination[394] on the basis that the buyer had technically examined the car and accepted it as it was.[395]

The expression 'by themselves' in Article 491 may indicate that the knowledge or ignorance of the defect should be assessed according to the buyer's personal idiosyncrasies. The term 'due care' in Article 491 may mean that the buyer should not neglect the appropriate examination, which is still to be conducted within the buyer's circumstances and abilities without amounting to a reasonable person's examination, especially if the buyer's abilities are less than those of a reasonable person. Demonstratively, in some cases, it was stated that the defect was considered hidden when it was unknown to the buyer and they were not able to know it.[396]

This subjectivity requires the consideration of the buyer's attributes. In the case of an accidental (unprofessional) buyer, it is simple to consider the defect hidden if the buyer cannot personally discover the defect easily, except by resorting to special assistance,[397] contrary to cases in which the alleged defects were clearly visible without the need of special technical expertise.[398] Conversely, in the case of a professional buyer who specialises in the goods in question, it may not be easy to claim hidden defects, especially as anyone with their experience might be able to discover the defect.[399] This subjective norm could make sellers refuse to deal with unprofessional and first-time buyers, preferring professional buyers instead, so the contract would not easily be terminated due to hidden defects.

391 Crowther v Shannon Motor [1975] 1 WLR 30.
392 A similar meaning is found in Al-Majalla Art. 341, 343.
393 Al-Majalla Art. 336.
394 Case 19/6/2004 Court of Cassation/Commercial 3 665/2003 p. 4, 5.
395 ibid. See also Case 17/6/2007 (n 1581) 5, 6.
396 Case 20/4/2002 (n 1094) 1–4; Case 24/4/2004 (n 1572) 2–4; Case 17/4/2012 (n 1572) 4, 5.
397 Al-Ahwany (n 497) 650.
398 Case 17/4/2012 (n 1572) 4, 5.
399 ibid; Al-Ahwany (n 497) 653; Al-Masry, *Commercial Contracts in Kuwaiti Law* (n 538) 81.

Some scholars, however, find that if the defect can be easily detected at the time of sale by usual examination[400] or with a usual person's care,[401] the seller is not liable,[402] and the buyer is considered to have accepted the commodity in its condition.[403] Al-Fadly's[404] and Al-Ahwany's[405] approaches are to ignore the phrase 'by themselves' mentioned in Article 491 and interpret 'due care' to mean the care of a reasonable person. If the buyer's personal abilities are less than a reasonable person's, they should seek expert advice;[406] otherwise, the buyer is considered negligent and the defect deemed apparent, not hidden.[407] Likewise, in some cases, it was stated that a defect could have been hidden when it was not apparent during a normal inspection that would usually be conducted by people in the circumstances in which the sale took place.[408] This makes the defect's concealment or revelation a relative matter subject to the judge's recourse to experts,[409] although an expert's opinion may not be binding. Conversely, in another case, the court emphasised that the buyer's knowledge by which the hidden defect claim could be excluded was actual knowledge, without considering any hypothetical knowledge. The buyer's acknowledgement in the contract that they had inspected the goods with due diligence was not taken into account.[410] Following a subjective criterion (by stating 'themselves') and an objective criterion (by stating 'due care') in the same rule is confusing and misleading, generating varying rulings.

In all cases, if the seller acts in bad faith by confirming that the commodity is free of a specific defect which is disputed or conceals the defect fraudulently,[411] the buyer shall have the right to terminate, even if they actually knew about the defect at the time of sale.[412]

#### *5.2.6.4 Comparative Analysis*

##### 5.2.6.4.1 POSSIBLE OUTCOMES UNDER THE THREE LEGAL SYSTEMS

*a) When Buyers Examine Goods at the Time of Sale* Reasonability is a general principle on which **CISG** is based; thus, the outcome of the examination is, at a

400 Al-Defery; Al-Sayrafy (n 254) 299.
401 Al-Ahwany (n 497) 675.
402 Al-Defery; Al-Sayrafy (n 254) 299.
403 Al-Ahwany (n 497) 675.
404 Al-Fadly (n 495) 125.
405 Al-Ahwany (n 497) 650.
406 ibid.
407 Al-Fadly (n 495) 124, 125.
408 Case 20/4/2002 (n 1094) 1–4; Case 24/4/2004 (n 1572) 2–4; Case 12/11/2005 (n 1213) 4, 5; Case 15/10/2006, 1250 (n 261) 5; Case 17/6/2007 (n 1581) 5, 6; Case 30/12/2008 (n 1213) 6; Case 17/4/2012 (n 1572) 4, 5.
409 Al-Fadly (n 495) 125.
410 Case 20/2/2006 Court of Cassation/Civil 81, 111/2003 p. 5.
411 KCIC Art. 491.
412 KCIC Art. 496(2).

minimum, according to a reasonable person. **Under SGA**, the decision on whether the buyer knew about the nonconformity or not may depend on the outcome of the buyer's personal examination. In *Bristol Tramways v Fiat*, it was stated that examining an omnibus just before concluding the contract would not have allowed the buyer time to discover the defects.[413] **Under KLaw**, the buyer's knowledge of the inferior quality can be assessed according to their actual findings after examining the goods, but this is conditional on the buyer's exercise of due care according to their ability. While this is true, some scholars and cases have applied an objective criterion.

*b) The Buyer Did Not Examine the Goods at the Time of Sale, Although It was Feasible* Buyers might be regarded as having presumed knowledge of the nonconformity **under CISG** when they are specialists or negligent. However, **under SGA**, presumed knowledge is not adopted, and in this case, the requirement of quality is not excluded. **Under KLaw**, the case might depend on the buyer's circumstances and if they have examined the goods with due care, although one case stressed that presumptive knowledge would not be considered.[414]

*c) When Sellers Act in Bad Faith* **Under CISG**, the seller's real or presumed knowledge of the nonconformity without disclosing it to the buyer makes the quality rule a requirement, even when the buyer could presumably *not* have been unaware of the nonconformity. However, the buyer's real knowledge of nonconformity will exclude the quality requirement, even if the seller acts in bad faith. **Under SGA**, there is no situation in which to apply a special rule when the seller acts in bad faith because only the buyer's real knowledge, by either drawing it to their attention or by actual examination, is considered. **Under KLaw**, the seller is considered as having acted in bad faith if they confirm the goods as being free of defects or hide the nonconformity deceitfully. The seller's knowledge of the defect without disclosing it to the buyer is not considered bad faith. A seller acting in bad faith will permit buyers to claim for hidden defects even if they actually knew of the nonconformity, contrary to CISG.

##### 5.2.6.4.2 CERTAINTY AND PRESERVING THE CONTRACT

To determine whether termination is an option, the consideration of reasonable findings of an examination **under CISG** could increase certainty, due to its predictability, more than the buyer's actual findings. Additionally, considering the buyer's presumed knowledge of nonconformity definitely lessens the likelihood of recourse to termination. **Under SGA**, pursuing the subjective findings of the buyer's examination to find out whether they knew of the inferior quality at the time of sale is unpredictable for the seller. Nevertheless, not adopting 'presumed

413 *Bristol Tramways v Fiat* (n 1719) 841.
414 Case 20/2/2006 (n 1936) 5.

knowledge' and not taking 'the rule of a seller acting in bad faith' raises the degree of certainty for both parties. This is true even though the likelihood of preserving the contract diminishes because when the buyer is negligent in examining the goods, they may still be permitted to terminate the contract due to inferior quality, contrary to CISG. **Under KLaw**, considering these two criteria – subjectivity according to the buyer and objectivity according to their due care – confuses the situation and reduces certainty. However, KLaw preserves the contract when it does not consider the seller's knowledge of the defect without disclosing it to the buyer bad faith. This knowledge does not allow termination when the buyer knows about the defect. However, KLaw deals with sellers acting in bad faith strictly by permitting buyers to claim termination based on hidden defect, even if they actually know about the defect, whereas CISG expressly prevents termination when the buyer has real knowledge of nonconformity, even if the seller acts in bad faith.

## 5.3 Procedural Requirements for Terminating Contracts Due to Inferior Quality

To avoid repetition, the procedural requirements under SGA and CISG, mentioned in Chapter 3, are applicable in cases of inferior quality. Therefore, this chapter will only mention relevant rules in terms of inferior quality. KLaw articulates special procedural requirements to hidden defects that are not applicable to other contractual breaches.

### *5.3.1 Inspection of the Goods*

#### *5.3.1.1 CISG*

Goods should be examined, according to Article 38(1), in 'as short a period as is practicable in the circumstances.' However, this short period does not mean that a prompt examination is required[415] but that the examination time should begin whenever practicable and last for a short period.[416] Nevertheless, in some cases, the buyer was obliged to 'act quickly' to examine the goods on receipt,[417] even non-perishable goods.[418] Case law has adopted some criteria to determine the required examination time:

a) **Detectability of Inferior Quality**: When the flaw is easily identifiable, the examination should be conducted 'within a few working days' of receiving the

415 Ferrari, *Contracts for the International Sale of Goods* (n 1291) 211.

416 *Tinned cucumbers case* (n 1301).

417 *Audio CDs case* (n 1296).

418 *Sport clothing case* (n 165). See also *Shoes case* (1990) 41 O 198/89 (District Court Aachen) <http://cisgw3.law.pace.edu/cases/900403g1.html>.

delivery.[419] In *Dr S Sergueev Handelsagentur v DAT-SCHAUB A/S*, when inconsistent production dates were stamped on the packaging, the buyer lost their termination right when they resold the goods without examining them.[420]

b) **Goods' Nature**: The inspection period is longer when the goods concerned are technically sophisticated and shorter when the goods are perishable.[421]

c) **Goods' Quantity**: The buyer does not have to inspect every single item; rather, it is sufficient to carry out spot checks by examining a small sample.[422] Hence, the buyer's defence in the *Tree case* that the shipment was too large to be inspected at all was insufficient.[423] However, in the *Shoes case*, on the shipment's arrival, the buyer examined a few samples, which were intact, but when their customers complained, the buyer notified the seller 16 days after the goods' receipt. The court found that the buyer delayed notifying the seller because the buyer had not examined all the shoes at the outset, which would have led to the discovery of the defects; therefore, termination was not an option. This conclusion could be justified because its reasoning was based on the buyer's expert knowledge and prior complaints from their customers regarding a previous order from the same seller.[424] According to the *Trekking shoes case*, the large quantity of goods necessitated resorting to experts.[425]

#### *5.3.1.2 SGA*

S.34 obliges the seller to give the buyer a reasonable opportunity to examine the goods to ascertain whether they conform to the contract. In *Poulton v Lattimore*, despite the fact that experts proved to the buyer that the seeds were below par immediately after they were delivered, the buyer sowed part of them and resold the remainder to sub-buyers, who claimed that the seeds were worthless. The court indicated that if the buyer had alleged they had sown the seeds as a means of examination, termination would have been permitted as the buyer did not have to believe the seller's affirmation of the seeds' status.[426] In *Winnipeg Fish v Whitman Fish*, it was found that in order to examine the goods, the buyer would have had to either thaw or cook them.[427] Therefore, the goods were permitted to be sold directly to the consumers.[428]

419 *Audio CDs case* (n 1296). See also *Chicago Prime Packers v Northam Food Trading Co* (2004) 01 C 4447 (Federal District Court) <http://cisgw3.law.pace.edu/cases/040521u1.html>.
420 *Sergueev v DAT-SCHAUB* (n 808).
421 Ferrari, *Contracts for the International Sale of Goods* (n 1291) 213.
422 ibid 218.
423 *Tree case* (11/2/2009) 172920/HAZA08–1228 (Court of Firsts Instance) <http://cisgw3.law.pace.edu/cases/090211n1.html>.
424 *Shoes case* (31/8/1989) 3KfHO97/89 (District Court Stuttgart) <http://cisgw3.law.pace.edu/cases/890831g1.html>.
425 *Trekking shoes case* (n 1311).
426 *Poulton v Lattimore* (n 1410) 97.
427 *Winnipeg Fish Co v Whitman Fish Co* (1909) 41 SCR 453 456.
428 ibid 468.

Despite the fact that there is no obligation for the buyer to inspect the goods under SGA, when the buyer chooses to terminate the contract[429] due to a violation of satisfactory quality, the buyer should inform the seller within a reasonable time[430] that the goods have been refused.[431] This requires the buyer's quick examination of the goods; otherwise, the right to reject the goods expires.

#### *5.3.1.3 KLaw*

An apparent defect at the time of receipt may oblige the buyer to refrain from taking the goods; otherwise, the defect will be considered accepted.[432] Therefore, when it has been proven that the buyer received the goods[433] without reservation, this defect does not raise the seller's liability.[434] However, if the defect is not apparent by sight, Article 492(1) states that the buyer 'must inspect the goods as soon as they are *able* to do so, in accordance with the *usual* practice,' indicating that the inspection time should be initiated subjectively, according to the buyer's situation, but the inspection method should be objective.

Inspection time can be interpreted in two different ways: The inspection should be conducted 'as soon as the buyer is *able* to do so' or 'as soon as the buyer is *enabled* to do so,' as Article 492(1) defines these two terms. If the judge adopts the latter criterion, the buyer needs to inspect the goods on their arrival, embracing a stricter approach, but if the judge adopts the former criterion, they will consider the buyer's personal situation in order to estimate the time at which they are able to inspect the goods. It is more likely that Article 492(1) adopts the personal criterion because the current law omits the phrase 'once the buyer receives the commodity,' mentioned in Article 401 of the old KCOC No. 2 of 1961.[435] Additionally, in some cases, it was stated that the buyer was entitled to claim termination even if the defects could be identified by the usual examination.[436] Moreover, in one case, the buyer received a car in January and discovered the defects by normal examination in March, but the defect was verified by specialists in May, causing no issue of examination time.[437] Furthermore, in another case, a quantity of cheese delivered in June 1969 and inspected in February 1970 was found to be unfit for human consumption but was not held defective as the buyer failed to prove that the defect existed at delivery.[438] The court did not mention the delay of the inspection,

429 *Harbutt's Plasticine v Wayne Tank & Pump* (n 1371) 646; Andrews, *Contract Law* (n 223) 442, 468; Chen-Wishart (n 77) 483 [12.2.4].

430 SGA s.35(4); s.36(1).

431 *Fercometal v Mediterranean Shipping* (n 1396) 792; McKendrick, *Sale of Goods* (n 202) 308.

432 Al-Ahwany (n 497) 627, 679.

433 Case 17/4/2012 (n 1572) 4.

434 Case 2/1/2005 (n 509) 8; Case 12/11/2006 (n 1535) 2–4; ibid 4, 5.

435 See Case 23/4/1989 Court of Cassation/Commercial 333/88 in Ministry of Justice, *Civil Provisions* (n 955) 292.

436 Case 15/10/2006, 1250 (n 261) 5

437 ibid.

438 Case 24/2/1972 Court of Cassation 1441/71 reproduced in Abdulreda (n 40) 574, 575.

probably because it was assessed according to the buyer's ability, and if the buyer had succeeded in proving the defect's existence at the delivery time, termination might have been permitted. Likewise, in other cases, the fact that a car did not actually pass into the buyer's possession but rather was handed over directly to the second buyer was considered[439] but did not affect the examination time. In another, the fact that trousers were tight at the knee made them defective,[440] although they conformed to the sample, indicating that the buyer did not properly examine the sample, reflecting their circumstances.

Some scholars and cases found that the examination of goods should be determined objectively in light of usual practice and what is customary, considering whether an ordinary person would have discovered the defect.[441] This makes the standard not a personal one, which varies from one person to another, but an abstract one.[442] However, the estimation of this abstract standard is entrusted to the trial judge as a matter of fact.[443] In one case, when the reason for not performing a proper inspection within the usual period was that the buyer trusted the seller as a friend and lacked experience in the goods,[444] their right to claim for hidden defect expired.[445]

In some cases, an 'average person' was used as a yardstick even when the buyer's expertise was higher than the average person's. The court of first instance and the appellate court decided that manipulation of both a chassis number and an odometer was not a hidden defect because it would have been possible for the buyer to discover it, especially as they worked in the field of trading cars. The buyer appealed, stating that it was proven by the expert's report that the defect was hidden, and this defence was accepted by the court of cassation, stating that the appellate court erred in asserting that the defect was not hidden because the buyer was a specialist car trader, especially as it would have been difficult for the average person to have discovered these defects without the assistance of technical experts.[446] Al-Fadly, conversely, states that, in the case of a professional buyer, their expertise should be considered, even though the defect may be difficult for a reasonable person to detect.[447] An unclear rule which is an amalgam of two different types of standards leads to contrasting rulings and may encourage 'rule shopping': choosing the rule which is in line with the litigant's benefit and striving to convince adjudicators of it.

439 Case 29/5/2007 (n 1093) 4, 5.
440 Case 8/11/1970 Court of Cassation/Commercial 228/70.
441 Case 30/9/1998 (n 1601) 6, 7; Case 29/5/2007 (n 1093) 4, 5.
442 ibid.
443 Case 30/9/1998 (n 1601) 6, 7; Case 12/11/2005 (n 1213) 4, 5; Case 15/10/2006, 1250 (n 261) 5; Case 29/5/2007 (n 1093) 4, 5; Case 17/6/2007 (n 1581) 5, 6; Case 30/12/2008 (n 1213) 6.
444 Case 30/9/1998 (n 1601) 4, 5.
445 See also Al-Ahwany (n 497) 676, 677.
446 Case 29/5/2007 (n 1093) 4, 5.
447 Al-Fadly (n 495) 125.

### *5.3.2 Notification of Inferior Quality*

#### *5.3.2.1 CISG*

According to Article 39, the buyer cannot terminate the contract when they fail to notify the seller of the nonconformity within a reasonable period after the buyer 'has discovered it or ought to have discovered it.' A particular method of notification is not stipulated;[448] thus, oral notice suffices, although this raises issues regarding its testimony.[449] As previously mentioned, there is a consensus that a notice with generic phrases is unacceptable; stating that 'the goods are not as we imagined,'[450] 'inferior and poor quality,' 'poor workmanship'[451] and 'the truffles were soft'[452] were considered improper notices in court.[453]

Some jurists follow a 'one-month' doctrine for notification, as Schwenzer finds that 'for durable goods, in the absence of any special circumstances, one should accept at least one month as a rough average period for timely notice,'[454] which was pursued by some courts[455] in order to promote uniformity.[456] However, in the *Automobile case*, it was stated that the decisive factor in evaluating the notification period was the circumstances of each case, and 'a schematic fixing of the time for the notice of defect is impossible.'[457] In the *Granulated plastic case*, the titanium dioxide content in granulated plastic used for manufacturing roll-down blinds was much lower than required, preventing the sunlight from being blocked out. The late notification of this nonconformity was justifiable since the inferior quality could be discovered only through quantitative chemical testing.[458]

#### *5.3.2.2 SGA*

As mentioned earlier, s.35(4) clarifies that there should be intimation to the seller within a reasonable amount of time that the goods are rejected; time may not

448 *Wire and cable case* (n 1306).

449 CISG Art. 11; *Agricultural machine case* (n 1323); *Poppy seed case* (3/5/2007) 43Cg34/05f (Commercial Court Vienna); Honnold, *Uniform Law* (n 320) 373; 238 <http://cisgw3.law.pace.edu/cases/070503a3.html>.

450 *Shoe soles case* (n 1325).

451 ibid.

452 *Truffles case* (24/1/1996) 13O142/95 (District Court Bochum) <http://cisgw3.law.pace.edu/cases/960124g1.html>.

453 Ferrari, *Contracts for the International Sale of Goods* (n 1291) 235. See also *GMS modules* (n 135).

454 Ingeborg Schwenzer, 'National Preconceptions that Endanger Uniformity' (2007) 19(1) Pace Int Law Rev 103, 11. See also Luca (n 815) 246.

455 See *New Zealand mussels case* (n 1329); *Machine for producing hygenic tissues case* (3/11/1999) VIIIZR287/98 (Supreme Court) <http://cisgw3.law.pace.edu/cases/991103g1.html>.

456 Luca (n 815) 246

457 *Automobile case* (11/1/2006) VIIIZR268/04 (Supreme Court) <http://cisgw3.law.pace.edu/cases/060111g1.html>. See also *Used shoes case* (n 1356).

458 *Granulated plastic case* (25/6/1996) 7O147/94 (District Court Paderborn) <http://cisgw3.law.pace.edu/cases/960625g1.html>.

necessarily be extended for the identification of specific defects. In *Bernstein v Pamsons*, it was stated that whether the defect was latent or patent was insignificant[459] because it was desirable to close the seller's ledger and to attain finality in commercial contracts.[460] However, some scholars find that the defect's nature may extend the reasonable period of time.[461]

As the word 'intimation' indicates, the rejection could be any expression other than notification; it does not have to be conveyed in a particular means,[462] language or form. It might be a sign or indirect phrase, such as saying that 'the goods are rubbish' without any obligation to be specific, as is the case in CISG. In *Vitol v Norelf*, it was sufficient that the buyer's communication or conduct plainly conveyed to the seller that the buyer wanted to put an end to the contract.[463] Moreover, accepting a repudiatory breach to terminate the contract is not dependent on providing a reason to validate termination.[464] The buyer may rely on a component reason that occurs later and was unknown to them at the time of the goods' refusal[465] to justify the earlier termination.[466]

#### *5.3.2.3 KLaw*

The buyer's failure of timely notification is considered either an implicit waiver of the hidden defect claim[467] or a penalty for the buyer's negligence,[468] and this, consequently, does not allow them to claim termination.[469] Article 401(1) of the previous KCOC stipulated that the buyer must notify the seller within a reasonable period, which is not mentioned in the current law; instead, Article 492(1) KCIC states that 'if the buyer finds a defect, *they must initiate to notify the seller*.' The word 'initiate' can be construed as either 'prompt notification' or 'prompt notification based on the buyer's situation.'

Ultimately, estimating the notification period[470] is a matter of fact that the trial court must evaluate in light of the circumstances of each case.[471] Case law has

459 *Bernstein v Pamson* (n 1411) 391.
460 ibid 396.
461 Bridge, *The Sale of Goods* (n 28) [10.55]; [10.78].
462 *Vitol v Norelf* (n 1404) 801, 802.
463 ibid 810, 811.
464 Cartwright (n 114) 283, 284.
465 Chitty (n 64) [24–014].
466 *Maredelanto* (n 78) 173, 174; *Micosta SA v Shetland Islands Council (The Mihalis) (Reparation)* [1986] SLT 193, 194; *Force India Formula One Team Ltd v Etihad Airways PJSC* [2011] ETMR 10 [116]; *Lowe v Machell* (n 473) [104].
467 Case 30/9/1998 (n 1601) 5–7; Case 20/4/2002 (n 1094) 1–4; Case 24/4/2004 (n 1572) 2–4; Case 30/12/2008 (n 1213) 1–4.
468 Abdulreda (n 40) 590, 591.
469 Case 17/6/2007 (n 1581) 5, 6; ibid Abdulreda 591.
470 Case 30/9/1998 (n 1601) 6; Case 20/4/2002 (n 1094) 1–4; Case 24/4/2004 (n 1572) 2–4; Case 30/12/2008 (n 1213) 1–4.
471 Case 30/9/1998 (n 1601) 6, 7; Case 17/12/2005 (n 1097) 3, 4; Case 15/10/2006, 1250 (n 261) 5, 6; Case 17/6/2007 (n 1581) 5, 6.

adopted varied criteria in order to determine the period during which notification should be initiated: 'on the buyer's personal discovery of a defect,'[472] 'once the defect has been discovered or within a reasonable period specified by customs and under the deal's circumstances'[473] or 'as soon as the buyer is able to do so according to what is customary.'[474]

If the defect is only detectable by special scientific, technical methods[475] or by using the goods,[476] but not by a standard inspection, the court might permit termination[477] and refuse the seller's defence, citing that the buyer examined the goods and confirmed their validity.[478] In this case, the buyer must, pursuant to Article 492(2), notify the seller as soon as they discover the defect; otherwise, they will lose the possibility of a hidden defect claim.[479] Relying on the buyer's discovery is subjective, based on their circumstances. An objective standard, such as stating that 'as soon as the buyer ought to have discovered the defect,' has not been added.

Although the notification of commercial matters should be conducted via official means or, at least, in writing in case of urgency,[480] in some cases, courts have regarded a request for the seller to repair a car as an implicit notification of the hidden defects.[481] In contrast, in other cases, frequent visits to the seller's garage for repair work did not amount to notification.[482] More problematically, in one case, the court rejected the seller's defence claiming that the buyer did not notify them. The court affirmed that filing a lawsuit with a request for termination was deemed to include a notification.[483] In contrast, Al-Ahwany finds that filing a lawsuit is not considered suitable for notification.[484]

### *5.3.3 Statute of Limitations*

#### *5.3.3.1 CISG*

Nonconformity will not be considered once a two-year period[485] (which is not subjected to suspension or interruption) elapses,[486] even if the inferior quality is

472 Case 15/10/2006, 1250 (n 261) 5; Case 17/6/2007 (n 1581) 5.

473 Case 30/9/1998 (n 1601) 6, 7; Case 20/4/2002 (n 1094) 1–4; Case 24/4/2004 (n 1572) 2–4; Case 30/12/2008 (n 1213) 6.

474 Case 31/3/1996 Court of Cassation/Commercial 3 439/95 p. 2.

475 Case 20/4/2002 (n 1094) 1–4; Case 24/4/2004 (n 1572) 2–4; Case 12/11/2005 (n 1213) 4, 5; Case 30/12/2008 (n 1213) 5, 6; Case 17/4/2012 (n 1572) 4, 5.

476 Case 14/12/1967 Court of Cassation/Commercial 127/67 reproduced in Abdulreda (n 40) 83.

477 Case 12/11/2005 (n 1213) 4, 5; Case 30/12/2008 (n 1213) 5, 6.

478 Case 14/12/1967 Court of Cassation/Commercial 127/67 reproduced in Abdulreda (n 40) 83.

479 EMKCIC 435.

480 KCOC Art. 108.

481 Case 12/11/2005 (n 1213) 4, 5; Case 15/10/2006, 1250 (n 261) 5; Case 30/12/2008 (n 1213) 5, 6.

482 Case 24/4/2004 (n 1572) 2–4; Case 2/1/2005 (n 509) 8.

483 Case 18/6/1996 (n 1226).

484 Al-Ahwany (n 497) 679.

485 CISG Art. 39(2).

486 Ferrari, *Contracts for the International Sale of Goods* (n 1291) 240.

latent and discoverable only upon using the goods or when time passes.[487] In the *Potato seedling case*, tons of potato plants were delivered in February 1998, and in September 1999, the buyer harvested them and resold them to farmers, who discovered that the plants had been invaded by *Ralstonia solanacearum* bacteria. In October 2000, the authorities ordered the contaminated harvest to be destroyed. The court rejected the buyer's claim of nonconformity due to the buyer's failure to notify the seller within two years of the actual receipt.[488]

#### *5.3.3.2 SGA*

The buyer is supposedly deemed to have accepted the unsatisfactory goods when a reasonable amount time elapses after they received the goods, and they have not rejected them or intimated this to the seller.[489] This reasonable time is the sole time limit within which termination may be used. In some example cases, the contract was affirmed, and the buyer lost their termination facility and could only claim damages when rejecting the goods one year after delivery,[490] five years after delivering pictures[491] and three days after delivering potato seeds.[492]

The seller's offer of remedying the defect by making the goods satisfactory is irrelevant[493] as the Law Commission stated that 'attempts at cure should not of themselves deprive the buyer of his right to reject the goods.'[494] Repairing a car as new without any cost to the buyer or even offering them a new car does not prevent the buyer from terminating the contract.[495] However, when the buyer asks the seller to rectify defects, the window of reasonable time closes[496] while the seller tries to repair the goods as s.35(6)(a) states that inquiry or agreement on the goods' repair is not considered an acceptance of the goods,[497] and if the seller fails to meet the quality requirement, the buyer may then reject them.[498] Yet some scholars find that waiting for the culpable seller's performance may lose the termination right through the passage of time.[499]

487 Honnold, *Uniform Law* (n 320) 362.

488 *Potato seedling case* (19/12/2006) 05/03275 (Appellate Court Rouen) <http://cisgw3.law.pace.edu/cases/061219f1.html>.

489 SGA s.35(4).

490 *Tele2 International Card Co SA v Post Office Ltd* [2009] EWCA Civ 9 [19].

491 *Leaf v Galleries* (n 1046) 89–91.

492 *RW Green Ltd v Cade Bros Farms* [1978] 1 Lloyd's Rep 602.

493 *Clegg v Andersson* (n 1427).

494 The Law Commission (n 230) [5.28].

495 *Bernstein v Pamson* (n 1411) 385.

496 *Jones v Callagher (t/a Gallery Kitchens & Bathrooms)* [2004] EWCA Civ 10 [24].

497 The buyer is always entitled to reject the goods after asking for them to be repaired. See *Lee v York Coach and Marine* [1977] RTR 35, 43.

498 *Fiat Auto Financial Services v Connelly* [2007] SLT (Sh Ct) 111; Bridge, *The Sale of Goods* (n 28) [10.82].

499 Stone; Devenney (n 64) 678.

Notably, the reasonable period may be extended when the buyer needs a pause to allow for contemplation of their best reaction to nonconformity.[500] In *Force India Formula One Team*, it was stated that the buyer needed time to recognise clearly the ultimate consequences and to consider their position before deciding either to accept repudiation or to affirm the contract.[501] This is especially pertinent if the repudiation of the contract could sever the relationship with the seller.[502] It was held in *Fiat Auto v Connelly*[503] that the continued use of the purchased vehicle did not amount to an act inconsistent with the seller's ownership, and the buyer had the right to reject the vehicle, especially as the buyer was waiting to make a judgement regarding whether to accept the vehicle and seek a repair or to reject it. The wait for the decision allowed the buyer considerable utility of the vehicle, which they used for 40,000 miles over a nine-month period. In *Clegg v Olle*, although the buyer knew that the yacht had an overweight keel,[504] it was decided that the buyer's indication that they refused remedial work until obtaining further information did not amount to acceptance of the yacht.[505] However, as Rix LJ stated in *Stocznia*, a buyer pondering their position for too long might be treated in law as having affirmed the contract.[506]

#### *5.3.3.3 KLaw*

According to Article 496(1), the right to claim hidden defects is lost if one year elapses, not subjected to interruption or stoppage,[507] commencing from the actual receipt of the goods, even if the buyer discovers the defect thereafter[508] and even if its discovery is something that needs special technical expertise.[509] Therefore, when a buyer filed a lawsuit one year after the delivery time based on the separation of a car's rear wheel,[510] they lost their termination right.[511] This short period in which to file a lawsuit based on a hidden defect[512] can be interrupted by a judicial

500 *Fisher Reeves & Co Ltd v Armour & Co Ltd* [1920] 3 KB 614, 623.

501 *Force India Formula One v Etihad* (n 1992) [122]. See also *China National Foreign Trade Transportation v Evlogia* (n 1414) 1022; *White Rosebay Shipping SA v Hong Kong Chain Glory Shipping Ltd* [2013] 2 CLC 884 [1].

502 Bridge, *The Sale of Goods* (n 28) [10.77].

503 *Fiat v Connelly* (n 2024).

504 *Clegg v Andersson* (n 1427) [53].

505 ibid [58].

506 *Stocznia Gdanska SA v Latvian Shipping Co (Repudiation)* [2003] 1 CLC 282 [87].

507 Al-Ahwany (n 497) 682.

508 Case 20/11/1989 Court of Cassation/Commercial 180/98 & Case 28/4/1997 Court of Cassation/Commercial 298/96 in Ministry of Justice, *Civil Provisions* (n 955) 452, 453.

509 EMKCIC 436; Case 22/5/1995 Appellate Court/Civil 2 17/95 p. 8, 9; Case 18/6/1996 (n 1226); Case 15/10/2006, 1250 (n 261) 4, 5; Case 15/10/2006 Court of Cassation/Commercial 2 876\2005\ p. 4, 5; Case 6/1/2009 Court of Cassation/Commercial 1 384/2006 p. 4, 5.

510 Case 31/3/1996 (n 2000) 2.

511 ibid.

512 Case 24/4/2004 (n 1572) 2–4; Case 8/3/2006 (n 1583) 14; Case 27/12/2007 Court of Cassation/Commercial 1 417/2006 p. 3, 4.

claim but not by notification,[513] even if it is conducted officially.[514] Thus, discovering substantial defects should urge the buyer to file a lawsuit requesting termination[515] and discourage them from asking for the goods to be repaired for the fear of the elapse of this period, especially as there might be uncertainty about the repair's result. In one case, discovering many defects in a jet ski and frequently visiting the seller's workshop to repair it lost the buyer their termination right because the lawsuit was filed after the lapse of one year.[516] Surprisingly, in one case, it was stated that since the buyer did not base their lawsuit on a hidden defect but instead made a general request for termination, the long prescription (ten years for commercial issues) was applicable, and the contract was terminated,[517] even after the expiration of a one-year period.

### 5.3.4 Actions of the Buyer/Seller Affecting Termination

#### 5.3.4.1 CISG

##### 5.3.4.1.1 ACTIONS OF THE BUYER AFFECTING TERMINATION

When buyers wish to exercise their termination right, the duty of restitution and the good faith principle[518] obliges them to take reasonable steps to preserve the goods[519] when they receive them,[520] when the goods are dispatched to the buyer and still possessed by the carrier[521] or when the goods are placed at the buyer's disposal.[522] The purpose of the preservation duty is to avert the goods' deterioration or abandonment at the place of delivery.[523] Two of these reasonable steps are:

**First**, if the seller unreasonably delays taking possession of the rejected goods, the buyer may send a reasonable notice to the seller of their intention to sell the goods by appropriate means.[524] Nevertheless, when the goods are susceptible to physical or monetary[525] deterioration or their preservation involves unreasonable

513 ibid; Al-Ahwany (n 497) 679.
514 Case 8/3/2006 (n 1583) 14; Case 27/12/2007 (n 2038) 3, 4.
515 Case 9/12/2001 (n 1600) 2–4; Case 15/10/2006, 876 (n 2035) 4, 5.
516 ibid 9/12/2001 2, 3.
517 Case 18/6/1996 (n 1226).
518 *Machine case* (19/12/2002) 19U8/02 (Appellate Court Karlsruhe) <http://cisgw3.law.pace.edu/cases/021219g1.html>.
519 CISG Art. 86(1).
520 Honnold, *Uniform Law* (n 320) 685.
521 ibid 684.
522 CISG Art. 86(2).
523 Huber; Mullis (n 1279) 362.
524 CISG Art. 88(1); *Cotton gin motes case* (2005) CISG/2005/01 (CIETAC arbitration proceeding) <http://cisgw3.law.pace.edu/cases/050407c1.html>.
525 DiMatteo et al (n 67) 161, 162.

expense, the buyer must conduct the above step where possible.[526] **Secondly**, the buyer may deposit the rejected goods in storage at a reasonable price at the seller's expense.[527] The obligation to preserve the goods is imposed on the buyer only when 1) these steps do not cause the buyer unreasonable inconvenience or expense, 2) the payment is not needed to collect the goods, and 3) the seller is not present at the place where the goods exist.[528]

##### 5.3.4.1.2 ACTIONS OF THE SELLER AFFECTING TERMINATION

The seller cannot rely on the buyer's failure to examine the goods and/or to send a proper notification of a nonconformity which the seller already knows about[529] or could not be unaware of.[530] This is to avoid imposing sanctions on the buyer for a delayed, deficient or defaulting notification where the seller does not need it.[531] The defects' nature and the seller's proficiency could assume the seller's knowledge of nonconformity.[532] In *Beijing v Connell*, when tons of rail press stopped operating due to the replacement of the A-5750 key, which was stronger and more durable, with a P-52 plate,[533] the seller could not have been unaware of this failure, raising the seller's liability even when the buyer notified the seller after the two-year cut-off period.[534]

#### *5.3.4.2 SGA*

When the buyer has a right to refuse the goods (according to their self-assessment), they are not bound to return the goods to the seller or even to place them with a third party.[535] It is sufficient to intimate to the seller that the goods are refused,[536] without the buyer being obliged to mitigate any loss.[537] However, as mentioned in Chapter 4, the buyer may lose the right to reject the goods and repudiate the contract if their actions are inconsistent with the seller's ownership of the goods. In *Clegg v Olle*, although the buyer knew that the yacht had an overweight keel, they used it and left their possessions on it for approximately six months, which could be considered an inconsistent act.[538]

526 CISG Art. 88(2).
527 CISG Art. 87.
528 CISG Art. 86(2).
529 DiMatteo et al (n 67) 120.
530 CISG Art. 40.
531 Honnold, *Uniform Law* (n 320) 376.
532 *Srl v BV* (n 1362).
533 *Beijing v Connell* (n 1836).
534 ibid.
535 *Grimoldby v Wells* (1874–75) LR 10 CP 391.
536 SGA s.36.
537 *Skandia Property (UK) v Thames Water Utilities* [1999] 7 WLUK 561.
538 *Clegg v Andersson* (n 1427) [53].

#### *5.3.4.3 KLaw*

##### 5.3.4.3.1 BUYER'S ACTIONS AFFECTING TERMINATION

Al-Majalla states that if it is not possible to return the goods in their condition at the time of contract conclusion, such as if a buyer converts the garment into a shirt and then discovers an old defect, the transformed goods cannot be returned, even if the seller is satisfied with the transformation, but they should reduce the price instead.[539] Conversely, Article 493 states that the hidden defect claim remains even if the goods are damaged, are lost or have deteriorated for any reason.[540] The buyer is not obliged to return the goods as they were at the time of receipt in order to claim termination as the loss of the commodity cannot lead to the loss of the buyer's right to claim a hidden defect.[541] Termination was held for selling a Chevrolet Caprice with a hidden defect even though the buyer misused and neglected the car's maintenance, causing it to decrease in value. The buyer, however, had to compensate the seller for this reduction.[542] Notwithstanding, according to Article 494, when the buyer disposes of the goods as an owner – for instance, by offering to sell them – after they learn of the defect[543] (this Article also relies subjectively on the buyer's knowledge), their conduct implies acceptance of such a defect,[544] preventing them from claiming termination,[545] unless the second sale contract mentions that the first buyer's right of hidden defect claim is transferred to the second buyer.[546]

##### 5.3.4.3.2 ACTIONS OF THE SELLER AFFECTING TERMINATION

The seller can claim neither the buyer's failure of the required examination, notification and/or timely litigation based on hidden defect nor extinctive prescription[547] when the seller clearly acted in bad faith, confirming the goods 'being free of the disputed defect[548] or concealing such a defect.[549] This is to prevent the seller from benefiting from their fraud,[550] which exceeds the buyer's default.[551] When this is the case, termination is subjected to a long statute of limitations: i.e. ten years from

539 Al-Majalla Art. 350; 345; 349.
540 KCIC Art. 493.
541 Al-Ahwany (n 497) 709.
542 Case 22/10/2005 (n 1492) 1, 2.
543 KCIC Art. 494.
544 AL-Majalla Art. 344.
545 KCIC Art. 494.
546 Case 28/12/2005 Court of Cassation/Commercial 10 2935/2005 p. 6, 7.
547 KCIC Art. 491; Art. 496(2).
548 Al-Defery; Al-Sayrafy (n 254) 302.
549 Case 15/10/2006, 876 (n 2035) in Ministry of Justice, *Civil Provisions* (n 955) 459.
550 Al-Ahwany (n 497) 658, 659.
551 Al-Sanhory (n 279) 726; Al-Fadly (n 495) 126, 127; Talaba (n 50); Al-Defery; Al-Sayrafy (n 254) 302.

the due date of the fulfilment of the obligation.[552] However, neither the seller's sole awareness of the defects[553] nor the sole use of exaggerated terms in praise of the goods[554] shall be considered deceitful.[555] Nevertheless, in one case, when the manager of the selling company admitted after concluding the contract that the vibration in a Mercedes was a common defect in the model in question, the court of first instance established that the seller had deliberately concealed their knowledge of the defect from the buyer, making the long prescription applicable to terminating the contract.[556] On appeal, the court upheld the previous decision despite the seller's defence that the manager's statement was not found to be fraudulent by deliberately hiding the defect.[557] Yet in another case, when a car broke down, the authorised agent refused to repair it because the true odometer reading was 114,636 km, not 53,771 km as shown. The sub-buyer filed a lawsuit, and the court decided on termination of the second contract. However, a court refused to terminate the first contract between an original buyer and their seller and decided on 1,500 KD in compensation,[558] even though the court recognised that the defect was hidden, reducing both the car's life expectancy and its value,[559] and despite the fact that it was proven that the original seller undertook the car's registration papers, where the difference in the odometer should have become clear.[560]

### *5.3.5 Comparative Analysis*

#### *5.3.5.1 Apparent Defect (by Sight)*

**Under CISG**, a buyer cannot refuse a shipment, and, as stated in *Fluorite* case, the fact that 'the [Buyer] did not reject loading at the shipment port does not mean the acceptance of goods whose quality do not meet the contract standards.'[561] Rather, buyers should notify sellers specifically about the defect and should also preserve the goods by taking reasonable steps, such as reselling the goods or depositing them. Requiring these steps to activate termination makes the buyer rethink the recourse to this remedy. Conversely, **under SGA**, refusing the goods is regarded as an acceptance of the seller's repudiatory breach, but the buyer should intimate to the seller the goods' refusal without the need to specify the flaw or the reason and without any obligation to return or preserve the goods. Similarly, **under KLaw**, not refusing the goods for apparent defects can be considered acceptance of the

552 KCOC Art. 118(1).
553 Al-Ahwany (n 497) 658, 659, 682, 683; Omran (n 1884) 80.
554 ibid Al-Ahwany 658, 659; Al-Defery; Al-Sayrafy (n 254) 302.
555 ibid.
556 Case 18/6/1996 (n 1226) 2, 3.
557 ibid.
558 Case 6/1/2009 (n 2035) 4, 5.
559 ibid 2, 3.
560 ibid 4, 5.
561 *Fluorite case* (2006) (China CIETAC arbitration proceeding) <http://cisgw3.law.pace.edu/cases/060200c1.htm>.

defective goods. The buyer should initiate notification to the seller of this nonconformity with its reason, but there is no obligation to return or preserve the goods. However, because Article 197 KCIC states that the contract must be executed consistent with the requirements of good faith and honour,[562] the buyer might voluntarily take steps to preserve the goods until their return to the seller. Nevertheless, there is a fear that this conduct might be interpreted as an acceptance of the goods as Article 493, in particular, guarantees that deterioration of the goods for any reason does not prevent the buyer from claiming termination.

This authorisation to refuse the goods under both SGA and KLaw puts the contract under the buyer's personal estimation, enabling them to reject the goods for minimal defects, easing the recourse to termination. However, this attitude is understandable under SGA as the legal outcome is predictable, and termination based on minor defects is generally permitted. This is contrary to KLaw, which gives this mechanism to the buyer with excessive vagueness, leading to a result that might clash with the judicial decision. On the other hand, CISG imposes the preservation duty without allowing the buyer to refuse the nonconforming goods and leave them unattended, which can expose them to changes in the weather. Exposure to the elements might substantially alter the goods' condition, and this would prevent the recourse to termination.[563] Notifying the seller of the nonconformity and specifying its nature under CISG make the situation clear, whereas SGA does not impose this clarification, and any general expression will suffice. Under KLaw, in some cases, requesting the goods' repair or filing a lawsuit was considered notification, expanding the recourse to termination.

#### *5.3.5.2 Hidden Flaws*

In *Heilbutt v Hickson*, defective army shoes contained paper in their soles.[564] Consider the following four hypothetical scenarios for this case:

##### A) FLAWS WERE DISCOVERABLE BY NORMAL EXAMINATION

The shipment involved carriage by sea to the buyer's port, but it was not examined on arrival because the buyer's specialist was indisposed.

**Under CISG**, the buyer should have conducted such examination as quickly as practicable, and this would have been assessed objectively, considering the involvement of the goods' carriage, so long as there was no reasonable opportunity to examine the goods before their delivery to the buyer's port. Notification, accordingly, should have occurred within a reasonable time of discovering the defect or when it could have been discovered, without considering the buyer's personal situation and a specialist not being available. **Under SGA**, there is no obligation to

562 KCIC Art. 197.
563 CISG Art. 82(1).
564 *Heilbutt v Hickson* (1871–72) LR 7 CP 438 443.

examine the goods, but late examination might have led to late acceptance of repudiatory breach, which should have been conducted within a reasonable amount of time. This time commences directly after the buyer is afforded a reasonable opportunity for examination. Such opportunity begins on the goods' arrival to the buyer's port. The buyer's personal situation might not have been considered, although it was taken into account in *Bernstein v Pamson*. **Under KLaw**, the examination should be performed as soon as the buyer is able to do so, and this might require consideration of both the goods' carriage and the buyer's situation. However, including the phrase 'according to usual practice' may change the equation, focusing the consideration on the objective circumstances, but this still depends on the court's conviction. Under CISG, the buyer's personal situation is not considered when estimating the required notification, making the situation fair and clear and supporting objectivity and reasonableness. Conversely, under KLaw, adopting objective and subjective criteria and giving the court the right to choose either of them is misleading. Using definite words in promulgating any law is extremely important to avoid different interpretations according to the litigants' interests.

B) DEFECTS WERE UNDISCOVERABLE UNLESS SHOES' SOLES WERE CUT[565]

The notification time for undiscoverable defects might be extended **under CISG** but should not exceed a two-year period from the actual receipt. Within that period, the seller has the right to cure the defect without suspending it. **Under SGA**, seemingly, differentiation between the type of defect and its discoverability is irrelevant. In this scenario, the buyer should have rejected the goods within a reasonable time, even though the defect was hidden,[566] as long as they had had a reasonable opportunity to examine the goods, considering the buyer's right to think about their position. If the buyer proved needed time to study the situation regarding the popularity of the defective shoes in the market, this would extend the reasonable time. This may make it possible to circumvent the function of a reasonable amount of time to end the buyer's ability to reject the goods by stretching it, if there is a good excuse. However, not recognising a prescription period for refusing the goods and repudiating the contract, contrary to CISG, minimises termination under the former more than the latter. If the seller successfully rectifies the defect without being asked by the buyer, the right to repudiate the contract might not be affected, and this lessens preservation of the contract more than CISG. **Under KLaw**, the buyer should notify the seller immediately after the buyer's discovery of the defect.[567] This short period, however, disturbs the contractual balance between the parties because it relies on the buyer's circumstances without considering their presumed discovery. However, the judiciary might have found that the notification should have been conducted promptly without considering the buyer's personal

565 ibid 453.
566 ibid.
567 KCIC Art. 492(2).

circumstances. It was plainly stated in one case that establishing whether the defect was a hidden one could not have been done by the usual examination and whether or not the buyer notified the seller of the defect as soon as they discovered it were matters of fact entrusted to the trial court,[568] even though these issues are essential for knowing their rules in advance.

Nevertheless, the buyer's termination right expires after one year elapses from the actual receipt without litigation, even if the buyer examined the goods in a timely manner and notified the seller of the defect. This short period might urge the buyer to refuse any attempts by the seller to cure the defect, making the recourse to termination considerable without accepting any compromise.

Notification in both SGA and CISG lasts for a reasonable time, but the starting points for such a period are different; it begins from the real/presumed discovery of the defect under CISG, but it begins after the expiration of a reasonable opportunity to examine the goods under SGA. This difference in starting points makes the notification time generally shorter and more certain and uniform in SGA as a reasonable time for examination and notification might not be extended according to the type of defect but according to the nature of the goods. In contrast, CISG explicitly mentions the 'discovery' element, and this forms the notification time according to the type of defect, thus attaining flexibility. Accordingly, contract preservation is more apparent under SGA than under CISG.

#### C) SHOES FILLED WITH PAPER ASSUME THE SELLER'S KNOWLEDGE

This assumption allows the transaction to be described as being in bad faith **under CISG**, exempting the buyer from any procedural default to terminate the contract. **Under SGA**, a seller in bad faith does not change the legal outcome. **Under KLaw**, this presumption might not be considered, especially if the seller is a retailer, unless the court finds otherwise. A seller acting in bad faith is regarded so only when they acted positively by confirming to the buyer the freedom from the disputed defect or fraudulently concealing it; only then would the buyer's procedural default not affect the termination right. For the sake of reinforcing good faith, preserving the contract may not constitute a priority under either CISG or KLaw, and estimating whether or not the seller acted in bad faith may differ according to the circumstances of the case, which lessens the degree of predictability, in contrast to SGA.

#### D) THE CONTRACT PRESUMABLY STATED, 'THE SHOES SHOULD NOT BE FILLED WITH PAPER'

This would be easily classified as a 'contractual description' under both **CISG** and **SGA**, and the aforementioned procedural requirements are mostly applicable to misdescription. However, the case is different **under KLaw**; the substantive and procedural conditions of hidden defects are inapplicable when requesting

568 Case 20/4/2002 (n 1094) 1–4.

termination due to misdescription.[569] The sole lack of an agreed description raises the seller's liability,[570] without requiring misdescription to be influential and regardless of the buyer's knowledge of misdescription at the time of sale.[571] This is true irrespective of the requirements of examination and timely notification[572] and regardless of the short prescription for the hidden defect claim[573] (applying the long prescription,[574] which is ten years from the due date of implementing the disputed obligation).[575] This distinction is apparently made because the misdescription is based on the contract, which must be respected and applied accurately, in contrast to hidden defects, which can occur accidently in any situation without the seller's knowledge. In case of the seller's deception, the conditions of hidden defects are inapplicable. However, there is a strong possibility of confusion between these two subjects.[576] In one case, although the expert proved that the goods complied with contractual descriptions but suffered from a manufacturing defect, the court considered the defect to be a misdescription, applying long prescription.[577] Additionally, in other cases, the court considered the following misdescriptions hidden defects: the difference in an odometer's mileage from that agreed,[578] selling a second-hand car rather than a new one as agreed[579] and selling a Mercedes 420 SEL rather than a 506 SEL as agreed.[580] This variation in legal characterisations might depend on the plaintiff/defendant's ability to persuading the judge according to the benefit of their chosen legal rule. This is not the case under CISG and SGA, which adopt an almost single set of procedural requirements to all kinds of nonconformity, leading to a uniform legal effect.

## 5.4 Conclusion

CISG does not exactly define the required quality,[581] and 'it is not possible to determine once and for all the precise degree of quality to which the buyer is entitled,'[582]

569 Al-Defery; Al-Sayrafy (n 254) 335.
570 Al-Ahwany (n 497) 725, 726; Shoala (n 1448) 361.
571 Egyptian Court of Cassation (28/10/1975) 608Y40QS 26 P 1345 reproduced in Shoala (n 1448) 293.
572 KCOC Art. 118; Case 11/2/2006 (n 1098) 2–4; Case 29/6/2010 (n 1475) 4–7; Al-Ahwany (n 497) 734; Al-Defery; Al-Sayrafy (n 254) 335.
573 KCOC Art. 118; Case 11/2/2006 (n 1098) 2–4; Case 29/6/2010 (n 1475) 4–7; Al-Ahwany (n 497) 734; Al-Defery; Al-Sayrafy (n 254) 335.
574 KCOC Art. 118; Case 11/2/2006 (n 1098); Case 29/6/2010 Court of Cassation/Commercial 656/2007 in Ministry of Justice, *Civil Provisions* (n 955) 295; Al-Ahwany (n 497) 734; Al-Defery; Al-Sayrafy (n 254) 335.
575 KCOC Art. 118.
576 See Saheb Al-Fatlawy, *Hidden Defects and Default of Specifications in Sale Contracts* (Dar Althaqafa 1997) 160, 161; Al-Defery; Al-Sayrafy (n 254) 295.
577 Case 29/6/2010 (n 2100) 4–7.
578 Case 6/1/2009 (n 2035) 4, 5.
579 Case 20/4/2002 (n 1094) 1–4; Case 17/12/2005 (n 1097) 2.
580 Case 9/12/1996 (n 1095) 4.
581 Poikela (n 83) 5.
582 Bianca; Bonell (n 155) 281 [2.9.2.].

and this may lead to several interpretations of Article 35(2)(a), by resorting to 'average quality' or to 'merchantable quality,'[583] each of which can render different conclusions.[584] It is likely that more than one standard must be taken to define the required quality; merchantability can be adopted, depending on the ultimate consumer's reasonable expectations,[585] and only when these expectations are substantially deprived and foreseeable can termination be activated. This task might be left to interpretation,[586] reducing certainty but attaining greater level of flexibility according to the circumstances of each case. CISG's procedural requirements, however, play a significant role in both achieving predictability and preserving the contract.

Generally, SGA is substantively and procedurally straightforward, leading to predictable outcomes,[587] as Lord Mansfield stated in *Vallejo v Wheeler*: 'In all mercantile transactions the great object should be certainty. [This is because] speculators in trade then know what ground to go upon,'[588] and '[W]hat is needed is not certainty of rule, but confidence in result.'[589] This clarity and almost automatic right to terminate the contract, however, can be exploited by speculating on the commodities' values in the market,[590] undermining the nature of the contract to be exposed to market risk[591] and allowing the buyer to obtain cheaper goods from another supplier[592] at the seller's expense. However, the SGA's procedural requirements successfully balance the equation, lessening these exploitable opportunities.

**Developing KLaw**: Its lack of clear conditions on hidden defects creates excessive uncertainty, intricacies and subjectivity, undermining the goal of contractual firmness and predictability[593] and permitting judicial speculations.[594] Through bewilderment, jurists may resort to different standards when defining, for instance, 'substantiality' or determining whether 'detriment' is an inherent element of a hidden defect claim or not, and this has certainly led to mystification and confusion between the rules. Even with recourse to case law, the cases are, substantively and procedurally inconsistent, involving various interpretations due to the discretionary power given to the judge in applying the law according to their own perspective where the only condition for this discretion is the provision of justifiable reasons.

583 Gillette; Ferrari (n 1625) 8.
584 *Condensate crude oil mix case* (n 1619) [103]
585 Poikela (n 83) 5.
586 Grebler, 'Fundamental Breach' (n 48) 409; Goode; Kronke; Mckendrick 2nd edn, (n 157) 249, 250 [8.72].
587 Mullis, 'Termination for Breach of Contract' in Guest (n 226) 142.
588 *Vallejo v Wheeler* (1774) 98 ER 1012, 1017.
589 Melvin Eisenberg, *The Nature of the Common Law* (Harvard UP 1988) 158. See also Ahdar (n 765) 40, 53.
590 Burrows, *Principles of English Commercial Law* (n 28) 76; McKendrick, *Contract Law* (n 206) 774.
591 Cohen (n 249) 583, 584.
592 Bridge, *The Sale of Goods* (n 28) [10.03].
593 *Yam Seng* (n 204) [123].
594 See Bridge, *Benjamin's* (n 28) [10–034].

Under KLaw, when assessing the extent of detriment suffered, there is a significant possibility of taking the buyer's personal circumstances into account, in contrast to CISG, in which the only detriment considered is that linked to the deprivation of expectation under the contract. Moreover, foreseeability of this detriment on the seller's part is another stipulation which strikes at the equilibrium between the parties. Subjectivity cannot be found under SGA due to its mechanical termination when breaching implied conditions. However, this approach may contradict economic reality and lack flexibility, which makes CISG's approach suitable for KLaw's reformation.

# 6 Conclusion and Assessment

This book has compared the rights of commercial buyers wishing to terminate contracts under CISG, SGA and KLaw when dealing with breaching sellers. By virtue of comparative analysis and the doctrinal legal research methodology, the synthesis of differences between the laws and legal system appraisals, have been done with a critical eye.[1] Because realism demands 'legal facts [to be] revealed by judicial decisions and discursive analysis which amalgamates all legal statements,'[2] the degree of judicial departure from statutory rules[3] and deeper comprehensibility of CISG, in terms of its divergence from the rules of the two selected non-contracting states, have been demonstrated. This approach has also revealed the following three points:

**First**, striking a balance between the need for 'certainty,' which necessitates rigid rules, and the need for justice, which involves 'flexibility' depending on the individual case, is not an easy task. Seeking absolute 'predictability, efficacy, equity and finality'[4] is not a realistic goal. It is true that reinforcing dependency on contractual promises instils confidence in social intercourse and enterprise, attains wealth and constitutes an important component of civilisation.[5] But, '[n]o legal system does or can attempt to enforce all promises'[6] since, in reality, many people prefer the occasional departure from these and abhor absolute rigidity without any flexibility in the viable system.[7] Terminating a contract for any breach has harsh consequences,[8] resulting in a series of pointless, laborious stages. The retroactive demise of a contract is time consuming and costly due to storage, insurance and reshipment charges. Setting strict criteria by which to claim termination has financial advantages that could be achieved by reducing the opportunistic behaviour

1 Honnold, 'The Uniform Law' (n 101) 349.
2 Halperin J, 'Law in Books and Law in Action: The Problem of Legal Change' (2011) 64(1) Maine Law Rev 59.
3 ibid 46.
4 Poikela (n 83) 67.
5 Cohen (n 249) 572, 573.
6 ibid.
7 ibid.
8 French Civil Code 2016 Art. 1229.

DOI: 10.4324/9781003466130-6

seen in some cases in which termination has been sought, which would also minimise the wastage of goods.[9]

**Secondly**, CISG has succeeded in both meeting the requirements of international trade and bridging the gap between civil and common law countries through the creation of provisions that do not side with any of these law families in order to prove neutrality. Neither the discrepancy in common law between 'conditions' and 'warranty' nor the distinction existent in civil law between 'hidden' and 'apparent' defects is found in CISG. Furthermore, it does not outline differences between 'misdescription' and sending goods of a 'different category.'[10]

**Thirdly**, Article 7 CISG requires an autonomous interpretation of the Convention and discourages recourse to the national law as an interpretative tool for any vagueness.[11] However, there is evidence that national courts have at times followed legal preconceptions in interpreting CISG's vague terms,[12] and this ends up with jurisprudential contrast.[13] It is certainly difficult for adjudicators to abandon their traditional legal way of thinking and transcend familiar steadfast principles to adjudicate with an unbiased mind.[14] Nevertheless, this study demonstrates that it is vital to completely ignore domestic principles and concepts when applying CISG in English or Kuwaiti courts[15] by virtue of conflict-of-law rules because each law has its theme, philosophy and aims, which at times clash with CISG. This is not only for the sake of attaining uniformity but also to avoid forum shopping.[16]

## 6.1 Clarity and Predictability of Legal Outcomes Versus Flexibility

The main criticism of **CISG** is around the abstract[17] and vague nature[18] of Article 25, containing 'cumulative conditions of positive and negative values,'[19]

9 Spagnolo (n 54) 52.

10 See Veneziano (n 1137) 41; Maley (n 186) 95.

11 Franco Ferrari, 'Uniform Interpretation of the 1980 Uniform Sales Law' (1995) 24 GaJIntl&CompL 183, 200; Phanesh Koneru, 'The International Interpretation of the UN Convention on Contracts for the International Sale of Goods: An Approach Based on General Principles' (1997) 6MJGT 105, 106; V Susanne Cook, 'The UN Convention on Contracts for the International Sale of Goods: A Mandate to Abandon Legal Ethnocentricity' (1997) 16 JL & Com 257, 258; Graffi (n 155) 339.

12 Poikela (n 83) 18, 19.

13 DiMatteo et al (n 67) 1; Eleonora Agro, 'The Impact of the UNIDROIT Principles in International Dispute Resolution in Figures' (2011) 16(3) UnifLRev 719, 719.

14 John E. Murray, 'The Neglect of CISG: A Workable Solution' (1998) 17 JL & Com 365, 367.

15 See Bashayer Al-Mukhaizeem, 'Application of CISG in Kuwait' (2020) 35 Arab Law Q 304.

16 Luca (n 815) 179, 180.

17 Enderlein; Maskow (n 150) 112; Bridge, 'Avoidance for Fundamental Breach' (n 158) 917; Hofmann (n 1267) 153.

18 Eörsi (n 1711) 341; Ferrari, 'CISG Case Law' (n 752) 254; Vincent Heuze, *La vente Internationale de Marchandise* (Librairie Générale de Droit et de Jurisprudence 2000) 394; Peacock (n 140) 102; Graffi (n 155) 339; Zeller, 'Fundamental Breach' (n 184) 81.

19 Grebler, 'Fundamental Breach' (n 48) 408.

which impair its interpretation.[20] This can lead to unexpected legal outcomes,[21] demand protracted and costly litigation to decipher its complexity and may leave decision-making to the discretion of the adjudicators, depending on their own biases,[22] or on local interpretations.[23] Grebler states that Article 25

> has been the object of recurrent criticism for both its form and its substance . . . that may account for the Convention not being adopted by a number of countries.[24]

However, as the German representative asserted at the 12th meeting of the UN Conference, 'fundamental breach could be defined only in vague terms.'[25] A transnational law's abstractness reflects its flexibility, especially as

> there is no "magic" formula which will provide an instant answer in every case. . . . (Even if there were, this would not resolve most disputes about defective goods, since most disputes are not about the law but about the facts.)[26]

Hence, the generality of Article 25 is restricted when judging 'on the circumstances of the contract and expectations of the parties,'[27] reducing the judge's discretion. Thus, ambiguity around the availability of termination depends on the parties themselves conveying their expectations, commercial purposes and mercantile interests in their contract,[28] which is based on a case-by-case analysis,[29] resembling calculus in mathematics.[30] This deliberate way Article 25 is phrased is meant to prevent the buyer from using any departure as a pretext for termination at the seller's expense[31] and to find the middle ground between the parties,[32] mediating between abstractness and concreteness.[33]

20 ibid 409.
21 Williams (n 1267) 21; Eduardo Grebler, 'The UN Sales of Goods Convention: Perspectives on the Current State-of-Play' (2007) ASILPROC 407, 408; Bridge, 'Avoidance for Fundamental Breach' (n 158) 921.
22 DiMatteo et al (n 67) 472; Grebler, 'Fundamental Breach' (n 48) 409, 411, 413; Bridge, 'Avoidance for Fundamental Breach' (n 158) 917; Kröll; Mistelis; Viscasillas (n 67) 340 [9].
23 Eörsi (n 1711) 336; Peacock (n 140) 100; Ferrari, 'Fundamental Breach' (n 161) 495; Bridge, 'Avoidance for Fundamental Breach' (n 158) 922.
24 Grebler, 'Fundamental Breach' (n 48) 407, 408.
25 Official Records (n 149) 12th Meeting 297.
26 The Law Commission (n 230) [3.11].
27 *Shoe leather case* (n 282).
28 Schwenzer, *Commentary on CISG* (n 15) 421, 422 [9].
29 Ferrari, 'Fundamental Breach' (n 161) 493; Grebler, 'The UN Sales of Goods Convention (n 2141) 413.
30 F. H. Lawson, *The Rational Strength of English Law* (Stevens & Sons Ltd 1951) 79.
31 UN, 'International Trade Law' (n 190) 31; Fried (n 1753) 119.
32 Burrows, *Principles of English Commercial Law* (n 28) 77, 78.
33 Spagnolo (n 54) 36.

Additionally, Article 25 is a declaratory provision and cannot be investigated in isolation,[34] thus requiring the use of other 'functional provisions' according to the type of breach.[35] Furthermore, 'global jurisconsultorium'[36] could be reached by following CISG's case law, available freely in sources online, such as the UNCITRAL database and Case Law of UNCITRAL Texts (CLOUT), the literature and the websites on CISG, all of which can play a role in enhancing uniformity and attaining legal clarity.

By contrast, **SGA** does not lend itself to acknowledging 'generic' requirements in the field of sale contracts because generality creates excessive uncertainty[37] and subjectivity, undermining the goal of contractual predictability, to which SGA has attached great weight.[38] As Mr Justice Leggatt affirmed, the favoured English legal method is to 'proceed incrementally by fashioning particular solutions in response to particular problems rather than by enforcing broad overarching principles.'[39] Additionally, as Megaw LJ stated, '[T]here is everything to be said for, and nothing against, a degree of rigidity in legal principle.'[40] Thus, termination is mainly connected with the strict but simplistic dichotomy of 'condition' and 'warranty,'[41] and this makes the law 'free from technicality,'[42] lessening discretionary power and preventing unexpected termination.[43] The attention paid to these concerns was one of the main reasons for holding certain terms as 'conditions' even though many degrees of breaches may occur,[44] enabling businesspeople to possess immediate and unequivocal knowledge about the legal outcomes of their actions.[45] Therefore, the reason for the English non-engagement with the Convention may have been the flexibility in defining a fundamental breach.[46] As was stated in the report of the Law Reform Committee:

> There are . . . certain differences which are not altogether insignificant and we think they are not such as to make the uniform law more attractive to traders than the existing UK law. Moreover they have the inherent disadvantage

34 Zeller, 'Fundamental Breach' (n 184) 90.

35 CISG Art. 49; Art. 64; Art. 7; Art. 8; Zeller, 'Fundamental Breach' (n 184) 81, 91.

36 Camilla Andersen, 'The Uniform International Sales Law and the Global Jurisconsultorium' (2005) 24(2) JL & Com 159.

37 Rogowska, 'Some Considerations on the Desirability of Accession to the CISG' (n 23) 34.

38 *Maredelanto* (n 78) 205; *Bunge v Tradax* (n 400) 715; *Kuwait Rocks Co v AMN Bulkcarriers Inc* [2013] EWHC 865 (Comm) [77]; *Yam Seng* (n 204) [123]; Fuller (n 81) 63; Ahdar (n 765) 40, 53.

39 ibid *Yam Seng* [123].

40 *Maredelanto* (n 78) 205.

41 Barry Nicholas, 'The Vienna Convention on International Sales Law' (1989) 105 LQR 201, 228; Peacock (n 140) 107; Bridge, *The Sale of Goods* (n 28) [10.15].

42 Mustill LJ in Rogers v Parish (n 1572) 942.

43 A similar meaning can be found in J Carter, 'Discharge as the Basis for Termination for Breach of Contract' (2012) 128 LQR 283, 299.

44 Smith *Atiyah's* (n 198) 200.

45 *Bunge v Tradax* (n 400) 720; Ahdar (n 765) 60.

46 Hofmann (n 1267) 153.

> that even slight changes of wording from that in the Sale of Goods Act result in losing the benefit of the certainty conferred by long-established case law on the interpretation of the Act.[47]

However, perfect legal certainty is unachievable,[48] and even within SGA, there are some aspects of indecision:

**First**, s.15A truly adds the element of justice and flexibility but also adds uncertainty because the estimation is subject to the discrepancy of subjective views held by individual judges.[49] **Secondly**, metaphorical concepts in the rule of 'intermediate terms,' such as 'going to the root' and 'frustrating commercial purpose' are too vague,[50] depending on the practical considerations in the eye of the judiciary.[51] Additionally, pursuing its consequential methods can be difficult as the buyer's wait for exacerbation of the consequences may be considered an acceptance of the goods. Moreover, the buyer's assessment can simply be refuted as the judge may find that the consequences do not meet the repudiatory breach's requirements.[52] **Thirdly**, 'satisfactory quality [for instance] does not provide ready-made [automatic] solutions to all the different questions which may arise,'[53] making a perfect definition of 'quality' difficult to attain because the issue depends on the facts of each case.[54] **Finally**, it is true that any 'description' mentioned in the contract should be complied with, and any minor difference gives the buyer the right to reject the whole delivery,[55] so long as it is worse than the slight breach mentioned in s.15A.[56] Nevertheless, as Gabriel states, '[S]tandards employed to distinguish promises . . . from opinions are not uniform.'[57]

Pragmatically speaking, excessive concern for the pursuit of certainty by 'hard-and-fast rules' can be a 'double-edged sword,'[58] due to its refusal to occasionally recognise the importance of some general concepts.[59] It could create stagnant and 'ossified law,' causing misalignment between law and practice[60] and not responding to the dynamic need for flexibility in the commercial realm.[61] This

47 Percy (n 90) 43 [4].
48 Iain MacNeil, 'Uncertainty in Commercial Law' (2009) 13(1) Edinb Law Rev 68, 78.
49 McKendrick, *Sale of Goods* (n 202) 491, 492; Fisher (n 429) 101, 102; Bridge, *Benjamin's* (n 28) [12–025].
50 *Ampurius v Telford* (n 474) [50]; Davies (n 196) 3rd edn 378 [25.2].
51 Peel, 15th edn (n 64) 974 [18–032].
52 Fisher (n 429) 101, 102.
53 Neo (n 1533) 368.
54 ibid 367.
55 Burrows, *Principles of English Commercial Law* (n 28) 77; Bridge, *Benjamin's* (n 28) [11–004].
56 Poikela (n 83) 61.
57 Henry Gabriel, *Contracts for the Sale of Goods: A Comparison of US and International Law* (OUP 2009) 141.
58 Burrows, *Principles of English Commercial Law* (n 28) 77.
59 Leggatt J in *Yam Seng* (n 204) [123].
60 Gonzalo Puig, 'The Misalignment of Commercial Law and Commercial Practice' (2012) 2 LMCLQ 317, 317, 327.
61 ibid.

could lead to unjust results. As Atiyah stated, '[W]e have the problem of trying to draft a simple statutory provision which will cover all eventualities.'[62] A modern trend in contract law of pursuing a 'never-say-never'[63] approach permits the open-ended nature of a rule to embrace individualised exceptions, reflecting reality for the sake of justice and practicality, presented in Article 25.

Under **KLaw**, the predictability of the outcome is of minimal importance in comparison to SGA or CISG, for two main reasons:

**First**, KLaw lacks clear substantive rules and a concrete general feature for terminating contracts. This makes the legal text a matter of concern because of its double entendre as there is no legal equation that makes the results predictable, and this can make it difficult to reach conclusions without any judicial conjecture. This lack of content may necessitate the recourse to a large number of cases to derive more concrete rules. However, resorting to cases may not be of much help as they suffer from inconsistency and variety in the adoption of criteria. Termination may be permitted even if no detriment is suffered by the buyer, allowing the buyer to speculate at the seller's expense. Imprecise standards and indeterminate and nebulous provisions lead to the waste of time and money[64] and may dishearten either party.[65] By contrast, concrete legal concepts achieve a balance between the parties, promote trust in contracts and trade exchanges and thus enhance prosperity in the commercial field.

**Secondly**, KLaw over-relies on judicial discretion to define and determine the breach's seriousness as there is not a clear yardstick. This lack of legal lucidity positions the judge as the main interpreter of the law according to their individual beliefs, culture, thoughts and convictions. This weakens the validity of law and perplexes the parties and their legal advisors. Worse still, this approach, which can reach unsettling solutions and multiple outcomes, may lead to so-called 'judge-shopping.' A variation of criteria in interpreting the law and the dependence on personal perspectives contradict legal precision and are incompatible with the nature of commercial contracts, even those concluded domestically. As McGrath J stated in the New Zealand case *Couch v Attorney-General*:

> The problem with a stand-alone outrageousness test is that it requires the court to make an assessment without reference to precise criteria. Judges must apply the remedy if, as a matter of impression, they consider it appropriate in the case. If this test is retained, there will be considerable uncertainty within the legal system as to when [termination is] available. Like cases will not be decided alike. This . . . will lead to many claims and multiple appeals against decisions where the minds of judges will reasonably differ.[66]

62 Twigg-Flesner; Canavan (n 30) 148.

63 Ahdar (n 765) 60.

64 ibid 39, 40, 53.

65 Jeremy Waldron, 'Vagueness and the Guidance of Action' in Andrei Marmor; Scott Soames, *Philosophical Foundations of Language in the Law* (OUP 2011) 75.

66 *Susan Couch v The Attorney-General* [2010] NZSC27 [243].

Furthermore, as Lord Hoffmann stressed in *Union Eagle*, the undefined discretion is rejected at the expense of the practical considerations of business to enhance parties' confidence,[67] and knowing the outcome of litigation beforehand would minimise the recourse to actual prosecution.[68] This persistent referral to the judge places KLaw in the lowest rank of accomplishing legal clarity, positioning legal centres on tenterhooks throughout the contract period and making the situation resemble a lottery.

## 6.2 Termination's Threshold

It can be argued that the motivation to precisely perform contractual promises is the binding nature of the contract, which can be applied through the right to termination.[69] Nevertheless, the principle of *favor contractus*, which favours the continuation of the contractual relationship between the parties, rather than terminating it for any breach, is essential. **CISG** has the tendency to protect the contract and complicate the route to termination. This is evident through the adopted systems of notification, additional periods,[70] curability right[71] and encouragement of less harsh remedies.[72] If the criteria adopted by CISG to identify a fundamental breach were more lenient, the 'damaged party [might] take advantage of the defaulting party's breach in order to revise an agreement based on a specific economic situation or to shift the risk of a change in the market conditions to the other party.'[73] Permitting termination for any breach may reduce the seller's chances of selling the goods at an advantageous price to another buyer when the goods' value dramatically diminishes, causing a more drastic loss than that suffered by the injured buyer. Despite the foregoing, it was argued that

> avoidance is the one-sided right of a party to terminate the contract by its mere declaration. Such termination of a contract is the hardest sword that a party to a sales contract can draw if the other has breached the contract.[74]

The aggrieved buyer is the one who assesses the 'substantiality' of a breach and declares the contract terminated,[75] and if the breaching seller objects to the termination and therefore resorts to a tribunal, the assessment will switch to the adjudicator, who might assess 'fundamentality' differently to the buyer. Nonetheless, CISG's plain philosophy lessens the chance of the buyer departing from it. The

67 *Union Eagle v Golden Achievement* (n 406) 519.
68 Cohen (n 249) 586.
69 Bridge, *The Sale of Goods* (n 28) [10.04].
70 CISG Art. 47(1); 49(1).
71 McKendrick, *Contract Law* (n 206) 774, 775.
72 Plate (n 372) 79; Williams (n 1267) 21.
73 Ferrari, 'Fundamental Breach' (n 161) 491; Grebler, 'Fundamental Breach' (n 48) 409, 410.
74 Magnus (n 135) 423.
75 E Sleem, *The International Sale* (Monshaat Alma'ref 2004) 82.

unforeseeability clause in Article 25, which reflects the Convention's reluctance to expand the exercise of termination,[76] minimises the opportunity of letting the contract depend only on the non-defaulting party's expectations. The duty is then put on a buyer to uncover all their purposes from the first step of a contractual relationship, and this clearly identifies the breaches leading to termination.[77]

Under **SGA**, 'The implied terms provide buyers with a healthy measure of protection against defective, disappointing, and substandard goods.'[78] However, as Treitel states, this makes it hard to think of an example of a warranty in a sale of goods contract since the scope of the implied conditions in SGA is ample,[79] and this is considered recognition that almost all contractual obligations in the sale of goods are conditions. Furthermore, as Lord Wilberforce emphasised in *Schuler v Wickman*, determining the materiality of the breach and the reasonable use of termination are not the role of the adjudicator in cases in which the term breached is a 'condition.'[80] This method was adopted due to SGA's tendency towards practicality by encouraging the parties to walk away from a tense transaction and seek a better deal elsewhere, rather than opting for the prolonged process involved in resolving the difficulties of the transaction and continuing the contractual relationship.[81] Nonetheless, this approach permits the exploitation of the termination facility on mere technical grounds[82] by speculating on the fluctuation of the commodities' market,[83] destabilising the contract's nature of being exposed to market-based risk.[84] Subsequently, the seller's costs incurred to fulfil their obligations are wasted.

**KLaw** depends heavily on contractual termination, which is considered the first penalty for any breach of the agreed contractual terms.[85] Requesting termination is permitted without the need for recourse to the 'reasonableness' criterion, for example. This approach regards termination as a 'rule,' while other remedies, such as specific performance, damages and price reduction, are regarded as 'exceptions,' creating disparity between the parties. The justification of this is that the contract is regarded as the law of the parties,[86] which should therefore be implemented and respected. However, uncompromised rigid enforcement and strict adherence to contracts may lead to unfair outcomes. It is true that the threshold for termination is procedurally high as it necessitates the recourse to court, but substantively, the threshold is low and unrestricted. In this situation, a party may be given the

76 Mullis (n 152) 344.

77 Honnold, *Uniform Law* (n 320) 278 [183].

78 Bridge, *The Sale of Goods* (n 28) [7.03].

79 Guenter Treitel, *Some Landmarks of Twentieth-Century Contract Law* (Clarendon 2002) 124.

80 *Schuler* (n 198) 263; Hofmann (n 1267) 151–153.

81 Burrows, *Principles of English Commercial Law* (n 28) 76; Cartwright (n 114) 281; Bridge, *The Sale of Goods* (n 28) [10.05].

82 Adams; Brownsword (n 218) 164.

83 Burrows, *Principles of English Commercial Law* (n 28) 76; McKendrick, *Contract Law* (n 206) 774, 775.

84 Cohen (n 249) 583, 584.

85 Abdulreda; Al-Nakas (n 257) 194.

86 KCIC Art. 196.

freedom to define the meaning of a vague term to their benefit and persuade the judge that termination is just.

The differences between the legal systems can be illustrated as follows:

*Table 6.1* General Differences Between the Legal Systems

| *Legal System* | *Clarity and Predictability of Legal Outcomes* | *Flexibility* | *Termination's Threshold* | *Judicial Discretion* |
|---|---|---|---|---|
| CISG | Medium (higher than KLaw but lower than SGA) | Very high (attaining fair outcomes) | High | Moderate–low |
| SGA | Very clear and predictable | Very low | Low<br>This could permit opportunism on the buyer's side when the contract becomes a bad bargain. | Low–very low |
| KLaw | Unclear and unpredictable, depending on the judge | Unclear, depending on the judge | Procedurally high (necessitating the recourse to court)<br>Substantively very low (no concrete stipulations) | Very high |

## 6.3 Recommendations for Reforming KLaw

It is clear from the analysis carried out in this study that KLaw is comparatively less practical, even in relation to internal contracts. For instance, KLaw adopts two opposing standpoints: by either delegation termination to the judiciary or making termination automatic, as seen in cases of delayed delivery. It also adopts a conglomeration of rules when terminating a contract in accordance with the type of breach, such as rules for 'misdescription' and rules for goods of a 'different category.' This multiplicity of rules leads to chaos when it comes to decision-making and risks confusion. Furthermore, in most cases KLaw does not assess the breaching seller's attitude or that of any average/reasonable person in their place as the assessment to terminate the contract is based largely on the affected buyer's conduct and situation. For instance, when goods of a different category are sent, the interpretation of 'substantiality' is very likely to depend on the buyer's situation, without any requirement for them to disclose their situation or any necessary information to the seller. This personal appreciation does not suit the neutrality of law, disrupts the contractual balance and leads to differing results in similar situations, as individuals are not identical in their way of life, culture, qualities or judgements.

Accordingly, this comparative study has demonstrated that 'there are many reasons which justify a reform of [Kuwaiti] law of contract, but the task appears difficult in a country which is naturally torn between tradition and progress.'[87]

SGA is, for the most part, unambiguous and could offer a valuable legal tool to practitioners who would be provided with certainty of the consequences of their legal actions and clarity of the most appropriate legal route to take when a contract is breached by the other party, without resorting to court. These benefits are clear, especially where SGA considers specific terms as 'conditions,' either by the power of law, such as in cases of misdescription, or by the power of precedents, as in cases of delay. Further certainty is granted regarding the pre- and post-contractual phases, which has little impact when estimating misdescription; this means that the contract is the only record of obligations. On the other hand, SGA still provides some flexibility by 1) adopting the notion of a reasonable time period within which to deliver the goods (when the contract is silent about the delivery time); 2) adopting s.15A for slight breaches, which makes the rejection of goods unreasonable, thus not permitting termination; and 3) when the 'satisfactoriness' of the quality of the goods is estimated according to a reasonable person's view. As both 'certainty' and 'flexibility' are often absent in KLaw, the strategies and guidance used in SGA could be employed by the Kuwaiti legislator to make Kuwaiti contract law more progressive.

Additionally, CISG must play a vital and more prominent role in reforming KLaw. Within KLaw, there should be a responsive movement towards modern requirements and receptiveness to international ideas and values, as well as consistency with the harmonisation process of commercial law, which is universally applicable.[88] Article 39 Al-Majalla encourages this improvement by stating that 'the change of provisions shall not be denied by the change of time.' Because one of the main aims of GCC's Unified Commercial Policy Law is to facilitate the flow of goods, promoting commercial and investment exchanges with the commercial world,[89] ratification of CISG could strengthen the economic power of these countries and enhances their 'businesses' opportunities abroad.'[90] Affiliation with CISG is vital not only for its macro importance to international commerce and bridging the divide between countries[91] but also for its micro benefits in improving domestic laws[92] and in establishing a homogeneous legal system. Accordingly, traders

87 Xavier Blanc-Jouvan, 'Towards the Reform of the Law of Obligations in France: The Reasons for the Reform' (2009) 83(4) TulLRev 853, 875.

88 Mattar (n 62) 201.

89 Barrbiz, 'Commercial Laws in the GCC' (2010) 1(3) 1; 8 <https://cdn.ymaws.com/www.wipp.org/resource/resmgr/newsroom_links/barrbiz_-_gcc_commercial_law.pdf>.

90 Roy Goode; Herbert Kronke; Ewan Mckendrick, *Transnational Commercial Law: Text, Cases and Materials* (OUP 2011) 737.

91 Poikela (n 83) 67.

92 Such as the domestic laws of Estonia, the Tokelau Islands and China. Chianale (n 87) 34.

will not be at the mercy of unpredictable regulations.[93] Furthermore, CISG's rules are a necessary prerequisite for healthy and trusted global trade because of the following:

**First**, there are tools in CISG that prevent the interference of subjective elements. CISG objectively attaches detriment to the expectations expressed in the contractual circumstances,[94] without leaving this task to the judge.[95] One of CISG's general principles is 'reasonableness,'[96] making the conduct of a 'reasonable person' a unified model, representing the public and a unilateral constant standard for everyone. This is to reflect the required behaviour in their insight, prudence, perception and alertness and to measure the parties' actions. Any personal circumstances of the buyer suffered as a result the detriment or their obscure characteristics are not considered, stabilising the legal situation, in contrast with the Kuwaiti orientation.

**Secondly**, requiring a fundamental breach to terminate the contract means that the aim of performing the contract is prioritised over termination.[97] The CISG's 'centrism' on Article 25 and its 'complementary and indivisible'[98] double features – namely, the negative impact of the breach on the injured buyer's contractual expectations and the foreseeability of such harm by the defaulting seller and a reasonable person[99] – combine flexibility and practicality. As the Bulgarian delegation stated in the 10th session commenting on the Convention's draft, account should be taken of the unequal position of the concerned parties to assess the components of a fundamental breach.[100] Article 25 plays a positive role in preventing any party from benefiting from the provision at the other party's expense.[101]

**Thirdly**, it is true that the English distinction between 'conditions' and 'warranties' is approached with precision,[102] but CISG is based more on pragmatism through theoretical standards which are to be applied and measured on each contract, attaining fair outcomes. Furthermore, the 'reasonable person' criterion makes the outcome predictable according to logical analysis of the case.

**Lastly**, one of CISG's aims is to balance the parties' interests: for instance, by obliging the buyer to preserve the nonconforming goods,[103] which might be

93 Bossche; Zdouc (n 5) 31, 32.
94 *Meat case* (n 171); Clausson (n 80) 96; Bianca; Bonell (n 155) 213–215; Naude; Lubbe (n 146) 377; Kröll; Mistelis; Viscasillas (n 67) 341, 342 [14].
95 Bianca; Bonell (n 155) 215.
96 CISG Art. 8(2), Art. 8(3), Art. 16(2)(b), Art. 18(2), Art. 25, Art. 33, Art. 34, Art. 35(2)(b), Art. 37.
97 Werner Lorenz, 'Reform of the German Law of Breach of Contract' (1997) 1(3) Edinb Law Rev 317, 326.
98 Egyptian representative, Official Records (n 149) 12th Meeting 295, 298.
99 Comments by Governments and International Organizations (n 330) 116.
100 ibid 112.
101 Babiak (n 57) 114.
102 R Graveson; E Cohn; Diana Graveson, *The Uniform Laws on International Sales Act 1967* (Butterworths 1968) 57.
103 Schlechtriem, 'Subsequent Performance' (n 349) 85.

considered 'acceptance of performance' under SGA.[104] However, under Klaw, the situation is unclear; the buyer may have a duty under the good faith principle to preserve the goods, but, at the same time, the buyer might refuse the defective goods in order to maintain the termination right, which can result in harmful repercussions for the seller.

These examples illustrate the importance of CISG as a 'model law' with which to encourage Kuwaiti legislators to revise current law in order to pursue universal progress in commercial transactions or, at the very least, as a tool to be incorporated into contracts on a voluntary basis, obviating the possible obscurity of KLaw.

104 ibid 91.

# Bibliography


- Abu-Hakima A, *The Modern History of Kuwait (1750–1965)* (Luzac & Company Limited 1983)
- Adams J; Brownsword R, *Understanding Contract Law* (5th edn, Sweet & Maxwell 2007)
- Adams J; MacQueen H, *Atiyah's Sale of Goods* (12th edn, Longman 2010)
- Amin S, *Commercial Law of Iran* (Bell and Bain 1986)
- Andersen C; Schroeter U; Kritzer A, *Sharing International Commercial Law Across National Boundaries: Festschrift For Albert H. Kritzer on the Occasion of his Eightieth Birthday* (Wildy, Simmonds & Hill, 2008)
- Andrews N, *Contractual Duties: Performance, Breach, Termination and Remedies* (Sweet & Maxwell 2011)
- ———. *Contract Law* (2nd edn, CUP 2015)
- Ballantyne W, *Commercial Law in the Arab Middle East: The Gulf States* (Springer 1986)
- Beale H, *Chitty on Contracts Volume II Specific Contracts* (29th edn, Sweet & Maxwell 2004)
- Beale H, Bishop W; Furmston M, *Contract: Cases and Materials* (5th edn, OUP 2006)
- Beatson J; Burrows A; Cartwright J, *Anson's Law of Contract* (30th edn, OUP 2016)
- ———. *Anson's Law of Contract* (31st edn, OUP 2020)
- Blair M, *Sale of Goods Act 1979* (Butterworths 1980)
- Bonell M, *An International Restatement of Contract Law: The UNIDROIT Principles of International Commercial Contracts* (3rd edn, Transnational Publishers 2005)
- Bonell M; Bianca C, *Commentary on the International Sales Law: The 1980 Vienna Sales Convention* (Giuffre 1987)
- Bossche P; Zdouc W, *The Law and Policy of the World Trade Organization* (4th edn, CUP 2017)
- Bridge M, *The International Sale of Goods* (4th edn, OUP 2017)
- ———. *The Sale of Goods* (4th edn, OUP 2019)
- ———. *Benjamin's Sale of Goods* (11th edn, Sweet & Maxwell 2021)
- Brownsword R, *Contract Law: Themes for the Twenty-First Century* (OUP 2006)
- Burrows A, *Principles of English Commercial Law* (OUP 2015)
- ———. *A Casebook on Contract* (7th edn, Hart 2020)
- Cartwright J, *Contract Law: An Introduction to English Law for the Civil Lawyer* (3rd edn, Hart 2016)
- Chen-Wishart M, *Contract Law* (6th edn, OUP 2019)
- Chitty J, *Chitty on Contracts Volume 1 General Principles* (33rd edn, Sweet & Maxwell 2019)
- Chuah J, *Law of International Trade* (6th edn, Sweet & Maxwell 2019)
- Cordero-Moss G, *International Commercial Contracts* (CUP 2014)
- Dalhuisen J, *Dalhuisen on Transnational Comparative, Commercial, Financial and Trade Law Volume 3: Financial Products, Financial Services and Financial Regulation* (5th edn, Hart Publishing 2013)

- Davies P, *JC Smith's the Law of Contract* (OUP 2016)
- ———. *JC Smith's the Law of Contract* (3rd edn, OUP 2021)
- DiMatteo L, *International Contracting: Law and Practice* (4th edn, Kluwer Law International 2016)
- DiMatteo L; Dhooge L; Pagnattaro M; Greene S; Maurer V, *International Sales Law: A Critical Analysis of CISG Jurisprudence* (CUP 2005)
- Eisenberg M, *The Nature of the Common Law* (Harvard UP 1988)
- Enderlein F; Maskow D, *International Sales Law: United Nations Convention on Contracts for the International Sale of Goods, Convention on the Limitation Period in the International Sale of Goods* (Oceana Publications 1992)
- Ferrari F, *Contracts for the International Sale of Goods: Applicability and Applications of The 1980 United Nations Sales Convention* (BRILL 2011)
- Folsom R; Alstine M; Ramsey M, *International Business Transactions* (11th edn, West Academic Publishing 2020)
- Fried C, *Contract as Promise: A Theory of Contractual Obligation* (OUP 2015)
- Fuller L, *The Morality of Law* (Yale UP 1969)
- Furmston M, *Law of Contract* (17th edn, OUP 2017)
- Gabriel H, *Contracts for the Sale of Goods: A Comparison of US and International Law* (OUP 2009)
- Gestel R; Micklitz H; Rubin E, *Rethinking Legal Scholarship: A Transatlantic Dialogue* (CUP 2017)
- Gillette C; Walt S, *The UN Convention on Contracts for the International Sale of Goods: Practice and Theory* (2nd edn, CUP 2016)
- Goode R; Kronke H; Mckendrick E, *Transnational Commercial Law: Text, Cases and Materials* (OUP 2011)
- ———. *Transnational Commercial Law: Text, Cases and Materials* (2nd edn, OUP 2015)
- Graveson R; Cohn E; Graveson D, *The Uniform Laws on International Sales Act 1967* (Butterworths 1968)
- Guest A, *Contemporary Issues in Commercial Law* (Sweet & Maxwell 1997)
- Harris D; Tallon D, *Contract Law Today: Anglo-French Comparisons* (Clarendon 1989)
- Honnold J, *Documentary History of the Uniform Law for International Sales: The Studies, Deliberations and Decisions that led to the 1980 United Nations Convention with Introductions and Explanations* (Kluwer Law and Taxation Publishers 1989)
- ———. *Uniform Law for International Sales under the 1980 United Nations Convention* (4th edn, Turpin Distribution Services 2009)
- Huber P; Mullis A, *The CISG: A New Textbook for Students and Practitioners* (Sellier 2007)
- Jacqueline I, *Kuwait: Social Change in Historical Perspective* (Syracuse UP 1982)
- Kritzer A, *Guide to Practical Applications of the United Nations Convention on Contracts for the International Sale of Goods* (Kluwer and Taxation Publishers 2002)
- Kröll S; Mistelis L; Viscasillas P, *UN Convention on Contracts for the International Sale of Goods (CISG)* (2nd edn, Hart Publishing 2018)
- Lawson FH, *The Rational Strength of English Law* (Stevens & Sons Limited 1951)
- Lookofsky J; Bernstein H, *Understanding the CISG in Europe* (2nd edn, Kluwer Law International 2003)
- MacCormick N, *Rhetoric and the Rule of Law* (OUP 2005)
- Macdonald E; Atkins R, *Koffman and Macdonald's Law of Contract* (OUP 2018)
- Marmor A; Soames S, *Philosophical Foundations of Language in the Law* (OUP 2011)
- Martin D; Snyder D, *International Transactions in Goods* (OUP 2014)
- Mazurenko V, *Interpretation of Contracts* (LAMBERT 2013)
- McKendrick E, *Sale of Goods* (LLP 2000)
- ———. *Goode on Commercial Law* (5th edn, Penguin Books 2016)
- ———. *Contract Law: Text, Cases, and Materials* (9th edn, OUP 2020)
- Örücü E; Nelken D, *Comparative Law: A Handbook* (Hart Publishing 2007)

- Peel E, *Treitel: The Law of Contract* (13th edn, Sweet & Maxwell 2015)
- ———. *Treitel: The Law of Contract* (15th edn, Sweet & Maxwell 2020)
- Percy C, *Hearing before the Committee on Foreign Relations United States Senate Ninety-eighth Congress* (2nd edn, United States Senate 1984)
- Saidov D, *Conformity of Goods and Documents: The Vienna Sales Convention* (Hart 2015)
- Salter M; Mason J, *Writing Law Dissertations* (Pearson 2007)
- Sarcevic P; Volken P, *International Sale of Goods* (Dubrovnik Lectures 1996)
- Schlechtriem P, *Einheitliches Kaufrecht und nationales Obligationenrecht* (Nomos 1987) <https://www.cisg.law.pace.edu/cisg/biblio/hyland1.html>
- ———. *Commentary on the UN Convention on the International Sale of Goods (CISG)* (2nd edn, OUP 1998)
- Schlechtriem P; Butler P, *UN Law on International Sales: The UN Convention on the International Sale of Goods* (Springer 2009)
- Schwenzer I, *Commentary on the UN Convention on the International Sale of Goods (CISG)* (4th edn, OUP 2016)
- Schwenzer I; Spagnolo L, *Towards Uniformity: The 2nd Annual Maa Schlechtriem CISG Conference* (2nd edn, Eleven International Publishing 2010)
- Smith S, *Contract Theory* (OUP 2004)
- ———. *Atiyah's Introduction to the Law of Contract* (6th edn, OUP 2005)
- Spagnolo L, *CISG Exclusion and Legal Efficiency* (Kluwer Law International 2014)
- Starck B, *Droit Civil Obligations* (Librairies Techniques 1972)
- Stiglitz J, *Globalization and Its Discontents* (Penguin Books 2002)
- Stone R; Devenney J, *Text, Cases and Materials on Contract Law* (4th edn, Routledge 2017)
- Treitel G, *Some Landmarks of Twentieth Century Contract Law* (Clarendon 2002)
- Twigg-Flesner C; Canavan R, *Atiyah and Adams' Sale of Goods* (14th edn, Pearson 2021)
- Twining W, *Blackstone's Tower: The English Law School* (Sweet & Maxwell 1994)
- Watkins D; Burton M, *Research Methods in Law* (2nd edn, Routledge 2018)
- Woodin M; Lucas C, *Green Alternatives to Globalisation* (Pluto Press 2004)


## Arabic Books


- Abdulreda A, *Hidden Defects* (Dar AlKotob 1998) 49; Abdulla AlHayan, *Explanation of Commercial Law* (Kuwait University 2015)
- Abdulreda A; Al-Nakas J, *Sources of Commitment and Proof* (Dar AlKotob 2015) 195.
- AboSaad M, *Sale Contract* (Dar AlFeker 2000)
- Abulil I, *The Contract and the Unilateral Will* (Dar AlKotob 1998)
- Ahmed A, *Commercial Contracts and Banking Operations in Kuwaiti Law* (Dar AlKotob 2015)
- Al-Ahwany H, *Sale Contract* (That AlSalasel 1989)
- Al-Azawy S, *Producer's Liability in Civil Laws and International Conventions* (DarAlthaqafa 2008)
- Al-Badrawe A, *General Theory of Obligations* (Part 1 Dar Alnahda 1968)
- Al-Danasory E; Al-Shawarbee A, *Practical Problems, Claims and Defences in the Contract of Sale* (Manshaat AlMaaref 2002)
- Al-Defery K; Al-Sayrafy Y, *Sale Contract in Kuwaiti Civil Law* (Kuwait University 2010) 201
- Al-FadlyJ, *Synopsis in Civil Contracts* (Dar Althaqafa 1997)
- Al-Fatlawy S, *Hidden Defects and Default of Specifications in Sale Contracts* (Dar Althaqafa 1997)
- Al-Jarmy M, *Termination of Contract: Comparative Study on Egyptian and French Law* (Dar AlNahda 1988)
- Al-Karjy M, *Termination of the Contract* (Dar Alnahda 1988)

- Al-Masry H, *Commercial Contracts in Kuwaiti Law and Egyptian Law* (AlSafar Bookstore 1990).
- ———. *Commercial Law of Kuwait* (Dar AlKotob)
- Al-Naqeeb A, *The General Theory of Responsibility Arising from Things* (Eweedat 1981)
- ———. *The General Theory of Liability Arising from Personal Action* (Eweedat 1983) 114;
- Al-Qarafy A, *The Differences–Written between Late 13th and Early 14th Century* (Part 4 Ministry of Islamic Affairs 2010)
- Al-Sanhory A, *The Sources of Commitments* (Dar Alnahda 1964)
- Al-Shawarby A, *Termination of Contract* (Manshat AlMaaref 1990)
- AlYaqob B, *Principles of Obligation in Kuwaiti Civil Law* (Kuwait University 2012)
- Al-Zehely W, *Islamic Jurisprudence and Its Evidence* (Dar AlFeker 1985)
- Ateya A, *Nullity and Termination of Sale Contract* (Dar AlFeker 2012)
- Ayob S, *The Concept of Fault in Contractual Liability* (Lebanese University 1996) 155.
- Basha M, *"Murshid Al-Hiran" on the Knowledge of Human Conditions in the Legal Dealings according to the Doctrine of Imam Abu Hanifa al-Nu'man* (Egyptian Library 1889)
- Dawood I, *Cognitive Imbalance in Contracts* (Dar Aljama Aljadeda 2014)
- Freez Z, *Kuwait Was my Home* (That Al-Salasel 1997)
- Mammon A, *Causal Relationship in Civil Liability* (Dar Alnahda)
- Muhammad A, *Sale Contract* (Dar AlFeker 1999)
- Omran A, *The Obligation of Information* (Academic Publications 1994)
- Sarko Y, *Commercial Contracts in Kuwaiti Commercial Law* (Kuwait University 1998)
- Shafiq M, *The UN Convention on the International Sale of Goods* (Dar Alnahda 1988)
- Shoala S, *The Civil Cassation Court in the Sale Contract* (Manshaat AlMaaref)
- Sleem E, *The International Sale* (Monshaat Alma'ref 2004)
- Talaba A, *Contractual Termination* (The Modern University Office 2004) 127–128
- ———. *Effectiveness and Termination of Sale* (Dar alFeker)
- Tnago S, *Sale Contract* (Manshaat ALMaaref)


## French Books


- Chabas F, *L'influence de la Pluralité de Causes sur le Droit a Réparation* (Librairie Générale de Droit et du Jurisprudence 1967)
- Demogue R, *Des Obligations en Général* (Librairie Arthur Rousseau 1923)
- Dessemontet F, *Convention de Vienne sur les Contrats de Vente Internationale de Marchandises* (Centre du Droit L'entreprise 1993)
- Heuze V, *La vente Internationale de Marchandise* (Librairie Générale de Droit et de Jurisprudence 2000)
- Marty G; Pierre Raynaud, *Les Droit Personnels Theorie Générale des Obligations Volume I Tome II* (Sirey 1962)
- Savatier R, *Traite de la Responsabilité Civile en Droit Français, Tome II* (Librairie Générale de Droit et du Jurisprudence 1951)


## Journal Articles


- Agro E, 'The Impact of the UNIDROIT Principles in International Dispute Resolution in Figures' (2011) 16(3) Uniform Law Review 719–734
- Ahdar R, 'Contract Doctrine, Predictability and the Nebulous Exception' (2014) 73(1) Cambridge Law Journal 39–60
- Ahmed B; Hussein H, 'Avoidance of Contract as a Remedy under CISG and SGA: Comparative Analysis' (2017) 61 Journal of Law, Policy and Globalization 126–142
- Akerlof G, 'The Market for "Lemons": Quality Uncertainty and the Market Mechanism' (1970) 84(3) The Quarterly Journal of Economics 488–500

- Al-Mukhaizeem B, 'Application of CISG in Kuwait' (2020) 35 Arab Law Quarterly 304–325
- Al-Nakas J, 'Contracts and Agreements Paving the Way for Contracting and the Importance of Differentiating between Contract and Agreement in the Pre-Contract Stage' (1996) 20(1) Law Journal 133–191
- Al-Shobry A, 'Contract Negotiation: Its Legal Framework and Its Impact on the Obligation' (2019) 4(1) Journal of the College of Islamic and Arab Studies for Girls in Damanhour 1178–1212 <https://jcia.journals.ekb.eg/article_57261_29f5e2784d007f9a504618d400102813.pd>
- Andersen C, 'Reasonable Time in Article 39(1) of the CISG – Is Article 39(1) Truly a Uniform Provision?' (1999) <https://www.cisg.law.pace.edu/cisg/biblio/andersen.html>
- ———. 'The Uniform International Sales Law and the Global Jurisconsultorium' (2005) 24(2) Journal of Law and Commerce 159–179
- Azzouni A, 'The Adoption of the 1980 Convention on the International Sale of Goods by the United Kingdom' (2002) 10 <http://www.cisg.law.pace.edu/cisg/biblio/azzouni.html>
- Babiak A, 'Defining "Fundamental Breach" under the United Nations Convention on Contracts for the International Sale of Goods' (1992) 6(1) Temple International and Comparative Law Journal 113–144
- Barood H, 'The Legal Value of Agreements in the Pre-Contract Negotiation Stage in the Field of International Trade Contracts' (2005) 13(2) Islamic University Journal 125
- Barrbiz, 'Commercial Laws in the GCC' (2010) 1(3) <https://cdn.ymaws.com/www.wipp.org/resource/resmgr/newsroom_links/barrbiz_-_gcc_commercial_law.pdf> 1–9
- Berman P, 'From International Law to Law and Globalization' (2005) 43 Columbia Journal of Transnational Law 485–556
- Blanc-Jouvan X, 'Towards the Reform of the Law of Obligations in France: The Reasons for the Reform' (2009) 83(4) Tulane Law Review 853–876
- Borges R, 'The United Kingdom and the UN Convention on Contracts for the International Sale of Goods (CISG): To Ratify or not to Ratify?' (2008) 14(4) The Journal of International Maritime Law 331–338
- Bridge M, 'Discharge for Breach of the Contract of Sale of Goods' (1983) 28(4) McGill Law Journal 867–927
- ———. 'Avoidance for Fundamental Breach of Contract under the UN Convention on the International Sale of Goods' (2010) 59(4) International and Comparative Law Quarterly 911–940
- Byers M, 'The Law and Politics of the Pinochet Case' (2003) 10(2) Duke Journal of Comparative & International Law 415–441
- Carter J, 'Discharge as the Basis for Termination for Breach of Contract' (2012) 128 Law Quarterly Review 283–302
- Chianale A, 'The CISG as a Model Law: A Comparative Law Approach'(2016) 1(2016) Singapore Journal of Legal Studies 29–45
- CISG Advisory Council, 'Opinion No. 19 Standards and Conformity of the Goods under Article 35 CISG' (2019) 2019(2) Nordic Journal of Commercial Law 34–63
- Clarke M, 'Time and the Essence of Mercantile Contracts: The Law Loses Its Way' (1991) 50(1) The Cambridge Law Journal 29–31
- Clausson O, 'Avoidance in Nonpayment Situations and Fundamental Breach under the 1980 U.N. Convention on Contracts for the International Sale of Goods' (1984) 6(1) New York Law School Journal of International and Comparative Law 93–117
- Cohen M, 'The Basis of Contract'(1933) 46(4) Harvard Law Review 553–592
- Cook VS, 'The UN Convention on Contracts for the International Sale of Goods: A Mandate to Abandon Legal Ethnocentricity' (1997) 16 Journal of Law and Commerce 257–264
- Curran V, 'Cross-References and Editorial Analysis, Article 40' <https://cisgw3.law.pace.edu/cisg/text/cross/cross-40.html>

- Devlin L, 'The Treatment of Breach of Contract' (1966) 24(2) Cambridge Law Journal 192–215
- Donboli J; Kashefi F, 'Doing Business in the Middle East: A Primer for US Companies' (2005) 38(2) Cornell International Law Journal 413–458
- Duca L, 'Developing Global Transnational Harmonization Procedures for the Twenty-First Century: The Accelerating Pace of Common and Civil Law Convergence'(2007) 42(3) Texas International Law Journal 625–660
- Eberle E, 'The Methodology of Comparative Law' (2011) 16(1) Roger Williams University Law Review 51–72
- Eörsi G, 'A Propos the 1980 Vienna Convention on Contracts for the International Sale of Goods' (1983) 31(2) American Journal of Comparative Law 333–356
- Erauw J, 'CISG Provisions 66–70: The Risk of Loss and Passing It' (2006) 25 JL & Com 203–217
- Ervine WCH, 'Satisfactory Quality: What Does It Mean?' (2004) Journal of Business Law 684–703
- Ferrari F, 'Uniform Interpretation of the 1980 Uniform Sales Law' (1995) 24 Georgia Journal of International and Comparative Law 183–228
- ———. 'CISG Case Law: A New Challenge for Interpreters?' (1999) 17 Journal of Law and Commerce 245–261
- ———. 'Fundamental Breach of Contract under the UN Sales Convention – 25 Years of Article 25 CISG' (2006) 25 Journal of Law and Commerce 489–508
- Ficetola L, 'Comparing Remedies for Breach of Contract in Italian and English Law' (2011) <file:///C:/Users/user1/Downloads/SSRN-id1990791.pdf> 1–19
- Fisher J, 'Uncertainty, Opportunism and the Intermediate Term: The Hong Kong Fir Principle in English and Irish Contract Law' (2015) 14 Hibernian Law Journal 96–110
- Flechtner H, 'Conformity of Goods, Third Party Claims, and Buyer's Notice of Breach under the United Nations Sales Convention ("CISG"), with Comments on the "Mussels Case," the "Stolen Automobile Case," and the "Ugandan Used Shoes Case"' <https://law.bepress.com/cgi/viewcontent.cgi?article=1065&context=pittlwps>
- ———. 'Transcript of a Workshop on the Sales Convention: Leading CISG Scholars Discuss Contract Formation, Validity, Excuse for Hardship, Avoidance, Nachfrist, Contract Interpretation, Parol Evidence, Analogical Application, and Much More' (1999) 18(2) Journal of Law and Commerce 191–258
- Forte A, 'The United Nations Convention on Contracts for the International Sale of Goods: Reason and Unreason in the United Kingdom' (1997) 26(3) University of Baltimore Law Review 51–66
- Gillette C; Ferrari F, 'Warranties and "Lemons" under CISG Article 35(2)(a)' (2010) 1 InternationalesHandesrecht <https://cisgw3.law.pace.edu/cisg/biblio/gillette-ferrari.html>
- Goff of Chieveley L, 'The Role of the Judge in England' (1994) 58(3) Rabel Journal of Comparative and International Private Law 443–448
- Graffi L, 'Case Law on the Concept of "Fundamental Breach" in the Vienna Sales Convention' (2003) 3 International Business Law Journal 338–349
- Grebler E, 'Fundamental Breach of Contract under the CISG: A Controversial Rule' (2007) 101 American Society of International Law 407–413
- ———. 'The UN Sales of Goods Convention: Perspectives on the Current State-of-Play' (2007) American Society of International Law 407–422
- Halperin J, 'Law in Books and Law in Action: The Problem of Legal Change' (2011) 64(1) Maine Law Review 46–76
- Harker J, 'The Nature and Scope of Rescission as a Remedy for Breach of Contract in American and South African Law' (1980) Acta Juridica 61–114
- Hayward B; Zeller B; Andersen CB, 'The CISG and the United Kingdom – Exploring Coherency and Private International Law' (2018) 67 International and Comparative Law Quarterly 607–641

- Henschel R, 'Conformity of Goods in International Sales Governed by CISG Article 35: Caveat Venditor, Caveat Emptor and Contract Law as Background Law and as a Competing Set of Rules' 2004 1(2004) Nordic Journal of Commercial Law 1–21
- Hobhouse J, 'International Conventions and Commercial Law: The Pursuit of Uniformity' (1990) 106 Law Quarterly Review 530–535
- Hoecke M, 'Methodology of Comparative Legal Research' (2015) 12 Law and Method 1–35
- Hofmann N, 'Interpretation Rules and Good Faith as Obstacles to the UK's Ratification of the CISG and to the Harmonization of Contract Law in Europe' (2010) 22(1) Pace International Law Review 145–181
- Holdych T, 'Warranties and Conditions in the Sale of Goods: A Market-based Assessment of English and European Community Warranty Law' (1998) 29 Cambrian Law Review 73–92
- Honnold J, 'The Uniform Law for the International Sale of Goods: The Hague Convention of 1964' (1965) 30(2) Law and Contemporary Problems 326–353
- Huneidi I, 'Twenty-Five Years of Civil Law System in Kuwait' (1986) 1(2) Arab Law Quarterly 216–219
- ———. 'The Legal Aspects of Doing Business in Kuwait' (1991) 2(12) International Company and Commercial Law Review 403–407
- Hutchinson T, 'Vale Bunny Watson: Law Librarians, Law Libraries, and Legal Research in the Post-Internet Era' (2014) 106 (4) American Association of Law Libraries 579–592
- Kalamees P, 'Hierarchy of Buyer's Remedies in Case of Lack of Conformity of the Goods' (2011) 18 juridica international 63–72
- Karl D, 'Islamic Law in Saudi Arabia: What Foreign Attorneys Should Know' (1991) 25(1) The George Washington Journal of International Law and Economics 131–170
- Koneru P, 'The International Interpretation of the UN Convention on Contracts for the International Sale of Goods: An Approach Based on General Principles' (1997) 6 Minnesota Journal of Global Trade 105–152
- Kourides N, 'The Influence of Islamic Law on Contemporary Middle Eastern Legal Systems: The Formation and Binding Force of Contracts' (1970) 9(2) Columbia Journal of Transnational Law 384–435
- Kumar M, 'The Political and Legal Status of Kuwait' (1962) 11(1) International and Comparative Law Quarterly 108
- Liang W, 'Does the CISG Put too Much Emphasis on Promoting Performance of the Contract? A Comparison with the English Law (2015) 1(2) International Journal of Management and Applied Science 31–36
- Liu C, 'Additional Period (Nachfrist) for Late Performance: Perspectives from the CISG, UNIDROIT Principles, PECL and Case Law' (2005) 4 <http://cisgw3.law.pace.edu/cisg/biblio/liu4.html>
- Lorenz W, 'Reform of the German Law of Breach of Contract' (1997) 1(3) Edinburgh Law Review 317–344
- Lubbe G, 'Fundamental Breach under the GISG: A Source of Fundamentally Divergent Results' (2004) 68(3) The Rabel Journal of Comparative and International Private Law 444–472
- Luca V, 'The Conformity of the Goods to the Contract in International Sales' (2015) 27(1) Pace International Law Review 163–257
- MacNeil I, 'Uncertainty in Commercial Law' (2009) 13(1) Edinburgh Law Review 68–99
- Magnus U, 'The Remedy of Avoidance of Contract Under CISG – General Remarks and Special Cases' (2006) 25 Journal of Law and Commerce 423–436
- Maley K, 'The Limits to the Conformity of Goods in the United Nations Convention on Contracts for the International Sale of Goods (CISG)' (2009) 12 International Trade & Business Law Review 82–126
- Mallat C, 'Commercial Law in the Middle East: Between Classical Transactions and Modern Business' (2000) 48(1) American Journal of Comparative Law 81–141

- Mann B; Holdych T, 'The Basis of the Bargain Requirement: A Market and Economic based Analysis of Express Warranties-Getting What You Pay for and Paying for What You Get' (1996) 45(3) DePaul Law Review 781–857
- Mattar M, 'Integrating the UNIDROIT Principles of International Commercial Contracts as a Source of Contract Law in Arab Civil Codes' (2017) 22(1) Uniform Law Review 168–201
- McCormack J, 'Commercial Contracts in Muslim Countries of the Middle East: A Comparison with the United States' (2009) 37(1) International Journal of Legal Information 1–28
- McDowellMudambi S; Doyle P; Wong V, 'An Exploration of Branding in Industrial Markets' (1997) 26(5) Industrial Marketing Management 433–446
- Mcmeel G, 'Prior Negotiations and Subsequent Conduct – The Next Step Forward for Contractual Interpretation?' (2003) 119 Law Quarterly Review 272–297
- Moss S, 'Why the United Kingdom has Not Ratified the CISG' (2005) (1–2) Journal of Law and Commerce 483–485
- Mullis A, 'Avoidance for Breach under the Vienna Convention; A Critical Analysis of Some of the Early Cases' (1998) Anglo-Swedish Studies in Law 326
- Murray JE, 'The Neglect of CISG: A Workable Solution' (1998) 17 Journal of Law and Commerce 365–379
- Naude T; Lubbe G, 'Cancellation for Material or Fundamental Breach: A Comparative Analysis of South African Law, the UN Convention on Contracts for the International Sale of Goods (CISG) and the UNDROIT Principles of International Commercial Contracts' (2001) 12(3) Stellenbosch Law Review 371–398
- Neo D, 'The Sale of Goods (Amendment) Act 1996: Satisfactory Quality, an Undivided Share in a Bulk and Other Amendments' (1997) 9(2) Singapore Academy of Law Journal 362–387
- Nicholas B, 'The Vienna Convention on International Sales Law' (1989) 105 Law Quarterly Review 201–243
- Nicholls D, 'My Kingdom for a Horse: The Meaning of Words' (2005) 121 Law Quarterly Review 577–591
- Nikolova S, 'UK's Ratification of the CISG – An Old Debate or a New Hope for the Economy of the UK on Its Way Out of the Recession: The Potential Impact of the CISG on the UK's SME'(2012) Pace International Law Review Online Companion 69–110
- Peacock D, 'Avoidance and the Notion of Fundamental Breach under the CISG: An English Perspective' (2003) 8 International Trade and Business Law Annual 95–134
- Piliounis P, 'The Remedies of Specific Performance, Price Reduction and Additional Time (Nachfrist) under the CISG: Are These Worthwhile Changes or Additions to English Sales Law?' (2000) 12(1) Pace International Law Review 1–46
- Pistis M, 'From *Caveat Emptor* to *Caveat Venditor* a Brief History of English Sale of Goods Law' (2006) Mondaq Business Briefing 1
- Plate T, 'The Buyer's Remedy of Avoidance under the CISG: Acceptable from a Common Law Perspective?' (2002) 6 Vindobona Journal of International Commercial Law and Arbitration 57
- Ploeg F, 'Natural Resources: Curse or Blessing?' (2011) 49(2) Journal of Economic Literature 366–420
- Poikela T, 'Conformity of Goods in the 1980 United Nations Convention of Contracts for the International Sale of Goods' (2003) 1 Nordic Journal of Commercial Law 1–68
- Puig G, 'The Misalignment of Commercial Law and Commercial Practice' (2012) 2 Lloyd's Maritime and Commercial Law Quarterly 317–336
- Roberts A, 'Comparative International Law – The Role of National Courts in Creating and Enforcing International Law' (2011) 60(1) International and Comparative Law Quarterly 57–92
- Rogowska A, 'Some Considerations on the Desirability of Accession to the CISG by the UK' (2013) 5(2) European Journal of Commercial Contract Law 31–43

- Saiegh S, 'Avoidance under the CISG and Its Challenges under International Organizations Commercial Transactions' (2005) 25(1–2) Journal of Law and Commerce 443–449
- STA Law Firm, 'Sale by Description – Interpretation and Ambiguities' (19/2/2018) Mondaq Business Briefing, 2–4.
- Schlechtriem P, 'Requirements of Application and Sphere of Applicability of the CISG' (2005) 36 Victoria University of Wellington Law Review 781–794
- ———. 'Subsequent Performance and Delivery Deadlines – Avoidance of CISG Sales Contracts Due to Non-Conformity of the Goods' (2006) 18(1) Pace International Law Review 83–98
- ———. 'Uniform Sales Law in the Decisions of the *Bundesgerichtshof*' <https://cisgw3.law.pace.edu/cisg/biblio/schlechtriem3.html>
- Schwenzer I, 'The Danger of Domestic Preconceived Views with Respect to the Uniform Interpretation of the CISG: The Question of Avoidance in the Case of Non-Conforming Goods and Documents' (2005) 36 Victoria University of Wellington Law Review 795–807
- ———. 'National Preconceptions that Endanger Uniformity' (2007) 19(1) Pace International Law Review 103–124
- Secretariat Commentary, Guide to CISG Article 31 <https://www.cisg.law.pace.edu/cisg/text/secomm/secomm-31.html>
- ———. 'Guide to CISG Article 35' <https://cisgw3.law.pace.edu/cisg/text/secomm/secomm-35.html>
- Shaaban H, 'Commercial Transactions in the Middle East: What Law Governs?' (1999) 31(1) Law and Policy in International Business 157–172
- Shen J, 'Declaring the Contract Avoided: The UN Sales Convention in the Chinese Context' (1997) 10(1) New York International Law Review 8
- Stannard J, 'So What If Time Is of the Essence?' [2005] Singapore Journal of Legal Studies 114–136
- Stewart A, 'What's Wrong with the Australian of Contract?' (2012) 29(1) Journal of Contract Law 74
- Tasneem F, 'Electronic Contracts and Cloud Computing' (2014) 9(2) Journal of International Commercial Law and Technology 105–116
- Thomson J, 'The Effect of a Repudiatory Breach' (1978) 41(2) Modern Law Review 137, 141
- Treitel G, "'Conditions" and "Conditions Precedent"' (1990) 106(Apr) Law Quarterly Review 185–192
- Varga C, 'Law and Its Doctrinal Study: On Legal Dogmatics' (2008) 49(3) Hungarian Journal of Legal Studies 253–274
- Veneziano A, 'Non Conformity of Goods in International Sales – A Survey of Current Caselaw on CISG' (1997) 1 International Business Law Journal 39–66
- Vick D, 'Interdisciplinarity and the Discipline of Law' (2004) 31(2) Journal of Law and Society 163–193
- Vuuren E, 'Termination of International Commercial Contracts for Breach of Contract: The Provisions of the UNIDROIT Principles of International Commercial Contracts' (1998) 15(2) Arizona Journal of International and Comparative Law 583–643
- Weir T, 'The Buyer's Right to Reject Defective Goods' (1976) 35(1) Cambridge Law Journal 33–38
- Werro F, 'Notes on the Purpose and Aims of Comparative Law' (2001) 75 Tulane Law Review 1225–1233
- Williams A, 'Forecasting the Potential Impact of the Vienna Sales Convention on International Sales Law in the United Kingdom' (2001) <https://cisgw3.law.pace.edu/cisg/biblio/williams.html>
- Yan M, 'Remedies under the Convention on Contracts for the International Sale of Goods and the United Kingdom's Sale of Goods Act: A Comparative Examination' (2011) 3 City University of Hong Kong Law Review 111–140

- Yovel J, 'The Seller's Right to Cure a Failure to Perform: An Analytic Comparison of the Respective Provisions of the CISG and the PECL' (2005) 1 Nordic Journal Of Commercial Law 1–19
- Zeller B, 'The Development of Uniform Laws – A Historical Perspective' (2002) 14(1) Pace International Law Review, Spring 163–177
- ———. 'Fundamental Breach and the CISG – A Unique Treatment or Failed Experiment?' (2004) 8 Vindobona Journal of International Commercial Law & Arbitration 81–94


**Official Reports**


- Central Statistical Bureau of Kuwait <https://www.csb.gov.kw/Pages/Statistics_en?ID=38&ParentCatID=4>
- CISG Advisory Council, 'Opinion No. 19 Standards and Conformity of the Goods under Article 35 CISG' <https://journals.aau.dk/index.php/NJCL/article/view/3396/2952>
- Department of Economic and Social Affairs Statistics Division, International Trade Statistics Yearbook Volume I (UN 2020) 2 <https://comtrade.un.org/pb/downloads/2019/VolI2019.pdf>
- European Commission, Internationalisation of European SMEs (Entrepreneurship 2010)
- HM Revenue and Customs, UK Overseas Trade in Goods Statistics: September 2020 <https://assets.publishing.service.gov.uk/government/uploads/system/uploads/attachment_data/file/934482/OTS_Release_092020.pdf>
- National Statistics, UK Overseas Trade in Goods Statistics: September 2020 <https://www.gov.uk/government/statistics/uk-overseas-trade-in-goods-statistics-september-2020>
- Report of the UN Commission on International Trade Law on the Work of its Tenth Session A/32/17 Vienna 23 May -17 June 1977, 31 <http://www.uncitral.org/pdf/english/yearbooks/yb-1977-e/vol8-p11-70-e.pdf>
- The Law Commission and The Scottish Law Commission, Report on a Reference under Section 3(1)(e) of the Law Commissions Act 1965 (Law Com No 160 Scot Law Com No 104 1987) <https://s3-eu-west-2.amazonaws.com/lawcom-prod-storage-11jsxou24uy7q/uploads/2016/07/LC.-160-SC.-104-REPORT-ON-A-REFERENCE-UNDER-SECTION-31e-OF-THE-LAW-COMMISSIONS-ACT-1965-SALE-AND-SUPPLY-OF-GOODS-1.pdf>
- UN, Commentary on the Draft Convention on Contracts for the International Sale of Goods prepared by the Secretariat (Secretariat Commentary UN DOC. A/CONF. 97/5 1978) <www.cisg-online.ch/index.cfm?pageID=644#Article23>
- UN, Official Records of United Nations Conference on Contracts for the International Sale of Goods (A/CONF.97/19 United Nations 1991) <www.uncitral.org/pdf/english/texts/sales/cisg/a-conf-97-19-ocred-e.pdf>
- UN, Report of the United Nations Commission on International Trade Law on the Work of its Tenth Session (A/32/17 Vienna 23 May–17 June 1977) <http://www.uncitral.org/pdf/english/yearbooks/yb-1977-e/vol8-p11-70-e.pdf>
- Yearbook of the United Nations Commission on International Trade Law 1977 Volume VIII 1, Comments by Governments and International Organizations on the Draft Convention on the International Sale of Goods, (A/CN.9/125 and A/CN.9/125/add.1 to 3) <http://dag.un.org/bitstream/handle/11176/262648/A_CN.9_125-EN.pdf?sequence=1&isAllowed=y>


**Electronic Resources**


- Akhilesh Ganti, 'Buyer's Market' (9/9/2019) <https://www.investopedia.com/terms/b/buyersmarket.asp>

- Caroline Banton, 'Delivered Duty Paid (DDP)' (22/4/2019) <www.investopedia.com/terms/d/delivery-duty-paid.asp#ixzz5Pq9Hgvbq>
- Indiana University, 'Legal Dissertation: Research and Writing Guide' <https://law.indiana.libguides.com/dissertationguide>
- Institute of International Commercial Law, 'CISG: Table of Contracting States' <https://iicl.law.pace.edu/cisg/page/cisg-table-contracting-states>
- Kuwait News Agency (KUNA), 'Kuwaiti Efforts in Establishing the Cooperation Council for the Arab States of the Gulf' (24/5/2002) <https://www.kuna.net.kw/ArticleDetails.aspx?id=1256299&language=ar>
- Robert Stein, 'Reasons Not to Use DDP' (27/8/2013) <http://mohawkglobal.com/global-news/reasons-not-to-use-ddp/>
- Translation of Surah Al-Mulk: Verse 13 <http://search-the-quran.com/search/Surah+Al-Mulk/8>
- UN Commission on International Trade Law <http://www.uncitral.org/uncitral/en/uncitral_texts/sale_goods/1980CISG.html>
- Will Kenton, 'Seller's Market' (12/5/2018) <https://www.investopedia.com/terms/s/sellersmarket.asp>

# Index

Note: Page locators in **bold** indicate a table.